ARCHIVES AND THE PUBLIC GOOD

Accountability and Records in Modern Society

Edited by
Richard J. Cox and David A. Wallace

QUORUM BOOKS
Westport, Connecticut • London

Library of Congress Cataloging-in-Publication Data

Archives and the public good : accountability and records in modern society / edited by
Richard J. Cox and David A. Wallace.
    p. cm.
  Includes bibliographical references and index.
  ISBN 1–56720–469–4 (alk. paper)
    1. Archives—Social aspects. 2. Archives—Administration—Case studies. 3.
  Records—Management—Case studies. 4. Common good. 5. Public interest. 6.
  Responsibility. I. Cox, Richard J. II. Wallace, David A., 1961–
  CD971.A73 2002
  027—dc21   2001057863

British Library Cataloguing in Publication Data is available.

Library of Congress Catalog Card Number: 2001057863
ISBN: 1–56720–469–4

First published in 2002

Quorum Books, 88 Post Road West, Westport, CT 06881
An imprint of Greenwood Publishing Group, Inc.
www.quorumbooks.com

Printed in the United States of America

The paper used in this book complies with the
Permanent Paper Standard issued by the National
Information Standards Organization (Z39.48–1984).

10 9 8 7 6 5 4 3 2 1

Contents

Introduction

Richard J. Cox and David A. Wallace

This book, like most books on its topic, originates with the editors' personal and professional experiences. At times we have followed different paths prior to our decision to collaborate on this volume, one of us having worked for years in traditional archives and records management programs, the other with years of experience in an untraditional archives with a mission to make previously classified federal records more readily accessible. However, over the past fifteen years our paths have also crossed as both teacher and student, remarkably at two different universities, and presently in the classroom educating future archivists, records managers, and other information professionals. Over this time we have become both colleagues and friends, all the while constantly rediscovering that we share similar convictions about the importance of records in our society and the need to educate professionals who understand that records are not only artifacts for use by historians and genealogists but that they are also essential sources of evidence and information providing the glue that holds together, and sometimes the agent that unravels, organizations, governments, communities, and societies. Even if the records of a society or organization are not used in the way they are intended, the process of creating and maintaining records takes on powerful symbolism for that society or organization.[1]

The immediate origins of this book were our convictions but also the perception of the need for record-focused case studies both for use in the classroom and to communicate and promote to a wider audience the significance of the roles records play in constituting society.[2] We are both incessant book buyers and readers, mostly focused on the search for studies—from as many disciplines

and perspectives as possible—on the nature and importance of records and record keeping, from the ancient world to the modern age. Across the years we
have each developed extensive personal libraries, but we have been frustrated
in choosing what our students should read about record keeping and accountability, often feeling overwhelmed by the vast quantity of monographs, biogra-
phies, autobiographies, festschrifts, textbooks, and even novels, on the general
notion of how records hold us accountable from our private to our public
spheres.[3] These books, whose impact upon the reader can be moving, alarming,
entertaining, depressing, or enlightening, often mute the issues about records
within their larger narratives. Records frequently provide the scaffolding for the
stories relayed and sometimes they even play central roles, yet they are rarely
explicitly surfaced as objects receiving concentrated attention, especially in
what has long been described as the Information Age, with its stress on the effective and efficient creation, management, and use of information. The importance of records and especially archives is often obscured.[4] The authors' focus
on the broader narrative they are constructing, while entirely appropriate,
serves to obscure recordkeeping dimensions that can profoundly shape social
interactions and memories of them. When teased out, the recordkeeping dimensions—such as control and access, preservation, destruction, authenticity, and
accuracy—demonstrate time and again that records are not mute observers and
recordings of activity. Rather, they often actively constitute an activity in themselves and are frequently struggled over as objects of memory formation. They
are often at the heart of struggles over what "memory" will be produced and so-
cially validated, issues that have become more essential in the postmodern age
with its varying emphases on texts and contexts.[5]

To counter our frustrations over the dearth of records-specific accountabil-
ity-focused studies we decided to approach a series of prospective authors on
their interest in writing case studies explicitly focusing on the intersection between record keeping and accountability. This call was enthusiastically received. Others in the wider recordkeeping community and those along its
margins had themselves been grappling with the accountability dimensions associated with records, and our request for a contribution was more than once
the final straw compelling thoughts to paper. For that we are grateful and hope
that this volume contributes to a widened understanding of the quite significant
roles records play in accountability.

The fourteen contributions to this volume revolve around four closely related themes tying the importance of records for accountability in society—
explanation (making laypeople understand what records mean), *secrecy, memory,* and *trust.* We believe that the case studies that make up this volume provide
powerful narratives for the classroom and can be read profitably by individuals
who wish to know how records support and help constitute organizational and
societal functions.

First, though, what do we mean by *accountability?* There are many definitions we could employ, from simple dictionary definitions to legal treatises. For

instance, the *Oxford English Dictionary* associates accountability with notions of "responsibility" and "liability" and being able to "answer for [the] discharge of duties or conduct."[6] For this volume, we employ a definition forged by experience and grounded in years of observation. Kevin Kearns, a professor of management, provides a "pragmatic approach" to the topic of accountability. In his view, accountability meanders through "legal and regulatory mandates," "negotiating with . . . clients, special interest groups, and other stakeholders," "discretionary judgments, calculated risks, and entrepreneurial ventures," and finally, advocacy involving the need to "interpret and communicate the needs of citizens to higher authorities who have the power and resources to meet those needs."[7] Kearns discerns that accountability systems possess "three core elements"—a "higher authority vested with the power of oversight and supervision, a measure or criterion used by the higher authority to assess compliance or performance of mandated activities, and an explicit reporting mechanism for conveying information to the higher authority."[8] Kearns argues that accountability means different things for different groups, but that it is real and can be mapped out in different kinds of organizations, cultures, and circumstances. Accountability represented by records is not merely restricted to a legal or organizational sense. As a family member explores the records of his ancestors, there is the sense that one generation holds another accountable to its legacy.[9] We can even stretch the notion of accountability provided by records as a means for us to understand just how people or government create images or re-create images of themselves, especially with the notion of speechwriters or ghost writers.[10] Accountability, as an idea suggesting the importance of records, needs to be explored in greater detail so that all its ramifications are understood, and we hope that this volume is a start to doing this.

The case studies that make up this volume confirm these notions by demonstrating how accountability can be served or undermined by recordkeeping practices in many contexts. They provide an understanding of how records and documents help compel, shape, distort, and recover social interactions, and all, to some degree, comment on what has come to be a discipline in its own right, the study of social, public, or collective memory.[11] While on the surface memory seems soft and fuzzy and accountability can be viewed in a legalistic manner, the concepts are much more closely related. The new scholarly interests in memory suggests a quest for meaning and even stability in the face of ever-changing technologies in an age in which the complexities of information and evidence are now well known.[12] Records appraised for legal or accountability purposes can, over time, assume symbolic or memory functions. Moreover, the role of archives to acquire and maintain records with continuing value to society is a form of accountability by providing a reasonably explicit memory function for that society. The archivist of Canada, Ian Wilson, reflected that notions like information, knowledge, accountability, and memory are all related or parallel responsibilities of archivists and archives, and ones that are not easily disconnected from one another.[13] It is easy to lose sight of how such notions are all at play at once, both by archivists as they develop working strategies to manage the increasingly complicated documentary heritage, and by the society with often simplistic notions of how and what archives and archivists do.

While Kearns, in his general discussion of accountability, does not explicitly discuss records (he mentions "red tape" and information systems), it is our contention that the chief value of records is, in fact, a broad accountability binding individuals with each other and with governments, organizations, and society across space and time. Records created in the normal course of business provide evidence of actions, decisions, and intentions, both legal and illegal, proper and improper, and wise and misguided. There is, in fact, historical precedent for such matters as the importance of records for accountability and evidence as we gain additional understanding about the roles records play in dramatic shifts in information technologies.[14] As records accumulate, they can evolve into sources of memory for individuals, organizations, and society. For some they can become symbolic. Over time a small proportion of what is created comes to be formally preserved in archival institutions.

It is records' power as sources of accountability that is for us their most salient feature, a feature that often bring them into daily headlines or into the courtroom. Over the past decade records have become key participants in both large- and small-scale events that both constitute and reshape our world. On the large scale, "truth commissions" in Argentina, Brazil, Chile, El Salvador, Guatemala, and South Africa have struggled to obtain access to the archives of former regimes. And across Europe, in Czechoslovakia, Poland, Germany, and Romania, debates have raged over whether access to Soviet-era records would do more harm than good in coming to terms with the past. In these instances records have been central to understanding the extent of repression and human-rights violations in these countries.[15] And in both the former Soviet Union and the United States, broadened access to millions of formerly classified archives are contributing to more realistic assessments of their often shocking activities throughout the Cold War era. In a profound sense, the combined release of these records across the globe represents a unique episode in world history. Never before have so many governments released so many documents in an effort to confront the past. Nothing like it was possible for most of the twentieth century. The linkages between political control and information control rendered earlier access attempts largely futile. The societal consequences of this outpouring of documentation remain largely unclear. However, the consequences will be great, as records are tied up with the most basic senses of personal and community identity, human impulses, and societal and organizational control.[16]

And such releases are not unique to the public sector. Private-sector enterprises such as the tobacco and chemical industries have been forced to release vast amounts of records documenting their knowledge about and refusal to take responsibility for their products' damaging consequences.[17] In addition, the long shadow of Nazi Germany and World War II continues to hold our attention as the remaining victims and perpetrators reach the ends of their natural lives.

Over the past decade reconciliation with and accountability for the impacts of Nazism have led to records-based investigations into plundered gold and art, payments for insurance policy and common property claims, and corporate complicity in the Holocaust.[18]

On the small scale, records appear daily in the global press, underscoring the roles they play in social and political accountability. A small representative sampling from stories appearing in the news media from late February through late March 2001 is illustrative, highlighting the roles played by records in investigations and access controversies, as well as the consequences resulting from their handling (including security, authority, and theft). On the investigatory front, a U.S. federal judge ordered the chairman of the Bank of New York Company to provide telephone records, tax returns, and credit card statements as part of a shareholder lawsuit accusing nineteen bank officials in a money laundering scheme; government investigators subpoenaed former White House officials and documents pertaining to highly controversial pardons granted by former president Bill Clinton during the final days of his presidency; court documents released in North Carolina demonstrated that automotive giant DaimlerChrysler engineered a massive "lemon-laundering" effort wherein the company bought back and recycled troublesome vehicles to unknowing consumers (between 1993 and 2000, the company bought back more than 50,000 vehicles); and an audit of Medicaid documents in Florida revealed that the state office continued to pay more than $3 million to health maintenance organizations, hospitals, pharmacies, and nursing homes for services for over 6,000 patients who had already died.[19]

On the matter of access, Mexican news agency executives pressed the president of Mexico to support a freedom of information law in Mexico to counter administrative secrecy and the hurdles encountered by citizens seeking government information; a controversy erupted over whether autopsy photographs of race-car driver Dale Earnhardt should be made public (Earnhardt died during a crash at the Daytona 500 car race, and the press wanted copies of the photos in order to conduct an independent investigation into the causes of the driver's death); the Canadian Blood Services (CBS), Canada's blood agency, came under criticism for developing what was perceived as too constrictive a freedom-of-information-access policy (the level of discomfort over CBS's secrecy stems from an earlier "tainted-blood" scandal that left thousands of Canadians infected with the AIDS virus and Hepatitis C, and critical documents bearing on this earlier scandal had been improperly destroyed); and a bill in the Arkansas legislature that would have allowed adoptees to see their birth certificates when they reached the age of 21 died in committee (this bill was the latest in a series of nationwide public policy debates over the confidentiality of adoption records and the rights of adoptees to access them).[20]

On security, there were the following stories: The online book service Bibliofind.com suffered a hacker attack into 98,000 customer records, forcing the Web site to go offline for a short period; Indiana University suffered a hacker attack resulting in the unauthorized downloading of the Social Security numbers of 3,000 students, the hacker taking advantage of a security hole that had inadvertently been left open by one of the server administrators; a couple availed themselves of identities of twelve people by collecting Social Security numbers from driving records (these numbers were used to illegally obtain credit cards under false identities), representing only a small part of the more than 40,000 complaints received from November 1999 through December 2000 by the Federal Trade Commission from consumers and identity theft victims; over the past several years the U.S. District Court and the U.S. Bankruptcy Court in northern California have been posting lawyers' filings and judges' opinions online, with personally identifiable details about credit card accounts, Social Security numbers, and details on the depression, homosexuality, and annual income and expenditures of named individuals, adding to the growing national debate over the privacy considerations of posting normally open court records online; and thousands of confidential instant messages between the CEO and top-level executives of a dot-com company were inappropriately posted to the World Wide Web, greatly disrupting the company's operations.[21]

On the roles records play as authoritative resources, there are the following stories: (1) A West Virginia man pardoned by the governor in 1996 is unable to assemble the records he needs in an effort to expunge his criminal record. The state archive is unable to locate the original application or other supporting documentation associated with the governor's decision, and the director of the state's Department of Archives and History points to the absence of an enforced requirement to deposit records as a contributing factor. (2) Sophisticated counterfeiting techniques make it increasingly difficult for employers in Arkansas to screen out false identification records and work documents. One counterfeiter captured by the Immigration and Naturalization Service claimed to have manufactured more than 700,000 work documents in less than one year. (3) A local government employee is under investigation amidst allegations that she altered records to benefit her husband's income bonus. (4) The New Jersey State Division of Youth and Family Services ordered workers to reconstruct missing information in more than 1,600 agency case files (documenting the actions of the state to protect some 3,000 abused and neglected children). One novice employee testified in court that she was instructed to create records for events that occurred well before her tenure.[22]

Finally, on records as objects of theft, there was one story about a Baltimore city police officer's arrest for breaking into the department's internal affairs office and stealing documents that allegedly implicated fellow officers. Another told of a Canadian lawyer charged with attempting to hire an individual to steal records associated with a federal investigation of a client. Yet another told of a legal consultant who was sentenced to sixty days in prison for leaking confidential Los Angeles police records, about seventy-nine officers accused of domestic violence, to a television reporter.[23]

The challenge with these newspaper stories is that often the significance of records is poorly explained and the role of archivists and other records professionals is absent. The importance of records and recordkeeping systems must be set forth by those who best understand them, namely archivists and records managers, and in this volume these fourteen essays attempt to do just that. The most critical function for records professionals might be *explaining* records and archives in ways that they can be readily understood.

EXPLAINING ARCHIVES AND RECORDS

How well understood by the public, policymakers, and even creators of records (which, after all, the public and policymakers are as well) are records and recordkeeping systems, the nature of archival principles, the work of archivists? James M. O'Toole's essay recounts his experiences in working with lawyers and in a courtroom in trying to make these functions and issues understandable, in the well-publicized case regarding the ownership of the Martin Luther King, Jr., Papers. O'Toole notes, as other archivists have, the need to seize "teachable moments" in order to explain archives.

Terry Cook describes the public reactions to the fact that Canadian government records are routinely destroyed as part of standard archival procedures at the national archive. The standard procedures were suddenly thrust into the glare of public scrutiny, for it seemed as if the national archive had been involved in a major conspiracy and subsequent coverup. Cook's essay is additional testimony to the care archivists and records managers must take in explaining their work and that of their institutions. In fact, Cook extends the notion of accountability right to the steps of the archive itself: "Archives of the state are not just repositories of historical sources for researchers to use in understanding the past; they are also political manifestations of and active agents of the dominant culture of society. Archives are not merely scholarly playgrounds for their staffs and researchers; they are also bastions of social memory and national identity. And what documents the archives chooses to keep or destroy (or lose as 'missing') are not the result of dispassionate historical research or bureaucratic processes, but rather sensitive, controversial acts for which archives can be held accountable in courts of law and of public opinion." We concur.

Another of the themes that arises from these essays is the need for archivists and their allies to engage the public in considering the importance of records. Many other fields or causes have had their public advocates, what some call public scholars or intellectuals. One thinks of Wallace Stegner and Bernard DeVoto and the early western environmental movement as but one example in which they brought critical issues into the public forum through their writings, public speeches, and other activities.[24] Many of the articles in this volume call for more forceful action by archivists about the need for information and other policies promoting the importance of records for an accountable government or accountable organizations. Leadership becomes a challenge, as well, as Anne

Van Camp and others note instances in which key archival agencies or professional associations have fumbled the ball in pushing for policy changes or in taking advantage of opportunities to explain why archival records are not just old artifacts kept in dusty museumlike structures.

As some of the essays demonstrate, archivists must take their cases directly to the public and policymakers. The description of the International Records Management Trust (IRMT) "Information for Accountability Workshops" suggests that records and other professionals can take a very active role in transforming the political climate regarding access to government records. The workshops are interesting because they bring together records professionals with government officials, citizens, and other stakeholders to grapple with issues relating to records and their values. Greg Bradsher argues that the National Archives and Records Administration's (NARA) work in making available records about Holocaust-era assets has "demonstrated the importance of NARA and archives not only to this country but to peoples, governments, and organizations in other countries." We think he is right, although we wonder what it is that cases like this taught society about archives. The motivation for a "full accounting" of what occurred during the Holocaust certainly seems to suggest a learning process about the importance of records for accountability purposes.

The public's misunderstanding of records and archives must seem to archivists and records professionals to be a mystery. After all, individuals have long been connected to records and vice versa. In the United States, for example, every decade the public is informed about the taking of the census, a massive and often controversial recordkeeping endeavor.[25] Archivists and records managers need to strive for a kind of archive literacy, just as others have argued for literacy about other pervasive societal information sources such as television and the computer.[26] Archivists and records managers need to move well beyond their traditional notion of advocacy in which the public and policymakers gain an appreciation for archives and records to making them understand *and* support the essential reason that records are created, how they need to be maintained, and what makes them significant.[27] In an age in which much is up for rethinking and redefinition (including even basic legal definitions), archivists must admit that the public perceives archives as *secret* and mysterious places.[28]

ARCHIVES, TRUST, AND ACCOUNTABILITY

The idea that archives are completely trustworthy places may be a reflection of particular professional psyches characterizing some archivists and records managers. O'Toole brings up important, troubling matters about professional ethics. He notes his own musings and discomfort in giving testimony criticizing colleagues, but weighed this against the greater importance of archives. Shelley Davis brings up similar problems, but she mostly reflects on being ignored and abandoned by colleagues in the face of a massive government mess in neglecting to preserve IRS records. How do archivists build trust with the public unless they take public stands on every important case involving a reliance on records for evidence and accountability?

As Davis and Chris Hurley remind us, governments are not hesitant about destroying records—very deliberately—in order to prevent investigations, as well as to generally weaken any sense of accountability. Unfortunately, in such cases we also know that archivists have not exactly played distinguished roles, often being part of the problem rather than part of the solution. Davis, not an archivist, speculates about this in some bewilderment about where archivists might have been. Hurley, an archivist, describes more pointedly the responsibility of the archivist, but notes that what happened in the Heiner affair was "misconduct" or, at least, some misplaced notions of archival responsibilities. Are archives and archivists, Hurley asks, only there to advise on "historical" values of records or do they have a broader role in accountability and related functions? As Hurley writes, "Sooner or later someone . . . is going to make the connection between the wrong they feel when the records needed to make their case are denied them and the compliant archivist who made that possible. When that day comes, archivists better have answers on where their responsibility lies." In the case described by Bradsher, openness, both from archivists and in public access to the records, seems to be the better course for affairs to take, for records make daily headlines, especially in matters like looted art and other stolen assets of Holocaust and other victims of World War II. His story elevates the kind of role that should be played by a national archive, but, alas, this national archive has more often been the focus of charges about a lack of energy in advocating a strenuous defense of records.

What archivists and other records professionals do about ethical issues seems to be a challenge, since records hold powerful sway over individuals, governments, and organizations because of the evidence they may reveal about misconduct. While all professional archival associations have ethics codes, even ethics committees, little practical work is often done about ethics. A few articles here and there relate to ethical issues. While our society is immersed in a great love affair with experts in everything and in trying to teach everything (such as ethics),[29] it seems that we need to hold onto some stronger notions of records purposes, such as accountability, and set directions for practical management that reflect on ethical matters as well. We continue to have troubling questions posed to us about the involvement of both government *and* government archivists in cases like the Heiner Affair in Australia or the Tuskegee syphilis experiments described by Tywanna Whorley in her essay in this book. If for no other reason, archivists and records managers must remember that society may remember because of records *and* that society may also recall the roles of records professionals because of the records they create and the records that survive in their repositories.

RECORDS, ACCOUNTABILITY, AND MEMORY

A lack of records can be a terrible blight, as Davis suggests in describing the absence of records in the IRS and the hostile, cutthroat environment she discovered there. The IRS was beset by a lack of records and corporate memory and by resistance both to change and to outside influence. Apart even from the issues of accountability suggested by the Jamaican bank problems, the mismanagement of records seems to be an important, if not critical, factor in that banking industry collapse. According to Victoria Lemieux, the misunderstanding about how records were created, the rules they needed to comply with, and the panoply of policies and regulations affecting them were all factors in the poor competitive position of the banks. So, Lemieux argues, it was not just poor management, but "weak management of the record creation and keeping processes." Some of this results from internal accountability and procedural safeguards, while some of the problems actually suggest local cultural traditions running counter to more Westernized notions of record keeping. In a sense, these banking managers lost track not just of how they needed to comply with external regulations but of their own corporate mission and tradition—their memory.

Memory problems are not just the absence of records. The value of records in holding individuals, governments, and organizations accountable can be graphically seen in the most dramatic subversion of records—their deliberate forgery. As David Gracy, in recounting a variety of cases about forgeries, notes, "every citizen who relies on the sanctity of recordkeeping systems and the integrity of individual records within those systems, especially systems of government, the contents of which are fundamental to entitling citizens to benefits, rights, and privileges, ought never cavalierly to take the incorruptibility of the system for granted." Indeed, considering forgery puts the archivist right back to fundamental principles and mission since, as Gracy writes, "essential . . . to detecting forgery is a knowledge of recordkeeping systems and of the structure of documents." The kinds of concerns raised by many about the reliability of records in electronic information systems long predate the emergence of computers, but they have existed since writing and recordkeeping systems first emerged. Wherever people commit activities to records, they will also attempt to fabricate or cover up documents.

Bureaucracies have long been the target of efficiency experts, administrators, and reformers, but they are also the victims of self-inflicted problems. Barbara Craig, in reviewing the Fabrikant Affair in Canada, in which a disgruntled university professor killed four of his colleagues, refocuses our attention on formal policies and procedures for creating and maintaining records, rules that we often view as bureaucratic nuisances of the worst kind. Craig, in this case, notes, "Freedom that is robust and defensible emerges logically, not paradoxically, from the attention paid to keeping complete and comprehensive records. Far from being only a lesser responsibility with only a brief claim on our attention, records making and keeping must be living commitments if they are to thrive." Craig's study reveals substantial problems in how the university kept records and the extraordinary efforts that it took to evaluate what documentation it had. Ultimately, it was the university's lack of memory that was at fault.

The issue of records for individual, corporate, and societal memory is an inherent part of the accountability function of records and recordkeeping systems, a matter that can be seen in major social and political controversies in recent years. We need to remember that records are critical to societal awareness and the memory of pivotal events, and that their use may be part of controversies forcing archivists to take stands on access to records—such as in the uproar about the Enola Gay exhibition at the Smithsonian Institution, prompting books and accusations from all parties in the case.[30] In our modern era, the past and its interpretation is under attack or being used by pundits of all political and ideological persuasions, suggesting that archivists and records managers need to be able to articulate why records are crucial for resolving such disputes while at the same time making record keepers sensitive to the possibilities of their being targeted as well. In cases as diverse as the debates about Afrocentrism, Thomas Jefferson and his relationships with his slave Sally Hemings, and the symbolism of monuments and the Confederate battle flag, it is possible, likely, and preferable that archivists take public stands—since records are critical to each case.[31] While society, in the absence of records or acceptable explanations, may fill in the gaps just by inventing, if necessary, events or their explanations,[32] archivists must sound off about the records that attest to the veracity of these events and explanations.

RECORDS, ACCOUNTABILITY, SECRECY, CENSORSHIP, AND CITIZENS

The importance of records to the public is also suggested throughout the essays, especially given the secrecy that can often surround such records (indeed, that organizations and governments want to keep records secret is testimony to their value for keeping these institutions and their employees accountable to society). The IRS case suggests the lack of any regard for the public by an agency with very powerful arms. Robin L. Chandler and Susan Storch's examination of the Brown & Williamson tobacco papers suggests that the public's right to know can outweigh proprietary and other interests, even in a situation where there are questions about the authority to make the records available—how they were obtained, who owns them, and other similar issues. And Whorley points out that in the absence of access to records, incidents of the Tuskegee Syphilis Study can take on meanings that detract from the very real horrors perpetrated.

Open access to government records is, according to Van Camp and other authors in this volume, the hallmark of a democratic government, and such openness is crucial to the notion of accountability being considered throughout this book. Van Camp's description of the records relating to foreign relations, especially in contrast to the more recently opened records of the former Soviet Bloc nations, provides a stark argument for the importance of more open government, the role of records in such openness, and the means by which openness can be accomplished. Kimberly Barata and her coauthors describe the legacy of secrecy in Sub-Saharan African governments, a "strongly entrenched culture of secrecy and conservatism" inherited from the colonial days, resulting in a "legislative and regulatory environment that discourages civil servants from making information available to the public." One might suppose that the situation is better in Western nations, but the descriptions of the IRS records management debacle and the Australian Heiner affair suggest that while the degree of secrecy might be different, openness is still a critical problem.

Secrecy is a particularly important theme, and has been one. Many have fought with governments about obsessive secrecy concerning their records and the information contained in them. Wallace indicates how excessive secrecy and manipulation of the documentary record impeded investigation into the Iran-Contra Affair and detracted from accurate portrayals of events. And Harris notes how secrecy became a justification in preventing South Africa from confronting the full scope of activities of its powerful intelligence services during the apartheid years.

As more records are opened, especially with the collapse of authoritarian regimes, revelations confound and surprise us, and the crucial role of the archivist should become even more obvious to the public.[33] DeVoto, for example, gave up on his idea to write histories about military campaigns during World War II when he discovered he could not have access to the records. DeVoto discovered that his enemy "resided in Washington in the person of the smug bureaucrat who always claimed to know better and constantly denied citizens needed information."[34] Others have sounded the same kind of alarm with nongovernmental records, like those documenting adoption.[35]

The power of records, even those seeming to have fairly routine value, is suggested by the concept of secrecy and can be seen in the Brown & Williamson case, where the release of the documents has served as a watershed for the development of government policy, the onset of tobacco litigation, and the battle against the control of information. Censorship, closely related to secrecy, is another theme that emerges from these pages, sometimes a forceful, explicit process and at other times a function implied. Verne Harris's account of the destruction of the public records in South Africa is, perhaps, the most chilling assessment because it is so blunt. Records are so critical that they have been important to societies that did not even develop formal—or Westernized versions of—writing systems.[36] Access to records, counter to secrecy or censorship, is a topic of importance throughout these essays. The Brown & Williamson case, as just one example, strongly suggests this importance, where the authors note that "given the gravity of the revelations about the tobacco industry, access to full text of the . . . collection was essential for informed public debate and long-term policy development within our democratic society." This same case points out the power of using the Internet to enhance such access.

Privacy and access to information may be the distinctive hallmarks of the modern Information Age, and as a result, archivists and records managers should have pivotal roles to play.[37]

CONCLUSION

The potential important role that archivists might play in arguing the importance of records in the public forum can be seen in the personal involvement of many of the authors in the cases they are describing. James O'Toole is an expert witness, and Shelley Davis is an official historian and insider (at least for a time). The authors describing the B & W tobacco papers write from firsthand experience. Greg Bradsher spearheads the efforts of the U.S. National Archives to play an active role in the Holocaust assets case. Terry Cook writes from firsthand experience. All belie the notion of the archivist as passive or conservative. Verne Harris, as an archivist, was involved in many of the situations he describes, bringing a personal perspective that is both powerful and emphatic. And Ann Van Camp describes her decade-long involvement as the first archivist appointed to the Historical Advisory Committee of the U.S. State Department.

There are many other case studies that could have been included in this volume, but it is more important to note that there are many more cases in which we could have hoped to have had archivists speaking out and arguing for the use of records to settle cases or resolve problems.[38] Who knows whether we will have many chances with future generations of archivists unless we build strong foundations for understanding records as supporting accountability and other such purposes. Think of the present generation. David Brooks describes this as a generation of people who are focused on careers (or goals of some sort), and who are also "extremely respectful of authority, treating their professors as one might treat a CEO or a division head at a company meeting." "The world they live in seems fundamentally just. If you work hard, behave pleasantly, explore your interests, volunteer your time, obey the codes of political correctness, and take the right pills to balance your brain chemistry, you will be rewarded with a wonderful ascent in the social hierarchy."[39] Who knows? Maybe this change will enhance an appreciation for the accountability value of records. Or it might just be indicative of a long hard road ahead. In either case, what is certain is that records and archives will regularly rise to the surface in accountability crises of all shapes and forms. It is hoped that this volume will serve as a weathervane indicating which way the winds can blow and serve as a resource to understand future accountability crises.

NOTES

1. For an organizational example of this, refer to Martha S. Feldman, *Order Without Design: Information Production and Policy Making* (Stanford, Calif.: Stanford University Press, 1989).

2. A representative sampling of the slim volume of writings explicitly examining the relationship between record keeping and accountability would include Edward F. Barrese, "Adequacy of Documentation in the Federal Government: Accountability Through the Record," *Information Management Review* 5 (Spring 1990): 53–58; Rachel Lilburn, "Ethics and Accountability in Public Sector Information Management,"

Archifacts, Apr. 1997, pp. 6–20; Sue McKemmish and Frank Upward, eds., *Archival Documents: Providing Accountability Through Recordkeeping* (Clayton, Australia: Ancora Press, 1993); McKemmish, "The Smoking Gun: Recordkeeping and Accountability," *Archifacts*, Apr. 1999, pp. 1–15; and McKemmish and Glenda Acland, "Archivists at Risk: Accountability and the Role of the Profession," paper presented at *Archives at Risk: Accountability, Vulnerability and Credibility*, Annual Conference of the Australian Society of Archivists, Brisbane, July 1999, available at sims.monash.edu.au/rcrg/publications/archive1.html.

3. Here is a sampling of recent studies with a strong focus on the role of records in different aspects of societal or governmental accountability: Gotz Aly, *"Final Solution": Nazi Population Policy and the Murder of the European Jews* (London: Arnold, 1999); Timothy Garton Ash, *The File: A Personal History* (New York: Random House, 1997); Seymour Hersh, *The Dark Side of Camelot* (New York: Little, Brown, 1997); Martha K. Higgins, *Political Policing: The United States and Latin America* (Durham, N.C.: Duke University Press, 1998); Adam Hochschild, *King Leopold's Ghost* (New York: Houghton Mifflin, 1998); and David A. Horowitz, ed., *Inside the Klavern: A Secret History of a Ku Klux Klan of the 1920s* (Carbondale, Ill.: Southern Illinois University Press, 1999).

4. A hallmark of the so-called Information Age has been the effort to control information, as depicted in James R. Beniger, *The Control Revolution: Technological and Economic Origins of the Information Society* (Cambridge, Mass.: Harvard University Press, 1986). Ironically, the very technologies aiming to control information either have depicted record keeping as bureaucratic obstacles to effective work, such as in Arno Penzias, *Digital Harmony: Business, Technology and Life After Paperwork* (New York: HarperBusiness, 1995), or have demonstrated that records can be more easily threatened by the very technologies creating them, as described by Tom Blanton, ed., *White House E-mail: The Top Secret Computer Messages the Reagan/Bush White House Tried to Destroy* (New York: New Press, 1995). If we worry about the future of traditional repositories, like libraries—an idea played with in the essays in R. Howard Bloch and Carla Hesse, eds., *Future Libraries* (Berkeley: University of California Press, 1995), then we should worry about places like archives and other repositories for records.

5. See Terry Cook, "Archival Science and Postmodernism: New Formulations for Old Concepts," *Archival Science* 1, no. 1 (2001): 3–24.

6. *Oxford English Dictionary*, 2d ed. (Oxford, Eng.: Clarendon Press, 1989).

7. Kevin P. Kearns, *Managing for Accountability: Preserving the Public Trust in Public and Nonprofit Organizations* (San Francisco: Jossey-Bass, 1996), pp. xv, xvi.

8. Kearns, *Managing for Accountability*, p. 36.

9. Ian Frazier, *Family* (New York: HarperPerennial, 1994), is a good example of this, but the considerable writings on genealogy and family history all attest to this notion of accountability as well. Nick Salvatore, *We All Got History: The Memory Books of Amos Weaver* (New York: Vintage Books, 1997) provides an example of how one individual maintained records about his life in order to guide subsequent generations. We can see this in diary writing as well, as described by Thomas Mallon, *A Book of One's Own: People and Their Diaries* (New York: Ticknor and Fields, 1984).

10. Carol Gelderman, *All the Presidents' Words: The Bully Pulpit and the Creation of the Virtual Presidency* (New York: Walker, 1997) is a good example of this.

11. For an introduction to such scholarly study, see Patrick H. Hutton, *History As an Art of Memory* (Hanover: University of Vermont/University Press of New England,

1993), and Matt K. Matsuda, *The Memory of the Modern* (New York: Oxford University Press, 1996).

12. There is growing public concern about how to communicate across the generations in an age when most things are viewed in ephemeral ways, as described by Stewart Brand, *The Clock of the Long Now: Time and Responsibility* (New York: Basic Books, 1999). Communication across generations is especially relevant, for we have seen how historical understanding can be forced aside, creating an environment lessening the accountability of public officials, organizations, and other individuals and institutions. For some provocative works about this, refer to Michael Schudson, *Watergate in American Memory: How We Remember, Forget, and Reconstruct the Past* (New York: Basic Books, 1992); Barbie Zelizer, *Covering the Body: The Kennedy Assassination, the Media, and the Shaping of Collective Memory* (Chicago: University of Chicago Press, 1992); Robert Brent Toplin, *History by Hollywood: The Use and Abuse of the American Past* (Urbana: University of Illinois Press, 1996); Toplin, ed., Ken Burns's *The Civil War: Historians Respond* (New York: Oxford University Press, 1996); and Toplin, ed., *Oliver Stone's USA: Film, History, and Controversy* (Lawrence: University Press of Kansas, 2000).

13. See Ian E. Wilson, "Information, Knowledge, and the Role of Archives," *Canadian Journal of Information and Library Science* 25 (Apr. 2000): 19–34.

14. See, for example, M.T. Clanchy, *From Memory to Written Record: England 1066–1307*, 2d ed. (Cambridge, Eng.: Blackwell, 1993); Patrick J. Geary, *Phantoms of Remembrance: Memory and Oblivion at the End of the First Millennium* (Princeton, N.J.: Princeton University Press, 1994); Jack Goody, *The Power of the Written Tradition* (Washington, D.C.: Smithsonian Institution Press, 2000); and Anthony Grafton, *The Footnote: A Curious History* (Cambridge, Mass.: Harvard University Press, 1997), and Grafton, *Forgers and Critics: Creativity and Duplicity in Western Scholarship* (Princeton, N.J.: Princeton University Press, 1990).

15. See Antonio González Quintana, *Archives of the Security Services of Former Repressive Regimes* (Paris: UNESCO, 1997). Available at unesco.org/webworld/reamp/secret_english.htm.

16. See, for example, Jean Bottero, *Mesopotamia: Writing, Reasoning, and the Gods* (Chicago: University of Chicago Press, 1992); Anne L. Bower, ed., *Recipes for Reading: Community Cookbooks, Stories, Histories* (Amherst: University of Massachusetts Press, 1997); Angel Rama, *The Lettered City*, trans. and ed. John Charles Chasteen (Durham, N.C.: Duke University Press, 1996); and Thomas Richards, *The Imperial Archive: Knowledge and the Fantasy of Empire* (London: Verso, 1993).

17. See tobaccoresolution.com; chemicalindustryarchives.org; and pbs.org/trade secrets/index.html.

18. See, for example, Konstantin Akinsha and Grigorii Kozlov with Sylvia Hochfield, *Beautiful Loot: The Soviet Plunder of Europe's Art Treasures* (New York: Random House, 1995); Tom Bower, *Nazi Gold: The Full Story of the Fifty-Year Swiss-Nazi Conspiracy to Steal Billions from Europe's Jews and Holocaust Survivors* (New York: HarperCollins, 1997); Hector Feliciano, *The Lost Museum: The Nazi Conspiracy to Steal the World's Greatest Works of Art* (New York: HarperBooks, 1997); Itamar Levin, *The Last Deposit: Swiss Banks and Holocaust Victims' Accounts*, trans. Natasha Dornberg (Westport, Conn.: Praeger, 1999); Lynn H. Nicholas, *The Rape of Europa: The Fate of Europe's Treasures in the Third Reich and the Second World War* (New York: Vintage Books, 1994); Isabel Vincent, *Hitler's Silent Partners: Swiss Banks, Nazi Gold, and the Pursuit of Justice* (New York: William Morrow, 1997); Jean Ziegler, *The Swiss, the Gold,*

and the Dead, trans. John Brownjohn (New York: Harcourt Brace, 1998); and Edwin Black, *IBM and the Holocaust: The Strategic Alliance Between Nazi Germany and America's Most Powerful Corporation* (New York: Crown, 2001).

19. "Banker Told to Submit Records, *New York Times,* Mar. 3, 2001, nytimes.com/ 2001/03/02/business/02BONY.html; "Clinton Officials Subpoenaed: Investigators Seeking Documents Related to Pardons," *ABC News,* Mar. 13, 2001, abcnews.go.com/ sections/us/DailyNews/pardons010313.html; "NC Documents Reveal DaimlerChrysler's 'Massive' Lemon Laundering," *PRNewswire,* Mar. 16, 2001, prnewswire.com/ cgi-bin/stories.pl?ACCT=104&STORY=/www/story/03–16–2001/0001449253 &EDATE=; and "Audit: State Medicaid Paid $3.2 Million to Dead Patients," *Naples Daily News,* Mar. 17, 2001, naplesnews.com/01/03/florida/d604198a.htm.

20. "Mexican Media Asks for FOI Law—President Said to Support Freedom of Information," *Editor & Publisher Online,* Mar. 1, 2001, mediainfo.com/ephome/news/newshtm/ stories/030101n12.htm; "Autopsy Records Are Public," *Savannah Morning News,* Mar. 16, 2001, savannahmorningnews.com/smn/stories/031601/OPEDautopsy.shtml; "Blood Agency 'Frightening' in Its Secrecy: Victims of Tainted Blood Denounce CBS's Policy of Hiding Information," *Ottawa Citizen,* Mar. 6, 2001, ottawa citizen.com/national/010305/5041647.html; "Bill Opening Access to Birth Records Fails," *Arkansas Democrat-Gazette,* Mar. 16, 2001, ardemgaz.com/week/Fri/ark/A_11yxgr-adopt16.html.

21. "Hack at Amazon-Owned Service Exposes Thousands," *CNET News.com,* Mar. 5, 2001, http://news.cnet.com/news/0–1007–200–5031805.html?tag=mn_hd; "Hacker Reportedly Gains Access to Records of 3,000 IU Students," *Evansville Courier & Press,* Feb. 26, 2001, courierpress.com/cgi-bin/view.cgi?200102/26+hacker 022601_business.html+20010226; "Lines Vary Between Public, Private Life," *Daily Skiff* (Texas Christian University), Feb. 26, 2001, http://news.excite.com/news/uw/ 010227/university-203; "Intimate Details Credit Cards, Social Security Numbers and Other Data Left Open to Prying Eyes When Court Documents Are Posted Online," *San Francisco Chronicle,* Mar. 15, 2001, sfgate.com/cgi-bin/article.cgi?file=/chronicle/archive/2001/03/15/BU60727.DTL; "ICQ Logs Spark Corporate Nightmare," CNET News.com, Mar. 15, 2001, cnet.com/news/0–1005–200–5148422.html.

22. "Documents Supporting Man's Pardon Not Found: Director of Archives Says Issue Part of Larger Problem," *Charleston* (W. Va.) *Daily Mail,* Mar. 28, 2001, daily mail.com/news/News/2001032724/; "Employers Learn to Sort Real, Fake ID Certificates," *Arkansas Democrat Gazette,* Mar. 7, 2001, ardemgaz.com/Wed/biz/ D1bnw immigration7.html; "Fire Clerk Denies Rigging Records," *Bergen* (N.J.) *Record,* Mar. 15, 2001, bergen.com/bcoast/charge200103153.htm; "Some Worry DYFS Case Audits May Taint Paper Trail," *Bergen Record,* Mar. 15, 2001, bergen.com/region/ dyfsnp 200103156.htm; "DYFS Supervisor Denies Doctoring Child Records," *Bergen Record,* Mar. 29, 2001, bergen.com/region/dyfs29200103292.htm.

23. "Officer Charged in Internal Affairs Office Break-in," *Boston Globe,* Mar. 13, 2001, boston.com/dailynews/072/nation/Officer_charged_in_internal_afs.html; "Canadian Lawyer Charged with Trying to Obtain Stolen Papers in Minneapolis," *Canoe.ca,* Mar. 15, 2001, canoe.ca/WorldTicker/CANOE-wire.Cda-Lawyer-Charged.html; "Man Gets Jail for Leaking Police Files," *Los Angeles Times,* Mar. 27, 2001, http://www. latimes.com/news/state/20010327/t000026473.html.

24. See John L. Thomas, *A Country in the Mind: Wallace Stegner, Bernard DeVoto, History, and the American Land* (New York: Routledge, 2000).

25. See Margo J. Anderson, *The American Census: A Social History* (New Haven, Conn.: Yale University Press, 1988).

26. David Bianculli, *Teleliteracy: Taking Television Seriously* (New York: Continuum, 1992) and Paul Gilster, *Digital Literacy* (New York: Wiley and Sons, 1997).

27. Elsie Freeman Finch, ed., *Advocating Archives: An Introduction to Public Relations for Archivists* (Metuchen, N.J.: Society of American Archivists and the Scarecrow Press, 1994), provides an excellent introduction to how archivists have thought about advocacy. Records managers have been much less focused on advocating their position.

28. The idea of basic redefining of the elements of the Information Age can be seen in James Boyle, *Shamans, Software, and Spleens: Law and the Construction of the Information Society* (Cambridge, Mass.: Harvard University Press, 1996). The popular public perception of archives as secret places may stem from notions about archives in institutions such as the Vatican; see Maria Luisa Ambrosini and Mary Willis, *The Secret Archives of the Vatican* (Boston: Little, Brown, 1969).

29. Gordon Marino, "Avoiding Moral Choices: Call in the Ethics Expert," *Commonweal*, Mar. 23, 2001, pp. 11–15.

30. Kai Bird and Lawrence Lifschultz, eds., *Hiroshima's Shadow: Writings on the Denial of History and the Smithsonian Controversy* (Stony Creek, Conn.: Pamphleteer's Press, 1998); Martin Harwit, *An Exhibit Denied: Lobbying the History of Enola Gay* (New York: Copernicus, 1996); Edward T. Linenthal and Tom Engelhardt, eds., *History Wars: The Enola Gay and Other Battles for the American Past* (New York: Metropolitan Books, 1996); and Philip Nobile, ed., *Judgment at the Smithsonian* (New York: Marlowe, 1995).

31. For some suggestive readings on this topic, refer to: Todd Gitlin, *The Twilight of Common Dreams: Why America Is Wracked by Culture Wars* (New York: Metropolitan Books, 1995); Mary Lefkowitz, *Not Out of Africa: How Afrocentrism Became an Excuse to Teach Myth As History* (New York: Basic Books, 1996); Lawrence W. Levine, *The Opening of the American Mind: Canons, Culture and History* (Boston: Beacon Press, 1996); Sanford Levinson, *Written in Stone: Public Monuments in Changing Societies* (Durham, N.C.: Duke University Press, 1998); Deborah Lipstadt, *Denying the Holocaust: The Growing Assault on Truth and Memory* (New York: Free Press, 1993); Gary B. Nash, Charlotte Crabtree, and Ross E. Dunn, *History on Trial: Culture Wars and the Teaching of the Past* (New York: Alfred B. Knopf, 1997); and Peter N. Stearns, *Meaning over Memory: Recasting the Teaching of Culture and History* (Chapel Hill: University of North Carolina Press, 1993).

32. See the classic study by Daniel J. Boorstin, *The Image: A Guide to Pseudo-Events in America* (New York: Harper Colophon, 1961).

33. Timothy Garton Ash, *The File: A Personal History* (New York: Random House, 1997); Richard Breitman, *Official Secrets: What the Nazis Planned, What the British and Americans Knew* (New York: Hill and Wang, 1998); Angus MacKenzie, *Secrets: The CIA's War at Home* (Berkeley: University of California Press, 1997); Michael Palumbo, *The Waldheim Files: Myth and Reality* (London: Faber and Faber, 1988); and Daniel Patrick Moynihan, *Secrecy: The American Experience* (New Haven, Conn.: Yale University Press, 1998).

34. Thomas, *A Country in the Mind*, p. 85.

35. E. Wayne Carp, *Family Matters: Secrecy and Disclosure in the History of Adoption.* (Cambridge, Mass.: Harvard University Press, 1998).

36. Elizabeth Hill Boone and Walter D. Mignolo, eds., *Writing Without Words: Alternative Literacies in Mesoamerica and the Andes* (Durham, N.C.: Duke University Press, 1994).

37. Philip E. Agre and Marc Rotenberg, eds., *Technology and Privacy: The New Landscape* (Cambridge, Mass.: MIT Press, 1997); Ellen Alderman and Caroline Kennedy, *The Right to Privacy* (New York: Vintage Books, 1997); David Brin, *The Transparent Society: Will Technology Force Us to Choose Between Privacy and Freedom?* (Reading, Mass.: Addison-Wesley, 1998); Fred H. Cate, *Privacy in the Information Age* (Washington, D.C.: Brookings Institution Press, 1997); Whitfield Diffie and Susan Landau, *Privacy on the Line: The Politics of Wiretapping and Encryption* (Cambridge, Mass.: MIT Press, 1998); Amitai Etzioni, *The Limits of Privacy* (New York: Basic Books, 1999); Michael Perelman, *Class Warfare in the Information Age* (New York: St. Martin's Press, 1998); Jeffrey Rosen, *The Unwanted Gaze: The Destruction of Privacy in America* (New York: Random House, 2000); Herbert I. Schiller, *Information Inequality: The Deepening Social Crisis in America* (New York: Routledge, 1996); H. Jeff Smith, *Managing Privacy: Information Technology and Corporate America* (Chapel Hill: University of North Carolina Press, 1994); Janna Malamud Smith, *Private Matters: In Defense of the Personal Life* (Reading, Mass.: Addison-Wesley, 1997); Reg Whitaker, *The End of Privacy: How Total Surveillance Is Becoming a Reality* (New York: New Press, 1999); and William Wresch, *Disconnected: Haves and Have-Nots in the Information Age* (New Brunswick, N.J.: Rutgers University Press, 1996).

38. Consider David Rudenstine, *The Day the Presses Stopped: A History of the Pentagon Papers Case* (Berkeley: University of California Press, 1996); Athan G. Theoharis, ed., *A Culture of Secrecy: The Government Versus the People's Right to Know* (Lawrence: University Press of Kansas, 1998); and Diane Vaughan, *The Challenger Launch Decision: Risky Technology, Culture, and Deviance at NASA* (Chicago: University of Chicago Press, 1996).

39. David Brooks, "The Organization Kid," *Atlantic Monthly*, Apr. 2001, pp. 40–54 (quotations pp. 41, 50).

EXPLANATION

Archives on Trial: The Strange Case of the Martin Luther King, Jr., Papers

James M. O'Toole

Records and documents are frequently brought into court as evidence. By giving silent but effective testimony, records help determine matters of fact and matters of law in both civil and criminal proceedings. The fundamental content of the law itself is enshrined in written statutes and regulations, at least in modern democratic societies. Writing also codifies the common law, as it is interpreted and applied in historical and evolving case law. Moreover, the routine documentation of human affairs may be brought to bear in resolving disputes between citizens. Letters, contracts, wills, deeds, and other records often prove significant in such cases, though they must be used carefully. In Western legal systems, for instance, records are generally understood as exceptions to the rules barring hearsay: Since documents cannot be cross-examined, as live witnesses can, they constitute a kind of third-party evidence that would not be admissible in trials if there were not independent means for authenticating them and thereby relying on what they have to say. Even so, records have some advantages over live witnesses. Because they were created contemporaneously with the questions at issue, records can be more reliable than witnesses, who are usually in the position of trying to remember events after the fact. For these reasons, records often join other "exhibits" as part of the body of evidence in court cases, as recent litigation involving Microsoft or the American tobacco companies has amply demonstrated. Indeed, archivists have long advanced the potential legal uses of records as one of the primary justifications for the maintenance of archival programs. Precisely because records offer a form of legal accountability, archivists argue, those records should be properly managed.

Less common are those occasions when records and documents themselves become the focus of a legal proceeding. Sometimes it is the use of records that is at issue, as in copyright cases: Was a particular use of written materials, whether published or in manuscript, a "fair use" under the terms of the copyright laws? The cases of the last thirty years on this subject, most notably the one involving the unpublished letters of the novelist J.D. Salinger, have addressed this question, though these cases have been resolved in ways that many archivists and scholars find troubling. However that may be, the records themselves are very much at issue in these sorts of cases. Even clearer examples of the centrality of records are those instances in which the ownership and possession of documents is the matter before the court. In recent years, the most striking instance of this kind of proceeding was the protracted case of the papers of Martin Luther King, Jr., a case in which I was personally involved. A lawsuit to determine the ownership of this valuable archival collection came to trial in the spring of 1993. On its face, this was a simple dispute over property. At the same time, it also raised a number of questions of significant interest to those concerned about the documentary record, broadly defined. What is the nature of archival materials? What is the purpose of archival processes, and how can we tell when these have been satisfactorily accomplished? What standards of professional ethics are involved in archival work, and how should general ethical principles be applied in particular cases? Can we determine the "proper" placement of historically significant documentation? A review of the case suggests some larger reflections on the role of records in modern society.

THE PAPERS

By the time of his assassination in April 1968, Martin Luther King, Jr., had become one of the iconic figures of the twentieth century and, indeed, of all American history. Thrust into leadership of the modern civil-rights movement as a young minister in his first pastoral assignment during the boycott of segregated buses in Montgomery, Alabama, in 1955–1956, King went on to found the Southern Christian Leadership Conference (SCLC), which became the nation's foremost civil-rights organization. For the first time in decades, the legal and de facto segregation of black Americans was systematically challenged and began to crumble, and the impact of that social revolution was felt everywhere in the country. At his death, King was still expanding his vision of nonviolent political action, joining the growing opposition to American participation in the Vietnam War and addressing issues of economic justice at home. Surely it was clear even before his death that he would be someone whom historians would study over and over into the indefinite future.[1] Thus, his letters, papers, sermons, and other documents were sure to be an important body of sources for historical study, and their proper preservation and management was a matter of great importance.

Shortly after he received the Nobel Peace Prize in 1964, King began to make arrangements for the preservation of his papers, but the matter was a complicated one. Then the pastor of a church in Atlanta, the city in which he had been born, he had focused most of his activity on the South, where legal segregation presented the most obvious first target of civil-rights activity. An archival repository in that region would thus seem the logical place for the documentation of his movement, but countervailing arguments worked against making that decision. The political and racial climate of the South during those years was uncertain and violent, with church burnings and the murder of civil-rights workers making news with chilling frequency. Would his papers really be secure in a southern library or archives, or might some opponent seek the symbolic satisfaction of attacking King and his legacy by destroying the historical evidence of it? Accordingly, King looked elsewhere in arranging for the disposition of his papers.

The precise origin of the plan to deposit some of them at Boston University (BU) is not wholly clear. King had attended the university's School of Theology in the early 1950s and had earned his ministerial doctorate there; it was also there that he had met his future wife, Coretta Scott King. Though he had had little contact with the school during the intervening years, he was open to an approach in the spring of 1964 from his alma mater, asking that he consider placing his papers in the library, in a newly created department of special collections. An informal exchange of letters took place between King and the director of the university's library, and soon the papers were being shipped from Atlanta. At the time, the collection consisted of fifteen file-drawer-sized transfer cases, eleven of them from the offices of the SCLC and four from the King family home. By the end of that summer, the papers, most of them dated prior to 1961, were physically in the library of Boston University, at its campus on the banks of the Charles River in Boston; a second, smaller shipment of papers was made the following year.[2]

To say that this was accomplished through an "informal exchange of letters" is to understate the issue that assumed center stage during the trial in 1993. No formal contract or deed of gift was ever signed between King and Boston University. Instead, in keeping with what was then a not uncommon archival practice, the transfer was effected by this informal exchange. University officials had drafted a short, two-sentence letter for King to sign, but King chose to write his own. It was the wording of that letter and the document's standing as a legal instrument that lay at the core of the later dispute. He began by naming the BU library as "the Repository of my correspondence, manuscripts and other papers, along with a few of my awards and other materials which may come to be of interest in historical or other research." He also expressed his intention to send other papers to the library from year to year, though (after the second transfer) he never did so. In effecting the physical exchange of the materials, however, he expressly retained for himself the legal ownership of them. "All papers and other objects which thus pass into the custody of Boston University remain my legal property," he wrote, going further to indemnify the school from any damage the papers might suffer "despite scrupulous care." He then stated another intention: that he would periodically designate a portion of the papers to become "the absolute property of Boston University as an outright gift from me." During his lifetime, he never acted on this intention and never legally transferred ownership of the papers to the school or to anyone else. Finally, he concluded his letter with a very significant sentence: "In the event of my death, all such materials deposited with the University shall become from that date the absolute property of Boston University."[3]

Where, then, did the matter stand at King's death in April 1968? Since the time of the transfer of the papers to BU, he had generated an even larger amount of material, and all that documentation remained in his offices and home in Atlanta. He had retained the legal ownership of all his papers, including those at BU, for he never executed the formal deed of gift to which he had alluded, and the school never pressed him for one. Expressed as it was as an "intention," his statement had little legal effect. We all "intend" to do a lot of things, one of the attorneys subsequently explained to me, but the law does not and probably cannot enforce all of them. The last sentence of his letter might seem to have resolved the matter, however, with the fact of his death automatically conveying ownership to BU, but this may not have been as legally straightforward as it seemed. Specifically, this expression on King's part might not conform to the so-called "statute of wills," which required that property transfers at death be accomplished in a particular manner and form—most important, that any bequest be witnessed by at least two third parties. The absence of witnesses to King's letter might thus render it invalid. Finally, did the letter constitute a binding contract between King and the university? If so, BU had certain obligations to fulfill, including that of providing "scrupulous care" to the papers. Failure to do so might invalidate the contract. These were the legal issues that the subsequent trial would have to resolve.

THE CASE

By the middle 1980s, Coretta Scott King and the other members of her family had established the Martin Luther King, Jr., Center for the Study of Non-Violent Social Change. Located in Atlanta, where it engaged in a variety of educational and public programs, the center also became the archival repository for those papers of King that were in his possession at the time of his death. Covering essentially the second half of his public career, these consisted of documents generated after 1961, including many of his most significant writings and speeches. A grant from the National Endowment for the Humanities in the middle 1970s had made it possible for the center to process King's own papers and to produce a finding aid for them; the grant had also supported the processing of other collections there, including the records of the SCLC and those of the Congress of Racial Equality and the Student Non-Violent Coordinating Committee. As the center became a locus for the study of King and his impact, it began to look northward to those records of the early years of his activity that were at Boston University. Rather than having all (or almost all) King's papers under one roof, the collection was split between two widely separated archives. Researchers had to travel to both places: Any number of topics discussed in the papers at one repository could be fully understood only after consulting the papers at the other. The fundamental unity of the collection, something that archivists have traditionally valued and that is implicit in the principles of provenance and original order, had been shattered, with predictably unhappy consequences. Accordingly, in 1987, acting in her capacity as executor of her deceased husband's estate, Coretta Scott King filed suit in the Suffolk County Superior Court in Boston for the return to Atlanta of that portion of his papers that were at Boston University.[4]

As with many legal cases, the preliminaries of this one dragged on for several years. Documents and depositions were assembled on both sides, and the legal process of "discovery" moved slowly forward. As part of the general maneuvering, BU even filed a countersuit against the family and the center, claiming that since King had designated the school as the repository of his papers, the material in Atlanta should now be sent to Boston and the entire collection housed there; this argument was quickly rejected by the court. At least one attempt at compromise was made, with the idea floated that the items in both collections be microfilmed and the whole reunited on film in a way that it could not be in reality. Another participant in the negotiations even suggested that the collection be "shared" by the two repositories—physically reassembled into one whole and shipped back and forth between Boston and Atlanta, spending six months per year in each place. It was "a classic lawyer's compromise," the author of this suggestion said to me at one point, realizing by then that it would have been completely unworkable and probably damaging to the papers. With the failure to find any middle ground, the case of *Coretta Scott King v. the Trustees of Boston University* came to trial early in 1993.

It was at this point that I became involved. Attorneys from the Boston law firm of Goulston and Storrs, which had agreed to represent Mrs. King on a *pro bono* basis, contacted me in early February at my office at the University of Massachusetts, Boston, where I was director of the M.A. program in history and archives. Since a collection of documents was at the heart of the case, the lawyers needed something of a crash course in archival theory and practice, hoping to gain an understanding of what archives were and what archivists did with the materials in their care. They also hoped to determine whether BU had fulfilled its responsibilities to give "scrupulous care" to the King Papers, and whether the university's custody of the collection had been in conformity with accepted professional practice. Moreover, the advocates needed a way to understand the organization of the very materials at issue; since the collection was split right down the middle, it was not clear how all the various parts of it fit together. Never having used archives themselves, the lawyers also needed to know how scholars extracted relevant information from such collections. How did researchers go about using papers of this kind, and what finding aids were available? For that matter, just what were these "finding aids" that they had heard about, and what was this "provenance" business that they seemed to encounter at every turn? If they hoped to present such information to a jury, they first needed to understand it themselves. If they hoped to convince that jury to sanction reuniting the King Papers in the one repository in Atlanta, they needed to find a way of conveying exactly what was at stake.

Our initial interview was an exercise in what had come to be identified in professional parlance as a question of "archives and society." By the early 1990s, archivists in the United States had been discussing for several years the public perception of archives and archivists, and they had been searching for ways to extend an appreciation of professional issues to a wider public, including especially those who had never visited an archives.[5] The two lawyers, who spent about an hour and a half in my office one afternoon, had already done their homework. They had contacted the Society of American Archivists (SAA) for relevant literature, and it became clear in the course of our conversation that they had read my textbook, *Understanding Archives and Manuscripts*, which had been published two years before. They were quick studies (as all litigating attorneys must be), and they came primed with well-defined questions. At the time, I looked on our conversation as a teaching opportunity, a chance to promote a wider understanding of archives. It was not until later that I realized that, beyond the technical questions, the lawyers were also assessing me and my potential as a witness. In addition to researchers who had used the collection, they also wanted to put on the stand a witness who could explain archives to the twelve ordinary citizens of Boston who would ultimately decide the case. Was I someone who could do that? Was I, to be blunt, presentable? Were there any quirks of personality that might get in the way of the message and the information they wanted to convey? How clear could I make the sometimes arcane principles of archival practice? Apparently, I passed muster on all these counts and at the beginning of March agreed to act as a consultant and expert witness on behalf of the King family and the center in Atlanta.

Almost immediately, I became immersed in the details of the case. Thick packages of depositions and other pretrial materials arrived at my office at school and at home—neighbors wondered what all these parcels arriving by taxi were—and I analyzed them for the archival issues that were involved. Especially important were copies of the finding aids that BU had prepared for the King Papers, and an initial review of these proved very troubling. The papers had become jumbled physically in the shipping from Georgia to Massachusetts nearly thirty years before, and the inventories suggested that little or no effort had subsequently been made to restore the original order. There was one run of correspondence, for instance, filed alphabetically and covering the years 1956–1957 that had not been put back together after having been separated in packing and transit: Files for the letters A–G were in boxes 13A–17 of the collection, while the files for the letters H–Z were in boxes 60–67. A series arranged alphabetically by state was similarly disordered: Boxes 10–13A contained New York through Wyoming (with Oklahoma under "U," for some reason), while boxes 48–51A held Alaska through Montana. I was subsequently asked how I knew that these separated pieces actually belonged together—well,

I just did, but finding a way to explain that archivally obvious perception took some effort. The conclusion nevertheless seemed clear: Some of the most basic work of physical and intellectual arrangement had not been done during the period in which BU had held the King Papers.

These impressions were confirmed when I visited the university's archives and special collections department to examine the papers in person. This visit had been carefully arranged in advance and was conducted according to an elaborate protocol. Together with two Goulston and Storrs lawyers, I met in the morning at the offices of BU's attorney, and we all went from there to the school's library. After registering according to the normal procedures, we were taken into the stacks to view the collection, which was housed on standard library shelves in the familiar gray acid-free boxes. The climate control and fire detection systems seemed adequate enough, but the collection was shelved directly under a large sewer pipe; there was no evidence that there had ever been any leakage from this pipe, but it seemed a cause for concern nonetheless. The three of us then returned to the reading room and spent the rest of the day calling for and examining the contents of approximately sixty boxes from the collection, while a paralegal from the BU lawyer's office sat watching us.

This examination confirmed my fear that even the most basic archival work of arrangement and description had not been performed, and I later testified to this at the trial. The intellectual disorder of the inventories matched the physical disorder of the collection. There were a great many misfilings, and some individual documents had been removed from files, with very imprecise "separation" records. A letter to King from Malcolm X, for example, had been removed and replaced with a photocopy marked "original removed, on display," apparently a reference to a long-ago exhibit; the current whereabouts of the letter were unknown. In sum, it seemed to me that, when the files had arrived in Boston, they had simply been unpacked and put on the shelves in that same random order, with no effort to reconstruct the record series in which the collection had been compiled in the first place. In fact, it seemed an example of the mistake I had seen beginning archival students make many times over the years—that of thinking that the physical order in which they first encountered a collection was the intellectual "original order" that archival theory demanded that they respect.

During a second visit to the library a few weeks later, we again examined some boxes from the King Papers, but we also looked at other collections to get a sense of BU's overall archives and manuscripts effort. How did the condition of the King Papers compare with that of the papers of other individuals? The department was well known in the Boston area and nationwide for its Twentieth Century Archives. Under the leadership of its longtime director, Howard Gottlieb, BU had come to specialize in collecting the papers of well-known figures in contemporary America, particularly those whose prominence was grounded in popular culture. Beginning at a time when many other archives had spurned such collections, perhaps because they were judged not "serious" enough, BU had actively solicited and preserved the papers of actors, movie stars, musicians, popular authors, and others; it was now an important center for research on such topics. Unfortunately (as it seemed to me), BU had apparently taken better care of some of these collections than it had of the papers of Martin Luther King, Jr. In contrast to the jumbled and disorganized inventory of the King Papers, the eleven-page finding aid for the Gene Kelly Papers was a model of clarity; the two-volume inventory of the Roddy McDowell Papers (designated as "restricted until the year 2100") seemed frankly laughable in its detail, including an itemized description of some of the costumes McDowell had worn in several of his movies. I concluded that, while the King Papers had essentially languished unorganized, the archives had lavished attention on collections that, while not valueless, were certainly of lesser historical significance.

Throughout all the pretrial activity, I was repeatedly called upon to explain professional archival matters, and indeed archival thinking, to the attorneys. This was not only challenging in its own right—(How did one convey, in simple terms, the knowledge peculiar to one professional guild to members of another? How did one express to outsiders matters taken for granted by one's own profession?), but it also demanded reflection on the source and validity of my own knowledge. How did I know what I thought I knew about records, and what evidence could I offer that I was correct? How, for example, did I know that those scattered alphabetical files of correspondence were really two parts of the same whole, even if physically separated? How could I be certain that they hadn't been filed that way in the first place and that BU was indeed thus preserving the original order? Why did I say that the informal and legally imprecise means of transferring the papers to BU in the early 1960s had been common among archives at the time? More seriously, were there ethical issues involved in my criticizing the way an archive with which I had had no previous contact had set its priorities and done its work? I was concluding in my own professional opinion that BU had not cared for the King Papers as it should have, but was there a difference between merely thinking that privately and testifying to it in court? Addressing these questions threw me back on my experience and on the professional literature, which itself had to be mediated for nonprofessional understanding. As we moved toward the trial itself, much time was spent in conversation with the attorneys, as I attempted to express these issues clearly and they pressed me for greater precision.

THE TRIAL

The trial that would decide the fate of the King Papers opened on Wednesday, April 21, 1993, in the Suffolk County Courthouse in Boston. I attended only some of the initial proceedings. After jury selection and opening statements, testimony began with the examination of Howard Gottlieb by Mrs. King's attorneys, during which time I was present. He spoke of the preparation of several successive inventories, each supposedly more "refined" than the previous one, but this did not correspond with my assessment. A security microfilm had been prepared for the entire collection about 1969, but no reorganization of the papers into a sensible series arrangement had been undertaken at that time. At one point, he testified that the collection had "got out of order" through researchers' use of it, a circumstance that, if true, seemed troubling. Much of this testimony was probably of interest mainly to me, as an archivist. Other important topics were covered, including some discussions between the family and the university about the return of the papers to Atlanta; these discussions began shortly after the assassination, but they were never concluded. Over the intervening days of the trial, several other witnesses, including Andrew Young and Coretta Scott King herself, appeared, but I knew of their testimony only through the accounts in the newspapers. In the meantime, I continued to work with the attorneys in preparation for my own testimony, which finally took place on April 29 and 30, 1993.

The first step in this procedure was to qualify me as an expert witness. Why should the court listen to what I had to say about the matter at hand? The lawyers had to establish that I was someone who knew something about archives and whose testimony in the case should be considered by the court. This was accomplished by essentially working through my résumé in a question-and-answer format: what academic degrees did I have, what archives had I worked in, what books and articles had I published, and what professional associations did I belong to? Once "qualified" in this way, the examiner next led me through my expected testimony. First, I was asked to describe what an archivist is and does; as in my earlier conversations with the attorneys, this too was an occasion to try to explain archives to a lay public. Next, I was led through a description of the usual archival practices and procedures: acquiring a collection, arranging it according to accepted principles, and preparing an inventory and other descriptive media for it. Though I was trying always to avoid jargon and other technical lingo, whenever I lapsed into it the lead attorney (who was by now reasonably fluent in this language himself) stopped me and asked for an explanation for the jury. Next we talked specifically about the King Papers at Boston University, and I described my examination of them and the conclusions I had drawn about their organization. The "punch line" to my testimony—which altogether occupied about an hour one afternoon and two hours the following morning—was to ask whether I thought the collection at BU had been handled in accord with sound professional practice. I answered that I thought it had not.

My cross-examination by the lawyer for Boston University was not as grueling as the years of watching courtroom dramas on television had led me to expect or to fear. He asked me for a few points of clarification on aspects of archival practice, but he was more interested in other matters. In particular, by probing me about the field of history that I studied and taught, he was careful to establish with the jury that I was not an expert on the life and work of Martin Luther King, Jr. Of course, I was not and had never claimed to be. The reason for this line, however, became clear soon enough. I was the final witness for the plaintiffs, and the first witness called by BU in defense was Taylor Branch, the definitive biographer of King, who spoke of his use of the papers in researching and writing *Parting the Waters: America in the King Years, 1954–1963*, the first volume of his projected three-volume work. No matter what state the papers were in, he had had no difficulty in using them, he testified, and this seemed to be the point which the university's attorneys wanted to get across. Over the next several days, other witnesses (none of whom I heard directly) were called by the defense, including John Silber, the sometimes controversial president of the university who had run unsuccessfully for governor of Massachusetts in the last election. On May 5, the case went to the jury.

In most trials, the judge's instructions to the jury play a critical role. How the judge defines and clarifies the issues of the case is crucial, for these instructions make clear both what it is that the jury must decide and the legal principles to guide them in making that decision. I was not present to hear these instructions, but the newspaper reports made it clear that they focused on the narrow question of the status of King's July 1964 letter to the university. Did that letter constitute a legally valid charitable pledge to give his papers to Boston University? Had BU taken particular actions in reliance on that pledge? Was the letter a clear expression of King's "donative intent?" If the answer to these questions was "yes," the legal requirements of the bequest had been fulfilled at the time of his death, and the university was the legitimate owner of the papers. The seven men and five women of the jury met for an hour that day, and returned for another five hours of deliberation on May 6. Early that afternoon, they returned with a verdict, later described to the press by one of them. By a vote of 10–2 (the minimum required), they determined that the letter was enforceable and that Boston University was indeed the legal owner of the King Papers that it held.[6] Attorneys for Mrs. King appealed this decision, but in 1995 the Supreme Judicial Court of Massachusetts upheld the jury's decision.

PROFESSIONAL ISSUES

From a purely personal standpoint, my involvement in this case was interesting and even exciting on several counts. For one thing, it gave me the chance to observe a court case from the inside. I know—indeed am related to—many lawyers, but I had never seen how they work in preparing and presenting a case. I was impressed by the amount of effort that goes into such an undertaking and by the amount of detail they must master in the process. It was likewise instructive to observe professional legal culture, to see both the strategy and the tactics of a trial. I was pleasantly surprised by the goodwill on all sides, even in contentious matters, and the commitment to resolve disputes in an amicable manner: It came to seem normal when the aggressively opposing attorneys of the courtroom ordered up lunch for themselves and several witnesses for both sides during breaks in the proceedings. Trials may not be the perfect means for resolving society's disputes, I concluded, but given a commitment from all the parties to abide by the results they are probably better than most of the alternatives. Beyond all this, as an archivist, the experience gave me the chance to reflect on several important professional issues.

Throughout, the case demanded that archival materials and processes be described to an audience far different from that which most archivists routinely encounter. The American archival profession now recognizes the importance of presenting archival concerns to a wider public, and a number of successful efforts at this have been sponsored by particular archives around the country. These are often exercises in preaching to the converted, however, or at least to those who are willing to be converted. Here was a case in which a basic level of archival knowledge had to be conveyed to an otherwise uninterested audience. The jurors had not sought out this opportunity to learn about archives—if the common supposition is correct, many of them had hoped to avoid it by trying to get themselves excused from jury service—but it was now necessary that they acquire enough comprehension of what archives did to address the issues of the case. Regardless of which side one took in the dispute, central to it was some understanding of how archives acquired the papers of prominent persons, what the archives then did to organize those collections, and how researchers were able to make use of them. Thus, though I was testifying on behalf of only one of the parties, my role was in some respects a broader one. Many archivists continue to acknowledge (at least in theory) the importance of seizing "teachable moments" about archives, hoping that over the long term greater public support for archival work will be forthcoming. Such moments arrive unpredictably, however, and the King case shows the importance of being ready to seize them.

More particularly, the case presented a graphic example of the problem of divided archival collections. The papers of this tremendously significant historical figure were split between two competing repositories, each jealously guarding its part of the whole and eager to hold onto its piece of King's legacy. Officials of Boston University testified that they had never used the King Papers for fund-raising purposes, either for the library or for the university in general; indeed, they seemed to resent the implication that they would exploit King's reputation in that way. Even so, they were clearly proud of their possession of some of his papers. The fact that King himself had, in the disputed letter of 1964, designated the school as the "Repository"—capital letter and all—of his papers seemed to hold great symbolic significance. At the same time, the King Center in Atlanta had by the time of the trial become the primary site for the preservation of King's public memory. This was not without its own difficulties, as subsequent disputes with the National Park Service over the birthplace and with various media organizations over the rights to the famous "I Have a Dream" speech would later indicate.[7] Still, the center had by the middle 1980s come to think of itself as the appropriate repository, with or without a capital R, for the papers. Even if one could understand the circumstances that had led to the division of the collection in the first place—most especially the 1960s desire to get the papers physically out of the dangerous South—both sides were now left with a serious archival dilemma: a collection that (most would probably agree) *should* have been a single, organic whole was instead split into two widely dispersed pieces. Archivists had long decried competition between repositories in acquiring collections, but this case addressed the consequences of a division already accomplished. What was the best way—best for the papers and best for any user of them—to resolve that problem?

CONCLUSIONS

In working on the case, I came to believe that it would be best to have the entire collection at the center in Atlanta. This was not an easy conclusion to draw, but I did so on the basis of what seemed best for the papers themselves. Of the precise legal question at stake—did King's letter constitute a legally enforceable charitable pledge?—I knew little, but as an archivist I could see the damage to archival integrity, to scholarship, and thus to long-term historical understanding of King and his movement that was caused by the division of the papers. Moreover, I was genuinely convinced that BU had not lived up to its responsibility to care for this priceless collection. The most basic work of arrangement and description, both intellectual and physical, had not been performed on these papers, as far as I could see; from the frankly amateurish look of the inventories, I even questioned the school's ability to do so. I remarked to a colleague that any student in one of my archival courses who had presented such an inventory as the product of an internship project would flunk and would deserve to. For those reasons, it seemed to be in the best interests of the papers to put them in a place where they might be better cared for. This was obviously a relative judgment, as all such conclusions must be. I was aware of persistent problems with the archival program at the center in Atlanta, and these were troubling. There was not a full-time archivist on the center's staff at the time, though one was hired shortly afterward. Moreover, since then, the center has been criticized for circumstances that make use of the papers inconvenient, and the family has been negotiating for the sale of its portion of the papers to the Library of Congress, an arrangement not yet (as of this writing) finalized.[8] Had the jury's decision gone the other way, would the papers in Boston really have been any better off in Atlanta? Perhaps not. Or perhaps might the fact of reuniting the collection into a single whole have given an impetus to an improved archival program there? Maybe, but that could have been mere wishful thinking. In any event, these concerns added uncertainty to the case and my participation in it. What were my own responsibilities here—to the profession, to the papers, even to History (with a capital letter of its own)?

The case also raised issues of professional ethics. The SAA code of ethics warns, rightly enough, against one archivist engaging in "irresponsible criticism of other archivists or institutions," and yet very strong criticism was at least implicit in my testimony.[9] Was that criticism responsible or irresponsible? I had been retained in part to analyze and to express a judgment about how the archives and special collections department at BU had cared for the King Papers.

My examination of the collection had led me to conclude that the department had done a very poor job, and I said so in response to a direct question at the trial. While I had not stated my concurrent fear that the department might not be capable of doing any better, this was a professional matter not to be taken lightly. I like to think that my motives were not compromised, but others may be better judges of that. In (at the time) twenty years of archival practice in the greater Boston area, I had had little contact with the staff at BU, either positive or negative. They had not been particularly active in the local professional community, but they had plainly built up a program that enjoyed strong support from the university. As director, Howard Gottlieb had been successful at winning public recognition through the news media, a skill of which some local archivists may have been jealous. The archival program at BU was, to that degree, an archives-and-society success story. Yet I had formed the opinion that there may have been less to it than met the eye. In such circumstances, what were my ethical responsibilities—speaking out or silence? Should I refrain from criticizing a colleague and his program? Or should I heed the injunction of another part of the ethics code, which demanded that archivists apply "sound archival principles" and that they "establish intellectual control over their holdings?" I myself had written that archives had a fundamental "responsibility to organize the[ir] records in a coherent and understandable way" and that they should do so "as quickly as possible" on receipt of a collection.[10] Those requirements had not been fulfilled, in my view: the King Papers were essentially as unorganized and incoherent in 1993 as they had been when they arrived in Boston nearly thirty years before. In deciding to testify on behalf of one side in the case, I had decided that what I took to be the good of the papers should take precedence, but I remained somewhat troubled by the criticism of colleagues that my actions necessarily entailed.

Finally, the King Papers case provided a new perspective on the nature of archival materials and why society values them. At first glance, this collection was like countless others that crowd the shelves of the nation's archives. It contained the correspondence, writings, and other documentary "leavings" of an individual's life, records that were originally created in response to specific, often mundane, circumstances but that had now taken on additional meaning and usefulness. Like other collections, this one could be used to reconstruct a person's life and career, potentially revealing to subsequent generations patterns and factors that were not apparent to the participants themselves. To say that this was just another collection of personal papers is to be deliberately perverse, however, precisely because of the person whose papers they were. If Martin Luther King, Jr., had simply been the pastor of a church in one southern city, his papers would probably have had only a local interest. But King's extraordinary life and career had transformed these papers into something else, perhaps even into relics of a certain kind. Every item he had touched, every letter he had written or signed, had the potential to convey a powerful connection between himself and any future reader. His autograph was certainly valuable in monetary terms, but archivists, historians, and ordinary citizens alike could feel the emotional power of these papers. Even the most mundane item in the collection had the power to transport people of the present back into the world, and even into the presence, of this singular man. Even the most innocuous item could evoke the drama of that earlier era, one in which sweeping and enduring historical change was underway. Was it not in part the very power of those emotions and symbols that made the struggle over this collection so passionate, that made Boston University want to keep the papers, and that made the King Center want to have them all in one place? The papers were valued not just for the information they contained, but also for their power to forge human connections across time and even to evoke larger human aspirations. In this particular case, there was, perhaps, an unhappy outcome for all concerned: the collection remained divided, with little cooperation between the two repositories; in neither place were the papers treated as well as they deserved. If, however, we can derive lessons about the nature of archival materials and the importance of their proper care, the case will have served a larger, more important purpose.

NOTES

1. There is, of course, a huge scholarly literature on King. The standard accounts are David Garrow, *Bearing the Cross: Martin Luther King, Jr., and the Southern Christian Leadership Conference* (New York: Morrow, 1986); Taylor Branch, *Parting the Waters: America in the King Years, 1954–1963* (New York: Simon and Schuster, 1988); and Branch, *Pillar of Fire: America in the King Years, 1963–1965* (New York: Simon and Schuster, 1998). Branch is planning a third volume, which will complete his life of King.

2. For a review of the early history of the papers, see Ron Chepesiuk and Gloria Kelley-Palmer, "The Martin Luther King Library and Archives at the Crossroads," *American Libraries* 25 (February 1994), pp. 148–151. Readers unfamiliar with Boston's academic geography should be careful to note the distinction between Boston University (where the King Papers were held), Boston College (my current employer), and the University of Massachusetts—Boston (where I taught at the time of my involvement in the case). These are three entirely separate universities, the first two private and the third public.

3. King to Boston University Library, July 16, 1964, copy in author's possession. The full text of the letter was published in the *Boston Globe*, May 7, 1993; it also appears in the decision of the Massachusetts Supreme Judicial Court that finally settled the matter: *Coretta Scott King v. Trustees of Boston University*, 420 Mass. 52 (1995).

4. For a useful summary of the early actions of the case, see *New York Times*, May 4, 1993; see also "Boston and Atlanta Maneuver over King Papers," *Wilson Library Bulletin* 60 (May 1986): 9.

5. The "Ur-texts" of this movement are David B. Gracy II, "Archives and Society: The First Archival Revolution," *American Archivist* 47 (Jan. 1984): 7–10, and Gracy, "Our Future Is Now," *American Archivist* 48 (Jan. 1985): 12–21. For extended discussions of several aspects of this larger issue, see also Elsie Freeman Finch, ed., *Advocating Archives: An Introduction to Public Relations for Archivists* (Chicago: Society of American Archivists, 1994).

6. See the accounts of the conclusion of the trial and the verdict in the *Boston Globe*, May 6–7, 1993.

7. The question of whether broadcasts of the "I Have a Dream" speech violate the family's copyright is still not entirely resolved; see the *New York Times*, Nov. 7, 1999. In early 2001 an altered film of the speech began to appear as part of the ad campaign for Alcatel Americas, a French company building voice and data networks, all with the blessing of the King family; see Paul Farhi, "King's Dream Becomes Commercial," *Washington Post*, Mar. 28, 2001.

8. On the possible sale, see the *New York Times*, Oct. 30, 1999, and the *Atlanta Journal Constitution*, Nov. 10, 1999. The Senate quickly authorized an appropriation for the sale, but the House delayed action pending a number of questions about the precedent such a sale might set. It is also unclear whether the SCLC papers and other collections at the center would go to the Library of Congress under the terms of this arrangement.

9. The "Code of Ethics for Archivists" had been revised in 1992; I was a member of the SAA Council that had approved and adopted the code. The text, with commentary, is available at archivists.org/governance/handbook/app_ethics.html.

10. James M. O'Toole, *Understanding Archives and Manuscripts* (Chicago: Society of American Archivists, 1990), p. 59.

"A Monumental Blunder": The Destruction of Records on Nazi War Criminals in Canada

Terry Cook[1]

"Tinker, tailor, archivist, spy": so ran the provocative headline of the lead editorial in the *Halifax Herald* on April 8, 1981. "It is utterly incredible!" the editorial writer exclaimed, "Key documents have disappeared from the vaults of the National Archives." The editorialist found this to be "inexcusable," "extremely sloppy," "lax," and a "dereliction of responsibility" for which archivists should be punished.

The *Herald*, founded in 1824, is one of Canada's oldest newspapers and still serves as the principal voice of the Maritime region. It publishes under the editorial motto "that no good cause shall lack a champion and that wrong shall not thrive unopposed." In alleged archival negligence in fighting the Cold War, the *Herald* detected both a cause to champion and wrong to be exposed. Records relating to Soviet espionage in the late 1940s were reported missing from the National (then Public) Archives of Canada. Prime Minister Pierre Trudeau had even confirmed in the House of Commons that some pages relating to the defection of Igor Gouzenko could not be found in the diary of the prime minister at the time or among the records of the Royal Commission that investigated the Gouzenko Affair. Trudeau added that a search for these records had "proved fruitless thus far." The *Herald* and soon other papers were outraged.

Igor Gouzenko's personal defection from the Soviet Union's Embassy in Ottawa in September 1945, together with revealing documents, created an international sensation when made public in February 1946. Gouzenko's documents first exposed the Western world to the depth of Soviet espionage activities. Two months later, in April 1946, Winston Churchill made his famous "Iron Curtain" address in Fulton, Missouri. Over the next three years, there followed in short order the Truman Doctrine, the creation of NATO, the Berlin Blockade, the East-West division of Europe, Communist victory in China, and the Korean War. The Cold War was on, in icy, and sometimes hot, reality. The Soviet Union, recent allies in fighting against Nazi Germany, had once again become, in less than five years, the West's implacable enemy.

"Gouzenko" everywhere, and especially in Canada, became the watchword for Soviet spying and Communist intrigue, for international conspiracy and Cold War duplicity. Popular culture in the following decades reflected these developments in best-selling "spy" fiction by John Le Carré and Robert Ludlum, among others, and in the endless stream of James Bond films and their many imitators. After thirty years of Cold War, just as the *Herald* was penning its editorial in 1981, Ronald Reagan and Margaret Thatcher were preparing for the final showdown with the "evil empire." In this world of spies and intrigue, there also remained, despite the excesses of the McCarthy witch-hunts of the 1950s, continual concern about the fifth-column "enemy within" as well as the obvious external enemies in the USSR, China, and their client states.

For the *Herald*, then, to have Gouzenko-related records "spirited away" from the nation's own archives was clearly a scandal of major proportions—hard evidence of the enemy within. The Cold War required continual vigilance and tough security at home and abroad, yet clearly the National Archives of Canada was asleep at its watch over the nation's documentary heritage. "If these documents have been stolen, as it appears they have been, evidently, security was lax." One could never relax one's guard in these times. The *Herald* thought "someone" out there "attached more value to these papers than did the government of Canada," and Canadians "are entitled to an explanation—and soon." The *Herald* asked, "Are the national records so casually kept that they can disappear without a clue as to their whereabouts?" Answering its own question, the editorial writer concluded: "This is an illustration of extremely sloppy housekeeping. It is an example of dereliction of responsibility on the part of those charged with the keeping of the Archives. There are, it appears, a number of knuckles which need to be soundly rapped."[2] Despite subsequent protests from the National Archivist that no records had disappeared from the National Archives, the damage was done. Other newspapers picked up the story and thereby hurt the reputation of the National Archives among potential donors and actual users.

Several conclusions may be drawn from this incident. Archives of the state are not just repositories of historical sources for researchers to use in understanding the past; they can also be perceived as political manifestations of the dominant culture of society. Archives are not merely scholarly playgrounds for their staff and researchers; they can also be active agents of political accountability, social memory, and national identity. And what documents the archives chooses to keep or destroy (or lose as "missing") are not simply the result of dispassionate historical research or bureaucratic processes, but rather of sensitive, sometimes controversial acts for which archives can be held accountable in courts of law and in the court of public opinion. The cultural wars can be waged on the archival doorstep. And the reputation, and thus influence, of archives and archivists can be negatively affected unless they engage constructively in public debates about the nature of memory, history, and the past.

FACING THE LEGACY OF THE HOLOCAUST

The Gouzenko records incident of 1981 was a fitting prelude to a more serious scandal four years later over the allegedly improper destruction of immigration records relating to Nazi war criminals in Canada. Once again, the National Archives was grilled for its questionable care of the nation's documentary heritage. Once again, the accusations of archival blundering flew, and this time they were sustained for a much longer period. Perhaps the traditional public trust in archives as objective and neutral guardians of the documentary heritage, now shaken by the Gouzenko attacks, was more easily assailed the next time around with the Nazi immigration records. There was, moreover, in the new scandal a Cold War connection with the Gouzenko issue just described, in terms of the postwar conditions of Europe and the arrival of Nazi sympathizers, collaborators, and war criminals as immigrants in North America.

With the wide-scale confusion caused with hundreds of thousands of refugees or "displaced persons" in European temporary camps in the immediate postwar years, a significant number of Nazi officials, soldiers, and scientists landed among camp inhabitants, as did collaborators from other countries who had aided the Nazi extermination machine. As one U.S. military commander told arriving social workers, "You've probably got everything in this camp except Hitler and I wouldn't be surprised if you turned up that bastard when you get started on the registration."[3]

Accurate registration in such chaotic circumstances was often difficult, as was screening out Nazis or suspected war criminals, whom government regulations certainly barred from entry to Canada. Heavy bombings, fires, and the collapse of much European government infrastructure had destroyed many relevant records of births, marriages, political activity, and military service, thus making it impossible to verify the accuracy of displaced persons' accounts of their backgrounds and wartime activities. Other records that did survive, for displaced persons from countries in Eastern Europe behind the Iron Curtain, were inaccessible to Western governments. In such circumstances, some former Nazis and their non-German collaborators, who were suspected of crimes against humanity in the Holocaust or during military campaigns, were able to adopt pseudonyms and slip through the camps, pass the immigration screening processes, and settle in new countries among thousands of their innocent compatriots.

The anticommunist fervor of the Cold War caused immigration officials and political leaders to turn a blind eye more than once to Nazi sympathizers whose anticommunist credentials were beyond question. In the post-Gouzenko world, former enemies were now Cold War friends, just as former Soviet allies were now enemies. Various anticommunist groups, such as churches, research institutions, and intelligence organizations, as well as the government itself, actually sponsored known Nazi sympathizers (not war criminals necessarily) as immigrants for their knowledge and skills needed to combat the Communist regimes. In Gouzenko's Cold War era, where stark East-West lines were being drawn across the map of Europe, sometimes not too many questions were asked. Even when questions were asked, for there certainly was no conscious conspiracy to bring Nazi war criminals to new countries, it was easy enough for applicants to lie and tell the hard-pressed camp officials the anticommunist rhetoric and wartime occupational activities ("I was just a farmer") they needed to hear.

For decades thereafter, Nazi war criminals were able to live comfortably as "quiet neighbors" in Canada, the United States, Australia, and parts of South America. They worked, paid taxes, got married, built homes, raised families, joined churches, and became integrated members of their new communities. They—and Nazism in general—posed no internal threat to their new postwar societies, in contrast to the perception, at least, surrounding Communism. And so, despite occasional crusading journalists, these quiet neighbors were left alone to live their lives. At the height of Cold War tensions from the 1950s to the 1970s, the recipient nations of these immigrants were simply not very motivated to dig into the pasts of now-model citizens. Furthermore, as one writer suggests, "our silence immediately after the Holocaust was not due entirely to apathy but, at least in part, to the inability to respond intelligently to such a massive wound to the human race." A "curtain of silence" in the 1950s fell over the Nazi exterminations "as if the world wanted . . . to treat it as an inexplicable aberration that had burned across Europe."[4] The Holocaust was not taught in history classes in schools and universities, and there were few books or public discussions on the subject. The past was forgotten. Without memory, living quietly next door to silent horror became possible. There were exceptions, of course, like the powerful and bestselling publication in 1952 of *The Diary of Anne Frank* or in 1958 of Elie Wiesel's evocative story, *Night* (English translation in 1960), but generally the pattern of apathetic response to old wounds remained undisturbed. The world moved on.

Of course, in the immediate postwar years, there were war crimes trials, and the development of the concept of war criminals. Nazi military units or individuals who in violation of international codes of military conduct had committed atrocities against Allied soldiers, including murders by execution, were certainly tried in the late 1940s. And there were the famous war crimes trials at Nuremberg of the surviving Nazi leadership, and the less well-known (but more extensive) trials of Japanese wartime leaders. By the later 1940s, with these two focused initiatives completed against Nazi and Japanese leaders and rogue soldiers or units, the Western Allies were anxious to put World War II behind them and move on to confronting Communists, not Nazis.

Jewish organizations and even the state of Israel—with the exception of the famous kidnapping and trial of Adolf Eichmann in 1962—did not initially press hard to bring to justice those Nazis living in the West. It has been suggested that many Jews themselves suffered survivor-guilt syndrome for escaping the Nazi death machine. Public silence and personal grief seemed for many the most appropriate response for remembering those dear ones who had been exterminated and for coping with surviving when so many loved ones had not. And the younger generation of Jews tended to see the Holocaust as "ancient history" and focused their energies on Israel, Vietnam, or other contemporary political issues. Although Simon Wiesenthal as the famed "Nazi hunter" began his work in 1947 and various members of the World Jewish Congress compiled lists of survivors and camp officials, complacency toward the presence of Nazi war criminals continued to prevail until the later 1970s.

Then things changed. Jewish survivors were finding their voice in novels, memoirs, poetry, and histories. As they did, concern for justice over the hideous genocide of the Nazis increased. Time was becoming critically important, for by the early 1980s when legal action finally began to be initiated against Nazi war criminals, even the youngest members of the surviving generation of adult-age concentration camp survivors were nearing the end of their lives, or mental competencies, as were many overseas witnesses required for successful prosecutions. The trail for finding reliable written documentation, especially in the USSR or Eastern Europe, was also growing increasingly cold. If justice were to prevail, it had to happen soon.

At the same time, there was a gradual awakening of interest in the Holocaust as a momentous historical phenomenon, with Holocaust museums and memorials, first established in Israel, gradually beginning to appear in Western countries. Holocaust studies—and an avalanche of publications—flourished as a cross-disciplinary pursuit in many universities. Equally, a small but vocal group of Holocaust deniers, often neo-Nazi and anti-Semitic in orientation, sought to minimize the numbers of deaths of Jews in concentration camps or deny that there had been any planned or systematic "Final Solution." Such zealots attracted media attention and, not surprisingly, alarmed Jewish organizations, Holocaust survivors, and fair-minded observers. The neo-Nazi assertions demanded rebuttal—and what better way than exposing in courts of law the actual war criminals who had perpetrated the Holocaust now being denied?

Finally, as the Cold War entered its final showdown in the 1980s, "human rights" became a politically sensitive issue, used internationally by the Western democracies to embarrass Communist regimes and win support of "neutral" Third World countries. It was hardly tolerable, then, for those same democracies to be harboring in their midst Nazi war criminals responsible for the greatest violation of human rights in the history of the world. As David Matas, a human-rights lawyer and prominent Jewish advocate, later reflected, "Our government cannot credibly combat racial discrimination but ignore racially motivated mass murders. Respect for human rights involves prosecuting for genocide."[5] And ethical jurists, such as Alan Ryan of the United States, who directed the Office of Special Investigations from 1980 to 1983 that was charged with investigating and prosecuting Nazi war criminals, argued convincingly that thirty years of silence and apathy was no reason for its continuance (as some suggested), nor could atonement for evil be earned merely by subsequent good behavior by Nazi immigrants living quietly in their new homes. Genocide unpunished invited its repetition by future dictators, and verbal condemnation of genocide without action remained only pious rhetoric.

CANADA CONFRONTS ITS "QUIET NEIGHBORS"

Against this background, then, a concerted effort began in some Western countries to identify and prosecute Nazi war criminals. In Canada, the focus of the case study being presented in this essay, the same apathy described above was found, after careful investigation, to have been pervasive in the country since the early 1950s. Even suggestions voiced at the end of the 1970s by a few politicians and Jewish organizations that Canada should follow the lead being set by Alan Ryan and his U.S. team of Nazi war criminal investigators was strongly—and effectively—resisted inside the federal bureaucracy, particularly by the Royal Canadian Mounted Police (RCMP) and the Department of Justice.

Suddenly, everything changed. The request by the West German government, made public in 1982, for the extradition of a notorious war criminal, Helmut Rauca, who had been living safely in Canada since 1950, brought stark publicity to the issue as well as raised public concern that other brutal Nazis might be living quietly in the country. A flood of subsequent allegations in the media, combined with the threat of neo-Nazism highlighted then by the hate-crimes trials of two prominent Canadian Holocaust deniers, Ernst Zundel and James Keegstra, raised more pressure for change. After the Rauca incident, a crusading solicitor general, Robert Kaplan, as the chief law enforcement officer of the federal government, quietly ordered investigations by the RCMP into some 100 Nazi suspects on lists provided by Jewish organizations. And a change of government after 1984, following two decades of Liberal Party rule, generally made new initiatives in public policy more welcome.

The flashpoint to these growing pressures came with the spectacular allegation by Sol Littman, a veteran journalist and Simon Wiesenthal Center representative in Canada, that Josef Mengele, the notorious "Angel of Death" at Auschwitz in charge of grotesque medical experiments and mass extermination, had applied from South America to come to Canada in 1962 and might still be in the country. Littman based his allegation on interpretations of documents obtained through the U.S. Freedom of Information Act (FOIA); he had also done extensive research at the National Archives of Canada. The press in Canada and abroad picked up the Mengele story in later January 1985.

Canada's most famous Nazi hunter, Sol Littman, came to his work later in life. One commentator describes how Littman "initially tried to put [the Holocaust] out of his mind because it was so horrible, but it kept coming back to him, bothering him. He compared it to having a pebble in his shoe. He found that he could ignore it and keep walking for only so long. Eventually, he had to stop and do something about it." Littman mastered the art of making sensational public charges, sometimes based on scanty evidence, as a way of goading complacent governments and media into action against Nazi war criminals. After three frustrating decades of apathy from Western governments such as Canada's, for a Jewish lobbyist to adopt such tactics may be understandable, but it earned resentment from government insiders, who branded Littman a "loose cannon" and "vigilante," and from ethnic groups who charged that he saw Nazi collaborators everywhere. Yet without Littman's research and promotional savvy, there simply would have been no formal investigation into Nazi war criminals and thus no airing of this dark issue.[6]

The federal government acted swiftly on Littman's charges. Within two weeks, on February 7, Prime Minister Brian Mulroney created a formal Royal Commission of Inquiry to investigate the charge that Canada was a haven for Nazi war criminals, including whether Mengele had entered the country, and to propose remedies for bringing Nazi war criminals to justice. A Royal Commission is the highest and most prestigious level of public inquiry in Canada. The new commission was to be presided over by the former chief justice of Quebec's Superior Court, Jules Deschênes (the commission of inquiry was commonly called the Deschênes Commission). After many months of hearing testimony from witnesses, conducting extensive historical and legal research, and reviewing thousands of archival and administrative documents, the commission offered its report to the government in December 1986 and a public version was released in early 1987 (a secret version naming names and summarizing evidence against each suspected war criminal has never been released).

On the particular issue of Josef Mengele's entry in 1962, Deschênes concluded "beyond a reasonable doubt" that the notorious Nazi had never entered Canada, nor attempted to do so, although, as Deschênes qualified, "unfortunately, the destruction of some of the government and police files in the long period which followed [the alleged entry in 1962] robs any inquiry of the possibility of achieving absolute certainty."[7] On the broader issue of Nazi war criminals, Deschênes concluded that Canada had been no better than many Western nations in letting the issue of war criminals lie dormant for three decades; that hundreds of potential investigations on suspected war criminals should be closed because the accused were dead, had never entered Canada or had left, or there was insufficient evidence to sustain a prosecution; that active investigation of some two hundred cases be seriously pursued (as detailed in the secret version of the report); that blanket condemnation of various ethnic groups of immigrants was not supported by the evidence; and that various extradition treaties and the Criminal Code should be amended to facilitate bringing war criminals to justice within Canada or elsewhere, whether such war criminals were Nazis or of some other origin from some future conflict. One strategy, used in the United

States, also received close attention and moderate commendation by Deschênes: the denaturalization and deportation of suspected Nazi war criminals who had lied about their past military or political activities in order to gain entry to Canada. Justice and punishment might not come necessarily from actual evidence of war crimes, as that would often be difficult to obtain in reliable form from Eastern Bloc and Soviet archives, or from fast-dying or mentally failing witnesses, especially with the passage of time changing physical appearances so greatly. Rather, justice could be served by the removal from "quiet neighborhoods," and the comforts and social benefits of host countries, of those Nazis who had entered the country under false pretenses.

The National Archives of Canada had many dealings with the Deschênes Commission. Despite the very heavy historical research dimension of the Deschênes Commission's mandate and work, the National Archives was not initially invited to join a new senior-level interdepartmental working group of nine agencies preparing the government's input for the commission or deciding how best to cooperate with the commission's historical researchers. When the National Archives itself eventually learned of the group's existence, and sought and received membership, it was welcomed in the person of Robert J. Hayward, an archival midlevel manager, who thereafter engaged in significant consciousness raising among government partners on the committee. Government officials were surprised to learn, for example, that not all older immigration and security records relevant to the commission's research work were at the National Archives of Canada; that many such records were subject to long retention in and destruction by the creating departments according to approved records retention and disposal schedules; and that "historical" records at the National Archives were themselves subject to the same restrictions imposed by the Access to Information Act and the Privacy Act as if the records were still active in their creating department. The National Archives further assisted by analyzing sources and preparing special search guides for the commission's historical researchers on the most relevant records on postwar immigration. It also presented as formal evidence with the commission copies of records in its custody, some received from immediate postwar United Nations units in Europe, containing various "lookout" lists of suspected war criminals that were important in assisting the commission to draw up its master list of cases to investigate. Of course, the existence of such lists in Canada's possession, now brought to light from the archival holdings, raised again the question of why Canada had done nothing with this knowledge for so many years. Other departments—quite aside from the commission's own researchers— used the National Archives as their "institutional memory" to remember (research and discover) their own role—or that of their predecessor agencies—in how they dealt with immigration in the immediate postwar period for which they were now being held formally accountable.

The role of the National Archives in records retention and destruction authority was not limited to internal bureaucratic explanation, research support, or document production. Formal explanation was required before the Commission.

When Sol Littman (who had made the original Mengele charge) testified in April 1985 that many immigration records were destroyed "in its peculiar wisdom" by the government, including virtually all overseas application forms, with only the formal landing records being retained permanently at the individual case level, Commissioner Deschênes' interest was piqued. A day of hearings at the Commission (May 14, 1985) was therefore devoted to the clarifying for Deschênes—and for those groups (and their lawyers) having formal standing before him—the nature of the records scheduling and record destruction process. Robert J. Hayward of the National Archives of Canada gave extensive testimony explaining the evolving context of federal records management policy and changing practices since 1945, and gave the Commission as formal exhibits all the relevant standards, guidelines, and administrative orders. Officials from various departments were thereafter called to account in sworn testimony for their agencies' specific retention and disposal practices against the general landscape that Hayward had painted. The intent was to show that the destruction of any records, such as the overseas application forms, had been done as a routine part of government business and under the formal authority of the National Archivist.

Had matters stopped there, the role of the National Archives of Canada in relation to Nazi war criminals would make an interesting footnote in archival history. The National Archives was shown to be much more than a storehouse of historical material—without at all diminishing its important contribution to the Deschênes Commission (and society at large) in that traditional role. The National Archives clearly demonstrated that it (and the archival profession generally) was concerned with public policy and the administration of law and regulation. The National Archives was revealed too as a vital player in the management of government information, most especially in authorizing its efficient disposal when no longer required for current operations. Now the National Archives was increasingly seen as the government's own memory of what it had done (or not done), and thus as an agency providing an important means by which government could hold itself accountable or defend itself when others held it to account. Many of these roles surprised senior officials of government when they learned of them through the Deschênes process, which says something rather unfortunate about the low profile of archives generally within public administration. Yet once National Archives had injected itself into the process, its expertise and contributions were appreciated, suggesting that, as in the Deschênes case, archivists everywhere need to be vigilant in promoting themselves as active agents rather than sitting on the sidelines waiting for calls to action that may never come.

QUESTIONS FOR THE NATIONAL ARCHIVES

Matters did not, in fact, stop there. Part way through the Deschênes Commission's hearings, a major scandal broke that thrust the National Archives of Canada into the nation's headlines. When Sol Littman testified in April 1985, as noted above, that the overseas immigration application forms had been routinely destroyed, which he judged to be "peculiar," the fact was not initially picked up by the media, but it was not unnoticed.

Among the government's senior bureaucrats, another set of discussions had been going on ever since the Rauca extradition in 1982 concerning the availability of older records to support prosecutions against war criminals (curiously— once again—without involving the National Archives). This group of senior mandarins was already concerned that, although scheduled for early routine destruction, the immigration application forms, some seemingly dating back to World War II, had apparently not been destroyed until as late as 1982 (as Littman was later to testify publicly). On May 22, 1984, the deputy solicitor general (the most senior civil servant in the department) wrote to his minister, Solicitor General Robert Kaplan, one of the first politicians to advocate prosecution of war criminals, that the Royal Canadian Mounted Police (RCMP) "does not offer an opinion upon whether such destruction involved a culpable act, or was 'simply' a monumental blunder. What is clear is that the loss of these records, whose destruction should not have taken place, has seriously impaired the ability of Canadian authorities, notably the RCMP, to investigate and take effective action against war criminals in Canada."

Kaplan later testified before the Deschênes Commission that, upon hearing this news, "We were absolutely furious about it. It just seemed incomprehensible at that particular time that my officials and the RCMP would be foiled in this way, if I can put it in that expression, by a file destruction policy working in thin air." Exchanges of letters at the most senior levels of the bureaucracy between the solicitor general, the RCMP, and Immigration occurred thereafter in the summer of 1984 (again without recourse to the National Archives, which did not even know that this furor about records destruction was occurring). The RCMP commissioner concluded this exchange of correspondence by asserting that "the efforts of the RCMP in the investigation of alleged war criminals may have been inadvertently hampered through the destruction of these records. However, this is something to which we can only speculate, since the files are gone and we will never know what they contained."[8] (In fact, the RCMP *could* have known something beyond speculation by investigating the sample of immigration case files retained by the National Archives of Canada from the larger group destroyed in 1982 and by reading the National Archives report describing the content of the files that were then destroyed. At this stage, however, no one was thinking about the Archives or its role in records appraisal and destruction, the process that separates the very small percentage of records to be kept permanently as the nation's archives from the vast majority that are shredded after their original operational use to their creator is finished.)

After Kaplan's public testimony before the Deschênes Commission on October 9, 1985, and his offering of the above correspondence as commission exhibits, all the internal discussions became public. The media now had its required hook. Here was conspiracy! Here was thwarted justice! Here was a "monumental blunder" in government, and perhaps a "culpable" act against the state! Here was the Cold War alive and well in Ottawa! At the very time in 1982 that the Rauca extradition case was breaking, when the government of the time under Kaplan's leadership was finally beginning to move against Nazi war criminals, the very records had been destroyed that would have been useful, at the very least, and perhaps essential, for discovering and deporting illegal Nazi immigrants who had lied their way into the country. Moreover, why were "routine" records apparently thirty years old being destroyed only now, since routine records are usually destroyed after two or three years at most? Was someone inside government still covering up Nazi tracks? "Missing Files Hinder Search for Nazi War Criminals," the *Globe and Mail* headlined on October 10, 1985. "Nazi Inquiry Told Vital Files Were Destroyed 'Mysteriously,'" blared the *Toronto Star* the same day. On November 7, the *Canadian Jewish News* asked, "Was [19]81 Crucial Year in Exposing Nazis?"—since the immigration records necessary for doing so all seemed to have been destroyed in 1982. Was it now too late? Had archival policy thwarted justice?

David Matas, author a few years later of *Justice Delayed: Nazi War Criminals in Canada*, and an active Jewish participant before the Deschênes Commission with formal standing as senior counsel representing the League for Human Rights for B'nai B'rith Canada, declared in the media that, in the records administration of the Government of Canada, "we've got lots of evidence of monumental blunder." He asserted that "its policy for record retention must be tied to the administration of justice, so that information relating to criminal cases will not be destroyed. We need a policy . . . that records be retained that could be useful for criminal cases and not just for historical cases."

The leading newspaper of the Canadian prairie provinces, the *Winnipeg Free Press,* picked up Matas's comments in December 1985 for its long lead editorial: "The Vanishing Files." It declared the issue of these immigration files being "secretly destroyed" to be the most "puzzling" and "bizarre" conundrum to come before the Deschênes Commission. The editorialist dismissed as "impudence" and "nonsense" claims of Immigration officials that these voluminous case-level records had been destroyed to save storage space. This the *Free Press* saw as "ridiculous in an era in which it is routine to put important information on easily-retrieved microfilm or computer floppy discs." The archival appraisal process of saving records on "a select group of immigrants only," rather than keeping all those records on each of "hundreds of thousands" of individual cases, the *Free Press* also rejected as "an equally lame excuse." The whole destruction by Immigration and Archives was a "scandalous act," the *Free Press* declared, requiring additional government investigation to ensure that it was only a monumental blunder, and that "no ulterior motives" were involved to undermine deliberately the administration of justice.[9]

In this atmosphere of national scandal and conspiracy, justice thwarted and continuing Cold War intrigue, Deschênes himself decided to divert a significant amount of commission time and resources to look into the alleged improper destruction of postwar immigration records. As he put it in his final report, "The Commission was thus led to investigate this somewhat strange situation, under the cloud of rumors of a conspiracy to destroy files which might have compromised people suspected of war crimes."[10] This records controversy, in the words of one archival participant, thus "produced something rare in the annals of Canadian judicial proceedings, extensive testimony dealing with the subject of records retention and disposal."[11] Special hearings on December 3, 1985, produced more than 300 pages of transcripts and were devoted to understanding the particular appraisal and disposal of immigration case-level records in 1982, as well as the general practice of archival selection for permanent preservation. Six witnesses were heard from the records management program of the Immigration Department, one from the Ottawa Federal Records Center, where some of the records in question had been housed before 1982, and one (the present writer) from the National Archives who was responsible for the appraisal decision of 1981–1982 and subsequent archival transfers of samples of immigration case files to the archives' holdings. Unlike the May 1985 session of the commission that sought to understand the general processes of record management and disposal, the December 1985 session investigated an allegedly improper and possibly conspiratorial application of those general processes in the one-time large destruction of immigration case files in 1982.

Before the special "records day" at the commission, I was interviewed by two lawyers at their request, one from the Department of Justice and one from the commission itself. Like Robert Hayward, I was then a midlevel manager at the National Archives of Canada. My responsibilities included the Immigration portfolio, and, in the absence of a regular archivist, I had personally investigated the records in question in 1981–1982 and recommended the destruction of most of them. Beyond confirming their understanding of the general appraisal and disposal procedures as Hayward had outlined in his May 1985 testimony, the lawyers were particularly interested in the 1982 disposal of records—and in minute detail (who called whom, when, why), the numbers of boxes of records before and after the disposal action, the exact sequence of steps and dates in the disposal and subsequent archival transfer, changes in the National Archives decisions on the time to retain Immigration records, the reasons and methods for archival sampling, and my awareness of any motives or actions by Immigration record staff that would support the conspiracy theory that records had been destroyed deliberately to cover up the presence of Nazi war criminals in Canada. They also requested and received copies of six documents, for example, records schedules, accession forms, and internal correspondence. They concluded, as I informed my superiors, "that my knowledge should be part of the public record and that I will be called to testify formally."[12] They were evidently also researching to prepare the questions that senior commission counsel would pose to all the witnesses involved in the 1982 destruction of records.

The first issue before the commission on December 3—the special "records day"—was to determine the value of the destroyed records for the commission's work and the prosecution of war criminals.[13] From an analysis by witnesses and commission staff of the remaining records in the archival sample, Deschênes concluded that the immigration case files destroyed in 1982 "did not contain material which would have been very useful in the hunt for Nazi war criminals. . . . the files did not contain documents or information relating to events prior to the immigrant's landing in Canada or concerning his past military or criminal history." On the second issue, concerning the large volume of records destroyed in 1982 just as Nazi hunting in Canada was beginning, the answer was simple, supported by voluminous documentation and statistics of the actions and timing of records storage, transfers, and accessioning: Immigration had disbanded its file retention and disposal unit in 1977 and reestablished it in 1981. Naturally, a large backlog had accumulated over those four years, to which records retention schedules were applied retroactively in 1982. In fact, destruction of similar Immigration case files had been occurring regularly since the 1950s, and the number destroyed in 1982, if spread over the five previous years of inaction when nothing had been disposed, averaged out to roughly the normal rate of destruction of previous decades.

Turning then to the larger issue of the possibility of a conspiracy, the commission's legal staff put the same question to each of the expert witnesses on records disposal and archival appraisal:

Did you ever give, or did you ever receive, or did you ever hear of instructions to destroy files other than in the ordinary course of business within the Department of Immigration, or to destroy files that in any way relate to the presence of [*sic*, i.e., "in"] Canada of a Nazi war criminal?

Each witness, the commission's report noted, "gave a negative answer without the slightest hesitation. The Commissioner has seen and heard those witnesses, and he knows of no reason why he should disbelieve one or the other of them and hold them to have been parties to such a grand-scale conspiracy." Indeed, former Solicitor General Kaplan had been recalled to the witness stand and was explicitly asked, in following up his initial testimony and correspondence offered in evidence, whether there was "a scintilla of evidence that there was any conspiracy relating to the destruction of these records," and whether there was "any evidence that it was a culpable act which led to the destruction of these records." He replied unequivocally: "I know of none" regarding the conspiracy, and "I have no such evidence" on culpable or criminal actions.

If not a conspiracy or crime then, was the incident still a "monumental blunder" of bureaucratic incompetence in the records management and archival areas? Here Deschênes said that this would only be true if the information in the files had been "crucial" to potential prosecutions, "a fact which . . . is far from established." By this, Deschênes meant that even if the overseas immigration application forms survived, they still would not provide a blanket solution for deporting closet Nazis immigrants. What Deschênes did find was, in his words, a group of employees performing their [record disposal] task under schedules approved by the proper [archival] authorities. They had never been advised that other authorities may wish to retain files that they were instructed to destroy. Nobody, from the deputy ministers down, has ever given them any specific instructions to derogate from their disposal duties.

The deputy ministers were, at the very same time as the records destruction of 1982, meeting behind closed doors to discuss Nazi war criminals, and in their discussions they were concerned about whether any records that would facilitate prosecutions existed, but they had never bothered to convey this concern to their own staffs or to the National Archives of Canada, nor did they appear to understand the records management and disposal policies and practices of the Government of Canada for which they were accountable in their own agencies. "Under such circumstances," Deschênes then asked rhetorically, "if the destruction was a blunder, whose blunder was it?" He made the point less rhetorically in his formal recommendation number 42 that concluded the section of his final report on the records destruction issue:

The destruction of a substantial number of immigration files in 1982–1983 should not be considered as a culpable act or as a blunder, but has occurred in the normal course of the application of a routine policy duly authorized within the federal administration. In any event, if a blunder there was, it arose out of the failure of the higher authorities properly to instruct of an appropriate exception the employees entrusted with the duty of carrying out the retention and disposal policy of their department.

Deschênes in his report also reflected upon the fact, in his understated way, that "as this inquiry was forging ahead into the labyrinth of Immigration and Archives administration, the more clearly it appeared that the 1982 destruction episode had been wrongly built up into an incident of dramatic proportions."

The records destruction issue continued to attract popular interest, however. Upon the release of the Deschênes Commission's final report, for example, the *Montreal Gazette* made the issue its lead story under the headline "Destruction of Files During Nazi Probe Is Called Routine." While the timing of the destruction and the Rauca case publicity originally "appeared suspicious," the *Gazette* noted that in "tracing the bureaucratic process that led to the destruction," Deschênes made it clear that there was no conspiracy, criminal act, or even blunder. The *Gazette* also noted Kaplan's retraction of his sensational charges and Deschênes's questioning of the assumed value of immigration application forms as useful evidence to demonstrate that any Nazi immigrant now in Canada had necessarily lied to enter the country.[14]

THE NATIONAL ARCHIVES EXPLAINS ITSELF

Despite the vindication of archivists and records managers by Deschênes in his report, there were, in the issues raised before his commission and in the media, serious implications for archival appraisal, and by extension for the preservation of society's memory. Indeed, archives did not escape some continued public criticism over the Nazi records. Nor should they have. In turn, the archival response to this criticism eventually led to a whole new perspective on appraising archives for permanent retention. Before such reflection and forward thinking occurred, however, there came the defense of present and past practice.

The blow-by-blow sequence of the various responses of the National Archives of Canada justifying its appraisal decision on the immigration case files, backed up by several lengthy internal memoranda, need not be detailed here, let alone the intricate details provided by the Immigration Department about what boxes of what kinds of records were destroyed when, while following which National Archives–approved records disposal schedules in force at any particular time. On the topic of the specific appraisal arguments advanced by the National Archives in these internal reports and public testimony and subsequent writings, the following ten points were made:

1. In regard to the charges of a criminal conspiracy to destroy evidence or protect Nazis, or even a monumental bureaucratic blunder, the actual timing of the 1982 destruction of immigration case files demonstrated that neither charge was valid. There was in fact no possible linkage to the West German extradition request for Helmut Rauca that *afterward* generated significant public concern that other Nazi war criminals might be in Canada. After significant discussion and research, the destruction of the case files was authorized by the National Archives on March 4, 1982. Helmut Rauca was arrested on June 17, 1982. Subsequent loose assertions (on which the conspiracy or blunder charges were based) that the records destruction and Rauca case had occurred "at the same time" were simply wrong.

2. Despite charges to the contrary, the archival selection criteria *were* sensitive to the political traumas of the war and immediate postwar period: The appraisal criteria employed in the March 1982 disposal action specified that *all* files still surviving from pre-1950 must be retained as archival, and that the random sampling of immigration case files that was to be employed should be applied only to post-1950 case records. And this decision was made more than three months *before* any knowledge about Rauca was available to the archives!

3. The backlog of records destroyed so controversially in 1982, like their predecessors in previous decades, were files created in Canada and did not contain the hotly contested overseas application forms or related overseas medical and security-screening forms. In fact, there were never any overseas case "files" created by Canada before 1952, by which date the immigration screening rules for Nazis had been changed, rendering the existence of the forms largely irrelevant. Only individual application forms, not files, were created, held temporarily overseas until the immigrant was admitted, and then destroyed. The files destroyed in 1982, were not, in short, the equivalent of their U.S. "counterparts" and could not be used (as the Americans had done with different types of files) to prosecute and deport "quiet neighbor" Nazis for immigrant entry fraud (i.e., lying on their forms).

4. The enormous volumes of modern government records require the destruction of the vast majority of them, in a prompt and efficient manner. No government has the

hundreds of millions of dollars that would be needed annually to build or rent endless warehouses to keep government case-level files in their entirety for extended periods of time, let alone indefinitely as archival holdings. For example, the immigration
case files created since World War II outnumber all archival records for all federal
departments for the entire history of the nation since Confederation in 1867. Society
barely supports archives on the modest scale on which they currently operate and
shows no inclination to increase that support by a factor of nineteen (that is, to keep
100 percent of the records created permanently or long-term, rather than the usual
archival 5 percent and often as low as 1 to 2 percent). Even if that were fiscally possible, keeping everything (by not doing archival appraisals to authorize destruction)
and thus allowing no separating of wheat from chaff, does researchers no favors, as
little information of value could be found in the resulting paper jungle.

5. The notion of microfilming or scanning to computer storage all the hard-copy or paper records was (and remains) a simplistic suggestion; the media conversion costs
would exceed that of building the warehouses for storing the original paper versions,
not counting the extensive cost of indexing the records so they could be found in
their new formats after the media conversions. And if scanned, one creates com-
puter-based records that themselves, because of hardware and software obsoles-
cence, and media fragility, must be migrated forward every few years, at great
expense, in order to remain readable and usable.

6. The immigration experience of *individual* Canadians, as well as the overall role and
processes of the Government of Canada in immigration policy, sponsorship, screening, transportation, and settlement, are all very well documented in individual immigration landing records and in citizenship/naturalization records, and in a wide
range of policy and subject files, as well as by selections of records of unusual, controversial, or precedent-setting cases and by samples of regular or noncontroversial
cases—all of which have been appraised and then designated (or scheduled) for permanent retention by the National Archives as part of the nation's memory. In short,
the National Archives was not insensitive to the need to document Canada's ethnic
and multicultural experience as sometimes charged.

7. The statistically valid sample of immigration case files that I insisted on taking, before
recommending the rest of the 1982 records for destruction under the National Archivist's authorization, was done in order to provide evidence of immigration processes, procedures, and daily government operations—in *addition* to all the other
records preserved as just noted under point 6 above. The decision was made in the
context of this much wider range of immigration records already preserved by the archives. And the commission's researchers used this sample for just that purpose: to
determine what kinds of documents had been created and filed as part of the immigration work at the time, and which were not.

8. The traditional use by most archives of inclusive dates to describe series of records in
appraisal reports and finding aids can be confusing to the uninitiated. A range of inclusive dates to describe several thousand files—for example, dates of 1945–1978,
as provided by the National Archives, when in reality what is held is one file from the
"start" date of 1945, three files from the 1950s, a few more from the 1960s, and
some thousand from the 1970s, up to the "end" date of 1978—misleads researchers
very much more than it informs them. This is especially true if the related list of file titles and dates is withheld from the researcher because of privacy considerations—as

with immigration case records of recent vintage. The use of such inclusive date ranges for the immigration case files led to the erroneous conclusion that many more files from the 1940s and 1950s had survived in the archival sample taken in 1982, or had been destroyed in 1982, than was actually the case.

9. Inclusive dates of a single file can be similarly confusing to the uninitiated. If immigration case records generally have a retention period of, say, five years before authorized destruction, why were records from the 1950s and 1960s being destroyed in 1982? That fact generated some of the conspiracy thinking. The reality is that destruction schedules (or timetables) are based on the last piece of correspondence in a file, not the first. Thus two files dated (i.e., containing material on the file from) 1948–1977 and 1973–1977 would both be properly destroyed, applying a five-year retention period, in 1982, even though a good portion of material on both files would have survived far longer than five years after its creation. Records disposal is at the file, not the document, level and is based on the most recent, not the earliest, piece of correspondence in the file.

10. For issues of accountability, a line must be drawn clearly between the responsibilities of the records managers and program officers (and ultimately the minister) of creating departments on the one hand, and, on the other hand, the appraisal archivists of the National Archives (and ultimately the National Archivist) when determining the long-term legal value of records. Establishing retention periods *for legal (and operational) purposes* is the responsibility of the creating department accountable for the function involved. Establishing which records have *permanent "archival and historical" value* to the nation well beyond the operational (including legal operational) lifetimes of their subjects is the responsibility of the National Archives. Whether voluminous records generated annually regarding medical research for testing and approving thousands of potentially dangerous new drugs, or for construction repairs on thousands of houses on Indian reserves, or for millions of immigrant applications, it is the responsibility of the creator to retain the records necessary to protect the legal rights of the government and citizens, and to determine how long that retention period should be. It is the creator, in these three examples, who is legally accountable for, and knowledgeable about, respectively, the legal repercussions of various drug chemicals in the body, fulfillment of Indian treaty obligations, and possible criminal prosecutions for illegal immigration or prearrival crimes. While some such records having long-term legal value to the creating departments may also have archival and historical value, and thus be transferred to the National Archives, that overlap must not be allowed to blur the line between the operational and legal accountability of the creator to retain records having any continuing (nonresearch) use and archival accountability for appraising which records will form the national memory.

The National Archives was not content with making many of these points before the Deschênes Commission or quietly within the federal bureaucracy. The two key National Archives witnesses before the commission also hit the publicity trail, with the full encouragement of senior management and the new National Archivist, Jean-Pierre Wallot. As Robert Hayward observed, "Editorials entitled 'Answers needed on Nazi records' or 'The vanishing files' are not everyday occurrences. The work of archivists, in deciding what records to keep and what records to destroy, is important and should be taken seriously. Destruction is an absolute act."[15] Hayward rightly asserted that it became important for the National Archives, after a year of negative headlines and scandal-mongering, to assure its various supporters through public education.

Hayward himself lectured on the subject and later wrote for a scholarly journal a detailed analysis of the National Archives role in the affair and its impact on professional archivists called to account for appraisal and disposal actions. I gave radio interviews and wrote four advocacy articles, three for professional audiences and one for a national audience. Each of the three articles set a different tone as the lead article of its publication: a hard-hitting exposé, naming names and condemning those who continued to attack the National Archives' position after its testimony had been made public, which was aimed at the professional archivists in Canada; an analytical piece stressing issues of public accountability, good records management, and transparency and accuracy in disposal documentation that was directed at the federal records management community; and an overview analysis of appraisal, naming no names (not even Deschênes's!) and explaining the principles of archival appraisal and how they led to the correct decision in 1982, which was targeted at researchers and general supporters of the National Archives. An op-ed piece for a nationwide audience was published in the *Toronto Globe and Mail* (Canada's newspaper of record, like the *Times* in New York or London): The editor supplied the double-entendre title: "For the Record: Archivists Honorable," with a subtitle: "Nazi Cases Not a Factor." That all these initiatives—save only Hayward's longer article—occurred during the spring and summer of 1986, that is, several months *before* the release of Deschênes's report, indicates the urgency that the National Archives felt to get its viewpoint well publicized. It is very rare for government agencies to comment publicly while federal investigatory commissions are still in the process of doing their work.

Part of that urgency was that the National Archives of Canada, after years of preparation, finally had a new archive bill before Parliament to replace its outdated 1912 legislation. The minister in introducing the bill to the critical second reading in Parliament (prior to its substantial debate and possible amendment) proclaimed in June 1986: "If a people is not aware of its past, it has no identity. It suffers from amnesia. It does not know its strengths. It does not know its weakness and cannot build on its experience. It cannot leap forward because it lacks the starting blocks of history." Given the sensitivity of the legislation in several quarters of the bureaucracy, and the long and delicate struggle to get it before Parliament, what the National Archives did not need was negative publicity remaining unanswered that it could not do its job properly—that it oversaw "monumental blundering." The legislation might be stalled, or rejected outright, or amended to impose some stringent oversight mechanism on the National Archives to monitor its now-questioned authorization of record destruction. Thus the National Archives felt obliged to counter the poor image it had recently been receiving.

In the article in the *Globe and Mail*, I asserted that the National Archives is indeed the "collective memory" of the nation, just as the minister claimed, as quoted above.[16] The serious charges leveled against the National Archives over the Nazi immigration case-file destruction had brought "into the public spotlight the usually quiet work archivists do in deciding which records will survive as the basis of our collective historical knowledge and which will go into the shredders." This appraisal work poses a central dilemma that archivists everywhere face daily:

Destroy the wrong records and you jeopardize the rights of citizens to redress, the need of government to consult records on a recurring basis, the demands of all manner of researchers to unravel the past and the cravings of a nation to understand itself. Keep too many records and you create a paper haystack in which few needles can ever be found, involving enormous storage, administrative and indexing costs that governments and society have shown no great willingness to bear.

After rehearsing many of the National Archives' ten arguments noted above about the Nazi immigration records, I concluded the *Globe and Mail* article with "it can be confidently stated that the records destroyed in 1982 did not contain the crucial information many thought and thus are irrelevant to the prosecution of Nazi war criminals living in the country and (beyond a valid sample) to documenting Canadian immigration history." The National Archives of Canada had done its job properly. And on the heels of all this controversy and subsequent vindication, the new archive bill was not diverted after all and soon passed into law.

The various impacts of the Nazi war criminals issue and the importance of having reliable records generally; the archival and other testimony before the commission; Deschênes's final report itself; and, throughout, the attendant media publicity and National Archives' responses—all these served to enhance understanding of the work of archives and archivists, within the government and in the country at large. While a few editorialists and even some friends of archives continued to misunderstand these issues, overall the Nazi records experience was salutary. As participant Robert Hayward observed in his analysis of this impact, "the Commission certainly gave the Archives exposure. Never before have Canadian archivists been called upon to explain publicly the way they do their job. Never before have editorials been written calling into question the work most of us have grown to consider routine and commonplace." Never before had a senior minister openly attacked the government's recordkeeping program as "monumental " blundering.

Given the National Archives' intensive involvement in the Commission's research and hearings and its multiple public explanations in 1985–1986 of the nature of archival appraisal, the Archives' traditional role "as the cultural storehouse of the nation's heritage" was enhanced to be sure. So too was its contribution now better understood (despite being ignored initially) to information management and government access (i.e., Freedom of Information) policy. The records disposal methodologies and procedures the Archives authorized for use by departmental officials (such as at the Immigration Department) were shown to be clear and well documented, rather than a matter, as Kaplan initially charged, of "working in thin air." And its own appraisal documentation for the destruction in 1982—detailing the records universe at the time regarding series, dates, and extents involved and outlining the justification for the keep-destroy and sampling decisions—was also, fortunately, in very good order, and available for inspection and then submitting as formal evidence. The archival processes overall were transparent and thus accountable. Hayward wondered, perhaps rhetorically, whether all archives could say the same if they were to be subjected (without advance notice) to such close scrutiny in their jurisdictions as the Deschênes Commission imposed on the National Archives of Canada?[17]

DEEPER QUESTIONS ABOUT ARCHIVAL APPRAISAL

Yet not all was well. The black hole in all this controversy was the actual destruction of post-1945 overseas immigration application forms (and, after 1952, the overseas immigration case files on which such forms would come to be filed). Here the National Archives wisely remained silent, at least publicly. The zeal of the media and some interveners before the Deschênes Commission, as encouraged by Kaplan and Littman's graphic testimonies, to expose a major scandal about Nazi coverups, or to cast blame on blundering civil servants, focused almost all public attention concerning "records" on the single destruction in 1982 of immigration case files. Once the Immigration Department and National Archives had demonstrated to Deschênes that postwar immigration case files had been destroyed following approved, routine procedures long before 1982, and that the 1982 destruction was exactly the same as its many predecessors and its large one-time extent easily explainable, then the "records" issue lost its appeal. And thus the very real Achilles' heel in the National Archives' actions was ironically missed (with one exception) by the rush to demonstrate conspiracy or blunder.

The key issue was why the overseas immigration application forms themselves had not been appraised by the National Archives as having archival value. That they had been destroyed routinely and accurately, following authorized National Archives procedures, reflecting archival appraisal decisions, was largely true, but not the point. Authorization for the destruction of overseas immigration case records (files and forms) had been granted by the National Archives in 1964 and updated in 1970. That raises several disturbing questions. By what authority had Immigration destroyed any such records before 1964 (especially in the critical 1945–1955 period)? And why is there no evidence in the Archives' own files authorizing such destructions before 1964? More critically, for the record destruction schedules of 1964 and 1970 that do authorize the destruction of overseas immigration records, why had none been designated as having archival value? On what grounds had the overseas application forms been authorized for destruction? And was it the right decision? And why was there no appraisal analysis in the National Archives' own files to indicate how this conclusion had been reached?

On whether this had been the right decision, Deschênes himself was ambivalent. On the one hand, he observed, as noted above, that the destruction of some of the government files had been "unfortunate," denying to him thereby the possibility of achieving "absolute certainty" on some issues. Such statements imply that the application forms, had they survived, might have been useful to the commission, and to Justice and RCMP officials, in verifying the presence of illegal Nazis immigrants in Canada. And he did accept David Matas's request that a formal moratorium be placed on the destruction of any surviving overseas immigration records that by oversight might still be in Canadian embassies or consulates in Europe for any immigration applicant born before 1927 (and thus at age 18 or older in 1945), thereby indicating again that the records might have value in pursuing war criminals. On the other hand, Deschênes also concluded, from surviving archival samples of the forms, that immigration applications would have offered no blanket panacea, unlike their American counterparts, to denaturalize and deport former Nazis, and that many other factors and evidence would have to be weighed in each individual case before deportation and denaturalization of any one Nazi could be successfully achieved in Canadian courts.

In this regard, Deschênes asserted that each case would have to be tested individually in a court of law to ascertain why the application form (even had it survived) for that person now on trial contained the fraudulent information it did, whether the immigrant was personally responsible for it being there, whether at the time he had understood the form (in a foreign language) that he was signing, and, more important, whether the Immigration agent in the 1940s had asked of the person in each case—there was conflicting evidence that this sometimes did not occur consistently—for particulars about the applicant's membership in the Nazi party or in those military units known to be involved in concentration camp or similar extermination assignments. The prospective immigrant had been under no legal obligation to provide this information voluntarily; he was required not to lie *only if* the information was directly asked for and it could now be proven decades after that he had indeed, personally, been asked for it. This was one of Deschênes's findings that most disappointed lobbying groups, for one could no longer *ipso facto* assume in all cases that any immigrant who could be shown to have been a Nazi must have lied to enter the country. Therefore, mass deportation with minimum legal appeals was not going to be as easy as previously thought. This line of reasoning evidently opened a large legal loophole, especially more than forty years after the applications in question had been created. This also shows that sometimes records are either more or less than strict evidence of the transactions that produced them.

David Matas, however, did not share Deschênes's doubts. He disagreed with the commissioner and he disagreed with the National Archives.[18] He alone (of non-National Archives' insiders) seemed to have grasped that the issue was not the destruction of 1982, but destruction period. Matas asserted that record management and archival policies, for more than three decades, were themselves evidence of "Canada's quiet code of inaction" against illegal Nazi immigrants: "the official record retention and destruction policies mirrored the government's apathy when it came to banishing war criminals from this country." It is a revealing and disturbing comment about the sensitive, politicized dimension of archival appraisal, and brings the culture wars and issues of public accountability very much to the archival door. For Matas here was doing nothing less than accusing archivists of being in full collusion with the state, destroying important records in order to maintain state authority and policy, even when that was morally wrong. The "immigration file destruction policies have left huge gaps in the records that can only hamper efforts to bring suspected war criminals to justice." Matas claimed that there were other choices: like the Americans, the overseas application forms could have been microfilmed, "but Canada chose not to."

While Matas repeated, to his discredit after hearing evidence to the contrary, that the 1982 destruction "occurred in the midst of the highly publicized Helmut Rauca affair," when it clearly preceded that publicity, he rightly objected to Deschênes's comment that if there was a blunder in the 1982 destruction, it was merely the left hand not knowing what the right hand was doing: senior government officials meeting in secret to discuss war criminal documentation, but failing to advise their own records management employees or the National Archives of Canada to retain immigration case files that had long been authorized to be destroyed.

For Matas, it was much more than that, for the "blunder" demonstrated once again the lack of enthusiasm by the government in pursuing war criminals vigorously. About Deschênes's conclusion, Matas argued that the commissioner missed the point:

Had the government been serious in its desire to deal with war criminals, guidelines would have required employees to check for immigration forms which might be useful in identifying suspected war criminals. Orders would have been issued from the top levels of authority to preserve any pertinent information in those files. And yet, none of the witnesses who participated in the destruction, including the archivists responsible for scanning files to pick out significant information, ever received any instructions to that end.... [A]ny determination of the relevance of these files should have been made prior to the destruction, not after the fact. In routinely destroying files, the government failed to consider their significance, in terms of information they might contain on Nazi war criminals, and for their potential contribution to social history.

This indictment is undoubtedly true for the government as a whole, although, as noted above, the National Archives in 1982 did not destroy or sample any pre-1950 records precisely because of these wartime sensitivities, and it was also very aware of the importance of a wide range of immigration records for "social history."

In assessing the 1982 "blunder" by senior officials, Matas underlined the politicized and controversial nature of appraisal and the related destruction of records, and how accountability and public policy can be thwarted by action (or inaction) by records managers and archivists. But what of the period before

1982? How sensitive had the appraising archivists been to the uses of overseas application forms to identify Nazis (or indeed other unsavory criminals from other countries more recently)? In this regard, Matas went even further. He asserted that any immigration document—not just the application form—should have been retained if it contained personal information. He offered the example of the extremely voluminous assisted transportation repayments case files. Any such case file would contain "names, addresses and signatures of immigrants. They could have been useful in locating and identifying Nazi war criminals in Canada." To the impossible costs of storage for tens of millions of such paper-based case records generated annually, he rather blithely offered microfilming as the solution. To the huge costs of microfilming, he offered nothing but a criticism of a failure of government will. One might wonder: why stop here? Why not keep or film every case file—income tax, unemployment insurance, pension, grants or loans to farmers, and potentially (depending on what the immigrant did in life in Canada) a thousand other types—that also contain names or addresses or signatures useful in locating immigrants living under false pretenses?

Here Matas underscored a fundamental archival reality: every record ever created has some potential use to someone, and no one can predict all the possible uses decades after creation that any record may invoke should it survive, nor the bitter disappointment that some future user might feel should that record have been destroyed as having no potential use, when that user has arrived at the archival repository precisely to use that record.

Archival appraisal for most of the twentieth century has, in fact, based its decision making on what to keep and what to destroy primarily on assessing actual or anticipated research uses of records, particularly for writing academic history. Archivists trained as historians, so the thinking went, would be able to anticipate what documentary sources current and future historians would need. Aside from its crystal-ball aspect of trying to predict the future, adopting a "value-through-use" approach to appraisal is fraught with difficulty: what about ever-changing trends in historiography to which the historian-archivist would be subjected that would render the resulting archival record a fragmented response, to say nothing of being skewered by lobbying by well-organized groups of users; what about a growing number of users of archives from a rich variety of non-historical disciplines (biologists, for example, or climatologists, or engineers) for which the archivist's historical training sheds little light; what about nonacademic (genealogists and railway buffs) and public policy users (such as Nazi hunters or Japanese-Canadian wartime displacement claims lawyers); what about archives as evidence for the protection of the rights of citizens (claims for past Aboriginal abuse or drug-testing victims); and what about archives being able to reflect marginalized citizens in society who do not use archives and thus would be excluded from any measurement of "use?" On methodological grounds alone, how can patterns of use themselves be measured as a valid predictor when there is no level playing field on which use occurs, some records being restricted from use by access provisions, physical frailty, or poor finding aids, and other records be-

ing very popular and heavily used in archival exhibitions and cited in many
books, thus creating a self-perpetuating loop of more and more use? Finally, the
use-based timetable for conducting archival appraisal at the end of the operational "life cycle" of the record, which is often several decades after the files had
 been created when some historical perspective on use has had time to develop,
is simply no longer possible. Given the huge volumes of modern paper records
and the technological transience of their computerized counterparts, appraisal
must now occur at or very shortly after the creation of the records.

Clearly, then, some new approach to appraisal was necessary, and the hard
questioning posed by David Matas served as a stimulus for such rethinking. If
the overseas application forms were now considered very useful—by Littman,
Matas, Kaplan, the RCMP, Justice, perhaps Deschênes, and no doubt others—
then it was hard to defend their appraisal and subsequent destruction on the
grounds that they were of no use.

This kind of soul-searching occurred quietly only inside the National Archives, for on the records destruction issue, as noted above, public attention was
drawn almost exclusively to the alleged conspiracy or blunder surrounding the
special destruction of 1982. When Deschênes's report was released in early
1987, that issue was laid to rest, reinforced by the media that this had indeed
been a routine housekeeping matter. The National Archives thus escaped judicial censure by Deschênes and public embarrassment in the media over the
deeper and more troubling issues of the reasons for the authorization of the destruction of the immigration application forms well before 1982, and over the
general paucity of appraisal theory and methodology, based on
"value-through-use," that it had followed (in common with most other Western
archives) since the midcentury. While David Matas was the exception who saw
this weakness in the National Archives' defense, his point was lost amid his own
misinformation about the 1982 destruction, thus making it easy at the time to
dismiss his observations.

Matas's observations were not dismissed inside the National Archives. Robert
Hayward put it best in asserting that the commission and media spotlight on the
archives "had the virtue of wonderfully concentrating the mind." The whole
process "forced the [government archives] division to look carefully at what it
was doing and sharpen its focus on how improvements could be made." Hayward and I, and the whole management team, "felt our work was open to public
examination and we were being held accountable for our actions, and that we
should take whatever measures were needed to improve our selection and
scheduling of government records. The Commission of Inquiry acted as a catalyst in that term's purest scientific sense."[19]

The first such measure was to improve the National Archives' documentation
of the appraisal and disposal (or records scheduling) process. The Archives had,
in fact, been very lucky with the controversial 1982 destruction approval and its
related appraisal and sampling of records. A temporary moratorium on transfers
to the National Archives in the early 1980s because of a short-term space crisis

meant that, in order to gain stack space for the archival sample of immigration case records, detailed written documentation had to be produced to convince senior management to allow the transfer. This documentation later became the backbone of the National Archives' testimony before the Deschênes Commission. That kind of detailed paper trail of accountability would not normally have been there; the National Archives now ensured that in future it would be. The necessity to link each transfer of archival records to the disposal authority and its related appraisal became obvious by the type of accountability for archival decision making that Deschênes demanded, and therefore changes in the Archives' accessioning procedures and record control databases were also implemented.

More fundamentally, the National Archives sought to clarify formally the relationship of its own archival and records management processes and departments' records disposal roles and responsibilities.[20] Eldon Frost, director of the government archival records division, to whom Hayward and I both reported as middle managers, informed the director of the records management division at the National Archives, "As a result of testimony which staff of this Division were required to give before the Deschênes Commission in 1985, it was identified," both within the division and under the direction of the assistant national archivist, "that we needed to scrutinize some of our divisional (and departmental) records scheduling practices." Reflecting these concerns, Frost later wrote an article for the national scholarly journal for archivists in Canada with the revealing title "A Weak Link in the Chain: Records Scheduling As a Source of Archival Acquisition."

To strengthen that link, records disposal practices for the Government of Canada, as led by the National Archives, were placed by 1990 on a planned, coordinated basis; the old ad hoc approach to accepting transfers by doing on-the-spot appraisals, as in 1982, usually in response to some departmental space crises, was formally ended. Unscheduled records dating after 1966 would no longer be accepted by the National Archives; rather, departments would have scheduled their records in a planned, holistic way before authority was granted for their destruction or archival preservation. Improved listing and controls of dormant records stored in federal records centers was required. Clarification of any destruction delegation from the personal purview of the National Archivist was determined. Followup procedures were anticipated to make sure that approved disposal schedules were being interpreted and implemented correctly. The setting of retention periods was also, except for records having archival value, clarified as being the accountability of the creating department or agency, not the National Archives. Creators determine the long-term operational and legal needs of their own records; archivists determine long-term social and memory requirements for a small percentage only of those same records. More generally, the National Archives supported reliable and accountable systems in all departments to manage records better in all media. Whether government agencies themselves learned the lessons of accountability through records, and the concomitant importance of having good records management systems, and whether the National Archives did all it could to inform departments of their responsibilities and to promote sound recordkeeping practices, may unfortunately still be very much in doubt.

On the narrower issue of managing the formal disposal process for records, the events surrounding the Deschênes Commission did mark the beginning of a major reengineering of appraisal and disposal at the National Archives, which in turn has had a national and international impact. Improved records management, clearer records schedules, and coordinated records disposal are only the shell, however, in which the critical keep-destroy appraisal decision takes place. Archival appraisal still remains at the heart of the process. Archival research to determine the best records to preserve as the nation's documentary heritage remains the core intellectual activity; records disposal schedules are the practical means for its implementation.

The National Archives realized in the wake of the Deschênes Commission that it needed to think anew its appraisal criteria. At first it did so still within the traditional "value-through-use" approach. And it also realized the need to develop more sophisticated methodologies for the statistical sampling of case files than those used in 1982. Various efforts were made over the next couple of years to bring these two projects to fruition, without success. Then, after an influential international "expert meeting" of several countries' representatives in Germany on archival appraisal that I attended in 1989 on behalf of the National Archives of Canada, I took over both the appraisal and sampling projects and soon created, with helpful advice from National Archives colleagues, a new approach to archival appraisal.

Quite frankly, I had been personally troubled by Matas's accusation that archivists of the 1950s and 1960s in authorizing the destruction of the overseas application forms had been in collusion with the state in undermining fundamental justice and human rights. I also felt the accuracy of Matas's core challenge to the traditional "value-through-use" approach for determining which records are designated as archival, which challenge was reinforced by archivists from other countries attending the meeting in Germany. As noted above, that "value-through-use" approach was a self-referential, almost incestuous methodology, where frequent use begets more of the same use and thus acquisition of more of the same records, and lack of (present or perceived) use leads to non-acquisition and thus important gaps in our collective memories. Such thinking resulted in the destruction of the overseas immigration application forms.

From this context, I developed a new appraisal concept and methodology that I called "macroappraisal." Macroappraisal finds value through a functional analysis of society, its major institutions, and the interaction of citizens with those institutions. It is the values of society contemporary to the record creation that should be reflected in the "values" assigned to records for archival retention. Removing the focus of appraisal from the billions of records created daily to the functional-structural context of their creation, and citizens' interaction with and influence on such functions and structures, macroappraisal aims to reflect in archival holdings, in a more balanced way, a broader spectrum of human experience in society and to mirror more closely therefore society's own values, rather than more narrowly the values of powerful records creators or those derived from anticipating use patterns.

In appraising the function of qualifying and admitting immigrants to Canada, for example, rather than just looking at one type of case file generated at headquarters in Ottawa (as in the 1982 disposal) and deciding their archival value in isolation, the archivist using macroappraisal would now assess against the overall program's activities, and transactions of the immigration function, and immigrants' responses to these, all the case-level records, comprehensively, at one time: the overseas application, health, and security forms; the landing record; the local immigration file created at the port of entry; the central headquarters immigration file; any assistance or special settlement files, created at any level; and the naturalization and citizenship or deportation files, including any files created by levels of appeals, boards of inquiry, or the courts; together with microfilmed versions in some cases and computerized database versions in others. More general policy, subject, and operational files above the case level dealing with the function of qualifying and admitting immigrants would also be considered at the same time. From this broad or "macro" view of all the information relating to the function, the archivist is better able to choose the best, most succinct record to document Canadian immigrants, and their interactions with the state, because the forest is seen as a whole, rather than just a few trees in isolation. (Any records not so chosen as archival, but having possible long-term legal value to the creating department, remains the clear responsibility of the creating agency to retain them by adopting longer retention periods or media conversions.) Macroappraisal seems to be striking a resonance in the modern archival world, and it has been adopted in various forms in Australia, South Africa, Netherlands, various American and Australian states, and some Canadian provinces, and it is being studied by other archives programs in other nations for possible implementation.

CONCLUSION

At the end of the century, the hunt for Nazi war criminals continues. Klaus Barbie is finally tried and imprisoned in France. Australia expels several Nazis found in the country. And in Canada in 2000, arrests continue of Nazis who committed atrocities or lied about their membership in extermination units in order to enter the country. Despite the passage of time, accountability is required; there is no statute of limitations for crimes against humanity. The archival record remains central to such accountability. President William Clinton created a special interagency working group in January 1999 to identify Nazi war criminals and those who protected them. Early on, the group initiated a large-scale effort to identify relevant records within the government and issued an appeal to all American archivists to bring any related records in other archives to its attention.

Critical to accountability in any sphere of human activity is the existence of reliable records as evidence of human and organizational activity. And for the records to be credible, the records management and archival processes themselves must be based on sound theoretical concepts of "value," on logical strategies and methodologies to locate such values, and on consistent practice, verifiable implementation, and transparent documentation. Archivists and records managers must likewise themselves be transparent and accountable for their decisions. Significant improvements in all these areas at the National Archives of Canada were a direct result of the impact of the Deschênes Commission investigations or the criticisms of David Matas.

Odd but true, the conclusion seems inescapable that Nazi war criminals entering Canada illegally in the late 1940s led indirectly, by the end of the 1980s, to better ways of determining how archival records should be selected to form society's collective memory. This perhaps atones a little for past apathies.

NOTES

1. I am very grateful for the good advice received from three readers to whom I gave an earlier draft of this paper: Robert J. Hayward, my National Archives of Canada colleague in the 1980s and now with the Office of Critical Infrastructure Protection and Emergency Preparedness, Department of National Defense, Government of Canada; Verne Harris, then at the National Archives of South Africa and now the University of Witwatersrand's Graduate School for the Humanities and Social Sciences and the South Africa History Archive; and Tim Cook, still with the National Archives of Canada; and to my two editors, Richard J. Cox of the University of Pittsburgh and David A. Wallace of the University of Michigan. Their collective comments have much improved the argument and style of what follows, but I am alone responsible for the final product and all its interpretations. I also want to acknowledge and thank Bennett McCardle who, during the height of the events described in this essay in 1985–1986, was an archivist working in my section at the National Archives of Canada; her prodigious research and analytical abilities produced many reports that were very helpful to me then, and remain so in writing these reflections. I have decided to use throughout this essay the current nomenclature of "National Archives of Canada" and "National Archivist," rather than the nomenclature of 1912–1987, "Public Archives of Canada" and "Dominion Archivist."

2. *Halifax Herald,* Apr. 8, 1981, for all preceding quotations.

3. Cited in Alan A. Ryan, *Quiet Neighbors: Prosecuting Nazi War Criminals in America* (San Diego: Harcourt Brace Jovanovich, 1984), p. 14.

4. Ibid., pp. 331–332, 337.

5. David Matas with Susan Charendoff, *Justice Delayed: Nazi War Criminals in Canada* (Toronto: Summerhill Press, 1987), p. 260.

6. James McKenzie, *War Criminals in Canada* (Calgary: Detselig, 1995), pp. 114, 117–118.

7. Commission of Inquiry on War Criminals, *Report, Part 1: Public* (Minister of Supply and Services: Ottawa, 1986), p. 69, for quotation, and pp. 67–82 for the research summary and conclusions on Mengele. Hereafter cited as Deschênes, *Report.*

8. Ibid., pp. 208–209, for quotations in this and the previous paragraph.

9. "Those Vanishing Files," *Winnipeg Free Press*, Dec. 15, 1985, p. 6. For the David Matas quotations in the previous paragraph, see "Immigration Files Destruction Routine, Inquiry Lawyer Says," *Winnipeg Free Press*, Dec. 4, 1985, p. 33.

10. Deschênes, *Report*, p. 209.

11. Robert J. Hayward, "'Working in Thin Air': Of Archives and the Deschênes Commission," *Archivaria* 26 (Summer 1988): 127.

12. Terry Cook to Eldon Frost, Nov. 28, 1985, File 8052–2, National Archives of Canada Records, copy in my possession, reporting on meeting of Nov. 26.

13. Deschênes, *Report*, pp. 208–214, for all quotations that follow on the commission's process and its findings concerning its extraordinary foray into records issues.

14. *Montreal Gazette*, Mar. 13, 1987, p. A2.

15. See Hayward, "Working in Thin Air," p. 132.

16. Terry Cook, "For the Record: Archivists Honorable," *Toronto Globe and Mail*, Aug. 11, 1986 (the minister's comments are cited in the same place).

17. Robert Hayward's analysis on the immediate impact of the commission is very sound; see his "Working in Thin Air," especially pp. 130–133, and for the quotations.

18. Matas, *Justice Delayed*, pp. 84–88, which focuses on his criticism of the destruction of the overseas application forms. In response to my article in the *Globe and Mail* defending the National Archives' actions, David Matas wrote a rebuttal letter to the editor, "Immigrant Files and Nazis," *Globe and Mail*, Aug. 21, 1986, attacking the article and the Archives' actions. My counter-rebuttal dated August 31, 1986 (in my possession), was not published by the editor of the *Globe and Mail*. Quotations in this paragraph come from these three sources.

19. Hayward, "Working in Thin Air," pp. 130–131.

20. See Federal Archives Division, Management Committee Minutes, Dec. 15, 1985, and Feb. 26, 1986, which were devoted to analyzing the lessons learned from the Deschênes experience (over a year *before* the release of the Commission's report) and, as a consequence, to improving archival appraisal and records disposal. These extended minutes were forwarded by Eldon Frost, director of the Division, to the director of the Records Management and Micrographic Services Division, with a covering memorandum on Apr. 8, 1986, that was copied to three of the National Archives' senior executive managers (copies in possession of the author). This and the next paragraph are based on these sources.

Information for Accountability Workshops: Their Role in Promoting Access to Information[1]

Kimberly Barata, Piers Cain, Dawn Routledge, and Justus Wamukoya

Open government is an essential requirement for good government. In turn, good government requires the participation of citizens. For this to happen there must be a free flow of information. In many countries policies are being introduced to inform citizens about the availability, allocation, and utilization of public resources. In an environment where information is withheld there will be inevitable tensions and mistrust; citizens can feel that government is somehow responsible for their misfortunes.

It is in this regard that the International Records Management Trust, Rights and Records Institute,[2] in collaboration with Transparency International[3] (TI), developed the Information for Accountability Workshops. The goal of this project was to encourage improved public access to government information in order to develop a more informed civil society. Accountability and transparency cannot be achieved in an environment where information is not available. Records management underpins accountability.

There is a natural relationship between the trust and TI because transparency relies upon open access to information and records. Specifically, the workshop approach is derived from a methodology developed by TI and adapted by the trust. The Information for Accountability Workshops provide government officials with an opportunity to identify and respond to citizens' legitimate demands for information on government programs. They encourage the public sector to educate citizens about what is publicly available and what is not and why not. The intention is to create an environment where citizens feel comfortable requesting information without fear of penalty. Ultimately, the availability of more information should enhance their confidence in government. The workshops are designed not only to encourage civil society to articulate citizens' needs for information from government, but also to focus the attention of policymakers, opinion formers, and senior civil servants on the need to strengthen record management systems as a primary delivery mechanism to supply that demand.

This essay focuses on the reasons that this initiative was developed and how the outcomes of it successfully build a case for strengthening records management systems in support of public sector accountability to citizens. In particular, it reports on two pilot workshops that were carried out in Tanzania (spring 2000) and Ghana (summer 2000) to test the methodology that was developed.

WHY IS IMPROVING ACCESS TO INFORMATION IMPORTANT FOR ACCOUNTABILITY?

Those who live in Western liberal democracies tend to take it for granted that freedom of expression and a free press are essential requirements for good government and a healthy democracy. The basic argument is that good government requires the participation of citizens. For citizens to participate effectively, the electorate must be well informed, and this means access to the facts about government activities. A free flow of information about what the government is doing on behalf of its citizens and how taxes collected from citizens are spent is essential for accountable government. The press has a key role in ensuring that this information is communicated to the public.

These principles are reflected in the Universal Declaration of Human Rights, in particular Article 19: "Everyone has the right to freedom of opinion and expression; this right includes freedom to hold opinions without interference and to seek, receive and impart information and ideas through any media and regardless of frontiers." Access to information held by governments is implicit in enforcing other human rights: "Everyone has the right of equal access to public service in his country" (Article 21[2]). "The will of the people shall be the basis of the authority of government; this will shall be expressed in periodic and genuine elections which shall be by universal and equal suffrage and shall be held by secret vote or by equivalent free voting procedures" (Article 21[3]). And "everyone has the right to education. Education shall be free, at least in the elementary and fundamental stages" (Article 26[1]). Underlying these rights is the assumption that governments are maintaining adequate records of their activities and that the citizen has reasonable access to the information contained in these records or direct access to the records themselves. Others have gone further and argued that since government acts on the citizens' behalf and is funded from taxes paid by the citizens, the records created by government actually belong to the people. Thus, the presumption ought to be that governments should make their records available to the public unless they can show good cause why they should be withheld (for example, national security).

These views are more or less the conventional opinion in most Western liberal democracies, particularly in the United States, where these rights are enshrined in its Constitution, and in Scandinavia, where freedom-of-information laws date back to the eighteenth century.

WHY IS ACCESS TO INFORMATION DIFFICULT IN SUB-SAHARAN AFRICA?

In other parts of the world interest in improving the flow of information between the government and the public is a much more recent phenomenon. In particular in Anglophone Sub-Saharan Africa, the situation is complicated by various historical factors. As former British colonies, these countries inherited a strongly entrenched culture of secrecy and conservatism within the civil service.[4] Institutional culture was codified in the Official Secrets Act and service regulations. In some countries, the colonial authorities introduced repressive emergency legislation in the immediate preindependence period to counter the activities of popular independence movements. When independence was achieved, some newly self-ruling governments found these laws convenient for suppressing dissent and so the laws were allowed to remain on the statute books. The result has been a legislative and regulatory environment that discourages civil servants from making information available to the public.[5]

Most of the Anglophone Sub-Saharan countries abandoned the "Westminster model" soon after independence and adopted (either de jure or de facto) single-party systems. The absence of effective multiparty systems diminished the importance of the free flow of information to the political process. In many cases there were human-rights violations. However, Western governments often turned a blind eye during the Cold War period if the government was regarded as taking an anticommunist position. In these circumstances, fundamental human rights, including Articles 21 and 26 of the Universal Declaration of Human Rights, were not always upheld. Even where they were incorporated in the constitution, in many cases they were not supported by enabling legislation or effective case law.

Another, less tangible factor has been that traditionally African society has emphasized respect for elders and leaders. Asking for information, especially where there is a large social distance between the person seeking information and the government official, can sometimes be construed as impertinence.

Recently the situation has changed, and this has created a climate in Sub-Saharan Africa more favorable to initiatives designed to improve the provision of information to the public for accountability purposes. The ending of the Cold War has removed an important incentive for Western governments to overlook human rights violations by African governments. There has been a growing impatience with the poor economic performance of African economies. This has been attributed to poor political leadership and economic mismanagement by African governments. Strengthening the role of civil society is increasingly seen as a strategy for improving accountability and thus encouraging better decisions and more effective government. The Rights and Records Institute recognizes the need to find ways of enabling the ordinary citizen to obtain access more easily to the vast quantities of information that every government has in its possession.

Growing public concern about and intolerance of corruption is also a factor. This is a phenomenon both in the countries providing development aid and in the recipient countries. The public is increasingly frustrated by wasted opportunities and the scandal of the few enriching themselves at the expense of the many. Increasing information to the public about how the money is spent is seen as a promising strategy for reducing the opportunities for corruption. For example, the governments of Ghana and Uganda are considering introducing freedom-of-information legislation as a component of their official anticorruption programs.

Many governments in Anglophone Sub-Saharan Africa have spent more than a decade reforming the public sector (Ghana, Uganda, and Tanzania are good examples). These reforms have included privatizing state-owned enterprises and reducing the number of civil servants. More important, they have attempted to improve the quality of services provided to the public. Concomitant with this change has been a growing realization that for this reform to work the citizen needs information about what services are being offered and how to complain if there is a problem. Senior public servants are aware of the need for change and are looking for solutions, providing that increased public access to information has support from the executive and the legislature.

Finally, the "information revolution" is also a factor. The elites of the countries in the region are well aware that future economic success for their countries will depend on their ability to participate in the information revolution. They are aware that even in the United States, the government has played an important role in the development of the Internet. Unless citizens and the private sector in Sub-Saharan Africa have access to government-held information comparable to that available to citizens and businesses in the industrialized countries, they will be unable to compete. Many see liberalizing the government's information regime as a necessary step.

WHY THE WORKSHOPS?

The Information for Accountability Workshops initiative was developed to meet an unfulfilled need. Although records are essential for the protection of basic human rights, the rule of law, and efficient public administration, the "donor community" (that is, the international and national aid and concessionary lending institutions, such as the World Bank, USAID) has not paid much attention to records management, nor has it made much investment in this area. Moreover, there are many examples where investment in computer systems to improve public administration were in danger of becoming "white elephants" because very little use is being made of the information these systems process. Information systems that are not used will not be maintained and very quickly deteriorate.

The Rights and Records Institute realized that it needed to find a way of enabling the ordinary citizen to more easily obtain access to the vast quantities of information that every government has in its possession. If the institute could stimulate public demand for information, this could lead to a culture of information use, which would ensure that information systems in the public sector needed for accountability would be maintained and be relevant.

Along with many other people in the field, we became concerned that reforms to support accountability in developing countries were being pushed through by the donor community with little opportunity for the people of the countries themselves to express their views. The Information for Accountability Workshops were designed to stimulate demand by the public for information from their governments through an open-ended discussion process. This deliberately avoids promoting a particular policy solution. Each country must decide what level of information disclosure and which policy options are appropriate for its own needs. The workshops simply provide a framework for the discussion to take place.

THE WORKSHOP METHODOLOGY

The workshop methodology has been developed to enable civil society stakeholders to articulate their information needs to public sector stakeholders. It provides a mechanism to help government officials to gain a better understanding of both their agencies' and citizens' priorities for obtaining various kinds of information. In many countries, access to information is a sensitive issue and considerable tact is required to successfully reconcile the different perspectives of the executive, the legislature, and civil society organizations. The workshop methodology provides a framework for participants to develop an understanding of both the needs and the constraints of the different stakeholders regarding access to information. The methodology is transferable and can be adapted to suit the focus and agendas of different countries.

An important element is the use of a case study to move from a discussion of broad concepts to a focus on practical outputs. The case study provides an opportunity for participants to work through the methodology within their own context and propose both practical "quick wins" and longer-term solutions. Examples of case studies would be specific sector projects (e.g., the building of a hospital or primary school, land reform, or the decentralization of a function to local authorities). Alternatively, proposals for implementing access to information legislation or strengthening the operation of existing legislation could be the focus. The first pilot workshop in Tanzania focused on information demands in connection with a specific primary education project. In Ghana draft access to information legislation provided the foundation for discussions.

The workshops were designed as interactive events to identify user requirements for ensuring accountability. They took the form of presentations, to familiarize participants with key issues and concepts, and mediated discussions in the form of "breakout groups." These discussions provided the opportunity to draw

out issues, such as the types of records needed to satisfy accountability requirements within the agencies or the means of accessing this information efficiently.
The workshops involved an analysis of the types of information available that
demonstrate accountability and the mechanisms that exist to deliver it. Typical
objectives were to

- determine areas of agreement and disagreement over access to information between different stakeholders
- prioritize information requirements according to local needs
- agree what information should be made available, to whom, and under what conditions
- assess the capacity of existing and planned information systems to provide efficient access to information and to ensure accountability, sustainability, and suitability to local needs, as well as to meet donor requirements
- identify ways of improving the process of appealing decisions made by civil servants
- identify priorities for improving government services to citizens
- improve the dissemination of information that satisfies local stakeholder needs (e.g., resolving pension claims)
- develop a sustainable program of action to address shortcomings identified in existing information systems

Not only will it be possible to replicate the workshop approach in other sectors
and other countries, but workshop tools were developed and can be used as
teaching materials for public management training. The tools provide the framework for the workshops.[6] They include a workbook that provides guidance for
running the two-day workshops to define and strengthen the information systems needed to support accountability and a sourcebook that serves as a com-
panion volume comprising background literature, case studies of access to
information initiatives around the world, annotated bibliography, and annotated list of relevant Web sites. Ultimately this new approach should provide
public servants with an opportunity to identify and respond to citizens' requests
for information, to improve the quality of the information available and to reduce the spread of misinformation. Furthermore, it can help to build confidence
in government and support for public service programs. Large numbers of the
workshop tools have been downloaded from a number of Internet sites where
they are freely available. One can assume that at least a small proportion of the
downloads were performed by people who were either contemplating running
their own workshops or adapting the tools for their own use. Only time can tell
what impact this will have.

CASE STUDY: TANZANIA

In November 1999 a team from the Rights and Records Institute carried out
a short background study in Tanzania. This was to identify issues that would be

relevant to the design of the workshop agenda and program for the first pilot workshop. The team consulted widely to determine relevant practical concerns and local realities. This was essential in a country where, paradoxically, even information about a lack of information was not widely available or discussed.

The Background Study

In the case of Tanzania, there is reason to believe that the general public lacks awareness of the nature of its rights. In addition, many lack the resources to litigate for the protection of these rights. Since human rights are an essential element of the democratic process, there can be no true democracy in a country where the majority of the people do not know their rights and duties. In such a situation, the public is bound to be misled, much to the advantage of demagogues.[7]

Individuals interviewed for the background study agreed that most citizens are not aware of their rights. Public advocates, including nongovernmental organizations (NGOs), the media and legal aid groups, are working to inform citizens of their rights and play a key role in public sector information and data collection and disbursement. However, the majority of Tanzania's citizens live in the countryside, and the activities of the local press, legal aid providers, and grassroots organizations extend only as far as the regional town centers. Therefore, radio serves as the predominant means for many citizens living in rural communities to obtain information. Efforts to educate citizens about their rights must be sensitive to the fact that while urban centers have systems to inform citizens, the communication systems of the urban centers may not extend easily to all parts of the country. Solutions are needed that ensure information is distributed equitably to all.

Every citizen has the right to be informed; yet public servants have no obligation to provide information to them. Article 18, clause 2 (Part III Basic Rights and Duties) of the Constitution of the United Republic of Tanzania of 1977 states that "Every citizen has the right to be informed at all times of various events in the country and in the world at large which are of importance to the lives and activities of the people and also of issues of importance to society." The rights and freedoms enumerated in Part III of the constitution are considered basic rights and are arguable before the courts.

Those interviewed during the study agreed that many citizens in urban areas are aware that Article 18 exists, but few know how to exercise their right to obtain information. Mechanisms do not exist to provide guidance to citizens on accessing current government information. The National Archives Act provides for the right of citizens to consult public records that are over thirty years old and have been selected for long-term preservation in the National Archives or any other archival repository, the selecting being the responsibility of the director of the National Archives. Legislation has been drafted to reduce the thirty-year closure rule on public records in Tanzania to twenty-five years, but this legislation has not yet been passed. At the moment, the National Archives building is almost full and virtually nothing after 1973 has been transferred to it. As a result, most public records that belong in the archives are still held in the ministries and are, therefore, inaccessible to citizens.

The view that citizens have a right to access more current information on government decisions and actions (i.e., records that are less than thirty years old) is not well supported by public servants. Rhoda Howard, a human-rights author, points out, "Constitutional provisions are in any case, a mere guide to statements of principle, to which adherence can be assumed only when the political culture engenders respect for the Constitution and when there are institutionalized mechanisms for forcing the government to respect it."[8] There is little by way of institutionalized mechanisms that require the government to facilitate the public's right to be informed. A Code of Ethics and Conduct for the Public Service Tanzania was issued by the Civil Service Department in June 1999. Section III, Part 5, of the code addresses the issue of disclosure of information: "A Public Servant shall not use any official document or photocopy such as a letter or any other document or information obtained in the course of discharging his/her duties for personal ends; Public Servants shall not communicate with the media on issues related to work or official policy without due permission; Official information will be released to the media by officials who have been authorized to do so according to laid down procedures."[9] Although the requirements in the code are reasonable, there is no corresponding obligation for public servants to provide information. As a result, when citizens or their representatives ask public servants for information, their questions are often met with a defensive reluctance to provide answers.

The legal community has called upon the Constitutional Commission to include a provision in the constitution that gives citizens the right to request information. To be effective, this provision will have to be supported by clear guidelines and procedures to facilitate access.

The procedure to release official information to the media is not adequate. The section on disclosure of information in the Code of Ethics and Conduct for the Public Service Tanzania is clear: "official information will be released to the media by officials who have been authorized to do so according to laid down procedures." Interviews with media representatives revealed that there are no known formal written procedures to substantiate this statement. Media professionals are expected to rely initially on information issued to them through press releases. Yet many press officers in the ministries are not trained journalists, and the general perception is that the information they produce is self-serving and not useful.

If journalists want to pursue a matter further they are asked to submit a questionnaire on letterhead and wait for a response; often no reply is forthcoming. The need for the government to reply is only an understanding, not an obligation. Media representatives can ask to interview officials and will often be given permission to do so. However, their success is likely to depend upon the strength of the informal networks they have cultivated within government. The Media Council of Tanzania is trying to address this situation by maintaining a register of developments likely to restrict the supply of information of public interest and importance. The council reviews this register and investigates the conduct and attitude of individuals, corporations, and governmental bodies toward the media. Reports of these investigations are made public through the press.

Informal networks for trading information provide the only reasonably reliable method of obtaining public sector information. When a citizen does not have access to a network, information is very hard to obtain. Networks take a significant investment of time and trust to evolve. The reliability of the information obtained and the speed with which it is provided may depend upon the character of the relationship. Individuals without a credible informal network often resort to speculation, suspicion, and misinterpretation. For example, much criticism has been directed at the media in Tanzania for reporting misinformation. Poor reporting is often the result of badly trained journalists. However, it is also a reflection of the inability to obtain additional information needed to report accurately the facts about stories as they break.

Even with a network, some information is still difficult if not impossible to obtain. The national accounts and Auditor General's Report are common examples. Although both documents are published for the benefit of Parliament, it is difficult to obtain a copy even from the government printing office. Budgetary information is perhaps the most sought-after information. Civil society groups need budgetary and financial information to assess government priorities and determine which problems are being ignored or undervalued. National and international NGOs expend significant resources to circumvent obstacles to obtaining government information and to gather their own data. The fact that they pay so much attention to other organizations' reports is a demonstration that there is no other way to get the information; if NGOs are unable to obtain material themselves or through other organizations, they often resort to using donor agencies to force government to release information.

Few Tanzanians recognize that they have a right to complain. Most citizens are afraid that complaining will bring them unwanted attention. There is no way of knowing who has what influence and therefore the extent of retribution any person can inflict. When people do complain it is often an indication that they have reached a point at which they feel they have little left to lose.

The Permanent Commission of Enquiry is the government body that functions most like that of an ombudsman, but it is not independent. The president appoints the chairman and not more than four other members who then report directly to him. The president is not obliged to follow the commission's recommendations, since there are no proper provisions concerning its authority in the constitution. Furthermore, the procedure for appealing to the commission is not well known, and the commission does not follow a transparent process and its reports are not published. As a result, the courts rarely respect the decisions of the commission.

An Ethics Inspectorate was established in 1998. It operates under the Civil Service Department (CSD) and according to the Public Service Act, thus placing the CSD in charge of civil-service ethics and promoting its authority throughout government. Despite advertising its establishment in the local papers, the inspectorate is a virtually unknown body outside government. The role of the inspectorate is to promote values in the civil service and to work to change attitudes. To achieve this aim, the unit publishes the *Code of Conduct* to let civil servants know what is expected of them. The inspectorate investigates complaints about the ethical behavior of public servants. Virtually all letters of complaint to the inspectorate come from other civil servants. The Ethics Inspectorate produces a report detailing the number of complaints reported, the number investigated, a summary of how the complaints were resolved, and appeals made. This report is not made available to the public.

The independent Swahili newspaper *Majira*[10] provides an informal communal channel for the public to voice complaints or to make an appeal to the government. Citizens send letters to *Majira*, which are then published unedited in the paper according to prescribed daily subjects (e.g., Thursday relates to politics, Friday to culture and education, Saturday to social services). The letters often have little effect. Although the paper tries to pressure the government on the public's behalf, the letters rarely receive an official reply. The Ethics Inspectorate does scan *Majira* daily for criticisms and accusations and then investigates accordingly. The director claims that if a complaint appears in the newspaper it will be followed up. However, the inspectorate does not communicate the results of these investigations to the person complaining or to the media.

The widespread culture of confidentiality is an obstacle to change. Approximately two-thirds of government records are classified confidential, and there is no standard procedure for declassifying them. Given the number of confidential records, there is reason to believe that the Official Secrets Act is being misinterpreted or misapplied. This may be partly to do with how the system operates. Nonconfidential (i.e., open) records travel slowly through the system, while confidential records are dealt with more quickly. Moreover, confidential registries tend to be more efficient than the open registries. As a result, the administration of the system provides incentives to designate records as confidential.

Governments have the right to withhold documents for reasons of legislative provisions, national security, and other reasons. However, accountability and openness cannot be achieved within an established culture of indiscriminate confidentiality and secrecy. If a public official is working on behalf of the rest of the population, then the people have a right to know what actions have been taken and why. Until this issue is addressed, there may be no use in pursuing a right of access to information.

The government has declared its desire to become more accountable to the citizens. Much of the existing legislation affecting the availability of information to the public has yet to be reviewed and may be in conflict with the objectives of openness, transparency, and accountability. There is a strong need to reexamine this legislation. For example, possession of confidential information is a criminal offense if the individual is not authorized to handle the information. One illustration of this is the case of a part-time journalist and small trader who was found in possession of a confidential letter written by a regional commissioner, containing instructions to refuse him a trading license for spurious reasons. The journalist obtained this letter and took the regional commissioner to court on suspicion of corruption. However, because the document was classified, the journalist was prosecuted for being in possession of a confidential document.

Policies, legislation, and standards supporting open access to information have been developed in many countries, but if introduced in Tanzania they may not be successful. The international community must be realistic about what degree of open government can be achieved in differing circumstances and resource levels. Governments should not be pressured to champion accountability initiatives that they cannot sustain. Emphasis should be directed toward ensuring that the underlying systems are in place to support new initiatives, that civil-service culture is considered, that reforms are relevant to the wider government program for poverty alleviation, and that there is political will to sustain the program.

In Tanzania, civil society generally has very low expectations of government. Many of those interviewed by the research team expressed the view that people are struggling simply to survive and to achieve their basic needs; access to information is not a priority. The workshop considered ways of sensitizing the public to the relationship between greater access to information and the ability to fulfill basic needs by encouraging greater participation in government programs and the ability to demonstrate clearly how the money is spent.

While the government does recognize that people need information, many officials are very apprehensive about opening access to government information or records. Some expressed reservations over whether there was any point, because the government is in charge of making decisions on behalf of the people. There is little to suggest that the government of Tanzania has the political will to strengthen and enlighten civil society. Civil society advocates will have to work actively with government and donor agencies to achieve meaningful change.

One area where the government and donor agencies are already working closely together is in reforming the public sector to improve services to citizens. Despite low expectations, the public is indeed entitled to know the business of government, because government is mandated to take actions on behalf of citizens. Civil society members should have the opportunity to comment on proposed reform of services that affect their lives. The government would benefit from increased participation by gaining broad-based support for the reform agenda. One measure of the success of government service delivery reforms would be the development of a clear and well-established consultative process that involves the input of citizens at various stages. For this to occur there must be open channels of communication and a free flow of relevant information; this includes knowing what information is available, how to obtain it, and how to appeal to government if information is withheld.

In 1991 the government of Tanzania launched a Civil Service Reform Program (CSRP). The overall objective of the program was to achieve a smaller, affordable, efficient, and effective civil service. Despite the achievements in structural and institutional reforms, little has been done to translate these results into improved services for the people of Tanzania. As a result, the government is opting for a more comprehensive program with a longer-term perspective, the Public Service Reform Program (PSRP). The PSRP aims to transform the public service into one that has the capacity, systems, and culture for client orientation and continuous improvement of services.[11]

The PSRP will require more than a decade of sustained reform efforts. The aim is to deliver quality public services under severe budgetary constraints. The program will require a number of performance indicators and measures to ensure that reform efforts are meeting their targets and are sustainable. However, performance targets often focus internally within government rather than on the public's ability to achieve their basic needs as a result of improvements to services. In particular, the program does not appear to ask "How can government improve service delivery if the public cannot ask basic questions about services?" In recognizing that it is a service delivery organization, the government will need to accept that the requirement for accountability will increase and, as a consequence, it will need to allow citizens to question actions taken on their behalf.

The Workshop

The Tanzania workshop took place in Dar es Salaam at the end of March 2000. The Rights and Records Institute worked in partnership with Transparency International Tanzania to develop a program focused on issues of relevance to Tanzania that were identified during the background study. The aim of the workshop was to provide a starting point for the government to determine what kind of information it needs to make available to demonstrate its accountability to citizens and, therefore, which information systems are most critical to allow transparency of public services. The ambition was to encourage the public sector to educate citizens about what information is publicly available and how they may obtain it, but also what is not available and why not.

In Tanzania, citizens know they can ask their elected officials to answer their queries. However, they also know that obtaining a response from the government regularly requires perseverance and courage. The workshop was an opportunity to raise awareness among government officials and citizens and a forum for participants to discuss the need for changing policies, procedures, and attitudes within the civil service. To this end, the Ministry of Education and Culture's District Based Support for Primary Education (DBSPE) program provided the focus for discussion because it has strong accountability mechanisms built into the program design (the level of responsibility and reporting are clearly defined).[12] Two of the five key objectives of this program are accountability and transparency. These aims can be achieved only through the effective delivery of information to stakeholders.

The workshop was a significant achievement in that it represented the first attempt to discuss the issue of public access to information in Tanzania, and it was successful in raising awareness and generating enthusiasm for new initiatives. Many of the concepts discussed were new to participants; this made it difficult for them to go much beyond identifying key policy issues and defining practical steps to address some problems further. The participants were drawn from Parliament, the Civil Service Department, the Office of the Controller and Auditor General, the Ministry of Education, and local institutions and groups such as the Kunduchi Primary School, the local branch of the Danish educational charity MS, the Tanzania School of Journalism, and the Faculty of Law at the University of Dar es Salaam.

Participants were asked to complete an attitude survey at the start of the workshop. The survey measured the perceptions of participants on information access in Tanzania. There was clear recognition that improving access to information is an important issue. Almost all participants (95.5 percent) agreed that government has an obligation to provide information to its citizens. In a culture where secrecy is the norm and disclosure the exception, this demonstrated a clear pressure for change. Tied to this, strengthening records management systems was seen by participants as more important than solutions such as providing for longer office opening hours or increasing staff resources.

The workshop identified a number of obstacles to accessing government information and, in particular, problems with the DBSPE program. As a group, the participants expressed concern that the culture of the civil service, existing laws, and civil-service regulations restrict the flow of information to the public. The restriction is made worse by citizens' ignorance of their rights and of where to go for information. Participants concluded that the civil service could not be held solely responsible for the problems of accessing public information. Until the public begins to demand information, no improvements are likely.

It was remarkable that the participants, who ranged from a primary school teacher to members of Parliament, were able to achieve consensus on many issues. The results to some extent confirmed the findings of the background study, but they also introduced new themes and emphases. The obstacles identified included

- *Centralized bureaucracy.* The information exists, but the public cannot get it. Ministries hold most information about their programs centrally. This is the result of a highly centralized political and administrative system. As a result, the tradition requires individuals to go to the center (Dar es Salaam) to request information or raise complaints.

- *Poor distribution channels.* In general, the distribution of information both within government and externally to the public is poor. Participants from the civil service who are not involved in the DBSPE program were surprised that they had never heard of it. The workshop revealed how poor the lateral communication is between ministries, particularly at a senior policy level. In addition, DBSPE program staff admit that more information needs to be disseminated to teachers and parents. There also needs to be more information going to the district councils. At present DBSPE holds meetings at this level, but the districts and schools are not left with any written information. The program needs to provide basic factual material aimed at these lower levels. The district educational officers get operational level materials (e.g., teaching materials) but virtually nothing about the program itself. The issue of information requirements and distribution was overlooked in the original program design.

- *Language limitations.* It is important that the government disseminate information in local languages. The DBSPE program recognizes that in addition to producing functional and operational documents, they need to create and distribute documents that publicize the program. For these documents to be useful, the program needs to publish more widely in the Kiswahili language, rather than English.[13]

- *Budget constraints.* Although programs such as DBSPE may have ample funds, it is often difficult to transfer monies between allocation areas. It is important for the new program to budget for the translation and dissemination of various types of information (especially operational, administrative, and publicity information).

- *Poor planning.* Operational and administrative planning often does not take account of the need to distribute a variety of information in different languages and formats. If a program is to demonstrate transparency in decision making and spending it should build information distribution mechanisms into its project plan.

- *Civil-service culture restricts access to information.* Many public servants find it difficult to know whether information is confidential and therefore whether to allow access to it. Guidelines are needed to inform civil servants on how to classify documents and to establish procedures for sharing information both across government and with the public.

- *Awareness that the laws should be reviewed.* Some members of Parliament intend to bring the issues discussed in the workshop to the attention of the speaker. In addition, an official within the Civil Service Department indicated that the issues raised might have an impact on the way in which the department revises the National Archives Act.

- *Recognition that there is a need for changing attitudes within the civil service.* An official within the Civil Service pointed out that attitudinal change would be addressed in the next phase of civil-service reform through service benchmarks. In addition, the permanent secretary for the Civil Service Department mentioned that specific programs can target public servants working in districts and local authorities to raise their awareness on the issue of reasonable public access to information.

- *Realization that material needs to be presented in a more user-friendly way.* In particular, participants agreed that documents such as the auditor general's report could be formatted better to make the information it contains easier to interpret.

- *Recognition of the importance of access to information to underpin a national anticorruption strategy.* Attention was paid to the need for better access to government information as an anticorruption measure. There was interest in incorporating these issues into the national anticorruption strategy currently under development by the Prevention of Corruption Bureau (PCB).

The workshop also raised a topic that had not previously been discussed in a public forum in Tanzania. It highlighted the lack of access ordinary citizens have to information that directly affects their lives. It was able to demonstrate the gaps in information provision of the DBSPE program both within government and to the public. In addition, it drew out the wider concerns of the lack of information delivery mechanisms and effective records management. The workshop succeeded in raising awareness among policymakers, politicians, and opinion formers. However, it would appear that more groundwork is needed to develop public interest in this area before more wide-reaching information policy changes are likely to be contemplated.

CASE STUDY: GHANA

In Ghana, the right to information is part of the general fundamental freedoms and human rights contained in chapter 5 of the constitution (articles 12–33). However, there has been no case law or legislation to put this right into effect. The workshop in Accra concentrated on freedom-of-information legislation. Although the format used was similar to that of the Tanzania workshop, there were significant differences between the two events.

The second pilot workshop was carried out in Accra, Ghana, at the end of August 2000. The Rights and Records Institute, in partnership with the national chapter of Transparency International, the Ghana Integrity Initiative (GII) developed a program for the workshop appropriate to the Ghanaian context. No research study was conducted in Ghana prior to the workshop, but the International Records Management Trust has worked in Ghana for many years. Still, the GII's input was essential to ensure that the balance of participants and the focus of the program was appropriate to the Ghana context and reflected current debate on access to information.

Freedom-of-information legislation has been a subject of much discussion in Ghana, and the Institute of Economic Affairs has produced a draft right-to-information bill. The introduction of freedom-of-information legislation forms a key element in the government of Ghana's anticorruption strategy, adopted in 1999. It brought together members of Parliament, senior government officials, and members of the media and professional and civil society organizations as part of the process of building consensus for enacting and implementing a freedom-of-information (FOI) law. Although there would be positive benefits from the introduction of a nonstatutory access to information policy in Ghana, the public debate had already gone beyond this point. A freedom-of-information act would establish a right in law for reasonable access to information that would strengthen the position of the individual vis-à-vis the state.

The workshop program differed from that in Tanzania to reflect this debate. It focused on the benefits and challenges of FOI; identifying the strengths and weaknesses of the draft right-to-information bill; and identifying the changes that may be required in information systems and institutional culture to make FOI operational. More important, the emphasis was on the practical steps that could be taken to ensure that the legislation is used to facilitate an improved flow of information. This includes looking at how to build support for legislation; raise awareness among citizens; and use FOI to strengthen and support the government's existing Civil Service Performance Improvement Program (CSPIP).

The participants of the Ghanaian workshop also differed significantly from those attending the Tanzania workshop. On the whole they represented the elite of Ghanaian society and included a much higher proportion of opinion formers, policymakers, public servants, and politicians. The list of attendees included the deputy minister of communications; the chairman of the National Media Commission; the majority chief whip; the executive secretary of the Law Reform Commission; the head of the civil service; a presidential policy adviser; and several senior members of the press corps. They were noticeably more informed on the broad issues of access to information. This enabled them to engage in more lively debates about policy options and abstract ideas.

The workshops in Tanzania and Ghana both generated considerable attention from the media. In both cases the workshops were mentioned on national television news and on local and national radio. However, the media attention in Ghana was much more intense. To some extent this reflected greater public interest in the topic and the attendance of so many "notables." It was also a reaction to a genuine news story—a diplomatic incident. At the opening ceremony of the Accra workshop the British deputy high commissioner (the deputy ambassador) took the opportunity to make strongly worded comments on the government's track record on corruption and economic policy. The *Ghanaian Chronicle* ran the front page story, "Your Government Is Corrupt! Says British Ambassador."[14] The broadcast media also took great interest.

The incident with the British diplomat illustrates a contradiction at the heart of the Information for Accountability workshops; the workshops attempt to achieve progress by addressing information policy in a neutral, technical, and nonpartisan manner. An incident of this sort could easily have undermined the whole workshop by alienating the government and civil service. Fortunately, this did not happen in Ghana, and on balance the story served to bring the workshop more strongly to the forefront of the national debate. However, access to government information *is* a political issue. These workshops are likely to be most useful where there is already a broad measure of agreement among the main political parties on the general direction of information policy.

The government of Ghana is not averse to a freedom-of-information bill. In a speech on access to information and civil service reforms, Dr. Robert Dodoo, head of the civil service, emphasized that "Information in the public domain which is locked-up, untouched and unused is wasteful. Parliament and the people have a right to the use of information, the right to be informed to enable them to take the right decisions." He went on to say that the "trend toward a free flow of information between the Civil Service and the public is likely to be an irreversible development in this century and the next millennium. There is hope for the achievement of a total partnership between the Civil Service, the Media, Government and the public to enable free flow of information to become an important aspect of our national development."[15]

The requirement for effective record management to underpin FOI legislation was also clearly understood. In the opening keynote speech, Hon. John

Mahama, minister for Communications, articulated this aim by stating that "It is my hope that a comprehensive look will be paid to removing all the hindrances preventing free flow of information, including strengthening the capacity of public institutions to generate, preserve and retrieve information in a timely manner. If these issues are not addressed we may successfully pass a Freedom of Information bill, but find out that there is no free information to be given." [16]

As in Tanzania, the outcomes from the workshop were relevant to public reform initiatives. The Civil Service Performance Improvement Program (CSPIP) and the Ministry of Communications National Information Clearinghouse Project were only two initiatives that demonstrate the government's recognition of the need to improve access to information for its citizens. The CSPIP program in particular includes initiatives to improve information to citizens through public education programs in each ministry, department, or agency, and establishing client service units in each of them. This program is also being extended to district assemblies. Client service units seek to clarify and simplify complaint procedures and publicize services and agreed performance standards. This is intended to reduce the gap between government and its citizens and increase transparency, thus minimizing opportunities for corruption.

The National Information Clearing House Project is part of the national communication strategy. It was launched in early September 2000 with the aim of establishing links between the electronic information systems operating within institutions of government to facilitate improved access to and the sharing of information. This includes building capacity through the provision of training and awareness raising with government; developing Web-based information systems within institutions; and developing a Web site for Ghana with links to various government institutions. Despite these and other efforts, the present legal framework in Ghana may hinder such reforms.

It is recognized that FOI legislation will not alone increase access to information about basic public services and the activities of government, information that is key to holding government accountable. Many records may currently be available under existing regulations, but mechanisms are not in place to facilitate access. Moreover, citizens are not aware of what information exists, how to access it, and to whom to complain if access is denied. A program of awareness raising and institutional change is the only means by which the problems can begin to be addressed.

The workshop succeeded in building a consensus on the need to strengthen and modify the original draft "bill" provided by the Institute of Economic Affairs. Before the workshop in Ghana, those engaged in promoting FOI placed greatest emphasis on the media's need for information. The workshop helped to refocus the debate on the important benefits to the ordinary citizen, including facilitating greater individual interaction with agencies regarding records and information services. Finally, participants achieved a better understanding of the practical issues involved in putting FOI legislation into operation.

Participants reached the consensus that the government simply cannot continue to do business as usual, and the government is not averse to introducing a freedom-of-information law. The participants agreed that holders of public office are accountable to the public, yet it is difficult if not impossible to obtain government information. Part of the problem is the colonial legacy of strict control over government information and a conservative civil-service tradition.

The government recognizes that information is essential for a healthy democracy. Transparency implies the ability to obtain information as well as giving relevant information at the right time. The participants agreed that information held by government is held on behalf of the people. They also concluded that the CSPIP and the National Information Clearinghouse Project are only two initiatives that demonstrate the government's recognition of the need to improve access to information to its citizens. However, the present legal framework may hinder such reforms.

Much was said in the workshop about the press reporting misinformation. On the other hand, lack of access to information fuels sensational journalism. All the participants agreed that access to information is a two-way street. There is a need to cultivate a healthy culture for both requesting and disseminating information. The draft access to information bill proved to be a strong and useful basis for raising the issue to the national level and for focusing the debate. As a result of participants' examination and debate over the draft bill, the following limitations and recommendations emerged:

Table 1

Limitation	Recommendation
Weak Legal Framework	repeal/amend existing Official Secrets Act and other relevant laws
	harmonize existing legislation (including the Public Records Act)
	ensure consistency with the constitution
Inadequate Appeals Procedures	institute redress outside the courts
	implement clearer appeals procedures
	appoint an independent appeals/complaints body to adjudicate access to information (suggested: Commission on Human Rights and Administrative Justice)
No Administrative Oversight	assign oversight of the legal interpretation of FOI to the attorney general
	designate oversight for policies and guidelines to the Ministry of Communications
Lack of Sanctions	institute sanctions for those who refuse access to information
Lack of Awareness	develop public education programs on FOI rights and procedures

The purpose of the workshop was to identify actions that would need to be taken if FOI legislation was to have a practical effect. Because of the proximity of the general election and the possibility of a change of political leadership, detailed planning would be unproductive. Instead, the participants recommended actions under the following headings (the detailed actions suggested have been omitted): build an appropriate infrastructure with the ministries, departments, and agencies; strengthen records management; improve civil-service culture; examine procedures; address language and literacy barriers; increase public awareness; and implement anticorruption measures.

CONCLUSION

National archives in developing countries operate in a particularly harsh economic environment. It is difficult to justify funding the necessary work of these institutions when the alternative might be to feed a hungry child or pay for essential medicine to save someone's life. The Information for Accountability Workshops project was conceived as an experiment to see whether it would be possible to take advantage of global trends in international relations, politics, and public attitudes to make national archives' records management programs more relevant to the immediate needs of society.

The donor aid community targets Sub-Saharan Africa as the region in greatest need of development assistance. The assistance strategy includes support for measures to support good governance and increase participation. Increasingly there is an understanding that accountable and honest government is not a luxury, but rather an essential component in a strategy for developing a sound economy and reducing poverty.

In many countries, constitutional provisions for access to information have often not been implemented and the legacy of secrecy laws has created a climate in many countries where information is not freely available. There are signs that things are beginning to change. More and more countries are developing formal anticorruption strategies that include legislation to strengthen public rights to government-held information. In addition, when governments move to a more customer-focused public service, there is greater need to strengthen information systems to improve the delivery of services.

It is hoped that the Information for Accountability Workshop program will point the way toward stimulating a more efficient relationship between the supply of and demand for public-sector information. Central to this is the need for effective records management systems that can deliver timely and reliable information to citizens. Unless the information exists and can be readily retrieved, legitimate public demand for information from government cannot be met. Increasingly, national archives will need to take a more proactive role in this area and demonstrate that they can make a positive contribution to a fairer and more accountable public life.

NOTES

1. The Information for Accountability Workshops were funded by the Danish Trust Fund for Governance, administered by the World Bank. We thank them for making it possible to develop this innovative approach. The workshop in Dar es Salaam received additional financial and logistical support from the British Council Tanzania. The workshop in Accra received additional funding and logistical support from the British Council Ghana along with separate funding from the Westminster Foundation for Democracy. The authors would particularly like to thank Mr. Joseph Rugumyamheto, permanent secretary, Civil Service Department, Tanzania, and Dr. Robert Dodoo, head of civil service, Ghana, for their support and advice. Both have been good friends to the International Records Management Trust over many years. Our colleagues from Transparency International Tanzania, Mr. Ibrahim Seushi, Mr. Edward Hoseah, and Mr. Brian Cooksey and from the Ghana Integrity Initiative, Mr. Emile Short, Mr. Yao Asamoah, and Mr. William Nyarko have also played leading roles in making this initiative a success. Finally, very special thanks are due to Mr. Jeremy Pope of Transparency International and Mr. Mike Stevens of the World Bank, without whose encouragement and active support throughout this experiment would never have taken off.

2. The Rights and Records Institute was an operating division of the International Records Management Trust. The institute's mission was to empower developing countries' governments to manage recorded information in support of citizens' rights and to make public service delivery more efficient, cost effective, and transparent.

3. Transparency International (TI) is a not-for-profit, nongovernmental organization established to highlight corruption internationally and through its national chapters. It seeks to address corruption through international and national coalitions that encourage governments to establish and implement effective laws, policies, and anticorruption programs. TI works to strengthen public support and understanding for anticorruption programs and enhance transparency and accountability in international business transactions and in public administration.

4. See, for example, David Vincent, *The Culture of Secrecy: Britain 1832–1998* (New York: Oxford University Press, 1998).

5. Robert Dodoo, "Access to Information and Civil Service Reforms," in *Proceedings of the Information for Accountability Workshop*, August 30–31, 2000, Accra, Ghana (London: International Records Management Trust, 2000).

6. These materials are available on the Web at irmt.org.

7. Andrew J. Chenge, "The Government and Fundamental Rights and Freedoms in Tanzania," in Chris Maina Peter and Ibrahim Hamisi Juma, eds., *Fundamental Rights and Freedoms in Tanzania* (Dar es Salaam: Mkuki na Nyota, 1998), p. 6.

8. Chenge, "The Government and Fundamental Rights and Freedoms in Tanzania," p. 6.

9. Civil Service Department, United Republic of Tanzania, *Code of Ethics and Conduct for the Public Service Tanzania*, June 1999, p. 5.

10. *Majira* has a circulation of approximately 45,000. However, its circulation is dropping from a high of 100,000 as a result of higher prices. The price increased because the government placed a tax on imported newsprint. There is speculation that this was done to drive some newspapers out of business.

11. The PSRP seeks to improve the performance of the government in service to all citizenry, communities, and the private sector. It will benefit all society by improving

the quality, efficiency, and effectiveness of public services. The project will also benefit private sector operators by improving the policy and regulatory environment and ensuring efficient use of public resources in promoting and delivering essential social services, including economic infrastructure. Furthermore, the program will ensure that taxpayers receive from the government value for money through strategic, transparent, and accountable use of resources by public service managers. In addition, the program will promote integrity in the public service. It will also benefit public servants by enhancing their pay to correspond to their competence and performance, promoting meritocracy, and fairness in public service appointments, improving their work environment, and promoting their public image. Tanzania—Public Service Reform Program. Public Information Document (PID) prepared May 14, 1999. Projected appraisal date: June 1999. See worldbank.org/pics/pid/tz608330.txt.

12. The District Based Support to Primary Education (DBSPE) program is a national program jointly funded (until recently) by DANIDA, the Royal Netherlands Embassy, the Republic of Finland, and the Government of Tanzania. By the year 2002 it is expected that DBSPE will cover 62 districts out of a total of 114 and reach approximately 6,500 primary schools. The DBSPE was a good case study because, for unit costs, current figures indicate that 50—60 percent (or more) of the expense of their children's education is being borne directly by parents. This is in contrast to the 1970s and 1980s, when parents only paid a small proportion of the costs. Despite their contribution, there are no guarantees about what parents will receive in return. As a result, there is a continued decline in contributions from parents, who lack confidence in the way funds allocated for education are spent. The workshop used the unavailability of this information as the focus for practical discussion.

13. In recognition of this need, the Rights and Records Institute has commissioned a Kiswahili version of the Workshop Proceedings that is available on the IRMT Web site (irmt.org) and in printed form in key locations in Tanzania.

14. *Ghanaian Chronicle*, Sept. 1, 2000. See allafrica.com/stories/200009010368. html.

15. *Proceedings of the Information for Accountability Workshop*, Aug. 30—31, 2000, Accra, Ghana, are available at irmt.org.

16. Ibid.

SECRECY

Implausible Deniability: The Politics of Documents in the Iran-Contra Affair and Its Investigations

David A. Wallace

The series of events that would come to be known as the Iran-Contra Affair trace their roots to nearly contemporaneous destabilizations in longstanding U.S. relations with Nicaragua and Iran. In July 1979 the U.S.-sponsored dictatorship of Anastasio Somoza Debayle in Nicaragua was overthrown by the Sandinista revolutionary army. And in November 1979 revolutionary forces that earlier that year had overthrown the U.S.-sponsored dictatorship of the shah of Iran, seized 66 U.S. government officials and held them hostage for 444 days. The aftermath of these changes to the "geo-strategic" balance of power with these former client states led the United States to enter into two separate covert actions that over time blended into one another.

As the Cold War rose like a phoenix out of the ashes of World War II, the United States entered into a wide variety of covert actions across the globe. As defined by the United States Central Intelligence Agency (CIA), covert actions comprise "Any clandestine operation or activity designed to influence foreign governments, organizations, persons or events in support of the United States' foreign policy."[1] Essential to the operation of a covert action is the concept of "plausible deniability." Since the U.S. does not wish its covert actions to always be traced back to itself—despite their obvious connections at times—it has developed a practice of disavowing knowledge about and responsibility for any particular covert action. At times the concept of plausible deniability has also been used to insulate the president from being made intimately aware of specific covert actions and their details. One powerful rationale behind this practice is that it plausibly protects the government from being held accountable for embarrassing or criminal revelations about its own covert actions.[2]

The Iran-Contra Affair's covert actions drunk deeply from the well of plausible deniability, and U.S. government officials repeatedly denied accusations about its covert operations in both Iran and Nicaragua. The façade of deniability collapsed upon the assorted investigations and trials associated with the scandal, as massive volumes of top-secret government documents and testimony entered the public record. Never before have the mechanics and documentation associated with a U.S. covert action become so publicly evident. The erosion of secrecy made possible through these revelations made their plausible deniability simply implausible.

This essay examines the role of information control and accessibility in the Iran-Contra scandal in light of the official investigations into it. The text that follows traces the roots of the scandal, provides a detailed look at the three key investigations initiated by it, and takes a deeper look at key information control and accessibility issues impacting upon the scandal and knowledge about it.

THE SCANDAL

Nicaragua[3]

The United States never embraced Nicaragua's new Sandinista government. Throughout the 1980s it worked actively to overthrow and replace it with the "Contras"—a U.S.-shaped and U.S.-supported counterrevolutionary army and political movement. As early as December 1981, President Ronald Reagan authorized a CIA covert action to support the Contras with arms, supplies, and advice. The U.S. government had convinced itself that the Sandinista government had become too closely allied with the Soviet Union, the Eastern Bloc, and Cuba and that the only recourse was to overthrow it. The Reagan Administration believed that the Contras would create a more democratic state despite the fact that powerful elements in the Contra leadership were made up of former National Guardsman from the deposed Somoza dictatorship, and that journalistic accounts of the Contras highlighted severe human-rights abuses.[4] The not-so-secret war against the Sandinistas was highly controversial, and U.S. policy ebbed back and forth on the rationales and means of support for the Contras.

In 1983 the U.S. Congress disallowed any funds for the Contras that could be used to overthrow the Sandinista government but still permitted U.S. $24 million for other activities. In 1984, upon finding that the CIA had mined Nicaraguan harbors without proper congressional notification, Congress shut off all funding for Contra military and paramilitary operations. Once Congress shut off the tap, the Reagan Administration sought to support the Contras through pleas to third countries and private sources. From mid-1984 through early 1986 the Reagan Administration raised nearly U.S. $37 million from these sources. In July 1985 U.S. National Security Council (NSC) staffer Oliver L. North, with the knowledge of two National Security Advisers, Robert McFarlane (from October

1983 to December 1985) and John M. Poindexter (from December 1985 to November 1986), had taken charge of this money to run the "secret" war against the Sandinistas. At North's disposal was an entity called the Enterprise, a private organization that would help conduct the covert war on the behalf of the United States. For well over a year the Enterprise served, in the words of congressional investigators, as a "secret arm of the NSC staff, carrying out with private and nonappropriated money, and without the accountability or restrictions imposed by law on the CIA, a covert Contra aid program that Congress thought it had prohibited."[5]

Despite the fact that the congressional ban on assistance to the Contras prevented the U.S. intelligence agencies from assisting the Contras, North received cooperation and assistance from elements within the CIA, National Security Agency, State Department, and Department of Defense. In Congress's eyes, the "operation functioned without any of the accountability required of Government activities. It was an evasion of the Constitution's most basic check on executive action—the power of the Congress to grant or deny funding for government programs."[6] By 1985 the covert war being managed by North had become a kind of nonsecret secret. President Reagan assured the public that no laws were being violated. Over the next year national security advisers McFarlane and Poindexter testified falsely before Congress asserting that the NSC was neither collecting money for nor militarily assisting the Contras. When North's Contra-related roles became exposed in the press, he also lied to Congress about his activities, later receiving a "well done" e-mail compliment from his boss Poindexter for his prevarication. The October 5, 1986, shooting down of one of the Enterprise's private Contra resupply planes in Nicaragua and the capture of the surviving U.S. citizen pilot led to the unraveling of the subterfuge on Nicaragua and fed directly into congressional investigations.

Iran[7]

In Iran, the United States reacted to the 1979–1981 444-day hostage crisis by seeking a halt of arms sales and freezing trade and financial transactions with the new revolutionary government directed by the Ayatollah Khomeini. Iran needed access to weapons and capital to support its recently launched war against neighboring Iraq. By 1983 the United States initiated "Operation Staunch," which sought the cooperation of many other nations in denying arms to Iran. In January 1984 the United States classified Iran as sponsor of "international terrorism" and held it responsible for several attacks that killed nearly 300 U.S. military and embassy personnel. Shortly thereafter, between March 1984 and June 1985, seven U.S. citizens, including a CIA station chief, were taken hostage in individual kidnappings in Lebanon by forces believed to be allied with Iran.

At this point the administration's rhetorical war against "international terrorism" was running at full steam, and in June 1985 President Reagan publicly asserted that "no deals" would be made between his administration and "terrorists." At roughly the same time the U.S. sanctioned Israeli arms sale to Iran of TOW antitank missiles and HAWK antiaircraft missiles. Later the United States would deal directly with Iran in delivering additional weapons as well as military intelligence on Iraq. These sales were privately justified as a means to obtain the release of the U.S. hostages in Lebanon and to renew relations with Iran. While some hostages appear to have been released as a result of these sales, the goal of obtaining the release of all the hostages remained elusive. The same members of the NSC that had come to oversee the covert Contra war took the reins of the Iran arms sales initiative. North once again turned to the Enterprise to assist in these transactions. By December 1985, North was actively vetting the idea of diverting profits from these sales to assist the Contra's in their efforts to overthrow the Sandinistas. As with the Contra covert action, the president failed to dutifully inform Congress of these covert machinations, despite a clear legal requirement that he do so.

On November 2, 1986, roughly one month after Nicaragua shot down the Contra resupply plane, a Lebanese newspaper reported that the United States had sold arms to Iran. Despite the Administration's vigorous denials, the story would not evaporate. On November 13, the president addressed the nation on television and asserted that the United States "did not—repeat—did not trade weapons or anything else for hostages nor will we."[8] This statement was false and it committed those privy to the arms sales to the task of developing a cover story that supported the president's public statements. Roughly one week later, at Attorney General Edwin Meese III's request, President Reagan authorized Meese to conduct an internal investigation into the Iran arms sales in order to determine what had transpired and when. Meese had earlier been informed by Justice Department officials that participants in a 1985 arms sale to Iran held conflicting views on the basic facts surrounding the transaction. It was during this investigation that Justice Department officials discovered a memorandum reporting the diversion of Iran arms sales profits to the Contras. On November 25, 1986, the attorney general reported the diversion at a news conference and the remainder of the Reagan Administration became largely gridlocked over the legalities of the Iran and Contra initiatives.

An independent counsel investigation into the Iran-Contra Affair concluded that Meese's inquiry was "more of a damage-control exercise than an effort to find the facts."[9] It criticized Meese for failing to take notes of critical meetings with the president, vice president, national security adviser, director of the CIA, and secretaries of Defense and State. The independent counsel also charged that, after discovering the diversion memo, Meese failed to "secure records" in the NSC offices, many of which were later destroyed by North and Poindexter.

THE INVESTIGATIONS

These revelations led to three separate major investigations: a three-month-long presidential Special Review Board (more commonly known as the Tower Commission), which ran from December 1986 to February 1987; an eleven-month-long joint House of Representatives and Senate investigation, which ran from January 1987 to November 1987; and a nearly seven-year-long criminal investigation by a specially appointed independent counsel, which ran from December 1986 to August 1993. The last investigation resulted in several criminal prosecutions and convictions.

As these investigations proceeded, each peeled back additional layers of the scandal and each underscored the critical roles played by documents in enabling, documenting, and obfuscating investigations into the scandal.

Tower Commission[10]

The Tower Commission provided the first and briefest formal review of the Iran-Contra Affair. It was created by a presidential executive order on December 1, 1986, and it released its final report in February 1987. It was overseen by John Tower, a longtime U.S. senator with a special focus on national security issues; Edmund Muskie, a former U.S. senator, secretary of state, and presidential candidate; and Brent Scowcroft, a retired Air Force general who previously served as a presidential foreign policy adviser. The Tower Commission was given broad and narrow charges by President Reagan. It was directed to examine the "proper role of the National Security Council staff in national security operations, including the arms transfers to Iran."[11] The commission itself was explicit in pointing out that it was not an investigative body seeking criminal offenses. Rather, its purpose was more elusive: "to gather facts, and place them in their proper historical context, and to make recommendations about what corrective steps might be taken."[12] While it had no authority to subpoena documents, it was able to assemble what it called a "vast quantity" and interviewed more than eighty individuals. The commission relied upon the forthrightness of the affected agencies in conducting "thorough searches" for relevant materials.

As the commission's investigation proceeded, it discovered that notes of important meetings did not exist. Many witnesses testified to the commission that the NSC suffered from institutional memory and recordkeeping difficulties. The commission felt that negligent record creation and retention forced it to become "too often dependent on mere recollection."[13] The commission appeared to be particularly irked by these oversights, noting that "no formal written minutes seem to have been kept" and that the "initiative lacked a formal institutional record."[14] This was seen as inhibiting an "informed analysis" as well as the ability to "learn lessons." Commission member Brent Scowcroft indicated that malfeasance may have played a part, commenting that "It may be that some went into the shredder, but we can't prove it."[15] The commission found no concrete evidence that documents had been purposely destroyed. It did, however, conclude that North withheld important information from it. (North's files were a primary source of "historical documentation" relied upon by the commission in its investigation.)

The commission's key findings concluded in part that the "whole matter was handled too informally, without adequate written records of what had been considered, discussed, and decided."[16] In its recommendations the commission pointed to the national security adviser to "ensure that adequate records are kept of NSC consultations and Presidential decisions." Such records were seen as "essential for conducting a periodic review of a policy or initiative, and to learn from the past."[17] Overall though, the commission recommended that "no substantive change" be made to the NSC system.

The Tower Commission proffered the conclusion that the president was ill served by his subordinates in regard to the Iran initiative and that the initiative suffered by foregoing regular policy vetting practices. On that ground, the initiative was seen as the handiwork of a small faction in the NSC that actively kept operational details from the president and some of his top advisers. Such a conclusion indicated a conspiracy between a small cohort of individuals that kept the president in the dark—namely North, Poindexter, McFarlane, and former CIA Director William Casey (who died of natural causes in March 1987)—and not a broader-based coordinated effort to operationalize potentially illegal policies and activities and then conceal them from Congress and the public.

Joint Congressional Committees[18]

In November 1987, a short nine months after the Tower Commission report was released, dual congressional select committees issued their final report. The select committees comprised twenty-six members of Congress (fifteen from the House of Representative and eleven from the Senate) supported by a staff numbering more than 150. The committees' official report was countered by a minority report issued by eight members of the select committees. The minority report characterized the scandal as a series of mistakes and not the constitutional and legal crisis painted by the majority final report. The minority report called the diversion "extremely unwise" and the "result of poor judgment." In addition, the minority report pointed out that during the attorney general's initial investigation of November 1986: "Witnesses were repeatedly instructed . . . that the President's interests would be best served if the Attorney General were given a full and accurate account of what happened. Yet McFarlane, North and Poindexter made false, misleading, or inaccurate statements to, and concealed directly relevant information from, the Attorney General and his representatives." In spite of these challenges, the minority report contended that the attorney general's investigation uncovered the essence of the scandal.

Formed in January 1987, these committees represented an "unprecedented step" in the history of congressional inquiry by combining the efforts of separate House of Representatives and Senate investigations. As noted above, Congress and the Reagan Administration had been battling over U.S. policy toward Nicaragua for several years before the scandal erupted publicly. Upon disclosure, Congress stepped in to investigate because, in its own words, the scandal "carried such serious implications for U.S. foreign policy, and for the rule of law in a democracy."[19] The committees' final report claims that its work helped to "ensure that the principle of accountability is enforced for all officials and policies."[20] To work toward that end, the dual simultaneous investigations pooled all the information it collected on four key areas: arms sales to Iran; the diversion of funds to the Contras; possible violations of federal law; and the roles played by NSC staff in the conduct of foreign policy.

Over the summer of 1987, the committees held more than forty days of nationally televised public hearings. It reviewed and generated a much larger volume of material than had the Tower Commission: more than 300,000 documents and more than 500 interviews. Its eleven-month investigation produced a far more damning picture of recordkeeping obfuscation and malfeasance, for example confirming that in November 1986 the NSC staff had created false chronologies of events and had destroyed "relevant contemporaneous documents" in autumn 1986. The committees reported that after learning that President Reagan had authorized Attorney General Meese to conduct an internal investigation, both North and Poindexter spent several days altering, shredding, and deleting official documents. In addition, North conspired to remove classified documents from the NSC. In his testimony to the committees, North stated that he informed Poindexter that he had purged all the documents associated with the diversion of funds. Unfortunately for all those implicated, North was wrong. A Justice Department official found a copy of the "diversion memo" that had been overlooked in the attempt to erase and falsify both official and unofficial document trails. While the committees noted that the destruction of evidence obscured their efforts to uncover some of the details of what actually happened, they were clear that they had demonstrated "beyond doubt that fundamental processes of governance were disregarded and the rule of law . . . subverted."[21] And they condemned "without reservation . . . the withholding, shredding, and alteration of documents."[22]

Like the Tower Commission, the congressional committees' investigation pointed to North, Poindexter, McFarlane, and Casey as the main culprits. They concluded that these key advisers conducted an illegal covert action that bypassed existing law and congressional notification requirements. These same individuals were castigated for lying, shredding documents, and covering up their actions. The committees also concluded that the initial investigation conducted by Attorney General Meese in November 1986 suffered from questionable lapses in process, such as not taking notes during key interviews with top administration officials and not sealing key NSC offices once the investigation was underway. Such lapses were seen to place a "cloud" on the forthrightness of Meese's investigation. Like the Tower investigation, Congress pointed out that no evidence surfaced to disprove the president's assertions that he did not know of the diversion. Both North and Poindexter testified that they purposely kept the president in the dark about the diversion. In spite of these denials, Congress placed ultimate blame at President Reagan's feet, concluding that he should have known about such activity and that he should have ensured that the rule of law was followed. In a biting conclusion, the committees charged that President Reagan "created or at least tolerated an environment where those who did know of the diversion believed with certainty that they were carrying out the President's policies."[23]

Independent Counsel[24]

Lawrence Walsh's independent counsel investigation was the longest and most exhaustive investigation into the Iran-Contra Affair. Before receiving this assignment, Walsh, a lifelong Republican, had a long and distinguished public and private legal career, including service as a deputy U.S. attorney general, a federal judge, and president of the American Bar Association. Appointed in December 1986 at the request of Attorney General Meese, Walsh and his team spent nearly seven years developing evidence of malfeasance and illegal activity. Walsh's charge included examinations of arms sales shipments to Iran between 1984 and late 1986; the financing of those sales; the diversion of proceeds from these sales to the Contras; and U.S. assistance to the Contras. Walsh's final report, released in August 1993, concluded, in part, that the arms sales to Iran went against stated policy and may have violated the Arms Control Export Act; support for the Contras violated the congressional ban on aid to the Contras; and, that following the public acknowledgement of the affair in late 1986, members of the Reagan Administration "deliberately deceived" both the Congress and the public about official knowledge and support for the dual initiatives. Walsh's report was not well received by those accused of illegal and questionable activity. Walsh's final report included a separate 1,150-page volume of comments and materials submitted by individuals seeking to reclaim their reputations.

Walsh concluded in part that "large volumes of highly relevant, contemporaneously created documents were systematically and willfully withheld from investigators by several Reagan Administration officials."[25] For example, in late 1992, Walsh discovered that President George H.W. Bush had failed to turn over relevant diary entries that were contemporaneous to the affair when he was vice president, despite two earlier requests for such information. In another instance, Defense Secretary Caspar Weinberger's contemporaneous handwritten notes were "deliberately withheld" from congressional investigators and the independent counsel until they were "discovered" in the unclassified portion of Weinberger's papers he donated to the Library of Congress, papers that no one would be allowed to access without his permission under the donor agreement he signed with the library.

Unlike the other two investigations, Walsh painted a vivid picture of a far wider conspiracy of commission and coverup. Walsh charged fourteen individuals with criminal acts. Of these eleven were convicted. Of the remaining three, one individual's trial was unable to proceed because the government refused to declassify documents bearing on the case, and the other two received "unprecedented pre-trial pardons" by President Bush during his last days in office in late 1992. Of the eleven convictions, North and Poindexter were found guilty of destroying government documents, McFarlane was found guilty of withholding information from Congress, one CIA agent was found guilty of lying to Congress and another of withholding information from Congress. Both North's and Poindexter's convictions were reversed on appeal because of a technicality, though Walsh asserted that these reversals "in no way cast doubt on [their] factual guilt."[26] Perhaps most significant, Walsh concluded that, contrary to the findings of the Tower and congressional investigations, the president's top advisers, including the secretaries of State and Defense and the director of the CIA, had participated in a scheme to make Poindexter, McFarlane, and North the "scapegoats whose sacrifice would protect the Reagan Administration in its final two years."[27]

In his concluding observations, Walsh found fault with both the executive and legislative branches of the government. As to the executive branch, Walsh concluded that it had willfully deceived both the public and the Congress. Walsh found that Congress prevented an accurate understanding of the scandal by granting immunity to both North and Poindexter in exchange for testimony in which they incriminated only themselves. Walsh contends that this immunity greatly complicated his efforts to bring criminal charges. Such action permitted the congressional investigation to proffer the cover story of a "runaway conspiracy of subordinate officers," thus avoiding having an "unpleasant confrontation with a powerful President and his Cabinet."[28] Walsh concluded that the conspiracy reached into the Oval Office and implicated the president, vice president, director of the CIA, and the secretaries of State and Defense and other high-level officials from these agencies.

Finally, Walsh points to the deleterious effects that document destruction and concealment had on his investigation. He pointed out that North and Poindexter's destruction of records "caused an irretrievable loss of information"[29] to the various investigations and to the oversight mechanisms for covert actions. In terms of concealment, he concluded that the discovery of "large caches of handwritten notes and other documents maintained by high officials"[30] indicated that many of these officials had a deep interest in creating a false history of events and that their late discovery detracted from efforts to identify those with "feigned memory lapses or [who had] lied outright."[31] In addition, the government's refusal to declassify documents forced Walsh to drop his central conspiracy charges against North and Poindexter and others as well as force him to drop a criminal case against the CIA's station chief in Costa Rica. While Walsh would argue that some of this protected classified information had already become public information, the Bush Administration refused to meet with Walsh to discuss the matter.

DOCUMENTS AND ACCOUNTABILITY IN THE IRAN-CONTRA AFFAIR: A DEEPER LOOK

From the first years of the Reagan Administration in the early 1980s up through 1993 when the independent counsel issued his final report, information control and manipulation of the documentary record associated with the

Iran-Contra Affair appears time and time again. The assorted investigations reported document alteration, destruction, and theft in efforts to cover up the details. They also discuss the role played by electronic mail (new technology at the time) and provide insight into contentious access battles over information control and what should be permitted to enter the public sphere. Being investigations into covert activity, most of the associated documents were security classified. Any divulgence had to be reviewed line by line. The Walsh investigation underscores the roles played by the "personal" documents created by several of the key participants, including diaries and notes, and how obtaining access to them can be as thorny as can access to top-secret documents. The remainder of this essay will explore in detail a series of episodes associated with the Iran-Contra Affair detailing intersections of information control and accountability.

Confounding Early Congressional Inquiries[32]

Throughout the summer and fall of 1985, covert U.S. support for the Contras expanded rapidly and included arms purchases, intelligence sharing, and funding. By late August 1985 Congress had formally requested information on the NSC's Contra-related activities. Congress's concern had been piqued by press accounts calling into question the administration's compliance with the congressional ban on assistance to the Contras. Representative Michael Barnes—chairman of the House of Representatives' Western Hemisphere Affairs Subcommittee of the Committee on Foreign Affairs—requested a search of NSC files for documents on North's association with Contra leaders since the aid ban had taken effect. To process this request, National Security Adviser McFarlane tasked his deputy at the time, John Poindexter, to review all relevant records. The actual search performed, however, came to be construed much more narrowly. A memorandum offering options for the document search, produced by an NSC information policy officer, argued the "search should be as narrowly focused as was the request. In this case, Congressman Barnes has focused on . . . [documents related to North's contacts with the Contras.] Fishing expeditions in all files relating to Central America and/or Nicaragua are NOT necessary to respond to the request" (capitalization original).[33] This narrow search excluded files in North's own office under the rationale that such files were "convenience files" generally made up of drafts and copies of documentation in the institutional and presidential advisory files. Potentially relevant documents in North's office were not examined in response to Barnes's inquiry. The joint congressional committees' final report found that North's office included memoranda not logged into any official NSC recordkeeping system, as well as e-mail messages, notebooks, and vital correspondence directly bearing on Barnes's request.

The NSC's information policy officer advocated "bury[ing]" Barnes with appointment and telephone logs that ultimately would be skeletal in nature and provide no "substance." Ultimately, the NSC decided to search only the formal institutional files and to let North sample his telephone and appointment logs and have him report back on their "potential relevance." The search of the official files yielded fifty relevant documents, of which some ten to twenty were given closer inspection. Of these, six documents were seen by McFarlane as raising "legitimate questions about compliance with the law."[34] He gave North a list of these problem documents, which North kept taped to his office desk.

Over the following two weeks North and McFarlane planned their response to Congressman Barnes. They agreed that North would go ahead and alter the six troubling documents. Beyond that, the two provide conflicting testimony. McFarlane testified that he did not use the altered documents and later destroyed them. North contended that McFarlane basically ordered him to purge the document trail. According to North, McFarlane "was cleaning up the historical record. He was trying to preserve the President from political damage."[35] In his September 12 response to Barnes, McFarlane made no mention of the document search. Ten days later Barnes reasserted his desire to review relevant documents in the NSC's possession. A memorandum drafted for McFarlane about this argued that Barnes should be told that McFarlane had no legal authority to give him access to NSC files. The memorandum stated that he could also argue that North's actions were "internal and deliberative in nature and are . . . not NSC agency documents. As Presidential advisory papers, they fall under the dominion of the President" and therefore would be unavailable.[36]

In a face-to-face meeting in mid-October 1985 between Barnes and McFarlane, McFarlane offered the congressman the opportunity to review a stack of "relevant" documents he had assembled, under the condition that they did not leave McFarlane's office. Barnes flatly refused this offer, as they only had scheduled the meeting to last one hour and Barnes would need to tap into his own staff's expertise to make full sense of the material. Two weeks later Barnes once more pleaded for a search for relevant records. This time McFarlane did not reply.

Evading Covert Action Reporting Requirements

The U.S. Foreign Assistance Act of 1961, as amended in 1974 by the Hughes-Ryan Act of 1974, mandates that any covert action undertaken by the CIA must be authorized by a presidential "finding," stating that the covert action under question is essential to protect U.S. "national security." Hence, under law, all covert actions—which can be initiated only by the president—require a finding and timely congressional notification. Timely notification was understood at the time of passage to mean within forty-eight hours. In January 1985 President Reagan issued a National Security Decision Directive that included presidential approval procedures for covert actions. In part it states that the president must approve all covert actions in writing with a finding and that such findings would be required for covert actions undertaken not only by the CIA but also those undertaken by other entities within the government.[37]

The congressional committees' investigation found that the findings process had been both subverted and ignored by the Reagan Administration in its Iran–Contra machinations. In December 1981 President Reagan signed a finding authorizing covert action to counter Cuba's activities in Central America and to stem Nicaraguan military assistance to an indigenous revolutionary movement in neighboring El Salvador. However, under this finding the CIA provided assistance to Contra forces whose objective was the overthrow of the Sandinista government—an activity not authorized within the scope of this particular finding. As noted by the committees, if a finding issued for one purpose is used for another purpose, the finding process becomes "meaningless" and a "blank check" that "defeats the notion of Presidential accountability."[38] In addition, North, McFarlane, and Poindexter's covert efforts on behalf of the Contras were never authorized by a finding, nor was proper congressional notification followed. Poindexter testified that he did not want "outside interference"[39] from Congress on his covert Contra operation.

On the Iran side of the scandal, no written finding or congressional notification occurred when the CIA and NSC contributed to a secret HAWK missile shipment to Iran through Israel in November 1985. Although the formality of the finding process was completely ignored, Attorney General Meese later tried to justify the actions taken by claiming that the president had made a "mental finding" that provided a sufficient legal ground on which to proceed. Later, at the CIA's insistence, a signed finding was produced in December 1985 that purported to "retroactively" approve the November missile shipment. However, this finding was developed in absence of the normal process of informing and collaborating with senior administration officials.

Poindexter kept the only copy of this finding in his office safe. In Congress's eyes, the use of a "mental" finding and the "retroactive" written authorization completely ignored the legal requirement that findings occur before any covert action is undertaken and that the president assume responsibility and be held accountable for it. Once the scandal erupted in late November 1986, Poindexter purposely destroyed what he thought to be the only copy of the December 1985 Iran arms sales finding signed by the president. Poindexter destroyed this key document only hours after assuring congressional investigators that he would look into what exactly had been occurring regarding Iran-Contra–related matters. Unfortunately for Poindexter, investigators were able to locate a CIA version of this finding. Poindexter claimed that he destroyed this finding in order to protect President Reagan from "significant" political embarrassment, since the finding was drawn up as a straight arms-for-hostages deal.

Once the scandal started surfacing, the White House insisted that President Reagan had never signed such a finding and that he had not known of the November 1985 arms shipment from Israel to Iran. In addition, the president claimed in a nationally televised speech on November 13, 1986, that he had never and would never engage in a trade of arms for hostages. Needless to say, no finding was ever issued that approved using profits from arms sales to Iran in order to shore up the Contras.[40]

In their main recommendations, the congressional investigators highlighted the proper role and use of findings. In fact, the subject of the appropriate and legal use of findings occupied the top eight recommendations of the majority report's twenty-seven recommendations.[41]

Creating Misleading Chronologies

By fall 1986, the two strands of the scandal started breaking the surface. One of the first moves made by the principals was the construction of a chronology of events associated with the Iran initiative. Over two weeks in November 1986, North, Poindexter, McFarlane, and others drafted a dozen different versions of this chronology. Asserting that the effort to build an authoritative chronology was "hamstrung by poor recordkeeping," at the NSC, the Tower Commission concluded that the multiple chronologies produced were often "conflicting and occasionally far from what we believed transpired." In its worst estimation of what this boded, the commission acknowledged that it suggested an "attempt to limit the information that got to the President, the Cabinet, and the American public."[42]

The congressional committees had a far darker interpretation of these chronologies, concluding that the honest "errors" in the documents suggested by Poindexter and McFarlane (North admitted willful misrepresentation) were in fact "wholesale distortions of key events."[43] Key misrepresentations included U.S. collaboration with and awareness of Israeli missile shipments to Iran in mid- to late 1985. In his testimony before the congressional committees, North admitted that the fictitious chronology of events had committed President Reagan to a "false story."[44]

Avoiding Exposure and Providing for a Coverup: NSC Document Alteration and Destruction in November 1986[45]

The internal investigation into the affair began on the morning of November 21, 1986. Attorney General Meese, acting as legal adviser to the president, asked for and obtained the permission of President Reagan to obtain a clearer picture of the Iran initiative. Poindexter was present at this meeting. Later that day and over the following days, both Poindexter and North destroyed and altered official documents. The joint Congressional committees concluded in their final report that this destruction left an incomplete record with which to assess the president's knowledge of and role in the Iran-Contra Affair.

On the afternoon of the November 21 North told his secretary, Fawn Hall, to alter several action memorandums he had written demonstrating his fund-raising and military involvement with the Contras when it was prohibited by the Congress. The documents indicated by North for alteration were those same six from the list McFarlane had given him a year before during Congressman Michael Barnes's request for a document search, described above. North kept this list of six documents taped to his desk. These documents were System IV documents. System IV was a document file designation for highly sensitive documents that dealt with intelligence matters and covert operations. To create a System IV document, an NSC staffer had to contact the System IV custodian and obtain a System IV reference number. A computer log tracked each time a System IV document was checked out, moved to another office, or approved. By 1985 more than 1,500 documents were maintained by the System IV custodian in the System IV system. On the afternoon on November 21, North requested and received these six System IV originals from the System IV custodian. After North hand-edited changes directly onto the originals, he gave them to Hall to prepare, in the words of Congress, "new originals."[46] Hall later testified that she had no recollection of ever making changes to completed System IV documents before this incident. After she finished, she destroyed the originals and then became distracted before she destroyed her own file copies of these originals and filed the doctored copies in their place. It was due to this oversight that congressional investigators were able to determine that an alteration had in fact occurred—it had found discrepant versions of the "same" document.

One alteration was uncovered when investigators determined that it was created on stationery that was available only at a time different from the document's supposed date of creation. What had distracted Hall was North's excessive document shredding. When investigators found the infamous diversion memo that led directly to the formation of the various investigations, North woefully reported to his former boss McFarlane that he had missed one.

Over the course of the afternoon of November 21, North and Hall and NSC staffer Robert Earl were estimated to have shredded an eighteen-inch-high stack of documents that included PROFS notes (an early e-mail software), messages derived from National Security Agency encryption devices that had been given to North, North's own telephone logs, and other documents bearing upon the Iran and Contra operations. Hall testified that while shredding was regularly done in the normal course of business, at no other day at work had she seen such an organized destruction of so many documents. North reported being told by CIA Director Casey a month earlier to start to "clean it up," meaning in part to start eliminating the damaging documentary trail. North reported that from that point forward he began to "shred more than the routine excess paperwork." While he normally shredded documents daily, during the final weeks of his NSC tenure he admitted to shredding "more than ever."[47] North's destruction became so bold that he continued to destroy documents even while Justice Department officials were on site at the request of the attorney general searching for documents relevant to the scandal.

Both North and Poindexter were convicted for these illegal acts of document destruction. However, because Congress granted both of them immunity for their testimonies describing the destruction, the convictions later secured by Walsh were vacated on appeal because of the belief that their nationally televised testimony tainted the witnesses who later testified against them.

E-mail As a "Nonlog" System[48]

Electronic mail was introduced into the White House as a pilot project in 1982. By 1985 it had become more widely available, and most NSC staff had access to e-mail at that time. The White House used IBM's PROFS [Professional Office System] e-mail software, a menu-driven package that enabled users to send e-mail with file attachments. To assist the national security adviser with his e-mail traffic, the White House Communications Agency engineered the software so that when most NSC staff sent him a note it would first be filtered through the NSC's executive secretary. As North's name began to be publicly linked to the Contras, National Security Adviser Poindexter admonished him to maintain a low profile and to not put things in writing about his operational activities. After McFarlane's conflict with Congressman Barnes over document access, North stopped entering his records into the NSC's official recordkeeping system. North's communications with his superiors from that point forward took place on memoranda not logged in the NSC records system and via PROFS e-mail messages.

On August 31, 1985, Poindexter sent North an e-mail with the subject line "Private Blank Check." By replying to this message, North was able to bypass the normal flow of Poindexter's e-mail through the NSC's executive secretary and communicate directly with Poindexter. In his memoir, North recalled PROFS as a "godsend" that provided a "free and uninhibited means of communication."[49] It reduced the need for meetings and phone calls, enabled time shifting beyond normal office hours, and reduced the amount of paper containing details about the Iranian and Nicaraguan efforts. Because of this heightened sense of security afforded by this mode of communication, Iran-Contra–related PROFS messages contain a frankness and candidness that is found nowhere in official government records. Two fairly representative messages amply demonstrate this point.

After he resigned from the NSC in December 1985, McFarlane retained a PROFS terminal at his residence. He regularly communicated with North about details of the operation. In one exchange McFarlane noted that he had been "thinking about the blowpipe [missile] problem," to arm the Contras. He asked North to ask the "CIA to identify which countries [excised due to security classification] have sold them to. I ought to have a contact in at least one of them. . . . If for any reason you need some mortars or other artillery—which I doubt— please let me know."[50] In another exchange, North informs Poindexter of one key arms-for-hostages shipment wherein Israel, operating as a U.S. proxy, would transfer HAWK missiles to Iran in exchange for Iran's securing the release of U.S. hostages in Lebanon. In exchange for Israeli cooperation, the United States would replenish the Israeli missile reserves. North was optimistic that there was a "distinct possibility that at the end of the week we will have five Americans home and the promise of no future hostage takings in exchange for selling the Israelis 120 mod[ified] HAWKS. . . . it isn't a bad deal."[51]

Once Attorney General Meese's investigation began in November 1986, both North and Poindexter realized the grave potential for damaging revelations if their e-mail became public. To eliminate any traces, between mid- and late November 1986, North erased 736 e-mail messages and Poindexter deleted an astounding 5,012 messages associated with the scandal and their "Private Blank Check" communications back channel. This erasure is all the more impressive when it is realized that each message had to be individually deleted, since there was no mass delete option. Unfortunately for North and Poindexter, the White House Communications Agency provided investigators with backup tapes that provided snapshots of North's and Poindexter's e-mail storage areas before and after the deletions. From them, investigators were able to zero in on the deleted messages. Although recovered late in their investigation, the Tower Commission found them most useful, commenting that these recovered e-mails provided a "first-hand contemporaneous account of events."[52]

These recovered e-mails would also prove to be critical for both the congressional and independent counsel investigations. And in an ironic twist of unanticipated consequences, these e-mails would come to serve as the seeds justifying a decade-long series of lawsuits against the government—colloquially known as the "PROFS" and "GRS20" (General Records Schedule) cases. These lawsuits would challenge the *entire* federal government's use and management of e-mail based on the precedents established for PROFS usage in the NSC. Over time these cases fundamentally altered attitudes over the official nature of e-mail messages, confirming that nonlog attitudes were counter to federal law.

Struggles over Classified Information[53]

As the investigation dragged on for years, a mountain of classified information was implicated as potential evidence and much was declassified and became publicly available. Not all participants were pleased by this development. North bemoaned the "wholesale declassification and exposure" of his office files. In his memoir he recalls his "horror" as a classified presidential finding was reproduced in newspapers across the nation. For North the real problem wasn't that the content was reproduced, which was bad enough, but rather that the actual form of top-secret documents was disseminated. North claimed that enemies of the United States could exploit these now public documentary forms of classified documents to create false yet "authentic-looking" documents to develop fake stories of U.S. misdeeds across the globe.[54]

Despite North's misgivings, the declassification and publication of secret government documents occurred on a scale rarely, if ever, before seen. Early in the independent counsel's investigation, Walsh and the affected agencies collaborated on developing methods and practices for the production of classified and other documents for use in developing cases for prosecution. To perform this work, the independent counsel created liaisons with the White House, Congress, Justice Department, State Department, Defense Department, CIA, and National Security Agency. These agencies normally assigned a team of lawyers to the task. Walsh's requests to agencies were quite broad, seeking "all materials relevant" to the scandal. In seeking documents, Walsh decided to issue written document requests instead of using more heavy-handed subpoenas. Walsh later called this action a mistake. Claiming naïveté, Walsh said he expected "honest compliance" from affected agencies.[55] Access to classified information became a major endeavor throughout the first round of criminal prosecutions. Each defendant was granted, at government expense, a "secure compartmented information facility" (SCIF) to review secret documents. Once these SCIFs were constructed, the independent counsel provided the defendants with hundreds of thousands of documents. An interagency government legal team met regularly with the independent counsel to clear classified documents for examination by the defendants. Especially sensitive documents were reviewed line by line before they were cleared for review by the various defense teams. Selected documents would still need to be declassified by a separate process for use in trial. The process of declassification was complex and often contentious. North's lawyers objected to every redaction on all the documents that were declassified for use by the independent counsel at North's trial.[56]

Walsh was particularly irked by the female liaison from the United States' largest, most powerful, and most secret intelligence agency—the National Security Agency—chiding her as someone who "was not easily deterred by facts, reason, or appeals to fairness" and who "grossly" exaggerated claims of national security.[57] In addition, lower-level government document declassifiers were seen as being of three types: useful "problem solvers"; those who were "automatically negative" and whose attitudes were "developed from opposing numerous Freedom of Information Act requests"; and those "allied, in spirit or in fact" with defendant North. A potentially trial-stopping development occurred when the affected agencies developed a "drop-dead list" of a dozen categories of information that they agreed on protecting even if the trial judge ordered their release.[58]

Eventually Walsh was forced to drop his main conspiracy charges against North and Poindexter and others because the government refused to declassify the documents Walsh needed for prosecution. In another instance the entire prosecution against the CIA's Costa Rican station chief was dismissed for the same reasons. Walsh claimed that the "secret" information that the government refused to declassify in these instances often had already become public by other means. The administration, however, refused to meet with Walsh to discuss the matter. To date, some 4.6 million documents related to the assorted Iran-Contra investigations remain sealed.[59]

The use of classified information in trials is governed by the Classified Information Procedures Act (CIPA). Enacted in 1980, the CIPA attempts to balance the needs for criminal justice with the sometimes contending requirements of national security protection. When defendants seeking a fair trial require classified information to support their defense, the government is obligated to review the sought-after classified information and to determine whether it can be declassified for trial. If the government refuses to declassify the documents that the judge has deemed pertinent to the defense, the trial cannot go forward. The government's refusal to declassify documents for the prosecution of the CIA station chief in Costa Rica accused of lying about his role in the Contra war forced the judge to dismiss the case. Walsh noted that this dismissal was the first time the government prevented a CIPA-related trial to go forward and implied an inherent conflict of interest when a national security agency refuses to declassify records to be used in the prosecution of one of its own employees.

For the criminal prosecution of North, Walsh reported that CIPA-related issues dominated and came close to overwhelming his prosecution. During pretrial discovery, North's defense received more than 100,000 pages of secret documents, which was only a fraction of what had been requested. As discovery was expanded for North, the government produced some 350,000 pages in one month alone (some seven months before the trial even started)! Walsh accused both North and Poindexter in using CIPA to request top-secret documents that they knew the government would fight mightily against releasing—in a sense playing the system to try to force a dismissal. North's trial alone required seven days' worth of separate hearings to evaluate the redactions the government made to documents that North said he needed for his defense. As a result of the intelligence agencies' refusal to declassify information that North felt pertinent to his defense, Walsh was forced to drop the primary conspiracy charge against North. In another instance, the trial against the head of the CIA's clandestine operations required eighty hours of hearings on classified information alone. Retired CIA officials spent countless hours evaluating millions of pages of top-secret documents for his defense. The issue of access to classified information provided an almost daily controversy that exhausted the independent counsel, the intelligence agencies, and the defense.

Tracking Down Personal Notes and Diaries[60]

In his overall conclusions, based on more than six and one-half years of investigation, Independent Counsel Lawrence Walsh charged in part "large volumes of highly relevant, contemporaneously created documents were systematically and willfully withheld . . . by several Reagan Administration officials."[61]

As early as the November 1986 Meese investigation, the subject of access to personal notes and diaries became a hotly contested issue. North's spiral-bound notebooks contained 2,600 pages covering his Iran-Contra activities from January 1984 through November 1986. They contained much classified information, including names and details of meetings, as well as confirming that top administration officials were "exposed" to North's Contra efforts. North was allowed to take his notebooks with him after he was fired in November 1986, causing the independent counsel to wonder why Attorney General Meese and his successor Dick Thornburgh did nothing to recover them while they had the opportunity to do so.

As his investigation proceeded, Walsh's team aggressively sought contemporaneous yet undiscovered notes, such as North's notebooks, that could shed new light on the scandal. Walsh had come to the conclusion that primary participants in the scandal "were reluctant to provide truthful information unless they were confronted with difficult-to-refute documentary evidence."[62] In one instance, 12,000 pages of notes taken by M. Charles Hill, the executive assistant to

George P. Shultz, Reagan's secretary of state, were reviewed in 1990 after being tracked down on the Stanford University campus where Shultz returned after leaving government service. To Walsh this amply demonstrated that highly relevant notebook entries had not been turned over when originally requested. Only Hill's notes that discussed the Iranian arms sales and that supported Secretary Shultz's congressional testimony were provided initially. (Other relevant notes were obtained from the State Department's executive secretary, Nicholas Platt.) Upon review, Walsh concluded that the new Hill notes and new interviews with Hill and Shultz raised concerns about the testimony of high-level administration officials on a 1985 HAWK missile shipment to Iran.

Within Hill's notes there was a comment by Shultz that Reagan's secretary of defense, Caspar Weinberger, "takes notes but never referred to them so never had to cough them up."[63] This passage led the independent counsel in October 1990 to re-request notes from Weinberger that may have not been provided earlier. Weinberger responded that he had not held anything relevant back and that it was not normal for him to take notes. Weinberger granted Walsh permission to review his personal papers that he had donated to the Library of Congress in August 1987. After an initial review of the classified portion of Weinberger's papers, nothing new or relevant was recovered. Nevertheless, in November 1991 a member of Walsh's staff found 7,000 pages of handwritten notes in the unclassified portion of Weinberger's papers, approximately 1,700 pages of highly classified information that were contemporaneous with the 1985–1986 period of particular interest to the independent counsel. (Upon this revelation, the Department of Defense recalled these materials from the Library of Congress for a formal security review.)

Walsh claimed that these notes demonstrated that Weinberger's notetaking was "purposeful, deliberate, and an important part of his daily routine."[64] They also provided a new set of unique contemporaneous documents bearing upon the scandal, including details on Weinberger's conversations with the president and other Cabinet officials. Walsh concluded that these notes contradicted Weinberger's earlier Iran-Contra testimony on knowledge about portions of the scandal's details, namely his awareness of an early HAWK missile shipment to Iran, the replenishment of Israeli TOW missile stockpiles that had been transferred to Iran, and Saudi Arabia's support for the Contras. In June 1993, in recognition of these revelations, Walsh decided to indict Weinberger on five felony counts, including perjury and false statements on his notes and notetaking practices. Walsh has argued that he had no choice but to prosecute Weinberger, after he had "lied . . . so arrogantly"[65] about the notes and how directly they contradicted earlier sworn testimony.

Weinberger would argue that far from secreting these documents away, they were available in a public institution, namely the Library of Congress. However, Walsh is quick to point out that under the donor agreement with the library, Weinberger's papers were his private property and access to the papers required his permission. In 1990 Weinberger prevented the General Accounting Office, the watchdog arm of the Congress, from accessing his papers for a study they were conducting on official records removals by former Cabinet members.

The discovery of a further set of notes late in the investigation in 1992, those of former Reagan White House Chief of Staff Donald Regan, provided Walsh with yet another set of contemporaneous Iran-Contra documents. Fortunately for Walsh, Regan kept a photocopied set for himself, since neither the White House nor the Reagan Presidential Library was able to find Regan's originals. Combined with Weinberger's notes and others, Regan's notes helped Walsh develop his theory of a far wider conspiracy that included President Reagan, Vice President George Bush, CIA Director Casey, Attorney General Meese, Secretary of Defense Weinberger, National Security Adviser Poindexter, and White House Chief of Staff Regan—namely, a conspiracy to protect exposure of the president's possible involvement in a November 1985 shipment of HAWK weapons to Iran, a shipment that Regan's notes reveal Meese to have admitted was probably illegal.

In December 1992, one month after President George H.W. Bush lost his bid for re-election, the White House told the independent counsel that Bush failed earlier to produce relevant Iran-Contra entries from his personal diary. Bush would nightly dictate observations on his daily events into audiocassette tapes, which were then transcribed and returned to him. The Tower Commission reported that President Reagan kept a handwritten diary at the same time that contained his perceptions of daily activities. Reagan produced for the commission a typed copy of the handwritten diary for the dates requested by the commission. It is interesting that the commission was not permitted to keep the typewritten Reagan diary transcripts. For the joint congressional investigation, Reagan provided extracts from his personal diary. Oddly though, he rejected a request by the investigation to "refer" to entries from it in its final report, arguing that he did not wish to set such a precedent for future occupants of the White House. President Bush's diary, in contrast, was to remain hidden from the independent counsel until right before he was to leave the Oval Office, six years after they had been originally requested.

By late 1992 Walsh's investigation had started its big wind-down. At roughly the same time that the White House submitted Bush's diary entries to Walsh—late December 1992 through January 1993—President Bush granted presidential pardons to Weinberger and a CIA officer whose Iran-Contra–related trials had yet to begin as well as to four others previously convicted by Walsh's team. Walsh noted that such pretrial pardons were without precedent and made him wonder aloud whether they were granted to prevent additional Iran-Contra–related revelations and possible convictions. Walsh was prevented from pursuing details in the Bush diary, since President Bush would meet with Walsh only to discuss his failure to produce the diary entries when they had been originally requested in 1987, not to discuss their content.

Bush's lawyer explained to Walsh that Bush, then vice president, claimed ignorance, despite compelling evidence to the contrary, about an agreement circulated to his office between the White House, Walsh, and the joint congressional committees that was to govern document requests for the respective investigations. This agreement clearly stated that it included relevant notes, diaries, and audiotapes. One telling diary entry exhibits Bush's consternation that Secretary of State Shultz not only kept notes of his meetings with the president but that he had turned them over to congressional investigators: "I found this inconceivable" wrote Bush, "I would never do it. I would never surrender such documents and I wouldn't keep such detailed notes."[66]

Walsh concluded in 1993 that if the assorted "caches" of document his team was able to ferret out late in his investigation had been made available when they were originally requested some six years previously, then his investigation would not have dragged on for so long and would have likely resulted in additional criminal indictments.

CONCLUSION: INFORMATION CONTROL, ACCOUNTABILITY, MEMORY, AND POWER

As the above recounting demonstrates, document creation, use, circulation, and disposal are deeply embedded in organizational activities—even covert actions that require the strongest confidentiality and secrecy. Information control not only drove the workings of the dual parts of the Iran-Contra scandal, it also became evident in the battles over access during investigations and criminal proceedings. The "conclusions" and "historical lessons" and criminal convictions that would be possible depended in great part on obtaining access to information. At times this information was destroyed, at times it was withheld because of security classification and for reasons of "national security," and at times it remained questionably hidden for years, beyond the reach of investigators. The exposure of the Iran-Contra Affair provided a rare view into the opaque world of covert operations and secret wars. The investigations and the voluminous testimony and documentary evidence provide ample verification that democratic governmental accountability is deeply contested and highlights the means by which it may be accomplished—or not.

Time and again, elected and appointed federal officials worked aggressively to hide, destroy, and manipulate the documentary trail bearing upon the scandal. Given the relative status of the key players in the scandal, very few oversight mechanisms were available to those who would seek to draw a complete picture of the scandal. And those mechanisms that were available, such as congressional and independent counsel investigations, were met with hostility, stonewalling, outright interference, and deception. Allusions to national security and lives at risk were often employed to divert and dissuade investigators, the media, and the public from peering too far below the surface.

From the narrative of this scandal it would appear that anytime a severe policy fissure erupts in the government, it can be certain that one of the first actions taken by the principals will be to take the communications channel below the normal radar beam. When this occurs, the resulting documentary trail will be aggressively protected, since it may later surface and contradict public statements and assurances. While one can make the argument that men and women of honor can be trusted to faithfully execute the law and cooperate with criminal investigations, the events described in this essay clearly indicate that such an argument is no more than wishful thinking. It would appear that aggressive oversight and power to seize the documentary record provides one of the few means by which democratic accountability can be secured in a national security context. It remains to be seen whether future investigators heed this lesson or hold themselves in check under the assumption that those being investigated will cooperate in good faith. The degree to which the good-faith position holds can be seen as a measure of the investigators' desire to uncover the truth. The good-faith argument eroded with each successive investigation into the scandal, with the Tower and independent counsel investigations providing bookends along this succession of investigations. As more became known about the scandal, the less the men and women of honor could be trusted to be truthful. Under such circumstances, only by having the power to seize and have unimpeded access to the documentary record will investigations have any hope of yielding an accurate accounting of events.

NOTES

Except for direct quotations, all notes have been collapsed under the section heading in which they appear. Substantive direct quotations are separately noted. Also, the author would like to acknowledge the assistance of Rob Bell in wading through the voluminous official testimony and published reports.

1. John Ranelagh, *The Agency: The Rise and Decline of the CIA* (New York: Touchstone, 1987), p. 216.

2. Kathryn S. Olmsted, *Challenging the Secret Government: The Post-Watergate Investigations of the CIA and FBI* (Chapel Hill: University of North Carolina Press, 1996), pp. 86–87.

3. U.S. Congress. House. Select Committee to Investigate Covert Arms Transactions with Iran; U.S. Congress. Senate. Select Committee on Secret Military Assistance to Iran and the Nicaraguan Opposition. *Report of the Congressional Committees Investigating the Iran-Contra Affair, with Supplemental, Minority, and Additional Views* (Washington, D.C.: Government Printing Office, 1987), pp. 3–6, 31.

4. For example, see Christopher Dickey, *With the Contras: A Reporter in the Wilds of Nicaragua* (New York: Simon and Schuster, 1985).

5. *Report of the Congressional Committees*, p. 4.

6. Ibid., pp. 5–6.

7. Ibid., pp. 3, 6–9, 157–161, 285, 296, 563; *The Tower Commission Report: The Full Text of the President's Special Review Board* (New York: Bantam Books, 1987), pp. 502–508.

8. *Tower Commission Report*, p. 503.

9. U.S. Independent Counsel, *Final Report of the Independent Counsel for Iran/Contra Matters*, vol. 1 (Washington, D.C.: Government Printing Office, 1993), p. xviii. More damningly, the Independent Counsel concluded that Poindexter and Meese "attempted

to create a false account of the 1985 arms sales from Israeli stocks, which they believed were illegal, in order to protect the President."

10. *Tower Commission Report*, pp. xvii–xix, 62–83, 60–94.

11. Ibid., p. 2.

12. Ibid., p. 16.

13. Ibid., p. xvii.

14. Ibid., p. 70.

15. Ibid., p. iv.

16. Ibid., p. 62.

17. Ibid., p. 90.

18. *Report of the Congressional Committees,* pp. xv–xvi, 10–22, 557, 564.

19. Ibid., p. xv.

20. Ibid., p. xvi.

21. Ibid., p. 11.

22. Ibid., p. 19.

23. Ibid., p. 22.

24. Independent Counsel, *Final Report,* vol. 1, pp. xiii–xv, xviii, 412–413, 421, 561–565.

25. Ibid., p. xiv.

26. Ibid.

27. Ibid., p. xv.

28. Ibid., pp. 561–562.

29. Ibid., p. 563.

30. Ibid.

31. Ibid.

32. *Report of the Congressional Committees,* pp. 122–127; Independent Counsel, *Final Report,* vol. 1, pp. 142–145.

33. U.S. National Security Council, memorandum for John M. Poindexter from Brenda S. Reger, entitled "Barnes Request," dated Aug. 20, 1985. *Report of the Congressional Committees,* p. 432.

34. *Report of the Congressional Committees,* p. 124.

35. Ibid., p. 126.

36. U.S. National Security Council, memorandum for Robert C. McFarlane from Paul Thompson, entitled "Meeting with Congressman Mike Barnes," dated Oct. 16, 1985. *Report of the Congressional Committees,* p. 752.

37. Olmsted, *Challenging the Secret Government,* p. 46; *Report of the Congressional Committees,* p. 864.

38. *Report of the Congressional Committees,* pp. 378–379.

39. Ibid.

40. Ibid., pp. 13, 195–197, 302, 379–381; Theodore Draper, *A Very Thin Line: The Iran-Contra Affairs* (New York: Hill and Wang, 1991), pp. 216, 501.

41. *Report of the Congressional Committees,* pp. 423–424.

42. *Tower Commission Report,* pp. 480–481.

43. *Report of the Congressional Committees,* p. 299.

44. Ibid., pp. 298–300.

45. Ibid., pp. 10, 21, 73, 132, 135n., 256–270, 290–291, 305–308, 485; Oliver L. North, *Under Fire: An American Story* (New York: HarperCollins Publishers, 1991), pp. 298–299; Independent Counsel, *Final Report,* vol. 1, p. xvi.

46. *Report of the Congressional Committees*, p. 307.

47. North, *Under Fire*, p. 298. All North quotations in this paragraph are from that page.

48. *Report of the Congressional Committees,* pp. 130–131, 138; North, *Under Fire,* p. 193–194; *Testimony of Oliver L. North, Part I,* pp. 27, 87; Independent Counsel, *Final Report,* vol. 1, p. 24; Lawrence E. Walsh, *Firewall: The Iran-Contra Conspiracy and Cover-up* (New York: W.W. Norton, 1997), pp. 63–64.

49. North, *Under Fire,* pp. 193–194.

50. *Report of the Congressional Committees,* pp. 130–131.

51. U.S. National Security Council, PROFS Message from Oliver L. North to John M. Poindexter, "Private Blank Check," Nov. 20, 1985.

52. *Tower Commission Report,* p. 17.

53. Independent Counsel, *Final Report,* vol. 1, pp. 27, 37–38, 108–111, 565; Walsh, *Firewall,* pp. 423–424.

54. North, *Under Fire,* p. 324. All North quotations in this paragraph are from that page.

55. Walsh, *Firewall,* p. 55.

56. Ibid., pp. 165, 175.

57. Ibid., p. 176.

58. Ibid., pp. 176–177.

59. "Harper's Index," *Harper's Magazine,* May 2001.

60. Independent Counsel, *Final Report,* vol. 1, pp. 43–44, 47–49, 118–119, 412–421, 473–478, 506; Walsh, *Firewall,* pp. 254–256, 358–359, 392–397; *Tower Commission Report,* p. 17; *Report of the Congressional Committees,* p. xvi.

61. *Final Report of the Independent Counsel for Iran/Contra Matters, Volume I,* p. xiv.

62. Ibid., p. 44.

63. Ibid.

64. Walsh, *Firewall,* p. 392.

65. Ibid., p. 397.

66. Ibid., p. 478.

The Failure of Federal Records Management: The IRS versus a Democratic Society

Shelley Davis

For nearly eight years I worked for the Internal Revenue Service (IRS). I did not process tax returns. In fact, I rarely saw tax returns. I did not work with the massive computer systems of the tax collector. In fact, I did not even have a computer my first two years with the IRS.

My job was truly unique for the tax collector. I was one of nearly 10,000 employees of the "National Office" or headquarters of the IRS in downtown Washington, D.C., but I was the only one with the job title of historian. In retrospect, I think the IRS of today seriously regrets ever hiring me. I turned out to be not only their first, but also their last, historian.

My revelations of massive document destruction at the IRS, essentially the wholesale loss of the history of one of our most important government agencies, rocked the tax collector—at least for a while. My revelations led to congressional hearings and even a new law. Unfortunately, despite a few positive signs, little has changed in the attitude or action of the tax collector toward its recordkeeping responsibilities for the American people. This is my story.

After sixteen years of working for the federal government as a professional historian, my career came to a jolting halt at the end of 1995 when I found myself facing allegations that I had wrongfully leaked sensitive information to a history professor from a small liberal arts college in Pennsylvania. While untrue—even hilarious in retrospect—the bringing of false charges against a federal historian who was merely trying to enforce federal law to protect federal records, has aroused little concern among my fellow professional communities—historians, archivists, and records managers. I live with a deep sense of contentment that I did the right thing by resigning in protest when I learned of the false charges. I also live with deep disappointment that I was essentially abandoned by my peers simply because I worked for an agency that is considered to be of little historical importance or interest.

The story of the demise of my career involved events I never dreamed could happen in the relatively calm and uneventful life I led as a federal historian. Before going to work for the IRS, the biggest excitement in my professional life was when the air force sent me to sleep in a tent on a training mission so that I could see what life was like for "regular" troops as I recorded their official history.

Life at the IRS, at least toward the end of my tenure, took on a surreal tone, as federal agents rushed in a federal vehicle from Constitution Avenue to Lancaster, Pennsylvania, to confront my alleged accomplice in his office on the campus of Franklin and Marshall College. I later was told that federal officers trailed me during my final months on the job. Old friends turned away as I walked the halls of the IRS, fearing that association with me would taint their careers. And I was locked out of a roomful of critical historical documents.

In that last event lies the key to my demise at the IRS. It was all about the documents, both documents that existed and documents that had seemed to vanish into thin air. The nearly eight years I spent with the IRS tells the story of the breakdown of federal records management on both a personal and a policy level. The system and laws in place to protect federal records failed totally when pitted against the powerful bureaucracy and intransigence of the IRS.

The result? The smattering of records from the IRS held by the National Archives increased slightly after my untimely departure from the agency, primarily the result of the accessioning of three rooms of documents I managed to squirrel away during my tenure. But there it stops. My career sacrifice, I have decided, has meant nothing in terms of reforming IRS records management, nor has it even incrementally increased the availability of IRS records to the American public. And that is a sad reality.

Of course, the foregoing implies that someone cares about IRS records. It appears to me, in hindsight, that that is simply not the case. I have often started discussions of my IRS experience by comparing records management at the tax collector with records management in the Defense Department or the Central Intelligence Agency or the Federal Bureau of Investigation. I begin by saying, "What would be the reaction if the press were to report that the Defense Department had destroyed all records from World War II—or all records from the Korean War—or World War I—or the Civil War" and so on. There would be a massive outcry followed by an investigation to get to the bottom of the loss, followed by an attempt to recreate what was lost, and a piling on of "60 Minutes," "20/20," and "Larry King Live" coverage.

So how does one explain the nearly nonexistent reaction from the press, the public, and (most alarming to me) my professional colleagues in the historical profession to my revelation that the IRS had systematically and intentionally (as well as unintentionally) destroyed its paper trail for the entire twentieth century?

Over the past several years, I was forced to come up with one rather disturbing, if self-evident, revelation. Here it is: They don't care.

It's that simple. The sad realization I reached after hitting my head against the wall to drum up support for my campaign to save IRS records was that as long as the tax collector didn't reach into *your* pocket, you wouldn't give a damn whether the National Archives had any IRS records. I was even more shocked to hear historians (yes, historians!) nervously laugh, then tell me that perhaps it was a good thing that there were no IRS records because this meant they could not be audited.

Never has a federal agency and its power been so misunderstood by those we expect to monitor that power—journalists, historians, and record keepers. The light bulb finally clicked on for me during a fancy Washington reception I attended at a well-known Washington think tank to celebrate the publication of a Washington book by a well-known Washington talking-head journalist. My own book about my experiences inside the IRS was to be published in a few months, so I was interested in testing the waters among the journalists in attendance.

I managed an introduction to William Kristol, an influential and well-known Washington commentator and political analyst also attending the reception. But Mr. Kristol did not do what I thought he would do when he learned that I had written a book about the IRS. He did not ask who I was to write about the IRS. He did not ask me what angle my book was taking. In fact, he asked nothing about the IRS or my book. What he did do was most revealing. Mr. Kristol launched into a five-minute story of the one time in his life that he received a notice from the IRS. Kristol outlined in detail how he had eliminated this irritating intrusion into his life. Once finished with his story, before I had time to comment, Kristol twirled and walked away, saying, "I've got to run."

Kristol's response was, in general, typical. It did not matter who the audience was when I tried to explain the importance of IRS records and why people should care that these records were being systematically destroyed as the agency continued to send irritating notices to millions of Americans each day. In the end, I came to the conclusion that the IRS—not the Central Intelligence Agency, not the Federal Bureau of Investigation, not our super-secret defense satellite reconnaissance organizations—was truly the most secret of all federal agencies. How can I say that? Simple. Destruction of records is more permanent than all the "Top Secret" stamps in the world. While other agencies may have a penchant for classifying every piece of paper they create to the highest degree possible, the bottom line remains—a classified piece of paper is still a tangible item, even if it is locked in a vault. The IRS shredded, burned, trashed, and destroyed nearly their entire record path. How could they do this? Again, simple. Because no one was looking. Because the journalists, like Kristol, were more focused on their mailboxes and whether they contained a notice from the IRS than on the tremendous investigative power Congress has placed in the hands of this agency. Because historians have not viewed the history of tax collection as interesting nor worthy of their attention. Yet it is. I learned that it is. If only I had the records to prove it.

How did this all happen? Let's begin at the beginning.

GOVERNMENT HISTORIAN

After slogging away as the historian for nearly two years in a mobile trailer temporarily positioned in a parking lot, I was frustrated with the necessary "compartmentalization" of the agency's work. I could not link document A to document B because such linkage would increase the classification level of document A to something no one could see during my lifetime.

I wanted to write accessible history. Before joining the super-secret agency, I worked for the U.S. Air Force, sometimes with classified records, but mainly writing historical accounts of unclassified events, many of which were fascinating and important. I wrote the official air force history of the response to the air traffic controller strike of the early 1980s, for example. I wrote a history of Scott Air Force Base in Illinois, an early dirigible base, even leading bus tours of the facility, showing off an old graveyard to the fascinated visitors. It was fun and fulfilling work and I learned about the importance of preserving government documents. I also learned of the laws, most notably the Federal Records Act, governing the handling of documents created by the federal government.

In a fit of frustration with the secret nature of the job I had taken when I relocated to the Washington, D.C., area in 1987, I began looking for other opportunities. I had no desire to leave the field of federal history. I loved my work. After growing up in an academic family, my father a distinguished professor of economics, I had decided I did not want to go the academic route. I had seen enough departmental politics and meaningless backstabbing during my father's tenure as department chair for several years during my teen years to cure me permanently of any desire to work in a university environment. I felt incredibly lucky to have landed in the relatively unknown field of federal history after completing my graduate work. The federal government seemed to me a haven where serious historians could labor away, researching and writing about important things. I absolutely loved my work.

One day, flipping through a recruiting list of all federal jobs, I stumbled across the fateful listing: Historian, Internal Revenue Service. I suppose, like Mr. Kristol, I should have focused on the time the IRS sent me a notice saying I owed several thousand dollars in back taxes three days before I was to be married and leave on an expensive honeymoon. (I did not owe the money and it was eventually straightened out.) Instead, I found myself wondering what kind of history the IRS had. I was also attracted by the salary—the IRS job offered the next rung up on the federal ladder.

I threw my hat into the ring. Nine months later, after the slow wheels of the bureaucracy churned through all the applicants, I found myself seated in a basement room of the IRS National Office being oriented to life inside the tax collector. After years of working for the Defense Department, which loves to celebrate its history in public ceremonies and parades, I was somewhat shocked to hear the stout woman at the front of the room recommend that we not tell people who we worked for. "You should say you work for the Treasury Department," she counseled. "It's just easier," was her explanation.

THE IRS

I soon learned that IRS employees dreaded encounters such as the one I had with Mr. Kristol. Tell someone at a neighborhood barbecue you work for the IRS and you'll be forced to listen to their story. Tell someone on the bus you work for the IRS and you'll be met with frowns and evil stares. Better to just not admit whom you worked for, was the advice offered to new employees.

Talk about no esprit de corps! As I wondered through the hallways of my new employer, I was struck by the barren walls. I was accustomed to walls and halls that celebrated the past: portraits of past military commanders, flags, medal winners, battle scenes, and equipment displays. But at the IRS, there was only a progression of one pale yellow hallway, another pale yellow hallway, followed by another.

It took me a few days to track down the people who carried the job title of records manager at the IRS. I wanted this to be one of my first stops, followed by a visit to the National Archives to view what I anticipated would be the vast holdings of IRS historical files. Both visits turned out to be disasters.

The top IRS records manager, a middle-aged woman who had spent most of her government years as a personnel specialist before being shuttled off to the backwater of the records office, knew virtually nothing of federal records management policy from what I could glean in our uncomfortable first encounter. She (somewhat understandably) appeared only concerned with managing tax returns—the actual 1040s and related forms. Understandable, I say, because nothing would thrust the IRS onto the front page of newspapers more quickly than mishandling tax returns. She told me about the time a box of 1040s fell from a truck during transfer from the IRS processing center to the federal records center where they would be stored for seven years. Fortunately, a worker recovered the box before anyone outside the IRS discovered the flub and all was well again. When I tried to steer the conversation toward the location and identification of IRS policy records, the women looked more confused than anything. She made it clear she was not interested in the same things I was interested in, but warned me "not to step on toes." That warning echoed throughout my tenure at the IRS. Although I initially heeded the warning, I later decided it was bad advice.

So much for help from the records management staff. Next, I turned to the National Archives, assuming that I could bury my disappointment in my encounter with the IRS records staff by surrounding myself with Hollinger boxes (commonly recognized storage containers for archival records) stuffed with records, picking and choosing among topics to research. Imagine my shock when the archivist led me to a few ramshackle shelves on a high floor of the National

Archives, just two blocks down Constitution Avenue from the IRS National Office. A small collection of boxes on these shelves contained documents from the Civil War era.

When I asked about more recent records, the archivist led me to an odd-shaped cabinet, rather like a library card file. He yanked open a drawer to reveal row after row of identification badges from, of all things, the Bureau of Prohibition. (Note to historians: The IRS enforced Prohibition through most of Prohibition's fascinating and violent history.) Beyond the identification badges, the archivist simply shook his head, telling me he was not aware of any other IRS records from the last century. If he had not been so kind and soft-spoken I probably would have started yelling right then and there, but that did not seem to be an appropriate response in the stacks of the National Archives.

Returning to my small cubicle at IRS headquarters, I pondered my discoveries, or lack of discoveries, so far. Surely, I thought to myself, the problem must be me. After barely a month on the job, I tried to convince myself that I had not looked in the right place for the treasure trove of IRS records that I knew awaited me. If only I could ask the right question of the right person. But every door I opened revealed another brick wall.

It did not help that many IRS officials I encountered seemed amused at the idea of having a historian in their midst. They had no clear concept of what they wanted me to do. I soon learned that my IRS adventure really began the day a mid-level executive read an airline magazine article that stressed the value of corporate history. At that time, the IRS was jumping onto every *Kum Ba Yah* bandwagon of management leadership, including those suggesting the federal government should imagine itself a business operation. The IRS executive figured, if corporations think having a corporate historian is a good thing, then the IRS must need its own "corporate" historian. They had not given a moment's thought to what they would do with their historian once they had one!

This might sound like a glorious opportunity, but only those unexposed to the byzantine organization, rigidity, and hierarchy of the IRS would think so! It was up to me to carve out my place in the IRS universe. At first, I found this a daunting task, but as the weeks ground into months and I failed to locate any significant stash of records, it became merely frustrating. I wanted to write. I wanted to research. I wanted to dig into sources, sort through documents, and read microfilm. But there simply was not anything to dig, sort, or read.

I kept myself busy reading whatever scraps I could find. A drawer here, a desk there, was sometimes stuffed with old papers. Whatever I found, I kept, trying desperately to build a small collection of IRS records. In the meantime, I proposed different topics to my supervisors, with varying degrees of success. Just when I thought I had figured out how to please one group of tax executives, my position would be mysteriously shifted in a seemingly endless series of staff reorganizations. In my travels through the IRS, I began to feel like a mouse trapped in a maze.

AN IRS DISCOVERY

Along the way, I joined a carpool to ease my commute. One day, a woman in my carpool who worked with IRS computers called to ask if I would be interested in stopping by her office to look at some old filing cabinets her boss wanted her to throw out. She mentioned that they were filled with "old things." "Yes!" I practically shouted from my swivel chair, nearly knocking over several desultory bureaucrats as I bounded up the three flights to her office.

My eyes almost popped out of my head as I pulled open the eight drawers of the two cabinets. In my brief tenure, I had picked up on the need to upgrade aging IRS computers, originally installed in the Kennedy Administration, as the most pressing issue facing the tax collector. Each year, Congress berated the IRS for not fixing its computers while the IRS begged for more funds to increase its ability to do more than patch a growing problem.

The cabinets of my carpool associate contained the original, primary, and utterly important records of the IRS computer program. The files began in the late 1950s and extended through the installation of the first set of nationwide computers by 1964. The records also covered the 1970s, when the IRS upgraded the system. If ever there was an important set of twentieth century records regarding the policies of the IRS, this was it—but there was no National Archives in sight to protect them.

My exuberance at finding an important set of records did not spill over to my carpool mate nor to her fellow office workers, who seemed merely amused and somewhat confused by my enthusiasm. They were more than happy to let me box up the records and cart them back to my cubicle. Now they would not have to haul them to the burn room, which is where they were headed before the serendipitous contact from carpool mate.

And that, in essence, is how the next five years proceeded at the IRS. The occasional stashes of records I discovered, I usually discovered by mistake or because someone wanted to avoid the task of throwing the stuff out themselves. Each time I tried to involve the records management staff in the process, they were uninterested. The normal (and legally required) process through which federal records eventually end up at the National Archives (with which I was very familiar from my years at the Defense Department) simply did not exist at the IRS. The few records control schedules that existed were outdated, having been written years before the woman trained as a personnel specialist took over the records program. When I tried to suggest tactfully that the records management staff look into upgrading and updating the schedules, I was quickly accused of "stepping on toes."

My experience at the IRS raises the question, where was the National Archives? While somewhat complex to explain, the easiest way to begin is by saying that the archivist assigned to monitor IRS records accessions was also responsible for several other federal agency records programs. In other words, he was busy and stressed. If no one was screaming about IRS records, then he had no reason to pay attention to IRS records. As the lone historian inside the

IRS, I simply could not scream loud enough to get his attention. The man, although exceptionally pleasant, also happened to be one of the most nonconfrontational human beings I have ever encountered, and so the few times I was able to push him to fight harder to protect IRS records, I got the feeling he did not know how to fight.

A LEGALISTIC INTERPRETATION

Whether by design or default (I believe it was a bit of both), the IRS took advantage of this situation. They also held the ace in the deck—something called Section 6103. This was the section of the Internal Revenue Code that governed access to records and the confidentiality of tax returns. The IRS assumed the convenient position that Section 6103 trumped everything when it came to federal laws, rules, and regulations, including the Federal Records Act. Until I came along, no one had noticed, and no researcher, archivist, or historian had seriously challenged the IRS on its overreaching interpretation of the law. No one, it seemed, cared.

The history of Section 6103 provides a fascinating study in federal policy, with links to the Lindbergh kidnapping and current phobias over intrusions into personal privacy. (I told you IRS history was interesting!) The history of access—or lack of access—to tax returns is a flip-flop history. In the history of tax collection in the United States, there have been periods when the policy included the open posting of tax returns. The philosophy behind this was that citizens will report income honestly if they know their returns are available to anyone. Today, we live with the opposite extreme, as the IRS takes the position of not even confirming the existence of a taxpayer, let alone the details of a tax return. Over the years, the access policy has turned with the political and sociological times. (Note to readers: great idea for a dissertation topic.)

The tie-in to the Lindbergh kidnapping comes with the advent of the "pink card" era of tax return confidentiality. In the late 1920s and early 1930s, the government had pulled back from complete access to tax returns, instituting a policy in which only basic data (name, address, and total income) was extracted from tax returns and then written on pink cards. Anyone could come to their local IRS office and rifle through the pink cards. But when the public became alarmed at the possibility that kidnappers had targeted the Lindberghs' daughter for kidnapping by easily learning of the Lindberghs' ability to pay a high ransom, the pink slips quickly vanished.

A SECRET IRS OFFICE

The current era of abject refusal to release information was born during the Watergate years of the mid-1970s. Almost lost in John Dean's revelation of Nixon's famed enemies list was another revelation. If the press had only pursued this less-renowned revelation by the White House counsel, the nation might have suffered an even greater shock than it did with the revelation of Nixon's list. Nixon's list, in the end, was not really used for anything. If you disagree with this, you have been a victim of the popular notion that the enemies list was more than it really was. You have also been outwitted by the IRS's ability to shield its true history. What John Dean also revealed, but the press overlooked and ultimately ignored, was the existence of an organization inside the IRS called the "Special Services Staff"—SSS, of all things.

The full history of Watergate has yet to be written because so far, no national medium has focused on the IRS side of the story. That is partially because most of the IRS records are long since destroyed. It is certainly easier—whether you are a journalist or historian—to pursue topics that actually have some documentation. There is more to this story. Some documents do exist, and I squirreled them away during my tenure at the IRS. The rest of the story, I am convinced, is the reluctance of researchers to bother the IRS, perhaps fearing personal reprisal from the tax collection in the form of an audit. I have heard it again and again and again from journalists and others. Why go after the one federal agency that can bite back on a very personal level? This alone is a very powerful tool in the hands of the IRS, one that merits study from scholars of social history or the political power of a government agency.

The SSS was a small, secret office tucked into the basement of the IRS headquarters that compiled its own enemies list. The shocking thing about the SSS is that its list of "enemies" was ten times as large as Nixon's list, and while the president had to rely on others to carry out his desires for retribution, the IRS could do as it pleased with the names on its list. Just how did a person land on Nixon's list? Most of those on the president's list were wealthy contributors to the Democratic party, journalists who wrote unfavorable articles, or members of the entertainment industry determined to be against Nixon. For the most part, they were well-known or well-to-do liberals. And how did one land on the IRS list? It could be as simple as writing a letter against the Vietnam War to a campus newspaper. Or by attending a rock concert. Or by subscribing to an "underground" newspaper. Or by demonstrating against the Vietnam War. In short, those on the IRS enemies list were not well known and not well-to-do. One might think that the nation might be outraged at the revelation that a federal agency had compiled secret files on American citizens for no reason other than their participating in the process of democracy. In the case of the IRS and the SSS, this assumption would be wildly incorrect.

I still find it hard to explain away the lack of interest in the SSS, whether in 1973 when John Dean revealed the existence of the SSS before Sam Erwin's Watergate investigation or in 1997 when I devoted a chapter of my book, *Unbridled Power*, to the secret machinations of the IRS. I simply do not understand the apathy toward one of the most shocking intrusions of federal power into individual lives as that shown by the IRS SSS. In the rush to demonstrate to the American people that they were doing something to stem the seemingly unbridled power of the White House, Congress enacted today's version of Section

6103 of the Tax Code, effectively shutting down access to tax returns. In a direct shot at President Nixon, the legislation prevented even the president from access to tax returns without approval from the IRS and the Treasury Department. On the surface, this sounded great to those focused on Richard Nixon. No one dug deep enough to understand its true ramifications and the power now placed in the hands of the tax collector to control information.

What Congress did in 1976 when it enacted the modern version of Section 6103 was to hand the keys to the candy store to the IRS. Not only did the tax collector escape the Watergate era unscathed, they ended up with complete control over their own information. Now when the IRS claimed information was not releasable because it contained "taxpayer information," there was no way to counter this position. The road to access dead-ended at the IRS. This included access for the National Archives. To appraise records, archivists must be able to see them, but the IRS position that nearly all its records contained "taxpayer information" effectively barred the archivists from appraising IRS records. The IRS had the power to pick and choose what it would let the National Archives look at—a power not even allowed the Central Intelligence Agency!

TRYING TO CHANGE IRS CULTURE

The IRS must rue the day they hired me as their "corporate historian." Until I came along, no one made even a peep about the empty shelves at the National Archives. But I was appalled at what I found (or did not find) in the records for this very powerful, very large (more than 100,000 employees) federal agency. Nonetheless, I bided my time, convinced that if I remained patient and methodical, I could eventually begin to change the outlook of the IRS toward its recordkeeping responsibilities. Also, it would have been nonsensical to charge out with the allegation that the IRS was destroying records without proof. All I had was emptiness; empty shelves that should have been full of records. I did not see how I could prove the prior existence of records long since destroyed.

As the years ticked by, I produced a series of monographs. I compiled a chronology of important events in tax history, gleaned mainly from secondary sources. I wrote a brief history of the Whiskey Rebellion, the tax rebellion that challenged the tax rebellion that spurred the American Revolution. I wrote brief accounts of IRS offices around the country in places like Detroit and Memphis to celebrate anniversaries. I lectured employees on IRS history, usually opening with a short quiz to demonstrate the links between tax history and the growth of the United States. In short, I tried to be a good corporate historian.

And then the dam began to break. If not for the unrelated convergence of two events in 1994, I might still be biding my time to "fix" the records problems at the IRS. In the end, I was given no choice but to take the actions that led to my forced resignation from the government. Sure, I could have retreated to my office, kept my mouth shut, and finished out my career building castles of Styrofoam® cups as one notorious government employee did to make a point about his "do nothing" job. I think the IRS would have been overjoyed if I had taken that route. They would have been happy to send me a paycheck for keeping quiet (using your tax dollars, of course). The federal government is replete with such individuals. Whatever the reason—being able to sleep at night I think headed my list—I decided that I had to speak up and speak out when confronted with two yet unconnected dots in the puzzle of the missing IRS records.

SPEAKING OUT

The first event involved an outwardly innocent Freedom of Information Act (FOIA) request from a history professor at Franklin and Marshall College in Lancaster, Pennsylvania. Professor John Andrew's 1993 FOIA explained that he was at work on a history of Young Americans for Freedom (YAF), a group I vaguely remembered from my college days. Andrew had stumbled upon references to IRS targeting of YAF for audit while researching a book about the 1960s that piqued his interest. He now wondered whether the IRS had any records of such targeting of political groups for audit. Andrew's request both stymied and confused the IRS. Unlike the FBI and other "more interesting" federal agencies, the IRS received virtually no FOIA requests from serious researchers (most FOIA requests sent to the IRS seemed to come from what the agency called "tax protestors"—people trying to get out of paying taxes by proving that the IRS did not really exist). Not certain what to do with Andrew's letter, the FOIA office asked me to handle it.

Intrigued with the opportunity to help a fellow historian, I remembered that one of the small collections of documents I had discovered might reveal something that could help Professor Andrew. Those documents, it turned out, proved to be my most important (and explosive) discovery at the IRS. I never would have known about them if I had not made a point of being friendly and open with all IRS employees I met. After befriending a seasoned member of the FOIA office a few years earlier, this career employee decided to share his "treasure" with me. He knew he held the keys to a collection of historical importance and, I think, he wanted to ensure that they would outlive his tenure at the tax collector. Behind a curtained wall in a nondescript IRS conference room, he revealed to me a vault door. Behind the heavy steel door he revealed the files of the SSS. All of them. Intact. The IRS had not saved this collection because they wanted to or because they felt any obligation to the citizens or because they recognized their responsibilities under the Federal Records Act. No, the IRS saved this small roomful of documents because Congresswoman Bella Abzug had pounded her fist and chastised IRS Commissioner Donald Alexander during the Watergate Hearings, warning him to not destroy any records, during a revealing (yet ignored) moment of the 1975 hearings.

As legends become truth, over the next two decades, Abzug's impetuous threat to Alexander became enshrined in IRS lore as an edict to not destroy just this one specific set of records. So, there they were, in all their glory. While I had never seen any references to Kennedy-era targeting of groups and individuals by the IRS, I knew the SSS files contained several boxes of administrative records. Professor Andrew's request gave me the push to digress from my anniversary celebration booklets and dig into some real history for a change.

It took only thirty minutes to find the documents that would end my career. In about the third file of the administrative records of the SSS was one that contained documents from a Kennedy-era targeting program similar to but smaller than the Nixon-era SSS. Mixed in with the records from a decade later, it seemed that the IRS had used these records to justify their establishment of the SSS— just in case anyone ever asked why they were clipping newspapers and creating investigative files on average American citizens. But, as we know, no one asked.

In all, I found about an inch of documents that answered Professor Andrew's request. I took copies of the documents to the FOIA office and returned to my anniversaries. Another year passed before I would think of it again. My memory was jogged only because Professor Andrew himself telephoned me wondering if I knew the status of his FOIA request. Stymied because of the significant time gap between my delivery of the documents to the FOIA office and their failure to arrive in the professor's office at Franklin and Marshall College, I trotted down to the FOIA office to inquire about the request.

The FOIA folks promised to look into it and again, I returned to my mundane tasks. The result was a letter that landed in Professor Andrew's mailbox a few weeks later informing him that yes, the IRS had some documents responsive to his request but no, he could not see them because they all contained the dreaded "taxpayer information." Frustrated, Andrew relayed this information to me. Andrew, it turned out, was an experienced FOIA veteran. From years of FOIA requests with the FBI, Andrew was accustomed to receiving heavily redacted documents, but the IRS response was something new. How could an entire set of administrative documents be completely filled with information that could not be released, Andrew wondered. I held back from saying anything to the professor, since I knew the IRS was lying. I had read the documents. They contained no taxpayer information. They were purely administrative papers related to a program that the Kennedy Administration developed to monitor nonprofit organizations. A few organizations were named in the documents, but they were not audit targets, only examples of the broad range of nonprofit organizations.

If I had been searching for evidence that the IRS was lying about which documents really did contain taxpayer information, I now had it. But again, rather than running to the press or Congress, I asked Professor Andrew to work through the system by appealing the IRS's denial of his FOIA request. Although the IRS tried to smear my name when I finally did go public, they could never truthfully call my actions impetuous. I patiently and methodically waited for the system to either work or not work, for the IRS to do the right thing or to lie, cover up, and hide behind 6103. In the end, the system did not work and the IRS did lie, cover up, and hide in their senseless effort to withhold any and all information about their activities.

While waiting for the IRS to respond to Professor Andrew's appeal, the second event leading to my demise occurred. Despite all the frustrations I caused the IRS, I am basically a friendly, outgoing, and agreeable person. As a result, I had many friends among my fellow IRS employees, many of them the sources who helped me fill what eventually became three rooms full of documents. In the late spring of 1994, one of these friends stopped by my office to unload a bit of tantalizing information. As a lawyer in the IRS office of General Legal Services, which handled all non-tax-specific legal questions, including records management, he had learned that the records management staff had requested authority to destroy the collection of presidential tax returns maintained in the commissioner's office. The lawyer was concerned that the presidential returns had historic value despite the IRS's unequivocal prohibition on release of "taxpayer information," which, of course, would include even the tax returns of the presidents in their view. I agreed with the lawyer's assessment and thanked him for sharing the information with me.

The IRS lawyer swore me to secrecy about his identity and left me to pursue the issue of the presidential returns as I saw fit. I quickly discovered that the plot was much thicker than an effort to destroy presidential tax returns. The records management office was actually trying to destroy nearly an entire room full of documents gathered from the commissioner's office over a period of about thirty years. The documents were stuffed into a cramped basement room, a room to which I had always had access even though the commissioner's office refused to turn the old documents directly over to me. I had used them over my tenure and knew that they contained some incredibly useful and valuable historical information. They also included some newsworthy items (if they ever saw the light of day), such as an internal IRS investigative file used to track down the employee who leaked copies of President Nixon's tax returns to the press, prompting a huge uproar and ultimately a change in history, prompting an unprecedented audit of a sitting president. Great stuff, potentially.

Upon learning of the insidious plot to destroy the presidential returns, I contacted the records management staff. As politely as I could, I asked what had prompted the "clean-out" project. The records staff offered that they were simply carrying out the wishes of the IRS deputy commissioner, the second-highest-ranking official in the agency and the highest career (who is not politically appointed) official. Rather than taking on my nemeses in records management, I decided to go directly to the deputy commissioner's office, whose assistant was a man with whom I had had a friendly relationship since preparing an anniversary history of a field office he had headed.

The assistant to the deputy commissioner showed confusion at my questions, appearing unaware of the actions the records management staff was proposing—which seemed to contradict assurances I had received from the records staff that they were merely acceding to the wishes of IRS leadership. Unsure whether the man truly had not ordered the cleanout or was simply trying to sidestep the issue, I plunged ahead. I chose to step on a few toes, feeling that this particular set of records was too important not to take whatever action was necessary to preserve them. I told the assistant that if he signed the approval line on the piece of paper the records management staff had left with him and concurred with the destruction of records, he would be violating the law by sanctioning the destruction of federal records without approval from the National Archives. I carefully explained how the Federal Records Act expressly prohibited such action.

As I prepared to go to war over these documents, I pulled out my copy of the Records Act, just to refresh my knowledge. I was fortified to read the segment that declared it illegal for a federal employee *not* to take action to save records that were known to be in danger of destruction. Simple, I thought. I naïvely believed that I was carrying out the requirements of the law. Not so simple, it turns out.

Despite my explanation and protestations, the assistant to the deputy commissioner refused to guarantee that he would not sign the document provided by records management, telling me bluntly that my guidance contradicted guidance he had received from records management. It was my word against theirs, apparently, and he said he had no reason to believe me over this group of employees who had been with the IRS far longer than I had. I was left with no alternative but to call the National Archives and inform them of the impending destruction. For the first (and unfortunately, the only) time, the National Archives sprang into action by issuing what can be described as a "cease and desist" letter. In straightforward language, the archives backed me up, informing the IRS that it could not legally destroy the records until it had a chance to appraise them.

And that, one might think, was that. If the assistant to the deputy commissioner did not want to take my word about the endangered records, he now had the full weight of the National Archives to convince him. Turns out, the National Archives didn't weigh much on the IRS scales of justice.

The powers that be inside the IRS were decidedly unhappy about my latest move. The day after the National Archives letter arrived, I was called into my supervisor's office. The meeting was not called to present me with any accolades for following the law or doing the right thing. Instead, I sat in shocked silence as my supervisor delivered a "verbal reprimand" for "going outside my chain of command." In other words, I had gone over my supervisor's head to do what was lawful. True enough, I could not argue, but my supervisor openly admitted that she disagreed with my position (and with the authoritative word of the National Archives, apparently). She believed I was, indeed, "stepping on toes." Her position was that if records management said the records could be destroyed, well then, destroy the records. The National Archives be damned. Thank goodness the rest of the government does not operate this way! The National Archives would be nothing but a hollow shell.

And so, there I was, officially persona non grata at the IRS, yet I felt strangely compelled to stick the battle out. For the records, and for patriotism, apple pie, and the right to know what the government is doing.

I believed I had some support at high levels (I did, but not high enough) and that if I just hung in there, I could win this battle. My focus for the moment was to ensure that the roomful of commissioner's records was not destroyed. But now, the commissioner's office saw me as nothing but trouble and promptly revoked my access to the room. I was left with no way to check on the documents. For all I knew, the documents had been secreted out of the IRS late at night and reduced to a heap of ashes.

Things were getting difficult. While many of my IRS friends stuck by me, some began pulling away, especially those with the most to lose if they endangered their jobs at the IRS. The atmosphere became so rife with tension that one day, somewhat on impulse after reading yet another poster on the wall about "reporting fraud, waste and abuse," I picked up the phone and dialed the number for the Treasury Department's inspector general. I had decided it was time to file a complaint against the IRS for violating the Federal Records Act. In my conversation with the anonymous person on the other end of the line, I specifically cited the records management personnel for attempting to destroy records without the approval of the National Archives, something they should have known was illegal, among other complaints about IRS record keeping.

That merely added to my woes. It soon became common knowledge that I had filed a complaint against my fellow IRS employees, an intensely loyal and self-protective group. Just when I thought things could not get any worse, Professor Andrew's FOIA reentered the picture. Months had passed since I advised Andrew to appeal the wrongful denial of his FOIA request. When he called in August 1995 I thought his message would be that, at long last, he had received the documents. But that was not what prompted Andrew's call.

The professor relayed that he had received a call from IRS Internal Security. They wanted to meet in his office in Lancaster, Pennsylvania, to discuss his FOIA request. Internal Security is the IRS's internal police force. I learned that my allegations to the Treasury inspector general's hotline had been turned over to the IRS rather than left in the hands of the higher authority. With the exception of a brief meeting with two Internal Security investigators who seemed bored and uncomprehending of the concept of records management, I had no evidence of any investigation into my complaints. Imagine my shock when those Andrew named as those who planned to drive the three hours between Washington, D.C., and Lancaster to meet with him were the very IRS agents to whom I had explained my complaint.

My mind reeled with the implications as I tried to imagine a connection between Professor Andrew's appeal of his FOIA and the investigators apparently assigned to investigate my allegation that the records management office had tried to circumvent the Federal Records Act. The documents in question came from two distinct collections. There was only one link, and that was me, the IRS historian. My worst fears were confirmed when Andrew called me after his meeting with the IRS agents. To my shock, Andrew was laughing as he recounted the meeting. He obviously thought the whole thing was a hoot. He described the agents as "bumbling Keystone cops" as he told me that the first words out of their mouths upon entering his office were "We're not investigating you, we're investigating the IRS historian." No matter how funny Professor Andrew thought the visit was, I failed to see the humor.

This was how I learned that the IRS had opened an official investigation of me. Some might call it a witch hunt. Apparently the charge against me was leaking sensitive information to Professor Andrew. Ludicrous as the charge was, I knew that I was really under investigation because I had finally ticked off too many people and stepped on too many toes. The basis for the charge, I later learned, was that the IRS assumed that I had asked Professor Andrew to make an FOIA request for specific documents, giving him complete citations to include in his request. Andrew's second letter to the IRS had requested specific documents, complete with dates and citations, but that list had not come from me. In fact, I never located any of the documents Andrew listed by specific reference in his FOIA. The citations, Professor Andrew patiently explained to the IRS investigators, came from footnotes in a 1976 post-Watergate congressional hearing related to the SSS. One of the reasons Andrew was laughing so hard as he recounted the visit from the IRS "Keystone cops" was that he had to explain what a footnote was to the IRS agents by pulling the hearing record from his office shelf and showing them the citations for the documents.

LEAVING THE IRS

At no point during the remaining months of my IRS tenure did anyone inside the IRS inform me that I was under investigation. But I was. Professor Andrew confirmed it and I later confirmed it using FOIA requests after leaving the agency. My decision to leave was neither easy nor swift. Walking away from a sixteen-year career as a federal historian took a great deal of effort and thinking through. I even approached several whistleblower support organizations in the Washington, D.C., area, only to be told that my issues were not as "newsworthy" as the myriad environmental claims that promised prominent headlines.

I analyzed my options after the secret but revealing August 1995 visit by the IRS to Franklin and Marshall College and decided to leave the IRS by the end of the year. That would give me time to organize my personal life, pay off some bills, and save some money in anticipation of my pending unemployment. I had no intention of going public with my tale of document destruction inside the IRS until I was well out the door, but that decision was changed by a twist of fate. At the end of November, I answered the phone one day to find a *Wall Street Journal* reporter on the line. He simply wanted a copy of an old (blank) tax return. I promised to copy the form and send it off, adding bluntly that he need not bother to call with similar requests after January 1 because there would be no historian inside the IRS to help him.

I had not meant to open the floodgate, but good reporter that he proved to be, he began asking questions. Not really thinking, I began to spill my story. As I heard the tap, tap, tapping of his computer in the background, I realized the magnitude of what I was doing. I still had a month left at the IRS and I was jeopardizing that by talking openly with a reporter. But it was too late, since I had already started. The reporter proved to be honorable. He worked closely with me to verify my story and get all the details right. In the end, it took him two weeks to finish. I ended up on the front page of the *Wall Street Journal* on Friday, December 15, 1995, leaving only two weeks of work for me to worry about.

I didn't need to worry. The IRS had already started what would become a multiple-year effort to minimize me as a problem. They chose the wisest route in responding to my newfound publicity by simply not responding. Rather than escorting me out of the building in a huff, something that would have prompted more negative publicity, they simply ignored me through those final weeks. A smart move. A move that dramatically lessened the press coverage of my claims. With no response from the IRS, there was not much to report. The historian says there are no records. Yawn. I think most people who heard this story at the time thanked their lucky stars, mistakenly thinking that this meant their own 1040 was among the shredded records and they could no longer be audited.

Just as I had not sought publicity, I did not intend to write a book about my experiences. I was now a "Washington" story and the literary agents came calling on their own. Exactly thirty days after I walked out of the IRS, wondering what was next in my life, I had a contract to write a book about my experiences. I welcomed the opportunity for several reasons. A book would provide me with an opportunity to expand on the brief publicity I had received to continue to try to save IRS records from outside the agency as well as provide a source of income for at least my first year of nonfederal employment.

The book was published in early 1997 and caused a minor stir but brought no changes at the IRS. Nonetheless, there were increasing rumblings in Congress that the IRS needed a good, long look. My public departure was one of the pebbles that started the avalanche rolling. I spent a good part of the spring of 1997 promoting my book and working with congressional offices explaining the arcane procedures and culture of the tax agency. It was gratifying to finally have fellow professionals listening carefully to my story and taking me seriously after so many years of being derided by the IRS.

The congressional investigation turned toward the type of issue that would garner the greatest media attention—cases of taxpayers who had endured years of abuse or intransigent bureaucracy from the IRS. I was there, too, but more as a side witness. The weeping witnesses forced to cash in retirement accounts to fend off the tax collector made the evening news rather than the historian revealing that the IRS had destroyed its history. Expecting the media to pick up on the causal link between the unbridled power of the IRS and the lack of records was too much to expect from reporters who needed a fast, hard-hitting, and emotional story.

SILENCE

Trying to explain that without records there can be no accountability did not grab the headlines that financial devastation did. I understood that and expected it. What I did not expect, and do not understand to this day, is the resounding silence I encountered from my professional associates. Where was the historical community when I made my revelations? Nowhere to be found. I sincerely believe that if I had been reporting document destruction and mishandling from virtually any other federal agency, the historical community would have joined the battle. And where was the National Archives during my long and lonely struggle? For the most part, the National Archives remained mute. They did respond to my emergency request to save the documents slated for destruction with a cease and desist letter, but this constituted their most forceful action. I longed for the power of the archivist of the United States to back me up, support the lone historian inside this powerful agency, but such help remained elusive.

Although the National Archives launched an evaluation of IRS records management practices at my urging, they mysteriously bowed to IRS requests to prohibit me from attending any of the meetings between the records management staff and National Archives personnel. I was never able to extract an explanation from my associates at the National Archives about this bizarre action. I was left to surmise that the financial dependence of the National Archives on reimbursement for document storage from the IRS forced them into timidity in the face of the tax collector. (Note: The ten federal records centers across the country are filled largely with tax returns and the IRS is one of very few federal agencies that reimburses the National Archives for this storage.)

When the National Archives released its report just before my departure from the agency, the most damaging information (that the IRS did not save its records!) was buried deep inside a text filled with mealy-mouthed gratitude for the "cooperation" of the IRS. Ironically, the report was based solely on IRS claims rather than an actual archival inspection of records because, not surprisingly, the IRS refused to let the archivists inspect records based on the bogus "taxpayer information" claim! My frustration with lack of help from the National Archives now turned to profound disappointment as I realized that the one federal agency with the power and knowledge to take on the IRS was unwilling to do so.

Despite this disappointment, the congressional hearings that dominated the first half of 1998 and kept the media spotlight on the IRS resulted in the passage of legislation that may ultimately have a minor impact on records management at the IRS. The massive bill signed in a White House ceremony by President Bill Clinton at the end of July 1998 included a small provision that at long last allowed the National Archives access to 6103-designated records "for appraisal purposes." Although this provision was characterized as a major victory, from my experience and personal knowledge of the personnel in charge of the IRS records program, I do not see much chance for change in the immediate future. To date, many of the same people sit in the records management office as on the day I joined the IRS. Until the IRS hires an outside and professional (i.e., certified) records manager to take control of this vital program, I do not believe records will flow as they should to the National Archives. While the IRS will claim that the National Archives has accessioned new records, the vast majority of these include those I jammed into three rooms before my premature departure from the agency.

Until historians take note of the long and fascinating history of the tax collection agency, there will be no pressure on the IRS to save its records. Historians were not much interested in the subject before I joined the IRS, nor while I was there, and do not seem to be picking up on it now, despite all my efforts, my book, and the congressional hearings. Somehow, historians have failed to make the connection between tax collection and America's financial, social, and military history. It is there, believe me, it is there. Until the National Archives becomes more proactive in demanding that the IRS open its records, nothing will change. As one National Archives employee told me along the way, "No one asks for IRS records, so why should we care?"

It has been a long and lonely ride to preserve and protect the history of our tax agency. The ultimate irony, I think, is that we celebrate our history as a nation who fought a war for independence based largely on issues related to taxation and yet we have let the history of the agency we created to enforce our own system of taxation languish into virtual nonexistence. The result, although we remain blissfully unaware of its potential consequences, is that we have granted the IRS powers above and beyond those of any other federal agency. One just has to wonder what the founding fathers would think of this.

Lighting Up the Internet: The Brown and Williamson Collection[1]

Robin L. Chandler and Susan Storch

This chapter explores the impact that the documents in the Stanton Glantz Research Files of the Brown and Williamson Tobacco Corporation (known herein as the B & W Collection) have had on the debate over tobacco control and the impact of the Internet on archival access issues. The B & W Collection is part of the Tobacco Control Archives (TCA) established at the University of California, San Francisco (UCSF), Library and Center for Knowledge Management (CKM) in the spring of 1994 to provide a centralized source of unpublished and published information about the grassroots tobacco-control movement, the people and organizations involved, and the resulting legislation generated. The papers became the subject of a lawsuit in San Francisco Superior Court when the Brown and Williamson Tobacco Corporation (B & W) sought to permanently remove the disputed material from the UCSF Library. On June 29, 1995, the California Supreme Court allowed UCSF to release the documents on the Internet, stating, "the public has the right to know." The collection was recognized by the TCA and the University of California to contain important revelations about the tobacco industry and the health effects of tobacco use. The public availability of the documents has generated debate about the nature of corporate accountability and individual responsibility. The accessibility of the documents has served as the catalyst for tobacco litigation, promoted the development of government policy, and ignited the battle against control of information. Class-action suits, individual smoker law suits, and states' reimbursement suits against the tobacco industry have proliferated now that litigants have the information that was hidden for so long by the tobacco corporations. The B & W Collection has proven to be very important evidence in these suits. The documents are an example of the advantages of delivering access to archival primary source material on the Internet. In addition, the release of the documents has fostered debate among archivists about the future of corporate archives and the preservation of business records, the provenance of research copies in faculty files, archivists accountability to their profession and their institutions, and the tension between the archival profession's avoidance of political advocacy and the profession's responsibility to promote the public's right to know.

In the past, the tobacco industry has used three primary arguments to prevent government regulation of its products and defend itself against product liability suits: First, there is no proof that smoking causes cancer or heart disease. Second, smoking is not addictive—it is a personal choice. And third, the industry is committed to delivery of scientific truth about the health effects of tobacco. Documentary evidence is now available that tests these arguments, and individuals can freely access this information, form their own opinions, make informed decisions, and actively participate in the ongoing public debate reformulating the boundary between corporate and individual responsibility. With this context in mind, this essay will explore the impact that the documents in the B & W Collection have had on the debate over tobacco control and the impact of the Internet on archival access issues.

We will begin by describing the background of the TCA and its mission, its documentation plan, and the acquisition and legal context of the B & W Collection. We will also discuss how the Archives and Special Collections Department participates in the mission of the library at UCSF to create a digital library, using the Internet to communicate scientific information. Finally, we will illustrate the impact the B & W Collection has had on the nation and on archival issues, especially those of access and the potential implications for archival appraisal of ongoing electronic media. Lastly, we will provide a summation of the effect of tobacco legislation and litigation on national health policies and some reflection on the Web as a means of public information dissemination.

TOBACCO CONTROL ARCHIVES

California has been and is a world center for the development of tobacco-control policies. California citizens have shaped public policy to protect individuals from second-hand smoke and prevent nonsmokers from becoming new smokers. California voters have approved tobacco-control ordinances that prohibit smoking in restaurants and public areas and passed statewide Proposition 99, which has raised the state's tobacco tax and made it the highest in the nation. Aimed at reducing the number of smokers in California, the tax pays for the development and implementation of educational programs, some of which have served as national models for tobacco education agencies. All this makes California a natural laboratory in which to study tobacco-control issues.

The TCA was established at the UCSF Library and CKM in the spring of 1994 to provide a centralized source of information about the grassroots tobacco-control movement, the people and organizations involved, and the resulting legislation generated. The mission of the TCA is to collect, preserve, and provide access to papers and unpublished documents relevant to tobacco-control issues. The central focus of the TCA documentation plan is the collection and preservation of papers concerning California's Proposition 99, the tobacco tax initiative passed by voters in 1989. Additional collecting areas include other California tobacco-control propositions and ordinances, Proposition 99 legislative "clones" passed by other states, the papers of University of California faculty members researching tobacco-control issues, the papers of persons and agencies who are active in the California tobacco-control movement (such as the American Cancer Society, the American Lung Association, and the California Medical Association), and the records of tobacco-control organizations such as the Americans for Nonsmokers' Rights. Recently, the TCA has expanded its documentation plan to include the implementation of educational programs funded by Proposition 99. The TCA also seeks to preserve the records of selected county public health department programs and agencies educating specific populations such as youth and immigrant groups. Though in its infancy, the UCSF Library and CKM TCA program was documenting the history of individuals and organizations in the tobacco-control movement prior to the donation of the B & W Collection.

THE B & W COLLECTION

In fall 1994, Stanton Glantz, a professor in cardiology at UCSF dedicated to tobacco-control research and an internationally recognized tobacco-control activist, donated the B & W Collection to the TCA. Glantz had received an estimated 4,000 pages of documents on May 12, 1994, from an anonymous source called "Mr. Butts," a reference to the cigarette character in the comic strip "Doonesbury." Merrill Williams, a paralegal for a law firm representing B & W, had allegedly made unauthorized copies of key internal documents that he then spirited out of the company's offices. Subsequently, many of these documents were copied and distributed, appearing in the national press during spring 1994. Some of the documents informed Phil Hilts's series of articles for the *New York Times* and served as evidence for Congressman Henry Waxman's Subcommittee for Health and the Environment investigating the tobacco industry. Ultimately, an entire set of the documents was made available to Glantz, and these are the documents that make up the B & W Collection. Glantz's series organization and indexing of the documents formed the core of the collection arrangement and description.

The B & W Collection served as the basis for research by Glantz and his colleagues John Slade, Lisa A. Bero, Peter Hanauer, and Deborah E. Barnes, culminating in the publication of the book *The Cigarette Papers* in 1996. In addition, the July 1995 issue of the *Journal of the American Medical Association* (*JAMA*) was based on scientific research and analysis of the information contained in the B & W Collection by Glantz and colleagues. Notably, this *JAMA* issue devoted to tobacco research was published by the American Medical Association despite fears of tobacco industry reprisals against editors and authors. In an effort to squash public funding or disrupt the tenure process, the tobacco industry often challenges the academic research findings of scientists and policymakers. In addition, the tobacco industry, working through grassroots organizations, sponsors lawsuits against professors engaged in tobacco research and questions their use of public university funds. *Cigarette Papers* authors Stanton Glantz and Lisa Bero have been the subjects of reprisals of this nature. In 1997 the Regents of the University of California were sued by the Californians for Scientific Integrity (CSI), an organization formed by the National Smokers Alliance (NSA). Not coincidentally nor without irony, tobacco-product manufacturer Philip Morris financially supports NSA. CSI charged that Stanton Glantz had skewed data in a 1994 study of the effect of smoking bans in restaurants and used state funds illegally to promote tobacco control. Responding to a CSI-funded and -sponsored critique of Glantz's study, Mervyn Susser, editor of the *American Journal of Public Health,* where Glantz's article was originally published, wrote in the October 1997 issue that "plainly the aim is to destroy Glantz's career."[2] In 1998 Glantz's research entitled *Effect of Advocacy on State Tobacco Policy Making* was in danger of being axed from the federal budget for the National Institutes of Health (NIH). Historically, the NIH budget has never been subject to line-item politically based fiscal oversight. While Congress and the executive branch provide broad research guidelines, NIH administrators have been entrusted with the authority to choose which projects warrant federal funding on the basis of scientific merit and the research value of the project. The powerful influence of the tobacco industry on Congress prompted this unusual budget debate.

In another case, a scientist with longstanding and well-documented tobacco industry ties wrote the dean of the Medical School at UCSF stating that Lisa Bero, an untenured faculty member of clinical pharmacy at UCSF, had done unethical work and should be fired from the University of California. The dean and the vice dean for Academic Affairs discussed the charge with Bero, reviewed her publications, and ultimately wrote the scientist a letter stating that "Bero is one of UCSF's up and coming researchers and that if [you] have further interest in [Bero's] work [you] should read [her] publications in the *New England Journal of Medicine* and the *Journal of the American Medical Association.*"[3]

THE LEGAL CONTEXT

Apart from the usual concerns of administering an archival collection, the B & W Collection became the subject of a lawsuit in San Francisco Superior Court when B & W sought to permanently remove the disputed material from the UCSF Library. On January 6, 1995, B & W learned of the documents' accessibility at the UCSF Library when selections were introduced as evidence into a Mississippi courtroom in *Butler v. Philip Morris*. Ron Motley, the attorney representing the plaintiff Burl Butler in the case, argued the admissibility of the documents in his brief since they had been widely distributed by the media and were maintained as an archival collection at the UCSF Library. Twenty-five days later, on February 3, 1995, B & W lawyers moved to review the documents at the UCSF Library and CKM for their authenticity. B & W also hired private investigators to place the Archives and Special Collections reading room under continual surveillance to track and photograph researchers using the collection.

Shortly thereafter, B & W's lawyers declared the documents stolen property and demanded their return as well as access to the names of all researchers who had seen the documents. Needless to say, these requests were denied. The request for named researchers was particularly troubling, since libraries traditionally protect the confidentiality of researchers' use of their collections. In February 1995 B & W's attorneys filed suit against the University of California, asserting legal entitlement or property rights to the documents. *Brown and Williamson Tobacco Corporation v. Regents of the University of California* (No. 967298) was filed in California Superior Court in San Francisco. Christopher Patti, the university's legal counsel, took the position that the library was in possession of copies, not originals, and therefore the documents were not "stolen property." What then were B & W's property rights in the documents? Searching for legal footing upon which to make its claim, B & W attempted to control the information contained in the documents, not the tangible physical property. B & W argued a property interest in the control of information. However, there is no existing legal right to control information because it is contained in a document owned by individuals or organizations. For reasons unknown, the B & W attorneys chose not to argue an intellectual property or copyright strategy to protect trade secrets.[4] In speculation, the answer may reside in the nature of the copyright law. Copyright protects "original works of authorship" that are fixed in a tangible form of expression and include literary works; musical works, including any accompanying words; dramatic works, including any accompanying music; pantomimes and choreographic works; pictorial, graphic, and sculptural works; motion pictures and other audiovisual works; sound recordings; and architectural works. Federal copyright law does not protect titles, names, short phrases, and slogans; familiar symbols or designs; mere variations of typographic ornamentation, lettering, or coloring; mere listings of ingredients or contents; or ideas, procedures, methods, systems, processes, concepts, principles, discoveries, or devices, as distinguished from a description, explanation, or illustration. Perhaps the B & W attorneys feared they would lose the copyright argument and risk loss of control of their designs, ideas, and discoveries. Instead, B & W attorney Barbara Caulfield argued "the attorney–client privilege covering the documents had created a property interest in the information itself, and sued on a theory of conversion, asking for a return of its 'property.' "[5] Ironically, the B & W Collection documents reveal that the attorney–client and work-product privileges are a strategy that tobacco industry attorneys had nurtured as a means of protecting the corporation for years.

As reported by Glantz, "By the early 1970s the evidence of the health dangers of smoking had accumulated to the point of causing serious legal problems for the tobacco industry," including increased regulatory pressure by the federal government and numerous product liability lawsuits on the basis that tobacco contains toxic substances.[6] As a defense against possible legal challenges, B & W attorneys began to routinely label documents "work product" or "privileged." The B & W Collection documents reveal that company attorneys took the atypical role of actively planning and supervising scientific research projects. To Glantz, this demonstrated that "Attorney control over company research apparently was deemed necessary to assert control over evidence produced within the company so that it could not be used to prove that the company's products were dangerous, even though the evidence developed by the company scientists clearly contradicted this view."[7]

In 1947 the U.S. Supreme Court ordained the "work-product rule" to protect an attorney's process of preparation for litigation. Attorney-client privilege was established to prevent the disclosure of any documents that contain confidential communications between an attorney and his or her client. (See the Appendix to this article on attorney–client privilege.) To avoid discovery of "confidential" information, the B & W attorneys developed two other methods: special procedures to maintain secrecy for handling documents sent to B & W from affiliated companies such as the British and American Tobacco (BAT) company; and the removal of certain documents from the company. A 1979 memo (marked restricted) from J. K. Wells, corporate counsel, states, "the scientific material should come to you under a policy statement between you and [BAT's laboratory in] Southampton which describes the purpose of developing the documents for B & W and sending them to you as use for defense of potential litigation . . . [C]ontinued law department control is essential for the best argument for privilege. At the same time, control should be exercised with flexibility to allow access of the R & D staff to the documents."[8] Six years later, Wells determined that certain company records should be declared "deadwood," removed and shipped offshore to Great Britain. (Ironically, these documents sent to Great Britain would form part of the discovery process in the tobacco litigation brought forward by state attorney general Hubert Humphrey III representing the State of Minnesota and Blue Cross/Blue Shield.) Wells states in a 1985 memorandum "[the] documents which I suggested were deadwood [are] in the behavioral and biological studies area. I said the 'B' series are 'Janus' series studies [mouse skin-painting studies demonstrating that tobacco tar is carcinogenic] and should also be considered as deadwood. . . . [H]ave the documents on my list pulled, put into boxes and stored in the large basement storage area. . . . [W]e would consider shipping the documents to BAT when we have completed segregating them."[9]

Recognizing the issue as one of access and dissemination of information, rather than possession of tangible property, counsel for the University of California argued that B & W still had possession of its property because the documents in the library's possession were copies, and that serious First Amendment issues were being raised by claiming the right to block dissemination of the information. It is common for First Amendment case law to address issues of publication and distribution, unfortunately, there is not much good case law that states the displaying of materials in a library is "speech" under the First Amendment, and therefore this argument was considered an extension of the law. Litigation currently underway may further define this legal dialogue concerning library display of materials and the First Amendment. In a related case on March 20, 2001, the American Library Association (ALA) filed suit in federal court challenging the Children's Internet Protection Act (CIPA). The 106th Congress passed CIPA, which mandates that libraries and schools receiving federal funding adopt a prescriptive Internet safety policy intended to filter or block materials considered harmful to minors. In January 2001, the ALA adopted a resolution in opposition to federally mandated Internet filtering.

The access strategy developed by the TCA of posting the documents on the Internet, however, constituted a form of distribution or publication. At this point, the B & W suit became a classic case of "prior restraint"[10] or an attempt to enjoin publication. Attempts to impose prior restraint are the most serious and least tolerable infringement of First Amendment rights and can be justified only by an extremely compelling interest in suppression.

This dimension of the lawsuit was very similar to the Pentagon Papers case, in which the U.S. government attempted prior restraint of publication in the *New York Times* and the *Washington Post* of the Pentagon Papers. In 1967 U.S. Secretary of Defense Robert S. McNamara commissioned a history of the U.S. role in Indochina from World War II until May 1968. Developing a serious opposition to the U.S. involvement in Vietnam over the course of his research, Daniel Ellsberg, a senior research associate at the Massachusetts Institute of Technology's Center for International Studies, leaked significant portions of the forty-seven-volume history to the press. On June 13, 1971, the *New York Times* began publishing a series of articles based on the "top secret" study. Stating that further public dissemination of the material would cause immediate and irreparable harm to the U.S. national defense interests, the U.S. Department of Justice obtained a temporary restraining order against further publication. During the next two weeks, the *New York Times* and the *Washington Post* fought the order through the courts. On June 30, 1971, the U.S. Supreme Court ruled in favor of the press, freeing the newspapers to resume publishing the material. The high court held that even though publication might have serious impact on national security, prior restraint was impermissible because the government had failed to justify restraint of publication.

B & W attorney Caulfield, a former federal judge, argued that the tobacco company's privilege claims amounted to a property interest that was being usurped by the university, which threatened to release the documents on the Internet. "We are a private party seeking to exercise our right to seek return of stolen property," Caulfield argued. In response to questions by Judge Stuart Pollak about the First Amendment and the Pentagon Papers case, Caulfield argued that "the University is not a newspaper." Rather, it is a "state agency" that does not have the same First Amendment rights as the press. In response, Judge Pollak stated "this is an academic center and the tobacco company's complaint was an effort to suppress information and prevent information from being used in a public dialogue. . . . [I] am particularly concerned with B & W's demand that the original documents deposited with the library be returned as well as all copies of them made subsequently." Caulfield responded by arguing that the return of all copies was essential to protect B & W's privilege, and she stated, "if there is a conversion [reproduction] of information that is privileged, all copies of that information are protected."[11]

In determining the B & W judgment, Judge Pollak held that B & W had no legitimate property rights over copies of the documents. Pollock stated that "UCSF had not committed a 'conversion' of B & W's private property by displaying the documents—some subject to attorney-client or work product privilege—because it had not acquired them illegally. What occurred here simply was not and is not a conversion. . . . the University did not participate in the theft of the documents."[12] The court, however, concluded that it could require the return of the documents if the balance of interests warranted this action. The court proceeded to balance the First Amendment concerns with B & W's interests in avoiding disclosure. The court held that there was a very strong public interest in permitting this particular information to remain available for use by the university or by others who may obtain it from the university. On the other hand, B & W's interest in avoiding disclosure because of possible liability in litigation was a weak argument. B & W's interests were further compromised by the significant disclosure of the documents to researchers. The court also expressed concern about B & W's pending actions, which would include the attempt to track down researchers who had used the collection and trace the documents that had been copied.

In reaching his decision, the judge noted the First Amendment concerns raised by B & W's request that the university be prevented from retaining or using the documents: "the nature of what is being requested would in fact impinge upon public discussion, public study of this information, which has a bearing on all kinds of issues of public health, public law, documents which may be taken to suggest the advisability of legislation in all kinds of areas. So there is . . . a very strong public interest in permitting this particular information, judging from what has been shown in the papers, as to what it concerns, permitting this information to remain available for use by the university or by others who may obtain it from the university."[13]

The B & W attorneys appealed the lower court's decision, arguing "others have quoted [the documents] publicly but 'no one else has threatened to make

B & W's confidential property available, in its entirety, to everyone with access to a computer terminal . . . [and] absent a stay, trafficking in stolen property will have succeeded, and this highly publicized case may well encourage other thieves to steal privileged documents and launder them through California—a state that, though it is the intellectual property capital of the world, will have declined to protect the property rights in confidential information."[14] On June 29, 1995 the California Supreme Court allowed UCSF to release the documents on the Internet, stating, "the public has the right to know." Within a year, half a million people had visited the Web page, a population equivalent to a traditional newspaper readership. Floyd Abrams, a New York First Amendment lawyer who specializes in the media, observed, "if Daniel Ellsberg were to have come into possession of the Pentagon Papers today, he would not need to find a newspaper to publish them."[15]

DIGITIZING THE DOCUMENTS

As media attention to the B & W Collection grew, so did the demand for using the collection. Anticipating that this high volume use by the public would continue, the TCA staff developed a reference strategy to create digital versions of the B & W Collection by scanning more than 4,000 individual pages. The goal was to produce a searchable and browsable interface for electronic versions of the B & W documents using the limited financial and staffing resources available. The initial strategy to produce a CD-ROM quickly evolved to include Internet access through the UCSF Library and CKM Web site.

Glantz imposed his own series arrangement on the documents. The series are based loosely upon creator or broad topic and include terms such as "Nicotine," "Additives and Pesticides," and "Public Relations and Lawyers." The series descriptions anticipate the *Cigarette Papers* table of contents, which includes chapter titles such as "Addiction and Cigarettes As Nicotine Delivery Devices," "Public Relations in the 'safe' Cigarette Era," "Agricultural Chemicals and Cigarette Additives," and "Lawyer Management of Scientific Research." Glantz and his staff abstracted and indexed the research files as well as assigned document numbers based upon the series using PC-based software. Applying this paper organizational structure to the creation of an electronic access environment, the B & W Collection was scanned as TIFF (tagged information file format) files, which provided electronic image reproductions of the paper originals. Optical character recognition (OCR) software was not utilized at the time. Document authenticity was deemed essential to guarantee the use of the information in the public debates about corporate accountability. Viewing digital "images" of the documents would support document authenticity. The images would illustrate the artifactual nature of the documents by revealing letterheads, signatures, and marginalia where available. The OCR could have been used in conjunction with the digital images to provide keyword search and retrieval functionality. Glantz's prepared abstracts and indexes minimized the need for the functionality OCR provided. In addition, the technological state of OCR in 1995 required intensive staff time to ensure accuracy of data, and these personnel resources were not available in the library at that time. The TIFF files were ultimately converted to GIFs (graphical image files) because they are supported by Web browsers and require less disk storage space, a critical factor for real-time transfer of files on the Internet, as well as for CD-ROM storage limits. Ultimately, the PC indexing database generated by Glantz was adapted for the Internet by using a "free- WAIS" application (free-WAIS is a text retrieval system based on the vector space model). Internet users can search the B & W Collection by keyword or choose from a list of series based on subject matter. This indexing makes the collection easy to access and use. To browse the collection, a user clicks on a series name to get a title list of each document with a brief abstract in that series. When the user selects a document number, he/she gets a detailed abstract (written by Glantz and his research colleagues), and can proceed from the abstract to the actual document(s). This ease of access would not be possible if the records were available to the user only in paper format, in which case the archivist would have to spend significantly more time with each patron to provide this level of detailed information about the records. On July 1, 1995, a subset of the collection was released on the Internet, and by August 1, 1995, the entire B & W Collection was available through the UCSF Library and CKM Web site.

INSIGHT INTO THE TOBACCO INDUSTRY

The B & W Collection forms an integral part of the TCA as the fonds[16] of a UCSF faculty member and an internationally recognized tobacco-control activist and because of the unique research information it provides. This collection was recognized by the TCA and the University of California to contain important revelations about the tobacco industry and the health effects of tobacco use. The papers in this collection reveal three important facts about the industry and about tobacco. First, research conducted by the tobacco companies into the harmful health effects of tobacco was often more advanced than studies by the medical community. "Of the thousands of chemicals in tobacco smoke, nicotine is the most important. Nicotine makes tobacco addictive. The addictiveness of tobacco keeps people smoking long enough and heavily enough for the other chemicals in tobacco to cause heart disease, cancer, and other diseases. . . . by 1963 B & W and BAT scientists and executives were internally acknowledging that nicotine is an addictive drug and that tobacco companies are essentially in the business of 'selling nicotine.'"[17] The papers contain many technical reports illustrating research studies conducted by the industry. For example, in 1962 BAT contracted with the Battelle Memorial Institute laboratory in Geneva, Switzerland, to conduct two research studies: Project Hippo I, designed to explore nicotine's role in hypothalamic functions including reduction of stress, inhibition of weight gain, and regulation of sex hormones; and Project Hippo II, designed to compare nicotine effects on the body with the newly developed tranquilizing agents including reserpine. In the essay *A Tentative Hypothesis on Nicotine Addition*, the Battelle scientists wrote, "nicotine helps people to cope with stress. In the beginning of nicotine consumption, relatively small doses can perform the desired action. Chronic intake of nicotine tends to restore the normal physiological functioning of the endocrine system, so that ever-increasing dose levels of nicotine are necessary to maintain the desired action."[18]

Second, through that research executives at B & W were aware in the early 1960s that tobacco use is causally related to lung cancer and heart disease and that nicotine is addictive. As early as 1950 two scientists outside the tobacco industry, Ernst L. Wynder and Evarts A. Graham, concluded in published scientific reports that smokers had a greater risk of lung cancer than nonsmokers did. Despite knowledge based on their own sponsored research that nicotine was addictive, the industry made a conscious decision not to make that information public and actively suppressed the information's availability to the U.S. surgeon general, who would publish the landmark report *Smoking and Health* in 1964. "The Hippo reports prompted a flurry of correspondence between BAT headquarters and the B & W executive suite in the summer of 1963, particularly over the question of what information, if any, to disclose to the US Surgeon General's Advisory Committee."[19] In a July 3, 1963, cable to Tony McCormick of BAT, Addison Yeaman, the B & W general counsel, stated that "submission of the Battelle research to the Surgeon General is undesirable."[20] Tobacco industry executives concluded that the tranquilizing effect of nicotine could be an effective means to counter the link being made by public health organizations that cigarettes had a causal relationship to lung cancer. Over the next few decades, this conclusion would lead the tobacco industry to sponsor unsuccessful research on the production of a safer cigarette—a nicotine delivery device—that would remove the harmful constituents from smoke.

Third, this research was hidden by the tobacco companies from the courts by laundering the research data through legal departments and claiming that it could not be released due to the principle of attorney-client privilege, as illustrated earlier in this essay, and by establishing guidelines for public statements made by scientists and affiliated companies outside the United States. In August 1970 David R. Hardy, the tobacco industry's principal outside counsel, wrote to B & W's general counsel about his fears of BAT scientists being subpoenaed for potential U.S. health litigation. The letter marked "Confidential, for Legal Counsel Only" describes BAT and B & W scientists attending a conference in Germany and publicly discussing their research stating "a mouse-skin safer cigarette is a worthwhile objective . . . [and] there is a possibility that the experiments taking place at Southampton . . . with the membrane of a chicken embryo might be showing genuine carcinogenic effects in days."[21] Fearful of the effect of court testimony by employees or admission of documentary evidence from BAT and B & W files that would strengthen the causal relationship between cigarettes and cancer in a trial, Hardy warned that careless statements must be avoided at all costs.

THE UCSF INSTITUTIONAL CONTEXT

When these papers were offered to the UCSF Library and CKM, the library administration and the TCA carefully considered many factors in their decision to accept them. Accepting the collection was consistent with the mission of the university to serve the public and the medical profession as well as the mission of the library to support the core functions of the university. UCSF is an academic health care campus, and as such its mission is to attract and educate students for future careers in the health sciences, bring patients the best in health-care service, encourage and support research and scholarly activities, and serve the community at large with educational and service programs. As part of the university, the UCSF Library and the CKM's mission is to advance science and foster excellence in teaching and learning; promote health through the collection, development, organization, and dissemination of the world's knowledge in the health sciences; develop a campus focal point for applications of information technology; and develop online tools, informatics curricula, and personal information management services for the health sciences.

The UCSF Library and CKM is at the forefront of the development of digital libraries. The digital goals of the library are to create and implement the "library without walls"; ensure timely access to health sciences information for faculty and students; provide efficient and integrated computing services in a distributed environment; develop data and knowledge bases, access software, and management and analysis tools for scientific communication; and study the changing nature of scientific communication and respond to those changes.

The archival program supports the overall education, health care, and research mission of the university. In addition, it helps fulfill the library's mission to support research and teaching in health sciences disciplines, as well as participating in the development of the digital library and a digital archive.

ACCESS AND THE INTERNET

As is the case with many repositories, the library budget severely limits staffing of the Archives and Special Collections Department. The project archivist for tobacco control is a part-time position funded fully through external grants. The UCSF Archives and Special Collections has used the Internet as a partial solution to its budgetary limitations because electronic information delivery promotes wider, faster, and more efficient distribution of information with minimal ongoing staffing requirements. The Internet also makes round-the-clock access to information possible for widely distributed patrons even when the archivist is not available. In addition to the B & W Collection, all the finding aids for collections currently open for research in the TCA, the AIDS History Project, and the Biotechnology Archives are available on the World Wide Web through the California Digital Library's Online Archive of California (OAC) database of encoded archival description (EAD) finding aids.[22] Collection descriptions and box and folder lists are available to browse and select materials as well as foster informed reference interviews prior to the patron's arrival at the library for research. To complete this snapshot of electronic access, it must be noted that most of our reference questions for TCA are instigated by patrons and completed by the tobacco project archivist through the use of an electronic mail account on the Web site. As part of Galen II, the digital library of UCSF, the TCA Web site provides links to the library's Knowledge Resources section. Knowledge Resources are electronic information resources in the health sciences selected by UCSF librarians for their high-quality information and reliable service. In general, Knowledge Resources provide links to the universe of information in which the UCSF archival and manuscript collections reside, and specifically they link to complementary resources on AIDS, biotechnology, and tobacco control that are useful to our archival researchers.

When Stanton Glantz and colleagues wrote their in-depth analysis of the B & W Collection, they planned to offer *The Cigarette Papers* manuscript to a commercial publisher. Fearing legal challenges, all commercial publishers turned down the manuscript prepared by Glantz and his colleagues. Ultimately an academic publisher, the University of California Press, accepted the manuscript—a logical choice, since the university had previously won the court decision about the B & W documents. The UCSF Library and CKM considered *The Cigarette Papers* an extension of the B & W documents and approached UC Press about electronic publication rights. The library and UC Press agreed upon an appropriate business model, and the book was published in paperback by the UC Press and in electronic format by the UCSF Library and CKM. For the first two years, the online version was available for use via personal and institutional subscriptions, but it is now freely available for public access. The entire text of the book is searchable, providing much broader access to content than through the index of the paper version. As an additional advantage, there are hypertext links from the references in the online version of *The Cigarette Papers* to the B & W documents themselves. Readers therefore have an opportunity to readily scrutinize Glantz's interpretation of the documents and draw their own conclusions. Glantz and Edith Balbach have subsequently written and released online a second book that draws upon the B & W Collection as well as other online documents: *Tobacco War: Inside the California Battles* is a publication of the UC Press and the eScholarship program of the California Digital Library and is freely available for public use.

The use statistics for the B&W Collection online from 1995 to 2000 illustrates fully the intensive interest in these tobacco documents. From July 1995 through February 2000 users accessed more than 4 million graphical image files, a file being the equivalent to one paper page in the B & W Collection. Although interest dropped off after the first month, it soon stabilized, and interest has been steadily rising over the past several years, as illustrated in Figure 1. The graph tracks statistics for four tobacco industry collections released on the Internet by the TCA: the B&W Collection, the Mangini Collection, the Mangini Select Set and Report, and the California Documents from the Minnesota Repository Collection.

Figure 1

UCSF Library/CKM Tobacco Industry Documents Use Statistics 1995–2000

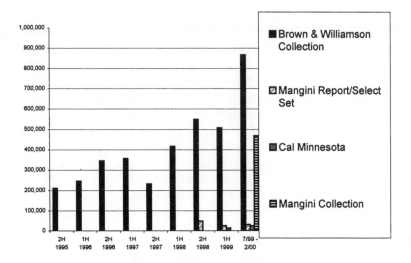

The Mangini Collection, including the Select Set and the Report, stems from litigation to end the Joe Camel cigarette advertising campaign. In 1991 the R.J. Reynolds Tobacco Company (RJR) was publicly charged in the *Journal of the American Medical Association* (JAMA) with targeting children through its Joe Camel campaign. Later that year, Janet C. Mangini, a San Francisco family law attorney, brought suit to end the Joe Camel campaign, becoming the first person to challenge the tobacco industry for targeting minors with its advertising. Ruling that Ms. Mangini should be permitted to prosecute her claims, the California Supreme Court wrote that the targeting of minors is oppressive and unscrupulous, in that it exploits minors by luring them into unhealthy and potentially life-threatening addiction before they have achieved the maturity necessary to make an informed decision whether to take up smoking despite its health risks.

The firm of Milberg, Weiss, Bershad, Hynes & Lerach co-counseled with Mangini and engaged RJR and its advertising agencies in discovery regarding the design and implementation of the Joe Camel campaign. Several million pages of documents were produced by defendants and reviewed by plaintiff's counsel. In addition, more than one hundred informal interviews and a number of depositions of RJR's outside advertising executives, internal marketing personnel, and research and development personnel were conducted in preparation for the December 1997 trial date. In May 1997 the City and County of San Francisco, together with the cities of Los Angeles and San Jose and ten other California counties intervened in the suit to help end the Joe Camel campaign. As the trial date neared, RJR approached the plaintiffs to determine whether the

Mangini action could be resolved if the campaign was pulled. RJR terminated the campaign and settled the case, stating that the "Mangini action . . . was an early significant and unique driver of the overall legal and social controversy regarding underage smoking that led to the decision to phase out the Joe Camel Campaign." A second important component of the settlement provided for the public release of RJR's confidential documents about youth marketing and the Joe Camel campaign. The approximately 100,000 pages of RJR documents available through the TCA Web site are now publicly available as a result of the settlement. In addition, the Web site provides an overview of *A Review of R.J. Reynolds' Internal Documents Produced in Mangini v. R.J. Reynolds Tobacco Company, Civil Number 939359—The Case That Rid California and the American Landscape of "Joe Camel."*

The California Documents from the Minnesota Repository are a fraction of some 40 million pages of tobacco industry documents currently held at the State of Minnesota Depository. The depository was created as a result of a successful suit by the attorney general of Minnesota, Hubert Humphrey III, and Blue Cross/Blue Shield of Minnesota against the seven major American tobacco companies. The suit was settled in 1998. The documents provide insight into industry plans to weaken enforcement of and support for California's 1995 smoke-free workplace legislation, AB 13; industry efforts to form a network of groups to present the tobacco industry position in order to create the sense of a grassroots movement; how well the industry understood the political nature of the anti-tobacco challenge; and how quickly the industry moved to engage the American Medical Association, the Western Center for Law and Poverty, and other groups to undermine the California tobacco-control program, which was funded by the 1988 passage of Proposition 99.

Use of the B & W Collection was especially high during and after the following events. In October 1995 the CBS television news program "60 Minutes" aired a story about the tobacco industry, which included an interview with Jeffrey Wigand, an industry whistle-blower. Use was again high in April 1996, the month in which the paperback version of *The Cigarette Papers* was published. Internet access to the documents rose steadily after the August 1996 resolution of the class-action suit *Grady Carter v. the Brown and Williamson Tobacco Corporation.* Use of the collection was also high during the negotiation of the Tobacco Settlement Agreement during the period of April to June 1997. Interest in the documents rose significantly between May and November 1998, during the U.S. Congress's consideration of tobacco industry legislation and the ultimate establishment of the Master Settlement Agreement. Use peaked again during the period prior to the U. S. Supreme Court's decision on the Federal Drug Administration's jurisdiction to regulate the tobacco industry in March 2000.

Internet reference use has been enormous, and it would have been impossible to successfully meet the demand in a traditional, supervised reading-room environment where staffing is minimal. The library's infrastructure and technical expertise to scan the collection and post it on the Internet provided a solution to the access problem. At the same time it must be recognized that the availability of the B & W Collection on the Internet has no doubt dramatically increased the collection's exposure and reference use.

THE IMPACT ON THE NATION

The release of the B & W Collection to the public has had a significant impact on the nation. The public availability of the documents has generated intense debate about the nature of corporate accountability and individual responsibility. The accessibility of the documents has served as the catalyst for tobacco litigation, promoted the development of government policy, and ignited the battle against control of information. Class-action suits, individual smoker lawsuits, and states' reimbursement suits against the tobacco industry have proliferated as litigants now have the information that was hidden for so long by the tobacco corporations. The B&W Collection has proven to be very important evidence in these suits. These previously hidden documents provided concrete evidence that could no longer be diluted by misleading tobacco industry public relations efforts. The papers in this collection reveal three important facts about the industry and about tobacco: first, that research conducted by the tobacco companies into the harmful health effects of tobacco was often more advanced than studies by the medical community; second, that through that research, executives at B & W were aware in the early 1960s that tobacco use is causally related to lung cancer and heart disease and that nicotine is addictive; third, that this research was hidden from the courts by laundering the research data through legal departments and resisting its release by invoking the principle of attorney–client privilege and by restricting public statements by scientists and affiliated companies outside the United States. These facts would fuel discussions about tobacco industry accountability and about the regulatory process of the three branches of the U.S. government.

New York Times reporter Philip J. Hilts wrote, "the natural end for a tangle like the tobacco wars is in court."[23] Class-action suits, individual smoker lawsuits, and states' reimbursement suits against the tobacco industry have proliferated now that litigants have the information that was hidden for so long by the tobacco corporations. The B & W Collection has proven to be very important evidence in these suits, as have documents made available by former employees of the R.J. Reynolds Tobacco Corporation and Philip Morris and information made available by executives of the Liggett Group. Represented by more than sixty law firms, the class-action suit *Castano v. American Tobacco Company*, Civil Action No. 94–1044, was filed on March 19, 1994 in the U.S. district court, eastern district of Louisiana. This action sought "damages from the tobacco companies only for the somewhat ambiguous injury of nicotine addiction."[24] In addition, the complaint charged the eight named defendants—the American Tobacco Company; the Philip Morris Companies, Inc. (the nation's largest tobacco company and maker of the most successful brand, Marlboro); the R.J.

Reynolds Company (the second-largest manufacturer and the maker of Camels); B & W; Lorillard, Inc.; the Liggett Group; the United States Tobacco Company (the biggest maker of snuff); and BATUS, Inc. (onetime owner of the Kentucky-based B & W)—with engaging in "fraud and deceit by misrepresenting that nicotine is nonaddictive; were negligent in not accurately describing their products; violated consumer protection statutes; breached an express warranty that their products were fit for consumption; and caused intentional, emotional distress on those who smoked their cigarettes."[25] The suit sought compensatory and punitive damages for each addicted smoker in the country. In an unexpected turn of events, the Liggett Group, the smallest of the U.S. tobacco companies, offered in March 1996 to settle with four of the five state suits in the Castano class-action suit. The four largest tobacco manufacturers filed suit against the Liggett Group, and in March 1997 a judge issued a restraining order blocking dissemination of the information. In May 1996, prior to this judgment, the appeals court decided against the Castano plaintiffs because of the unwieldy definition of class in the case, and because variations in state law could swamp common issues. Almost immediately, the plaintiffs filed separate state class-action suits in more than a dozen states currently in litigation.

In August 1996 B & W lost an individual-smoker suit in Florida when the jury awarded U.S. $750,000 in damages to smoker Grady Carter. A report in the *New England Journal of Medicine* stated "lung cancer had developed in the 65 year old Carter after he had been smoking for forty-three years. The jury found that B & W had failed to properly warn Carter of the risks of smoking before law required the warning labels."[26] The primary evidence used against them were documents from the B & W Collection, and the jury was convinced that the company knew that smoking was harmful and should have informed the public about the addictiveness of nicotine. The transcript of the case has been posted on the World Wide Web with hypertext links to the documents in the B & W Collection that were cited in the evidence.

In 1994 and 1995, Mississippi, Minnesota, West Virginia, and Florida filed lawsuits in state court against the tobacco industry to secure reimbursement for health care expenditures for ailments arising from tobacco use. They were shortly joined in their endeavor by forty-one other states. Led by Hubert "Skip" Humphrey III and Mike Moore, the state attorneys general negotiated a settlement with tobacco industry attorneys between April and June 1997. The landmark agreement, which would settle all pending class-action suits and other pending actions by states against the tobacco industry, was announced to the American public on June 20, 1997. It "promis[ed] to change the way cigarettes are marketed, to provide U.S. $368.5 billion over twenty-five years to compensate states for the costs of treating smoking-related illness, to finance nationwide anti-smoking programs and to underwrite health care for millions of uninsured children. Because the settlement proposal needed to bind all fifty states, it had to be drafted and enacted in the form of Congressional legislation in order to give it the force of law."[27] The settlement was presented to Congress on June 26, 1997.

Congressional leadership, both Democrats and Republicans, perceived the tobacco settlement proposal as complex and believed leadership from President Clinton would be required to make it law. On September 17, 1997, President Clinton outlined five broad principles to serve as the basis of legislation, but he did not formally endorse the proposal. The five principles were a combination of industry payments and penalties to reduce youth smoking by raising the price of cigarettes by up to U.S. $1.50 a pack; full authority for the FDA to regulate tobacco products; a voluntary ban on advertising to youth; legislation for broad disclosure of industry files; and moves to reduce secondhand smoke and to protect tobacco farmers and their communities. Clinton "made no mention of U. S. tobacco sales abroad . . . the fastest-growing markets and the key to the industry's long-term profitability . . . about 1.1 billion people smoke . . . about one-fifth of the world's population."[28] The World Health Organization has documented that smoking is declining in developed countries by 1.4 percent annually, but in the developing nations it is increasing by 1.7 percent a year.

Stemming from the president's agenda, many legislative bills were introduced codifying provisions of the tobacco settlement and introducing alternative proposals. A bipartisan bill sponsored by Senators John McCain, Slade Gorton, John Breaux, and Ernest Hollings became the chief platform on which the tobacco settlement was debated in the U.S. Senate. The McCain bill was stronger than the June 20 settlement agreement in many ways. The bill required the tobacco industry to pay "[U.S.] $516 billion over twenty-five years to help states and the federal government bear the medical costs of smoking-related illness; raised cigarette taxes by $1.10 per pack over five years; [enabled] the Food and Drug Administration to regulate the tobacco industry; and drastically [reduced] cigarette marketing, advertising and promotion."[29] In April 1998 tobacco industry attorneys announced the company's withdrawal of support for the congressional legislation, aggressively painting the bill as a tax-and-spend proposal. The tactic apparently worked, because on June 17, 1998, the Senate failed twice on procedural votes to advance the bill to a final Senate floor vote. Ultimately the tobacco industry attorneys and the state attorneys general achieved individual financial settlements for the states of Minnesota, Mississippi, Florida, and Texas and a deal, known as the Master Settlement Agreement, was struck to settle the remaining thirty-seven pending state cases on November 23, 1998.

The U.S. Food and Drug Administration (FDA) proposed regulating tobacco as a drug, because of the pharmacological nature of nicotine, previously denied by the tobacco industry. On August 28, 1996, the U.S. Food and Drug Administration (FDA) asserted jurisdiction over cigarettes and smokeless tobacco under the Federal Food, Drug and Cosmetic Act. Under this act a product is a drug or device subject to FDA jurisdiction if it is intended to affect the structure or function of the body. The FDA determined the pharmacological effects of tobacco are intended because newly disclosed evidence from tobacco manufacturers has revealed that the "manufacturers know that nicotine causes pharmacological effects, including addiction, and design their products to provide pharmacologically active doses of nicotine. The FDA thus concluded that cigarettes and smokeless tobacco are subject to FDA jurisdiction because they contain a 'drug,' nicotine, and a 'device' for delivering this drug to the body."[30] Because of the TCA, the evidence and scientific information are available to prove that nicotine is an addictive drug and that tobacco smoking is detrimental to the health of both smokers and passive smokers.

Although controversial, this jurisdiction of tobacco was upheld in federal district court in North Carolina when, on April 24, 1997, Judge William L. Osteen, Sr., ruled that the FDA has the power to regulate tobacco as a drug. These regulations were signed by President Clinton, and they declared nicotine to be an addictive drug and imposed a variety of restrictions on advertising tobacco products, including prohibiting the sale of cigarettes or smokeless tobacco to persons under eighteen, requiring anyone under the age of twenty-seven seeking to buy tobacco products to show a picture identification, and limiting vending-machine cigarette sales to adults-only locations such as bars. Reversing the decision of the lower court, the U.S. Supreme Court ruled 5–4 on March 21, 2000, that the Food and Drug Administration lacks the power to regulate tobacco products, granting a huge legal victory to the tobacco industry. Writing the majority opinion for the bench, Justice Sandra Day O'Connor stated that "by no means do we question the seriousness of the problem that tobacco use, particularly among children and adolescents, poses the single most significant threat to public health in the United States. [But] it is plain that Congress has not given the FDA the authority that it seeks to exercise here."[31] Speaking for the dissenters, Judge David Breyer wrote that "the 1938 federal Food, Drug and Cosmetic Act's basic purpose—the protection of the public's health—supports the inclusion of cigarettes within its scope . . . addiction, sedation and weight loss are precisely the kinds of product effects that the FDA typically reviews and controls."[32] A major setback for the Clinton Administration's campaign to curb teenage smoking, it seems unlikely that Congress will consider new legislation in the area for several reasons, including the failure to pass Senator McCain's tobacco legislation in 1998 and because of the Master Settlement Agreement between the states' attorneys general and the tobacco industry. However, the ruling limiting the authority of the FDA did not affect either the scores of lawsuits brought by local governments seeking to recover medical costs attributed to tobacco use or the civil actions by private individuals claiming health damages.

The *New York Times, Wall Street Journal*, the *Washington Post*, the *Journal of the American Medical Association*, the ABC and CBS television networks, and the University of California have all successfully released information to the public about the industry since the availability of the B & W Collection. Media news coverage has focused on the use of fear of litigation to suppress stories about the adverse effects of tobacco use and stories about the tobacco industry's campaign of misinformation and manipulation of the political process. The B & W story has been covered extensively by all forms of media, such as the

Chronicle of Higher Education, the *Los Angeles Times, Mother Jones* magazine, the *Nation, Frontline,* and *60 Minutes.*

IMPACT ON THE ARCHIVAL PROFESSION

Archivists have also been affected by the availability of the documents. Despite negative e-mails such as one from a Texas law student claiming that our actions have led him to become a corporate lawyer devoted to defending poor hapless big industry against evil criminals like ourselves, the overwhelming public response has been positive. For example, in an e-mail message received on Wednesday, August 14, 1996: "I think that information concerning the dangers of tobacco or any other drug or product should be given to the general public. I do not believe that any manufacturer should be allowed to simply conceal important information about any product. In other words, the court was justified in its decision to deny a restraining order against UCSF." Another message the same day said, "My cheers and praise to those person(s)! With thanks from a non-smoker, who, along with most of the US, believed for years that the tobacco companies were lying and covering up information . . . and these documents tell the truth! At last."

The TCA staff announced the availability of the collection on the Archives and Archivists Listserv, an Internet discussion group in July 1995. During the subsequent three weeks, archivists discussed, often heatedly, issues arising from the release of the documents. Topics of discussion included the impact of the documents' availability on repositories collecting business records; corporate archives retention schedules; the destruction of sensitive materials and corporate liability issues; the provenance of copied documents in faculty files; property rights versus intellectual property rights; the problem of accepting stolen documents; a comparison with the Pentagon Papers Case and the responsibility of archives to make information available to the public; academic freedom and freedom of speech; and the tension between the archival profession's avoidance of political advocacy and the profession's responsibility to promote the public's right to know.

The archival staff at the UCSF Library and CKM followed the Archives and Archivists Listserv debates with interest and concern. Our professional colleagues offered many varied opinions about our decision to release the documents. The TCA had received the research files of a prominent UCSF faculty member active in the development of tobacco-control policy. The documents were photocopies that had been organized and indexed by a scholar in the course of his research, and the archives maintained that order in making the photocopies available to other researchers, while the original documents remained in the possession of their creators. While cognizant of the listserv discussions and appreciative of the comments, it was clear that the UCSF Archives and Special Collections had followed the core mission of an archival repository within a college and university, which includes "serving as a resource and laboratory to stimulate and nourish creative teaching and learning as well as serving research and scholarship by making available and encouraging the use of its collections by members of the institution and the community at large."[33]

Looking beyond the debates of the Archives and Archivists Listserv, the B & W Collection prompts considerations worthy of future discussion by the archival profession. The availability of the B & W Collection on the Internet dramatically illustrates how the juxtaposition of information about the recent past with widespread and instant access can facilitate immediate public action. Archivists are applying appraisal theories such as documentation strategy and documentation planning to the preservation of records recently created. The UCSF Archives and Special Collections uses these appraisal theories in the collection and preservation of records concerning AIDS, biotechnology, and tobacco control. While the majority of records appraised remain in paper format, in time many of these contemporary records will be created primarily in electronic formats. In the case of the AIDS and biotechnology projects, these projects document subjects in which protecting confidentiality is of great concern, because the materials can contain information about patient's health-care treatment or patent licensing subject to litigation. Simultaneously the department is engaged in efforts to foster access to these materials either through selectively scanning documents consciously protecting confidentiality and privacy, or by participating in efforts to provide digital finding aids through the California Digital Library's Online Archive of California (OAC).

Archivists working within this emerging electronic environment must give serious thought to issues of confidentiality, privacy, and the proprietary nature of information, as well as to the exposure created by instant global access. Mary Jo Pugh noted that our finding aids, created mainly as tools for our physical management of collections, all too frequently "tend to capture only the order, not the substance, of the records." Pugh highlighted the extent to which our access systems of the time (before the advent of the World Wide Web) relied heavily on the mediation of an archivist to assist end users in translating their subject-based queries into our provenance-based descriptions.[34] Archivists have taken their rightful place at the information-age table, but the space and time buffer between collection and user, and hence our ability to mediate, is rapidly collapsing.

The Internet is a tool that can readily provide a solution to the difficulties of making records available for research, as it has with the B & W Collection, but will the use of this tool affect how we appraise contemporary records? To preserve privacy and confidentiality in a digital environment, will archivists choose to devalue certain records and destroy them, or choose to make access restrictions greater and thereby virtually eliminate access? Increasingly the tools of the Internet and the format of electronic records will be important in how archivists approach their work and how they perceive their responsibilities to their institutions and their profession. Archivists must, however, keep in mind that the challenges to access presented by these new information technologies also hold technical solutions. For example, electronic methods can mask specific identities while at the same time supplying general information about individuals for research use. When appraising, accepting, organizing, and providing access to materials in a paper environment or an electronic one, archivists must strive to maintain an even balance between their institutional and professional responsibilities to protect privacy and preserve confidentiality with the public's right of access to vital information. Enhanced information delivery through the Internet will magnify the impact of our decisions, but archivists must seek creative technological solutions to balance the availability of information with the right of privacy.

ARCHIVISTS' CONCLUSIONS

The UCSF Library and CKM archival program has striven to balance institutional responsibilities to serve the University of California community and professional archival responsibilities with the public's right to know by making the B & W Collection available for research. Internet access to information supports the mission of the library and the archives to provide more health science information to the university community and the public. One of an archivist's most important responsibilities is to make primary source material available to the public. Prior to their release on the Internet, the information contained in the B & W Collection was already being made available to the public as excerpts filtered though news media analysis and congressional committee investigations. The documents had become part of the public domain and were no longer confidential material subject to an archivist's responsibility to respect that confidentiality. Given the gravity of the revelations about the tobacco industry, access to full text of the B & W Collection was essential for informed public debate and long-term policy development within our democratic society.

In addition, the B & W Collection was a litmus test for the advantages of providing access to archival primary source material on the Internet. It has shown the difference that archivists can make in allowing access to information that will benefit the public and the solutions that Internet access provides for limited archival staffing and minimal funding. In this case, the release of the B & W Collection has greatly contributed to public revelations about the tobacco industry and the subsequent development of national health policy during the Clinton presidency. The posting of these documents on the Internet, their usage, and their subsequent impact have affirmed the power of information and the important role archives continue to play in making information available. It also confirms that the Internet is a powerful distributor of information that can circumvent traditional publication formats to reach a globally distributed public.

Finally, *Brown and Williamson v. University of California* litigation did not create new case law on the Internet. It did, however, emphasize that the Internet provides libraries and archives with the ability to make important information widely available in a manner clearly protected by the same constitutional rights that protect newspaper publication and introduced the prior restraint argument to the Web environment.

EPILOGUE

On January 31, 2001, UCSF publicly announced that the American Legacy Foundation (ALF) had granted U.S. $15 million to the campus to establish the National Tobacco Documents Library (NTDL). The funding from ALF (created in March 1999 as part of the Master Settlement Agreement) establishes a permanent Internet source based at the UCSF Library of more than 40 million pages of tobacco industry documents and the development of a research center for the study of the material. The 40 million pages of once-secret documents were made publicly available through the successful suit by Attorney General Hubert Humphrey III of Minnesota and Blue Cross/Blue Shield of Minnesota against the seven major American tobacco companies. The case settlement resulted in the creation of a tobacco industry–supported document depository and an Internet site of the 40 million pages of documents available until the year 2010. However, no permanent support was mandated beyond 2010 by the lawsuit. The ALF endowment has enabled the UCSF Library to permanently provide access to the 40 million pages of digital resources that were only temporarily available through the tobacco industry Web site. This new material will complement and enhance the existing archival collections forming the TCA. As noted in a news story on the new research center, the center "will expand on the tobacco-control research already underway by eighteen faculty at UCSF by promoting further study of tobacco-related documents, train scholars in the field, . . . [and] play a key role in educating community groups on the tobacco industry's advertising practices and aggressive marketing to children and minority groups."[35] On a complementary path, pioneering efforts are now underway to facilitate scholarly publication about the tobacco industry documents. In July 2001 the California Digital Library eScholarship program held its first meeting to discuss the establishment of a digital repository for new tobacco and tobacco-control research. eScholarship is dedicated to facilitating scholarly communication, especially experiments in alternative production and dissemination of scholarship. The increasing availability of tobacco industry documents through the UCSF Library and CKM Web site will likely stimulate a rise in tobacco research, increasing the need for efficient and expedient publishing mechanisms.

In 1994 the UCSF Library and CKM established the TCA as a program within the Archives and Special Collections Department. Within a year, the archives had opened a Pandora's box of tobacco documents from B & W, unleashing a chain of public health events that continue to unfold across the nation and the globe. In 1995 the World Wide Web was just two years old. Government, businesses, and educational institutions were exploring the Internet's uses, but the idea of providing a significant research collection online was largely untested. Today organizations such as the California Digital Library are committing resources to building significant online digital collections to support research, teaching, and education. The release of the B & W Collection on the Internet enabled journalists, public health officials, scientists, legislators, lawyers, and the public to discover, analyze, and judge the business practices of the tobacco industry and consider issues of corporate accountability. This has enabled the launch of public debate in Congress; the engagement of the executive branch in policy formation; and consideration by the courts of issues related to the best means to provide for the public's safety. In the course of these discussions, actions, and deliberations, additional significant discoveries were made with the release of increasing volumes of tobacco industry documents.

The administration of George W. Bush is currently preparing the next chapter in the federal government's regulation of the tobacco industry. On June 19, 2001, Attorney General John Ashcroft stated publicly that the Department of Justice's (DOJ) case against Big Tobacco might be weak. Previously, during fall 2000, federal district court judge Gladys Kessler permitted the DOJ to proceed against the tobacco industry for violating the Racketeer Influenced and Corrupt Organizations (RICO) Act. As this essay goes to press, the Bush Administration is considering action to pardon the tobacco industry, effectively safeguarding the industry from any further federal litigation.[36]

Professor Stanton Glantz displays the framed quotes of two philosophers on the wall of his UCSF office: Machiavelli and Kermit the Frog. In 1513 Machiavelli wrote, "and it ought to be remembered that there is nothing more difficult to take in hand, more perilous to conduct, or more uncertain in its success, than to take the lead in the introduction of a new order to things. Because the inventor has for enemies all those who have done well under the old conditions, and lukewarm defenders in those who may do well under the new ... thus it happens that whenever those who are hostile have the opportunity to attack they do it as partisans, whilst the others defend lukewarmly." In 1993 Kermit the Frog stated, "Life's like a movie. Write your own ending. Keep believing, keep pretending." Without a doubt, the battle will rage on. Public health advocates will strive to protect the citizenry from the hazards of smoking and the tobacco industry will counter with strategies to withhold and manipulate information about their products and internal processes.

APPENDIX: ATTORNEY-CLIENT PRIVILEGE

Along with an independent judiciary, the sacrosanctness of the confidential relationship between a lawyer and his or her client are bastions of an ordered liberty. Yet the protection from compelled disclosure accorded to the attorney-client relationship is predicated upon the tacit assumption that lawyers are consulted for the purpose of abiding by rather than in order to devise means to break the law. As the fundamental trust that a society reposes in lawyers, rightly or wrongly, erodes, so too will erode the protection afforded by the attorney-client privilege.

The attorney-client privilege is the oldest of the testimonial privileges protecting confidential communications. It was accepted as early as the reign of Elizabeth I. The purpose of the privilege was to prevent the attorney from being required to take an oath and testify against his client. It was then considered that such testimony against one to whom loyalty was owed would violate the attorney's honor as a gentleman. Accordingly, the attorney, rather than the client, held and asserted the privilege. See J. Wigmore, *Evidence* (McNaughton rev., 1961): §2290 at 542–543.

Today the privilege is the prerogative of the client. The client, not the lawyer, holds the privilege. The client has the ultimate authority to raise or to waive the privilege. An attorney may not testify about communications made by a client unless released by the client. The practical consequence of the privilege is that there can be neither compelled nor voluntary disclosure by the attorney of matters conveyed to the attorney in confidence by a client for the purpose of seeking legal advice. Thus the privilege exists as a privilege against testimonial compulsion of the attorney in respect to matters conveyed to the attorney by the client and no testimonial compulsion of the client on matters communicated to the attorney for the purpose of seeking the attorney's legal counsel. In practice, the privilege is strictly construed. In practice that means that not everything conveyed by a client to an attorney is immune from subsequent compelled disclosure in civil litigation or from a grand jury subpoena in the criminal context. Many communications that clients and attorneys like to believe will be privileged are not.

The rationale that today justifies the privilege is that information is given in confidence to an attorney by a client so that the attorney may give reasonably informed professional advice. If a client is concerned that what is told the attorney will return to haunt the client, necessary information will be withheld and legal advice will be predicated on half-truths. Disclosure that is made will be made with an unquiet mind. Legal advice designed to urge voluntary compliance with the law would be thwarted.

Fisher v. United States, 425 U.S. 391, 403 (1976) states "As a practical matter, if the client knows that damaging information could more readily be obtained from the attorney following disclosure than from himself in the absence of disclosure, the client would be reluctant to confide in his lawyer and it would be difficult to obtain fully informed legal advice."

Hunt v. Blackburn, 128 U.S. 464, 470 (1888) states "The rule which places the seal of secrecy upon communications between client and attorney is founded upon the necessity, in the interest and administration of justice, of the aid of persons having knowledge of the law and skilled in its practice, which assistance can only be safely and readily availed of when free from the consequences or the apprehension of disclosure."

Although today the privilege is the prerogative of the client, nonetheless as the legal expert, it is the attorney who is necessarily the guardian of the client's privilege. It is the attorney who must advise the client when the privilege exists and counsel the client to assert the privilege. It is the attorney who is called upon to review documents to make sure that privileged ones are not inadvertently disclosed.

The practical consequence of the privilege is that there can be neither compelled nor voluntary disclosure by the attorney of matters conveyed to the attorney in confidence by a client for the purpose of seeking legal advice. Thus the privilege is a privilege against testimonial compulsion of the attorney in respect to matters conveyed to the attorney by the client. Nor can the client in most instances be compelled to disclose what has been conveyed to the attorney for the purpose of seeking the attorney's legal counsel. Thus the privilege tends in most instances to be a two-way street, protecting from compelled disclosure what is said or written to or by an attorney to the client for the purpose of seeking legal counsel. See Edna Selan Epstein, *The Attorney-Client Privilege and the Work-Product Doctrine*, 4th ed. (Chicago, Ill.: American Bar Association, 2001).

NOTES

1. The authors would like to acknowledge the contributions of several individuals in the preparation of this article. They are Lisa Bero (professor of clinical pharmacy, UCSF), Karen Butter (university librarian, UCSF), Catherine Candee (director of scholarly initiatives, CDL), Stanton Glantz (professor of cardiology, UCSF), William Landis (manuscripts librarian, UC–Irvine), and Christopher Patti (general counsel, University of California Office of the President). In addition, they would like to thank Waverly Lowell and Michael and Max Manga for their patience and support during the process.

2. Peter Pringle, *Cornered: Big Tobacco at the Bar of Justice* (New York: Henry Holt, 1998), p. 309.

3. Electronic mail correspondence from Lisa Bero to Robin Chandler, Apr. 18, 2001.

4. Copyright is a form of protection provided by the laws of the United States (title 17, U.S. Code) to the authors of "original works of authorship," including literary, dramatic, musical, artistic, and certain other intellectual works. This protection is available to both published and unpublished works. Section 106 of the 1976 Copyright Act generally gives the owner of copyright the exclusive right to do and to authorize others to do the following: reproduce the work in copies; prepare derivative works based upon the work; distribute copies of the work to the public by sale or other transfer of ownership, or by rental, lease, or lending; perform the work publicly, in the case of literary, musical, dramatic, and choreographic works, pantomimes, and motion pictures and other audiovisual works; display the copyrighted work publicly, in the case of literary, musical, dramatic, and choreographic works, pantomimes, and pictorial, graphic, or sculptural works, including the individual images of a motion picture or other audiovisual work. See U.S. Copyright Office, *Copyright Basics.* Available at loc.gov/copyright/circs/circ1.html#wci.

5. Matt Siegel, "University Counsel Battles Brown and Williamson over Tobacco Documents," *American Lawyer* (July 1995): 48.

6. Stanton A. Glantz, et al., *The Cigarette Papers* (Berkeley: University of California Press, 1996), p. 235.

7. Ibid., p. 236.

8. UCSF Library and CKM, Brown and Williamson Collection, #1824.01. Memorandum from J.K. Wells to E. Pepples, "Procedure for Handling BAT Scientific Documents," Nov. 9, 1979.

9. UCSF Library and CKM, Brown and Williamson Collection, #1835.01. Memorandum from J.K. Wells to file, "Document Retention," Jan. 17, 1985.

10. Prior restraint literally means prior to publication, but in practice it is about censorship. Alerted that an event is going to happen, a temporary restraining order is obtained to stop the event, which in this case is to stop publication. Petra Reinecke, attorney-at-law, San Francisco, CA, personal communication.

11. "Judge Says Library May Display Brown and Williamson Documents," *Mealeys Litigation Reports: Toxic Tort* 4 (No. 6, June 16, 1995).

12. Ibid.

13. Glantz et al., *Cigarette Papers*, p. 10.

14. "California Supreme Court Denies Stay of Release of B & W Documents," *Tobacco Industry Litigation Reporter*, July 3, 1995, p. 13.

15. Pringle, *Cornered*, p. 75.

16. Fonds: A term widely used in Europe to designate for control purposes the archives of a particular type of institution or organization. Archival education programs use this term in close association with the term *provenance*. Provenance in archival theory is the principle that archives of a given record creator must not be intermingled with those of other record creators. The principle is often frequently referred to by the French expression, *respect des fonds*. A corollary, frequently designated as a separate principle, is the principle of sanctity of the original order (or respect *pour l'ordre primitif*). See Richard Lytle, ed., *Management of Archives and Manuscript Collections for Librarians* (Chicago: Society of American Archivists, 1980), p. 117.

17. Glantz et al., *Cigarette Papers*, p. 58.

18. UCSF Library and CKM, Brown and Williamson Collection, #1200.01. C. Haselbach and O. Libert, *A Tentative Hypothesis on Nicotine Addiction* (London: BAT, 1963).

19. Glantz et al., *Cigarette Papers*, p. 70.

20. UCSF Library and CKM, Brown and Williamson Collection, #1200.12. Cable from A. Yeaman to A. McCormick, July 3, 1963.

21. UCSF Library and CKM, Brown and Williamson Collection, #1840.01. Letter from D. Hardy to D. Bryant, Aug. 20, 1970.

22. The OAC union database (available at oac.cdlib.org) comprises more than 5,800 finding aids using the EAD document type definition (DTD). EAD is an encoding standard developed to create machine-readable finding aids. EAD allows for the presentation of extensive and interrelated information, preserve hierarchical relationships between levels of description, allows for navigating within the hierarchical information structure of the finding aid, and supports element-specific indexing and retrieval. See Sharon Gibbs Thibodeau, "Development of the EAD Document Type Definition" (1995), available at lcweb.loc.gov/ead/eadback.html.

23. Philip J. Hilts, *Smoke Screen: the Truth Behind the Tobacco Industry Cover-up* (Reading, Mass.: Addison-Wesley, 1996), p. 195.

24. George J. Annas, "Tobacco Litigation As Cancer Prevention: Dealing with the Devil," *New England Journal of Medicine* 336 (Jan. 23, 1997): 304.

25. Pringle, *Cornered*, p. 52.

26. Annas, "Tobacco Litigation," p. 306.

27. John M. Broder, "Cigarette Makers in a $368 Billion Accord," *New York Times*, June 26, 1997, p. 1.

28. Pringle, *Cornered*, p. 314.

29. Tobacco Control Resource Center, *The Multistate Master Settlement Agreement and the Future of State and Local Tobacco Control: An Analysis of Selected Topics and Provisions of the Multistate Master Settlement Agreement of November 23, 1998* (Boston: Tobacco Control Resource Center, Northeastern University School of Law, March 24, 1999), p. 5.

30. David Kessler et al., "The Legal and Scientific Basis for FDA's Assertion of Jurisdiction over Cigarettes and Smokeless Tobacco," *Journal of the American Medical Association (JAMA)* 277 (Feb. 5, 1997): 405.

31. "Justices Void Tobacco Rules: Unanimous on Health Threat, Court Splits on Whether FDA Had Authority," *San Francisco Chronicle*, Mar. 22, 2000, p. A1.

32. Ibid., p. A13.

33. *Guidelines for College and University Archives* (Chicago: Society of American Archivists, 1979), p. 2.

34. Mary Jo Pugh, "The Illusion of Omniscience: Subject Access and the Reference Archivist," *American Archivist* 45 (Winter 1982): 34. Cited in Bill Landis, "Virtual Archives and Description Standards." Presentation at the RBMS Annual Conference, June 13, 2001.

35. Tanya Schevitz, "Central Spot for Tobacco Papers: UCSF to Offer Public Access to Them on the Web," *San Francisco Chronicle*, Feb. 1, 2001, p. A13.

36. Richard Daynard, "DOJ Takes a Risk: Bush Administration Prepares to Grant to Tobacco Industry a Pardon for Past Misconduct" (Boston: Tobacco Control Research Center, June 19, 2001). Available at tobacco.neu.edu/PR/Backgrounders/dojsettle.htm.

BIBLIOGRAPHY OF INTERNET SITES

Carter v. Brown & Williamson. Available at bottary.com/tobacco_menu.htm.
eScholarship Tobacco Control Repository. Available at escholarship.cdlib.org/.
Frontline. Available at pbs.org/wgbh/pages/frontline/smoke/.
Journal of the American Medical Association (JAMA). Available at ama-assn.org/public/journals/jama/jamahome.htm.
Tobacco Control Archives. Available at library.ucsf.edu/tobacco.
The Cigarette Papers. Available at library.ucsf.edu/tobacco/cigpapers/.
Tobacco War: Inside the California Battles. Available at escholarship.cdlib.org/ucpress/tobacco-war.xml.
UCSF Library & Center for Knowledge Management (CKM). Available at library.ucsf.edu/tobacco.

MEMORY

The Tuskegee Syphilis Study and the Politics of Memory

Tywanna Whorley

For African Americans, the collective past is always present. More important, remembering historical events or experiences, specifically the institution of slavery, the Civil-Rights Movement, or where you were the day Martin Luther King, Jr., delivered his "I Have a Dream" speech, tend to blur "the boundaries of the personal and the public, the individual and the collective."[1] The boundaries tend to blur even more when memories recall acts of violence, brutality, and exploitation, such as lynchings, race riots, and being used as guinea pigs.[2]

The Tuskegee Syphilis Study provides an opportunity to explore how this experience has refined the politics of memory by using governmental archives, interviews, museums, and public policy to continue to hold a government accountable for its actions. This underscores how a community's memory can function as a mechanism to ensure accountability. Paul Antze and Michael Lambek state that "memory has found a prominent place in politics, both as a source of authority and as a means of attack."[3] In the case of the Tuskegee Syphilis Study, remembering has taken on several meanings, which tend to overlap one another. For example, blaming and holding those responsible, legitimizing the experiences of the participants, all while continuing to heal. In a study of memory, David Thelen states, "the struggle for possession and interpretation of memory is rooted among the conflict and interplay of social, political, and cultural interests and values in the present."[4] Former president Bill Clinton's formal apology on behalf of the government underscores how the Tuskegee Syphilis Study continues up to the present to be a high-profile and controversial incident. This essay will discuss how archives, museums, and interviews are used as vehicles for remembering the Tuskegee Syphilis Study. These mechanisms provide insight into how the Tuskegee Syphilis Study came about, the involvement of the U.S. government, how the participants and their families cope with this tragedy, and how the "study" continues to shape collective memory, from the creation of a museum dedicated to the experiments to influencing public policy on human experimentation, especially for federally funded projects.

BACKGROUND OF THE TUSKEGEE SYPHILIS STUDY

In 1928 the director of medical service for the Julius Rosenwald Fund, a Chicago-based philanthropy, approached representatives of the U.S. Public Health Service (PHS) to discuss ways to improve the health of African Americans in the South. At that time, the PHS had just completed a study of the prevalence of syphilis among more than 2,000 African American employees of the Delta Pine and Land Company of Mississippi. Twenty-five percent of the sample had tested positive for syphilis, and the PHS and the Rosenwald Fund worked together in treating these individuals. This arrangement led to the expansion of the treatment program to five counties in the South. Macon County, Alabama, was one of the sites that reported between 35 and 40 percent of all age groups testing positive for this disease.[5] Before the treatment phase of the project could be implemented, the Great Depression came, causing the Rosenwald Fund to withdraw financially. Without the financial support of this philanthropic organization, the PHS could not carry out the treatment program.[6]

At the same time, there was a debate festering among health researchers about racial differences in the effects of syphilis. Instead of ending the program, Taliaferro Clark, head of the PHS, decided to continue. Clark felt the treatment project could be salvaged by conducting a prospective study on the effects of untreated syphilis on living subjects, "the longest nontherapeutic experiment on human beings in medical history."[7] Although much was known about the natural history of syphilis, Clark wanted to know more about the effects of the disease on African Americans. At the time, there was no empirical knowledge about whether syphilis affected African Americans differently from whites. Clark realized that here was a "ready-made situation . . . for carrying on the proposed study" of the impacts of untreated syphilis on African Americans.[8] The PHS enlisted the support of the Tuskegee Institute, where the John A. Andrew Memorial Hospital was established. Since the Tuskegee Institute had a history of service to local African Americans, its participation guaranteed the execution of the experiment. In return, Tuskegee Institute received money, training for its interns, and employment for its nurses. In addition, the PHS solicited help from church and community leaders and plantation owners to encourage participation.

The fact that most African Americans of that time lived outside the world of modern medicine resulted in a willingness on the part of black men to participate in the study. For many who participated, the examination by the PHS physician was the first medical examination they had ever received. In addition, the participants received free examinations, food, transportation, and a fifty-dollar burial stipend. The stipend also proved to include an agreement between the deceased participant and his family granting the right to perform a postmortem examination.[9] The study included 399 men infected with syphilis and a control group of 201 not infected with the disease. The infected men were never told that they had syphilis. They were merely told that they had "bad blood." Throughout the "study," the men never received any kind of formal treatment for their disease. With the cooperation of state and local physicians, the researchers managed to prevent these men from receiving any kind of treatment or discovering what "bad blood" really meant.[10] During World War II, about fifty of the participants were ordered by their draft boards to undergo treatment for syphilis. The PHS convinced the draft boards to exclude study subjects from the requirement for treatment. More important, in 1943, when the PHS began to administer penicillin to patients with syphilis, the participants in the study were denied this medicine. In 1952 the PHS enlisted local health departments to track participants who had left Macon County as well as help to continue to prevent them from receiving treatment. As a result of such duplicity, the study was able to continue for forty years.

On July 25, 1972, a front-page headline in the *Washington Star* read, "Syphilis victims in U.S. Study Went Untreated for 40 Years."[11] The article revealed the gory details of the Tuskegee Syphilis Study. It highlighted how the nature of the experiment shifted from not offering treatment to the infected men for the purposes of study to the active denying of treatment. The story also appeared the following day in the *New York Times*. As a result of the *Washington Star* story, the study was officially ended in November 1972, when the federal assistant secretary for health and scientific affairs appointed an ad hoc advisory panel to review the study. The nine-member panel included members from the fields of medicine, law, religion, labor, education, health administration, and public affairs. The panel found that the men had agreed freely to be examined and treated, though many went untreated. However, the panel also concluded that there was no evidence to indicate that researchers had informed the infected men of the study or its real purpose. It was discovered that the participants had indeed been misled and had not been given all the information necessary to provide for informed consent. With regard to informed consent, the panel stated that human subjects should not be "subjected to avoidable risk of death or physical harm unless he freely and intelligently consents."[12] These men were not given the opportunity to choose. Thus, the advisory panel found that the Tuskegee Study was "ethically unjustified," and concluded that no formal protocol ever existed for this experiment.[13]

The PHS officials maintained that they did nothing wrong. However, by the time the story broke, more than 100 of the infected men had died, while others suffered from serious cardiovascular problems. More important, as a result of nontreatment, many of these men infected their wives, who in turn passed the disease on to their children. On July 23, 1973, Fred Gray, a civil-rights attorney, brought a U.S. $1.8 billion class-action civil suit against many of the institutions and individuals involved in the study. Calling the experiment "a program of controlled genocide," Gray demanded U.S. $3 million in damages for each living participant and the heirs of those participants that had already died.[14] The lawsuit was settled out of court. In December 1974 the government agreed to a U.S. $10 million out-of-court settlement.[15] This settlement was distributed as follows: living syphilitics received U.S. $37,000; heirs of deceased syphilitics received U.S. $15,000; living controls received U.S. $16,000; and heirs of deceased controls received U.S. $5,000. In addition to the out-of-court settlement, the government promised to give free medical and burial services to all surviving participants. The Participants Health Benefits Program, formerly known as the Tuskegee Health Benefits Program, was established to provide such services to the twenty-two wives, seventeen children, and two grandchildren with syphilis they may have contracted as a direct result of the nontreatment provided to the participants in the study. In 1996 the program cost the federal government U.S. $21 million.

GOVERNMENTAL ARCHIVES

The story of this American tragedy is told by James Jones in his landmark book *Bad Blood.* Considered to be the most comprehensive account of the study, Jones admits in his acknowledgments that "I first came across materials on the Tuskegee Study in 1969 while investigating another topic in the National Archives. Needless to say, I did not know that the experiment was still going on then."[16] More recently, in Susan M. Reverby's edited volume *Tuskegee's Truths: Rethinking the Tuskegee Syphilis Study,* Jones reiterates "I had seen other examples in my archival research of nontherapeutic medical research studies and I had no way of knowing that the Tuskegee Study was still active. I was, after all, in an archive."[17] Jones believed that the Tuskegee Syphilis Study had to be over because the records were in an archives and therefore inactive. Jones is not alone in his thinking about this perceived role of archives in society, specifically governmental archives. Many historians have the notion that archives consist of records of the past that do not have value unless they give it life through the form of a narrative. However, Jones discovered as a researcher that his notions of an archive inhibited his ability to realize that he himself had unearthed a horrible experiment that was still going on at the time of his research at the National Archives.

Archives are vital to society for many reasons. Among the most important functions that archival records fulfill is that they serve as instruments of accountability and building blocks of collective memory. John McDonald succinctly expresses the relationship between records and accountability as follows: "Without records, there can be no demonstration of accountability. Without evidence of accountability, society cannot trust in its public institutions."[18] Both Fred Gray, the attorney representing most of the participants, and James Jones reported difficulties in obtaining official records concerning the government study. Gray asserts that in preparing the case for trial, he filed a discovery motion, requesting any and all information that the government may have that may be relevant to the lawsuit. According to Gray, the response to the motion to produce documents during the early part of the study was met with "no records available so far as the government knew."[19] James Jones states that in 1975, when he tried to gain total access to the records of the study, his efforts were impeded by the Justice Department. Only after soliciting the assistance of a law firm in Washington, D.C., and filing Freedom of Information Act (FOIA) requests did the Justice Department acquiesce. The government did not begin to discuss the possibility of settlement until after the records concerning the study were found in the National Archives, revealing that an ongoing medical experiment was conducted with no one involved knowing where the papers pertinent to its initial design and early activities were kept.

The plethora of documents revealed that PHS physicians knew from the inception of the study that the participants believed they were in a treatment program. The files consisted of records created during the course of the study that related to individual patients; publications based on findings of the study; correspondences between medical personnel; administrative records; photographs of various medical tests or procedures; and minutes. More important, the documents clearly revealed how meticulous these physicians were in carrying out the initial steps of the study in the early years. For example, the government physicians wrote and visited local doctors in the area, gave them a list of patients in the study—both syphilitics and controls—and secured their cooperation in the study, which included not treating anyone for syphilis because it would spoil the data. The doctors sent annual letters to participants telling them the federal doctors were coming again to treat their "bad blood." In addition, the PHS obtained the cooperation of the Alabama Board of Health and the local draft boards in 1941 to make sure that these men were not called for wartime physicals that would disclose their syphilis and make treatment mandatory. Initially, those deprived included syphilitics and the controls who developed syphilis in the intervening years and had received no treatment for it. More shocking is the fact that these doctors knew that syphilis could be acquired or congenital. As a result of concealing the severity of the disease from the participants, their wives and children were not only exposed but went untreated as well.

Today the original records are housed at the National Archives and Records Administration's (NARA) Southeast Region Center in Atlanta, Georgia. These records also include affidavits relating to the federal court case; agendas and committee hearings; and materials relating to the public scrutiny to which the study and the agency were subjected once the study was exposed. Currently, there are thirty-eight boxes of records. Of the thirty-eight boxes, twenty (4–20a) pertain to the administrative files and are open to the public. Boxes 21 through 35 and 1 through 3 contain patient information and are restricted until the year 2030 in order to protect the identities of the patient and their families. The federal Freedom of Information Act (FOIA) process contains an exemption that allows federal agencies to withhold information based on privacy interests (see: 5

U.S.C. §552 (b)(6)). The exemption is permissive, not mandatory, so that agencies can choose not to withhold government records that satisfy an exemption for nondisclosure. Exemption (b)(6) allows the withholding of government records that are personnel, medical, and similar files whose disclosure would constitute a clearly unwarranted invasion of personal privacy.

Those who work in the Center for Disease Control's (CDC) FOIA office claim exemption (b)(6) when responding to requests by researchers or the general public who desire to see patient records from the study. Before transferring custody to the National Archives in 1992, the Tuskegee records were in the possession of the CDC. The authorized disposition of the records is permanent, meaning that they will be preserved for the foreseeable future. The records are deemed historically important because of continued public interest as well as for their legal ramifications. Although the statutory language of the FOIA privacy exemption does not state explicitly that the privacy interests protected by the statute diminish upon the death of the person mentioned in the record, a number of federal courts have suggested that these privacy interests either disappear or are reduced in that case. The National Archives is now facing this issue with the Tuskegee medical files. The Tuskegee records are the only records in the custody of NARA that have restrictions even though most of the participants are deceased. Generally, NARA releases records about an individual after the individual's death. Access to all the Tuskegee records is a hotly contested issue amongst the National Archives, researchers, and African Americans. For many African Americans there will continue to be distrust until the government grants access to all the information it has on the study.

Such distrust has manifested itself in the African American community through the development of myths to explain historical events. As pointed out by David Thelen, "from actors' conflicts and negotiations over memory are born traditions, legends, myths, rituals, and more formalized cultural expressions of collective memory."[20] Mistrust of the government and the medical establishment has led to myths about the Tuskegee Syphilis Study. For example, many believe that the men involved in the study were deliberately injected with the disease. The Tuskegee Syphilis Study also emerged as justification by the participants to expect dishonesty and nondisclosure from investigators concerning research risks. "Even if you give informed consent, like the Tuskegee thing—those men were told they would be treated but they weren't."[21] Thus, the well-publicized existence of the Tuskegee records is a double-edged sword for the government. On the one hand, the unrestricted records provide evidence of the government's involvement in the study, ensuring some accountability, yet the inaccessibility of the patient records continues to perpetuate myths.

INTERVIEWS

Archival materials acquire a new meaning in the light of conversations with the participants in the study. Many of the narratives about the study would not have been as powerful if it were not for interviews with former participants and their families. On the value of oral history, Ronald J. Grele has pointed out that such sources "are but one form of documentation. In some cases they are not the best form; in others they are the only form. When used with care and modesty, they increase our understanding of our past and reveal hidden levels of discourse."[22]

By discussing their experiences, the participants in their own way documented the Tuskegee Syphilis Study and broke the silence that had surrounded the participants and their families. When describing the spinal tap procedures done to him, Charles Pollard stated that "they give me one of them back shots, and it put me down—put me down on the ground on my hands and knees for weeks. They stuck them needles in me for forty years so you couldn't feel good. They never did tell me what was wrong with me."[23] In Carol Kaesuk Yoon's 1997 *New York Times* article "Families Emerge As Silent Victims of Tuskegee Syphilis Experiments," Albert Julkes, Jr., the son of a participant, noted, "You get treated like lepers. People think it's the scourge of the earth to have it in your family." Lillie Head, the daughter of participant, lamented that "it was something to be ashamed of, so it wasn't talked about." Herman Shaw, a survivor of the study, offered one of the few memories of a wife's reaction to learning the truth about the study: "She was somewhat shocked, may I say, because it was a disease. It wasn't anything that we'd heard about and nobody seemed to know about." Thus, the lingering shame and distrust of the government for what they did to the participants and their family members and their community in the past is documented through the voices of the victims in the present. Publicly retelling their experiences has placed the Tuskegee Syphilis experiment upon the public stage. More important, memorializing the participants of the clinical tragedy would cement their experience within public memory.

REMEMBERED IN MUSEUM

A museum in Tuskegee, Alabama, was established in 1998 to memorialize the victims of this clinical tragedy. The Tuskegee Human and Civil Rights Center's objective is to draw public attention and pay tribute to the victims of the study. Attorney Fred Gray has commented that "these men wanted a center representing their contributions and the contributions of other people of this area in the field of civil rights. This center will serve as a reminder that the healing process is ongoing."[24] One of the survivors summed up the event by saying that "we will never really be able to tell our children and grandchildren what we went through for forty years, but maybe they'll be able to see a little of it here."[25]

African American museums have held a dual responsibility to tell the African American story while at the same time telling a broader American story. In addition, the African American museum has become a public forum for addressing something that is uncomfortable about our collective past. The Tuskegee Syphilis Study would constitute one of many examples of poor treatment in African American history. The institution of slavery and the Civil-Rights Movement, although a shared heritage, were not experienced in the same way by whites as by African Americans. Yet these subjects allow us to stimulate reconciliation and healing as well as self-knowledge for African Americans and others who are moved by the common experience. The museum dedicated to remembering the participants will certainly refine for the current generation those values and visions that sustained the African American community throughout the eras of slavery, race riots, segregation, and exploitation.

PUBLIC POLICY

The Tuskegee Syphilis Study has come to symbolize the medical misconduct and blatant disregard for human rights that took place in the name of science. The participants of the study underscore the point that the burden of medical experimentation has historically been carried by those unable to protect themselves. By failing to obtain informed consent and offering incentives for participation, the PHS doctors were performing unethical and immoral experiments on human subjects. The Tuskegee Study was an immoral experiment from the onset. Moreover, similar comparisons can be made with inhumane medical experiments on humans living under the Nazi Regime during World War II as well as to other U.S. government experiments that tested drugs and chemical and biological weapons on unwitting U.S. citizens. Arthur Caplan, director of the medical ethics program at the University of Pennsylvania in Philadelphia, described the Tuskegee study as "America's Nuremberg." Caplan, author of *When Medicine Went Mad: Bioethics and the Holocaust*, has said that "Tuskegee was really the experiment that set American medicine on its ear. I think Americans had this belief that they couldn't or wouldn't do the kind of evil things that the Germans did. Tuskegee was a gigantic wake-up call."[26] The outcry over the Tuskegee study led to experimental reforms, including the requirement of informed consent, the creation of institutional review boards, data and safety monitoring boards, and continuing ethics education for researchers.

The researchers and their accomplices involved in the study, however, were not prosecuted. According to James Jones, when the story broke and throughout the investigation, the PHS physicians continued to deny any wrongdoing. There was nothing in their public statements to indicate even an ounce of contrition. No apologies were ever uttered. On the contrary, as noted by Jones, "the health officials who had exercised direct responsibility for the experiment made it clear that they had acted in good conscience."[27]

On May 16, 1997, President Clinton did what the PHS officials refused to do twenty-five years earlier when the experiments came to light. He offered a formal White House apology to the participants and their survivors of the study. Even though there was an official apology and measures put into place to prevent people from being treated again like laboratory rats, the underlying fact is that the Tuskegee experiments were not an isolated incident. Rather, they were part of a larger disturbing trend of unethical secret experimentation on humans throughout the twentieth century. Americans have not only been left to suffer silently from syphilis, but also have been injected with Plutonium 239, blistered with mustard gas, and sprayed with bacteria. Like the Tuskegee experiments, the victims of these other experiments were usually the most vulnerable members of society: poor African Americans, hospital patients, and children.[28] Striking a balance between protecting vulnerable classes of subjects and seeing that minorities are adequately represented in and reap the benefits of clinical trials has become a challenge for investigators. Because of the Tuskegee Syphilis Study, the African American community has long been suspicious of the medical establishment. As a result, it has been difficult to get African Americans to participate in clinical trials of any kind.

The fact that the government was running a long-term study when no one in charge had any idea of what the original protocols were, or where they were, is itself shocking. Measured by the ethical standards of the 1970s, these records demonstrated not only that the study was ethically wrong but that it had been, from the start, a program built upon deception. The central fact about the forty-year study was that its scientific rationale made no sense. No researcher involved in the study ever published a single comprehensive summary of its findings. The absence of such a record may have fostered the impression that no substantive findings of any real significance were obtained. But Jones notes in the appendix to his book that PHS scientists, physicians, and nurses associated with the study published a total of thirteen articles between 1936 and 1973 based solely upon its findings. These papers appeared in a wide variety of peer-reviewed journals, including *Public Health Reports, Journal of Chronic Diseases*, and Archives of Internal Medicine. After reviewing the records of the "study" however, the Ad Hoc Tuskegee Syphilis Study Panel concluded in 1973 that "the conduct of the longitudinal study . . . is judged to be scientifically unsound and its results are disproportionately meager compared with known risks to human subjects involved."[29] The exposure of the Tuskegee Syphilis Study prompted the National Research Act of 1974 which mandated that institutional review boards approve all federally funded proposed research involving human subjects. As a result, the Tuskegee Syphilis Study records are relevant to the notions of accountability, ensuring that the contemporary biomedical community justifies its experiments through a formal protocol process as well as a formal human subjects review process.

CONCLUSION

Memory is deeply implicated in concepts of accountability. The Tuskegee Syphilis Study did not just happen to the 625[30] men and their families living in Macon County, Georgia. The African American community connected with the experience because of the racial identity of the victims. Their sense of a collective past is used as a means to force the U.S. government to be accountable for its actions. Through the vehicles of public archives, interviews, a commemorative museum, and public policies, the African American community is able to remember the participants of the study, their ordeal, and the government's role. Paul Antze and Michael Lambek contend that "memories are never simply records of the past, but are interpretive reconstructions that bear the imprint of local narrative conventions, cultural assumptions, discursive formations and practices, and social contexts of recall and commemoration."[31] The remembrance of the Tuskegee Syphilis Study is a prime example of an American tragedy that continues to be hotly contested in both private and public memories.

NOTES

1. Roy Rosenzweig and David Thelen, *The Presence of the Past: Popular Uses of History in American Life* (New York: Columbia University Press, 1998), p. 149.

2. Jonathan D. Moreno, *Undue Risk: Secret State Experiments on Humans* (New York: W.H. Freeman, 2000); see also Oklahoma Commission, Final Report of the *Oklahoma Commission to Study the Tulsa Race Riot of 1921* (Feb. 28, 2001). Available at ok-history.mus.ok.us/trrc/freport.htm.

3. Paul Antze and Michael Lambek, eds., *Tense Past: Cultural Essays in Trauma and Memory* (New York: Routledge, 1996), p. vii.

4. David Thelen, "Memory and American History," *Journal of American History* 75 (Mar. 1989): 1127.

5. James Jones, *Bad Blood: The Tuskegee Syphilis Experiment* (New York: Free Press, 1981).

6. Ibid., pp. 87–88.

7. Ibid., p. 91.

8. Ibid., p. 94.

9. Ibid., pp. 132–150.

10. Ibid., p. 162.

11. Jean Heller, "Syphilis Victims in the U.S. Study Went Untreated for 40 Years," *New York Times*, July 26, 1972, pp. 1, 8.

12. "Selections from the Final Report of the Ad Hoc Tuskegee Syphilis Study Panel, Department of Health, Education, and Welfare, 1973." In Susan M. Reverby, ed., *Tuskegee's Truth's: Rethinking the Tuskegee Syphilis Study* (Chapel Hill: University of North Carolina Press, 2000), p. 166.

13. The Association for the Advancement of Blacks in Health Sciences, *America's Dirty Little Secret*. Available at aabhs.orgtusk.htm.

14. Jones, *Bad Blood*, p. 216.

15. Ibid., p. 217.

16. Ibid., p. xi.

17. James Jones. Foreword. In Susan M. Reverby, ed., *Tuskegee's Truths: Rethinking the Tuskegee Syphilis Study* (Chapel Hill: University of North Carolina Press, 2000), p. xi.

18. John McDonald, "Accountability in Government in an Electronic Age" (June 25, 1998). Available at irmt.orgr/resources/maljm2.doc.

19. Fred Gray, *The Tuskegee Syphilis Study: An Insider's Account of the Shocking Medical Experiment Conducted by Government Doctors Against African American Men* (Montgomery, Ala.: Black Belt Press, 1998), p. 90.

20. Thelen, "Memory and American History," p. 1127.

21. Giselle Corbie-Smith, Stephen B. Thomas, Mark V. Williams, and Sandra Moody-Ayers, "Attitudes and Beliefs of African Americans Toward Participation in Medical Research," *Journal of General Internal Medicine* 14 (1999): 541.

22. Ronald J. Grele, "On Using Oral History Collections: An Introduction," *Journal of American History* 74 (Sept. 1987): 577.

23. Dan Hulbert, "Tuskegee Horror Remains Real," *Atlanta Constitution*, Jan. 14, 1990, p. M1.

24. "Patients of Tuskegee Experiment Remembered in Museum," *Lexis-Nexis Academic Universe-Document* (1998). Available at web.lexis-nexis.com.

25. Ibid.

26. Howard Wolinsky, "Steps Still Being Taken to Undo Damage of 'America's Nuremberg,'" *Annals of Internal Medicine* (Aug. 15, 1997). Available at acponline.org/journal/annals/l5aug97/currnazi.htm.

27. Jones, *Bad Blood*, p. 219.

28. In March 1997 the Department of Energy paid U.S. $6.5 million to the families of seventeen individuals who were injected with plutonium and uranium in secret government Cold War era experiments. In November 1996 Energy Secretary Hazel O'Leary paid U.S. $4.8 million to the families of another twelve victims of government radioactivity experiments. For a historical overview of children and research, see Leonard H. Glantz's article "Research with Children," *American Journal of Law and Medicine* 24, Nos. 2–3 (1998): 213–244.

29. "Selections from the Final Report of the Ad Hoc Tuskegee Syphilis Study Panel, Department of Health, Education and Welfare, 1973." In Susan M. Reverby, ed., *Tuskegee's Truths: Rethinking the Tuskegee Syphilis Study* (Chapel Hill: University of North Carolina Press, 2000), p.166.

30. Originally, 600 African American men were chosen for the study. However, over the course of 40 years, some men left the study (17%) and were replaced. As a result, at the end of the study, the total number of men who participated was 625.

31. Antze and Lambek, *Tense Past*, p. vii.

Turning History into Justice: The National Archives and Records Administration and Holocaust-Era Assets, 1996–2001

Greg Bradsher

"Everyone should understand the role of the records in establishing and legitimizing identities and liberties." So began a letter to the editor of *Time Magazine* (Mar. 17, 1997) by John W. Carlin, Archivist of the United States. "The dramatic case of the search for Nazi gold is an excellent example of the value of records not only in documenting historical facts but also in preserving essential evidence," he continued. "For us at the National Archives and Records Administration [NARA]," Carlin concluded, "the role of preserving and providing access to this essential evidence of history is at the core of our mission." Indeed, NARA's holdings of records relating to Nazi gold and other Holocaust-era assets, and its ability to make those records available in a timely manner, has demonstrated the importance of NARA and archives not only to this country but to peoples, governments, and organizations in other countries.

Since March 1996 NARA's Archives II Building in College Park, Maryland, has been visited or contacted by well over 1,000 researchers (individual claimants; historians; print and broadcast media; journalists; authors; representatives of foreign governments and organizations; nongovernment organizations; and law firms) interested in records relating to Holocaust-era assets. The Nazi-looted and unclaimed assets they researched, among other things, were gold and diamonds, cultural property (including books, archives, manuscripts, and Jewish communal property), Jewish assets in Swiss banks, art, unpaid and unclaimed insurance policies, and restitution for slave and forced labor. Many of the researchers spent weeks, months, and even years at Archives II going through millions of documents. Not since the "Roots" phenomenon of the mid-1970s that focused increased attention on genealogical records has NARA experienced such a large and sustained research activity on a single topic.

NARA's Nazi gold phenomenon resulted, in part, because of the desire of many people worldwide to know what happened to the assets of Holocaust victims. It also resulted from the desire for a full accounting of the role played during and after the war by the U.S. government as well as by the neutral countries and other nations in their dealings with the Nazi-looted assets. These desires began more than fifty years ago and will undoubtedly continue well into the future. Archives, in the United States and abroad, have been central in the process, and those held by NARA have been critical to uncovering facts about Holocaust-era assets.

WHAT WAS TAKEN AND WHAT WAS RECORDED?

From 1945 to 1995, most researchers coming to the National Archives who were interested in World War II focused on the military, diplomatic, and intelligence aspects of the war, as well as war crimes and the Holocaust. Few were interested in the economic and financial aspects of the war, and even fewer were interested in the assets. For most scholars, the Holocaust is the greatest murder in history. Few addressed it as the greatest robbery in history. The Nazi era witnessed the direct and indirect theft of well over $150 billion of assets of victims of Nazi persecution.[1] The process of taking assets began with Aryanization of Jewish property in the 1930s, followed by the looting of real, personal, intellectual, and cultural property (including more than 600,000 pieces of art) throughout the war; and the looting of gold from the central banks of occupied countries (some $5 billion worth in today's dollars). The process even involved the taking the gold fillings, rings, and other valuables of those murdered in the "Final Solution."

There was also the indirect loss of wealth by victims of Nazi persecution. To protect their assets, many Jews in Europe during the 1930s sent funds to one or more of the Swiss banks, of which there are over 400. The Swiss in the mid-1930s even adopted a Bank Secrecy Law to keep account information secret so that Nazi authorities could not learn whether a Jew had an account in Switzerland. This was critical to the depositors, for Nazi Germany exacted the death penalty for anyone sending hard currency out of the country. Many of the depositors who were victims of Nazi persecution did not survive the war, and often neither did their heirs. Thus the Swiss banks, which never close an account, kept the deposits, estimated today to be worth anywhere from $1 to $20 billion. In addition, survivors and heirs found it difficult, if not impossible, to withdraw funds for lack of a secret bank account number or the lack of a death certificate, paperwork that the Nazis did not create at the death camps. Some Swiss banks, pushed by Israel and others in the early 1960s, undertook a relatively inadequate attempt to ascertain how much they held and to return it. About $2.5 million was identified and began to be returned to depositors or their heirs in 1964.

Many Jews in the 1930s bought property and death insurance policies believing that insurance would provide them or their heirs with financial protection. During the war, German authorities systematically confiscated the insurance policies of Holocaust victims, subsequently cashing in policies once the insured were murdered. Survivors and heirs after the war found it difficult, if not impossible, to have insurance companies honor policies. Often lack of a death certificate or lack of a copy of an insurance policy precluded payments. Some of Germany's postwar reparation payments to Holocaust victims and heirs and to the state of Israel were related to confiscated insurance policies, which secured indirect payments to some people.

Another form of indirect loss of monies was Nazi use of forced and slave labor. Some 12 million people, many from Poland and Russia, were forced into labor on behalf of the Third Reich. Some were minimally compensated, but many more were not compensated at all. Many died, as well, while being forced to work. For example, more than 20,000 laborers lost their lives while working in underground assembly sites for the production of V-2 rockets. Countless hundreds of thousands of others lost their lives while being worked to death in factories connected with the concentration camps.

RESTITUTION EFFORTS 1945–1995

While a case can be made that the U.S. government knew that the Holocaust was taking place in Europe and that it did not do as much as it could have to help minimize the deaths of European Jews, there is no denying that the Allies were well aware of the thefts taking place in Nazi Europe and did take action both during and after the war. Today, at the National Archives at College Park, Maryland, proof of Allied actions to prevent the thievery is documented in well over 20 million pages of records.

The process of identifying, locating, and recovering of Nazi-looted assets had begun well before the end of World War II. Federal agencies took an active role in trying to identify and locate looted assets. Early in 1944 the U.S. government became increasingly concerned about Nazis attempting to shield their assets outside Germany for personal use, as well as for building another strong Germany after the war. The U.S. government was also concerned about the neutral countries taking looted gold from the Germans in payment for military and other supplies. Because of these concerns, in late 1944 the Departments of State and Treasury and the Foreign Economic Administration initiated an effort, codenamed variously the "Safehaven Program," the "Safehaven Project," and simply "Safehaven," to identify and stop the movement of Nazi assets out of Germany and then to locate, recover, and restitute them.[2] These three agencies, besides having their own intelligence-gathering programs, relied heavily on the Office of Strategic Services, U.S. embassies, other U.S. federal agencies, and the British Ministry of Economic Warfare, to acquire information about the movement and location of Nazi-looted assets, especially gold. This information was gathered not only to use in negotiations with the neutral countries about their dealings with the Nazis but also for restitution purposes after the war. The quantity of Safehaven files and other economic warfare records created during the war was very substantial.

To the Allies and to the occupied countries, the recovery of looted central bank gold was a most important issue. The neutral countries were warned often after 1942 not to accept gold from Germany because it had been looted. Many continued to do so despite the warnings and threats. As a result, nothing could be done about that gold until after the war, but the Allies could do something about the gold Germany still held. During the first week of April 1945 units of the U.S. Third Army found hidden in a mine at Merkers, Germany, stacks of gold bars, bags of gold coins, millions of dollars' worth of foreign currencies, art treasures, and other valuable assets. When an accounting of the gold was undertaken, it was determined that the gold was worth about $238.5 million (equivalent to some $2.5 billion today). During subsequent weeks the U.S. Army uncovered gold valued at about $14 million in Reichsbank branches as well as $9.7 million from other sources. In addition, the U.S. Army uncovered other significant bodies of Nazi loot, including gold wedding rings found at concentration camps.[3]

When the war ended, the Allies determined that the Nazis had begun the war with a gold reserve of about $120 million and had seized much more than $600 million in gold from occupied countries, especially Belgium and the Netherlands. The Department of State estimated that the Germans had sold roughly $300 million to Swiss banks and had laundered about $140 million through Swiss banks in payment for goods from Portugal and Spain. Using gold in payment, the Nazis also directly purchased goods from other countries, primarily Sweden and Romania, in the amount of $61 million. And it was determined that the U.S. Army had located a total of some $240 million worth of gold, mostly recovered at the Merkers mine site.[4]

The Allies, at a reparation conference held in Paris late in 1945, established procedures for the restitution of the gold looted by the Nazis from the central banks of Europe (so-called "monetary gold"), as well as for the restitution of "nonmonetary gold" (e.g., gold watches and wedding bands). The procedures called for the nonmonetary gold to be restituted to individuals and groups of individuals through the auspices of an international refugee organization. The procedures called for monetary gold to be turned over to a newly established Tripartite Commission for the Restitution of Monetary Gold (Tripartite Gold Commission/TGC), which would decide how much gold would be returned to each country from whose central bank gold had been looted. The TGC, composed of American, British, and French representatives, restituted most of the gold in the 1950s after reviewing claims by various countries. In 1996 the TGC, headquartered in Brussels, Belgium, was in the process of deciding how to allocate the remaining $60 million worth of gold (in today's dollars).

At the Paris Conference it was decided that the United States and Great Britain would lead in negotiating with the neutral countries for the return of Nazi-looted gold. Negotiations with the Swiss took place in spring 1946 in Washington, D.C. The resulting Washington Accord provided that the Swiss return gold worth only about $58 million. This gold was turned over to the TGC to be restituted to the countries with claims before the commission.

The advent of the Cold War, the restitution of most of the monetary gold by the TGC in the 1950s, and other factors resulted in diminishing interest in all the questions surrounding Nazi-looted assets. It should be noted that immediately after the war, survivors were primarily concerned with putting their lives back together and did not have the energy or means to regain what was lost. And many Jews were reluctant to pursue what was rightfully theirs, mostly out of fear that their efforts would fuel anti-Semitism and because they did not want to re-live the horrors of the Holocaust era. Also, many initial claims were met with re-sistance and obstruction from the holders of the assets, which discouraged subsequent efforts to regain property. Unfortunately, few countries, companies, or banks made any concerted efforts, if any at all, to find the heirs of victims.

Nevertheless, some restitution was forthcoming. The government of the Fed-eral Republic of Germany beginning in the 1950s made substantial (over $60 bil-lion, or about $100 billion in today's dollars) reparation payments to Holocaust survivors, to heirs, and to the state of Israel and signed bilateral agreements with more than a dozen countries to set up pensions and annuities for victims in West-ern Europe. During the Cold War the communist regimes in Central and Eastern Europe prevented Holocaust survivors and heirs from receiving such payments. The people behind the iron curtain became known as double victims. There was some Jewish interest in dormant and closed bank accounts in Switzerland, but not enough to cause a groundswell of international action. Nor was there much inter-est in the role played during the war by Switzerland and the other neutrals. The issues surrounding looted assets exited from center stage. For forty years there was not much interest in Nazi-looted assets and almost no research.

RENEWED INTEREST AND THE RECORDS

In early 1996 World Jewish Congress (WJC) leaders, headed by its president Edgar Bronfman, asked U.S. Senator Alfonse D'Amato, the head of the Senate Banking Committee, to investigate the supposedly large quantities of dormant Jewish bank accounts in Swiss banks. The WJC believed that there were billions of dollars in accounts that had been established by Jews as a means of safekeep-ing for their assets and that the Swiss banks were making it difficult, if not impos-sible, for survivors of the Holocaust and heirs of victims of Nazi persecution to retrieve them. In late 1995 the WJC had been offered $32 million to settle the matter. This amount they considered an insult.

When the senator agreed to look into the matter, it touched off a renewed in-terest in Holocaust-era assets. For NARA the interest first manifested itself in late February 1996, when D'Amato wrote government agencies to ascertain whether they had any relevant records. NARA was the only agency to respond positively. In March 1996 D'Amato's legislative director, Gregg Rickman, sent Miriam Kleiman, who had been hired by the WJC and loaned to D'Amato, to Archives II to look for information about dormant Jewish bank accounts in Swiss banks and the role of Swiss banks before, during, and after World War II. Very early in her research Kleiman located records that contained detailed information about Jewish deposits in a Swiss bank. Within a month of her discovery, D'Amato's Senate Banking Committee held hearings on Nazi-looted assets and the Swiss bank accounts and shortly thereafter began a major worldwide research effort into Holocaust-era assets.

Researchers began arriving at Archives II in relatively small numbers in late spring 1996. The reference staff began providing records to these researchers, little realizing the amount of staff time that would be devoted to researchers in search of relevant records and that more than four years later they would still be providing such reference services. Realizing NARA would be pushed for information about records, I quickly prepared a three-page finding aid to Safehaven-related records and then expanded it to ten pages, and I thought that would be the end of my involvement with the subject. The trickle of researchers that began in March became a small stream after the Senate Banking Committee hearing in April 1996. It was not too long afterward that researchers representing Senator D'Amato, the World Jewish Congress, and the Swiss Bankers Association (SBA) had found a home at Archives II, with others following. On any given day during the summer the Archives II research room had between fifteen and twenty-five researchers doing research in what the staff termed: the "Nazi gold" records. And what had actually begun as a quest for information on Jewish assets in Swiss banks quickly broadened to include Nazi-looted monetary, or central bank, gold held in the neutral countries of Switzerland, Sweden, Spain, Portugal, Argentina, and Turkey, as well as the gold recovered after the war in Germany.

The records the researchers used were found within thirty record groups and comprised more than twenty million pages of documentation. The records were like a magnet, drawing increasing numbers of researchers as the summer progressed. The records included those of various military and naval organizations; the Foreign Economic Administration; the Foreign Claims Settlement Commission; the Federal Bureau of Investigation; the Department of Commerce; the Bureau of Foreign and Domestic Commerce; the Office of War Information; the Foreign Broadcast Intelligence Service; the Office of Censorship; the Office of Strategic Services; the Department of the Treasury; the Department of Justice; the Office of Inter-American Affairs; the Office of Alien Property; the High Commissioner for Germany; the Foreign Funds Control; the Federal Reserve Board; the United States Strategic Bombing Survey; the Department of State, including embassy and consulate records; captured German records; war crimes records; the records of the U.S. occupation of Germany, Austria, and Italy; and the records of the Roberts Commission, an organization established, in part, to identify looted art. Most of these records have been accessible for decades but were frequently overlooked or underutilized.[5]

THE SUMMER OF 1996

The research that was taking place at Archives II and the revelations that were being made about information in the records about Swiss bank accounts and looted gold caused governments to act. Initially the Swiss banks, responding to revelations about the bank accounts, appointed an SBA ombudsman to look into the truth of the allegations. He reported that there were just a handful of dormant accounts that might relate to victims of Nazi persecution and that their value was less than $9,000. Immediately the Swiss were attacked for not taking the matter seriously and talk of a boycott of Switzerland banks began. Responding to the pressure, the SBA and the Swiss government persuaded Paul Volcker, former head of the U.S. Federal Reserve Board, to head up an international committee (formally named the Committee of Eminent Persons) to audit the dormant bank accounts to ascertain how much of these accounts belonged to the Holocaust survivors and heirs. He hired three major accounting firms, and by the end of 1996 the audit had begun. To assist the so-called Volcker Committee, the Swiss government suspended Swiss bank secrecy laws for five years. The Swiss government also appointed Ambassador Thomas Borer to head up a Swiss Federal Task Force to deal with the issues confronting Switzerland.

The British also acted. Several members of Parliament, including Lord Janner and Foreign Secretary Malcolm Rifkind, took an active interest in Nazi-looted gold. During summer 1996 they assigned the Foreign and Commonwealth Office (FCO) to prepare a report on the Nazi-looted gold. The report, written by Gill Bennett, the FCO's chief historian, was published in September 1996.[6] Bennett's report helped raise questions internationally about the gold, and indirectly about the actions of Switzerland during the war. The report had a great impact in the United States. It set in motion the involvement of the U.S. government and provided political impetus to the process of seeking the truth about the past and putting that information to work in the process of providing compensation to the victims of Nazi persecution.

THE INTERAGENCY GROUP ON NAZI ASSETS, 1996–1997

During late summer 1996, at a fund-raiser for the Democratic National Committee, Edgar Bronfman raised the Swiss bank case with First Lady Hillary Clinton and expressed his desire for her to arrange a meeting with the president, which occurred the next day. At that meeting Bronfman explained the Holocaust restitution issue. Clinton agreed to help with the issue and to work with D'Amato. In early September 1996, the president tasked Stuart E. Eizenstat, then undersecretary of Commerce for International Trade, as well as special envoy of the Department of State on Property Restitution in Central and Eastern Europe, to prepare a report that would "describe, to the fullest extent possible, U.S. and Allied efforts to recover and restore this gold [gold the Nazis had looted from the central banks of occupied Europe, as well as gold taken from individual victims of Nazi persecution] and other assets stolen by Nazi Germany."

To accomplish this task Eizenstat established in October an eleven-agency Interagency Group on Nazi Assets. I joined the group as NARA's representative. William Z. Slany, the Department of State's chief historian, had the responsibility of drafting the group's report. He in turn asked me to prepare a finding aid to relevant records. This finding aid served as a research tool and was published as an appendix to Slany's report when it was published. Slany formed his research team, consisting of researchers from the Departments of Defense, Treasury, Justice, and State, the U.S. Holocaust Memorial Museum, the Central Intelligence Agency, and the Federal Reserve Board. They soon made Archives II their home.

While the Interagency Group was starting its assignment, events were transpiring that would have significant impacts on the Holocaust-era assets issues. Early in October class-action lawsuits were filed in the U.S. District Court in Brooklyn against the two largest Swiss banks, Union Bank of Switzerland (UBS) and Crédit Suisse, alleging that they had blocked the survivors' efforts to reclaim money that was directly deposited in the banks or that the Nazis had looted and stored in the banks. The plaintiffs sought $20 billion in compensation. The lawsuits (eventually consolidated into one lawsuit) and the publicity surrounding them provoked a diplomatic furor, and, eventually, an anti-American backlash in Switzerland. As 1996 ended, the outgoing Swiss president accused the United States of using the Holocaust to undermine Switzerland's success as a financial center. The Swiss ambassador to the United States charged that his country was being blackmailed. Other Swiss leaders and banks made what many consider major mistakes. Perhaps the most egregious was discovered by a Swiss bank guard early in 1997: bank archivists attempting to destroy bank records.

Trying to stem the criticism, the Swiss in December 1997 passed a law against the destruction of relevant records and created an independent commission of experts to spend five years studying the Swiss role in World War II. Swiss professor Jean-François Bergier was named chair of the Independent Commission of Experts—Switzerland: World War II (often referred to as the Bergier Commission), and several Americans were named to the commission. Also early in 1997, the Swiss established a $200 million fund for Holocaust survivors, which would grow to more than $400 million by 1999. President Bill Clinton also took action. He sent Eizenstat to mediate talks between the plaintiffs and the banks. The settlement talks, which involved at various stages not only Eizenstat but also a federal district court judge, Senator D'Amato, and a number of Jewish leaders, would continue until August 1998.

During November 1996 the TGC contemplated dissolving itself by disbursing its remaining gold. The U.S. government requested of the British and French TGC members that the TGC continue its existence until such time as records could be studied to determine what percentage, if any, of the TGC's gold contained nonmonetary gold. The records at NARA would play an important role in demonstrating that some of the gold was tainted, that is, contained nonmonetary gold. If this was true, then some of the gold should not go back to the central banks of the countries that had been looted by the Nazis, but rather should be given to individuals who had been victims of Nazi persecution.

During winter 1996–1997, NARA's reference resources were tested. Not only were there regular Nazi gold researchers to help, but once the Interagency Group threw itself into the task of gathering information to be incorporated in the government's report, the summer's river was, by January 1997, at flood stage. Frequently researchers were competing for the same records. The pressure to provide timely and equitable service was immense.

In addition to handling researcher requests for records, NARA became involved during the winter and the following spring in the accessioning of relatively large bodies of relevant classified and declassified records. This resulted from Eizenstat urging agencies to transfer such records to NARA where they could be made available. In November 1996 NARA accessioned some 1,400 cubic feet of Department of the Treasury records and the following spring more than 100 cubic feet of records from the Federal Reserve Board. These records, and other newly accessioned records, were declassified under great pressure to make them immediately available.[7]

THE MEDIA AND THE SWISS DISCOVER NARA'S HOLDINGS

The fall of 1996 and the following winter found the media discovering that an important aspect of the Nazi gold story was NARA: its records, its staff, and its researchers. Journalists and documentary filmmakers began appearing on a regular basis. The first stories highlighting NARA's role appeared in November 1996 in *USA Today* and in early February 1997 in *Le Monde*. *Time* ran a cover story in late February regarding the quest for records relating to Nazi gold. On March 30 the *Baltimore Sun* ran a lengthy piece under the headline "Hunt for Nazi Treasures Begins at National Archives." On the same day the *New York Times* ran a story under the headline "Over Here, Paper Chase for Nazi Gold."

By spring 1997, NARA had become a magnet for the media. The media, unable to obtain stories from those government historians researching and drafting the Eizenstat Report, found that much of the document base upon which the report would be derived was in NARA. Not only were the documents reviewed and filmed, but also researchers and NARA staff members were interviewed. Feature stories appeared in the *New York Times* and many of the nation's leading newspapers. Major periodicals such as *Newsweek* and *US News & World Report* also contacted NARA for information. The History Channel, the Arts and Entertainment Network, the Public Broadcasting Service, the Cable News Network, and other television networks ran specials based on interviews with NARA staff and researchers. Press interest has continued since May 1997. All the major television networks and a wide variety of print and visual media have regularly contacted NARA, as have Swiss, German, and other European TV and radio stations, numerous filmmakers, newspapers, and magazines. And as NARA drew researchers and the media, it began attracting the Swiss.

The Swiss, because their country was the initial and primary focus of the Nazi gold story, and because much of the story was based on NARA's holdings, during 1997 began developing ties with NARA. This NARA–Swiss connection became a very close one, in part, because of an agreement between the U.S. and Swiss governments. This agreement, signed in early 1997 by Eizenstat and Ambassador Borer, provided that their respective countries, including national archives, would closely cooperate. Beginning in late spring 1997 numerous Swiss, besides the Swiss media, began coming to NARA. Among them were a member of the Swiss Parliament; the first secretary of the SBA; Bergier and four other members of his commission; and members of the Swiss embassy staff. Researchers representing the SBA began their research at Archives II in spring 1996 and were joined in July 1997 by a research team from the Bergier Commission. Other researchers, including accountants from the Volcker Committee, also found NARA a useful source of information. During 1997 NARA and the Swiss Federal Archives developed close ties. There have been frequent communications between Christoph Graf, the director of the Swiss Federal Archives, and NARA to discuss ongoing research and NARA's critical role.

THE FIRST EIZENSTAT REPORT IN SPRING 1997

The finding aid was completed, with the assistance of many NARA staff and researchers, in mid-March 1997. Described in some 300 pages were at least 15 million pages of documents, created or received by some thirty federal agencies, relating to World War II economic warfare, restitution and reparation activities, the financial and diplomatic aftermath of the war, and the Safehaven Program. Also described in the finding aid were relevant captured German records, war crimes records, and records from the National Archives' Gift Collection.

Research was launched, at the beginning of spring 1997, into looted art; unpaid insurance policies (as a result of three class-action lawsuits in April against some of the world's largest insurance companies); and nonmonetary gold, that is, victims' gold from the death camps, such as dental gold. The Interagency Group on Nazi Assets and other researchers were most interested in the nonmonetary gold, and NARA had the task of finding relevant records. Among the most significant bodies of records uncovered have been those of the Reichsbank's Precious Metals Department. These records were greatly sought after because it was believed that these records would document conclusively how much of the looted German gold acquired by the Allies was composed of nonmonetary gold. The Precious Metals Department records I located on April 1 after an intense search of several days consisted of some seventy reels of microfilm contained in a small box within a recently accessioned Federal Record Center box of records from the Department of the Treasury. There was great excitement. The microfilms, which dated back to 1948 and were not accessioned by NARA until November 1996, were not in the best condition. However, NARA reproduced the microfilm and made it available to researchers on April

4, 1997. The discovery of the records was the subject of two Associated Press stories. Unfortunately, the records were found too late to be comprehensively used by the Interagency Group.[8]

On May 7, 1997, the Interagency Group on Nazi Assets, headed by Eizenstat, issued its report and my finding aid was published as the appendix to the report.[9] At the rollout of the report at the Department of State, Eizenstat had an enlargement of a page of the Precious Metals Department records on an easel behind him, to emphasize the importance of the nonmonetary gold issue and the fact that some of the monetary gold could be tainted and thus restitutable to individuals instead of countries. The report, based primarily on NARA's holdings, focused on what U.S. officials knew about Nazi looting of gold and other assets, when they found out about German actions or the actions of neutrals or non-belligerent nations, and how the United States attempted to trace the movement of looted gold and other assets into neutral and nonbelligerent nations, and how it attempted to recover the assets from these nations as well as from occupied Europe. The report was quite critical of the Swiss and the other World War II neutrals.

THE SUMMER OF 1997

Within days of issuing its first report, the Interagency Group on Nazi Assets was asked by political leaders to prepare another report. In summer 1997, researchers from the Department of State, the Central Intelligence Agency, and the National Security Agency, representing the Interagency Group on Nazi Assets, began to do their research again with NARA's assistance. In the wake of the Eizenstat report, more researchers found their way to College Park. Not only were the researchers continuing to seek information about Nazi-looted gold and related topics, but the boundaries of research had widened to include questions relating to looted securities, looted works of art, unclaimed and unpaid insurance policies, forced and slave-labor practices, Swiss refugee policies and practices, and wartime trade between the neutrals and the Axis powers. During the summer the House Banking and Finance Services Committee sent researchers to Archives II to obtain information on heirless assets in America.

After two news stories in July 1997, based on NARA's holdings, about the Vatican's involvement in Holocaust-era assets, researchers began focusing on the roles of the Vatican and the Croatian Ustashas and their dealings in Jewish assets. And the Interagency Group, headed by Eizenstat, was assigned by the president to write another report on the neutrals and their dealings with the Axis and the fate of the assets seized by the Ustashas. During the summer, as the research widened to more countries and more subjects, and as NARA continued accessioning records, researchers expressed a great desire for an expanded finding aid to relevant records. I produced a 300-page supplemental finding aid in fall 1997, which was placed on the Department of State's Web site in November 1997. I continued working on more finding aid information, since researchers were continuing to demand easier access to relevant records.

ASCONA, SWITZERLAND, AND LONDON

Professor Bergier and his colleagues during summer 1997 believed it would be useful for those involved in research on Holocaust-era assets to meet to discuss matters of mutual concern. They invited twenty-five individuals to meet in late October in Ascona, Switzerland, to attend a conference on Nazi gold records to discuss research methodology and archival resources and various concerns of the increasing number of commissions and governments involved in the search for Holocaust-era assets. William Slany and I represented the United States. Also in attendance were representatives from Argentina, Canada, Great Britain, France, the Netherlands, and Belgium. After the conference during the first week of November, I traveled to Bern, Switzerland, where I visited the Swiss Archives and met with the Swiss federal archivist to discuss issues of mutual concern; met with Bergier Commission staff; and went to the U.S. Embassy, where I briefed Madeleine Kunin, the U.S. ambassador to Switzerland, on Holocaust-era assets research and what NARA was doing to make records accessible. While I was in Switzerland, the banks published a long list of names of dormant accounts, supplementing the first such list they had published in July. It is interesting that the ambassador's German-Jewish mother's name was on the list. She had not known of her mother's dormant account.

In mid-November Secretary of State Madeleine K. Albright came to Switzerland to discuss the Swiss bank situation. Speaking to the Swiss Parliament on November 15, she said that "doing all we can to discover the truth about the Holocaust and events related to it, and to act on the consequence of that truth, are among the vital tasks of this century." Throughout the world, many countries, organizations, groups, and individuals shared this belief. In 1997 and 1998 commissions were appointed in Sweden, Portugal, Argentina, France, Belgium, Norway, the Netherlands, Switzerland, and half a dozen other countries to address issues relating to victims of Nazi persecution, postwar restitution efforts, dormant bank accounts, and a variety of related subjects. Archives, it was clear to everyone involved, were an important element in the search for truth and justice.

Representatives of these commissions and others, representing forty-one nations, met in December 1997 in London for a conference sponsored by the British Foreign Office to discuss looted gold, coordinate research efforts, address methodological issues, and encourage governments to open their archives and to make their records fully accessible.[10] An important objective of this conference, called the London Gold Conference, was the disposition of the remaining gold held by the TGC. By then it was quite clear that some of the gold held by the TGC was tainted with nonmonetary gold. The United States and others urged that countries should forego the final TGC payout and donate their share to a Nazi Persecutee Relief Fund. Nazi victims who lived in the former Soviet Union were the first to get aid from the fund because in many cases they did not get compensation that was paid to Holocaust survivors who lived in Western Europe. To get this fund established, Eizenstat committed the U.S. government to contributing $5 million even though the United States was not liable to TGC claims. By the following summer some dozen countries had contributed their TGC share and the total surpassed $50 million.[11] At the conclusion of the London conference, Eizenstat announced that the United States would hold another Holocaust-era assets international conference the following year in Washington, D.C.

WINTER AND SPRING 1997–1998

During winter 1997–1998, while the Interagency Group on Nazi Assets was conducting their research at NARA, I was busy at work preparing a revised and enlarged finding aid. This finding aid, some 750 pages, was placed on the United States Holocaust Memorial Museum's Web site in March 1998. The finding aid included a substantial amount of information about looted art as an increasing number of researchers (including lawyers and claimants) were looking for documentation about artworks. It should be noted that during this winter many U.S. art museums began checking the provenance of their holdings. Much of the wartime Nazi-looted art was returned to the countries of origin after the war ended. But thousands of art works stolen from Holocaust victims were not returned to the rightful owners or their heirs. Many of these were believed to be in private and state-owned museums around the world, including the United States. The United States was an active art market after the war, and looted art works are now being found here, in private collections, commercial galleries, and museums.[12]

In spring 1998 researchers began systematically looking into slave and forced labor, the wartime activities of U.S. corporations and banks, and refugee policies of various countries, particularly that of Switzerland. A lawsuit was initiated in March 1998 against Ford Motor Company for supposedly maintaining a slave-labor operation at its Cologne plant during the war. During the remainder of the year several lawsuits were filed against U.S. and foreign banks for their handling of Jewish accounts, as well as the banks and German corporations involved in slave labor. About fifty lawsuits were filed in U.S. courts against more than 100 German and Austrian companies for their slave-labor practices. The plaintiffs in the suits asked for $20 billion in damages. Responding to the suits, Volkswagen relatively quickly established a multimillion dollar fund for compensation to former slave laborers.

Questions began being raised in 1998 about looted archives, books, and Jewish communal property. A substantial quantity of Jewish communal property, religious and secular, was confiscated during the Holocaust and nationalized after the war by communist regimes in Central and Eastern Europe. Restitution of and compensation for confiscated communal property began to be addressed systematically in the 1990s, after the dissolution of the communist regimes. The renewed interest in Holocaust-era assets spawned efforts to push individual governments to either restitute or compensate.

The U.S. Congress in early 1998 adopted the Holocaust Victims Redress Act that authorized $20 million for restitution payments and $5 million for archival research. In signing this act into law on February 13, 1998, President Clinton noted that it "recognizes the need for long overdue archival research . . . to set the historical record straight." Clinton also stated that one of the aims of his administration was to "bring whatever measure of justice might be possible to Holocaust survivors, their families, and the heirs of those who have perished." Subsequently Congress appropriated $5 million for the Nazi Persecutee Relief Fund and made another appropriation in 2000.[13]

THE SECOND EIZENSTAT REPORT

The second Eizenstat report was issued on June 8, 1998.[14] The report, building upon the first one, provided a more detailed analysis of the economic roles played by the neutral countries and the factors that shaped those roles. Prominent in the report was a focus on those countries' trading links with both the Axis and the Allies, as well as on their handling of looted assets, especially gold. Also addressed in the report was the fate of the Croatian Ustasha treasury and the Vatican's role during and immediately after the war. Noted in the report was the fact that Nazi Germany financed a substantial portion of its war effort by paying for its wartime imports from the neutral nations in gold, much of it looted from occupied Europe and some of it stolen from the victims of the Holocaust. Most of this looted gold was sent to the Swiss National Bank, which converted it into Swiss francs or deposited it in the accounts of other central banks. Also noted in the report was that the postwar negotiations that the United States, Great Britain, and France conducted with the wartime neutrals was protracted and failed to meet fully their original goals: restitution of the looted gold and the liquidation of German external assets to fund the reconstruction of postwar occupied Europe and to provide relief for Jews and other nonrepatriable refugees. The failure resulted from the intransigence of the neutrals after the war, dissension within Allied ranks, and competing priorities stemming from the onset of the Cold War. Less than 10 percent of the looted gold acquired by the neutrals was returned to the TGC to meet the claims from the central banks of fifteen countries.

If the importance of archives, especially those held by NARA, and the role of NARA in assisting in the task of turning history into justice, was not fully appreciated during 1996 and 1997, it certainly was by summer 1998. This was made abundantly clear before a congressional committee on June 4. On that day the House Committee on Banking and Financial Services held a hearing to discuss Eizenstat's work and discuss legislation creating a U.S. commission to study Holocaust-era assets that might have come into the custody or control of the U.S. government. After his testimony, Representative Carolyn Maloney asked Eizenstat about the importance of records and access to them. Eizenstat responded that "Mr. Bradsher of the National Archives has really done truly heroic work in opening and indexing and cataloguing . . . all of this information. This is the information we have relied upon." Slany added, "The National Archives has . . . made available now, on an expedited basis, the records which we have been able to identify. And as Ambassador Eizenstat has mentioned, there is a finding aid which is ever-expanding because we keep finding more records. This finding aid is available on the web electronically, on the Holocaust Memorial Museum's web site, and it allows scholars to have the same kind of understanding and access to the records that we in the government agencies were able to use."[15]

SUMMER AND FALL 1998

The summer of 1998 saw progress in both the art and insurance issues and an initial settlement of the Swiss bank lawsuits. In June the American Association of Museum Directors adopted guidelines calling for a review of their members' collections to identify works of art of dubious provenance during the critical years 1933–1945. The guidelines also asked museums to set aside such legal defenses as statutes of limitations, which could bar returns to prewar owners, and to sit down with claimants to discover the facts about ownership history. By the end of the year, the search for looted art, according to two British authors, "had become the greatest treasure hunt in history."[16] Several countries, including France, established commissions to look into looted art in their countries. The records at NARA increasingly became a source for provenance researchers.

The summer also witnessed the insurance issue heating up, with various state insurance commissioners threatening to revoke the licenses of certain European-owned insurance companies in their states unless the European parent companies made their records open for inspection. The National Association of Insurance Commissioners, which began holding hearings in Philadelphia and New York City during the spring, pushed for a resolution of the insurance issue. In October the International Commission on Holocaust-Era Insurance Claims (ICHEC) was established by five European insurers, U.S. and European regulators, and Jewish groups to settle unpaid insurance policies issued between 1920 and 1945. Former Secretary of State Lawrence Eagleburger was selected to head the commission. The commission immediately began working with all major parties to resolve claims. To show their goodwill, two of the major insurance companies set up a $90 million fund to cover claims. The two companies, Italy's Assicurazioni Generali and Allianz AG of Germany, would increase this figure to $150 million.

In August UBS and Crédit Suisse settled the lawsuits against them by agreeing to pay $1.25 billion to claimants. This lawsuit against them, which was filed in October 1996, was intended to recover bank accounts. By the time of the settlement, the suit had extended its original reach. In addition to Nazi victims with Swiss accounts, the settlement ultimately identified four other groups of potential claimants, including those whose looted assets had found their way into Switzerland, slave laborers, and refugees who were turned away by Switzerland. The details of the settlement would take another two years to resolve, after having been worked out by a U.S. federal court.

The Archives II's textual research room during the summer continued to be filled with researchers looking at records relating to the various aspects of Holocaust-era assets. The high-water point of researchers came on September 1, 1998, when there were 47 of them. Many of these researchers represented law firms engaged in litigation and many were foreigners. Foreign researchers and representatives of a dozen foreign commissions looking into their countries' handling of victim assets found NARA an important resource to supplement the information available in the archival records in their own countries. Representatives of foreign banks, governments, archives, and corporations also came to Archives II.

The August 1998 Swiss bank settlement prompted several top German firms to come forward and announce that they would set up a restitution fund. This was simply a stopgap measure, since the lawsuits against the German firms were still active. The lawsuits forced the hands of governments. U.S. government officials, including the president, took a strong interest in resolving the issue of claims by forced laborers because they feared it could damage U.S.–German relations. German Chancellor Gerhard Schröder believed that the German government should not only contribute to the fund but also become an active partner in the resolution of the slave-labor issue. Eizenstat and a German counterpart began negotiating, setting up a negotiating track parallel to the one of the litigants. Eventually both Clinton and Schröder intervened. Clinton sent a personal letter to Schröder in early December 1998 reminding him of the issue's importance for German–U.S. relations. Schröder, for his part, arranged a crucial contribution of almost $1 billion from the German government to the corporate fund.

By summer 1998, there were upwards of twenty national commissions looking at what had happened to assets in their respective countries. Many of those involved in the assets issue believed that the United States should have its own commission to look at Holocaust-era assets that came into the control or custody of the U.S. government. Legislation to create a U.S. commission was introduced in Congress in late spring 1998. Congress enacted a law in July establishing the Presidential Advisory Commission on Holocaust-Era Assets in the United States and in October President Clinton appointed World Jewish Congress president Edgar Bronfman to chair the group. Eizenstat, eight members of Congress, and ten others made up the commission membership. And growing out of the desire to declassify still-classified government records, Congress in October enacted the Nazi War Crimes Records Disclosure Act of 1998. This law required federal agencies, including NARA, to review and recommend for declassification records relating to war crimes of the Nazis [and their allies], Nazi war criminals, Nazi persecution, and Nazi-looted assets.

WASHINGTON CONFERENCE, NARA SYMPOSIUM, AND ISRAEL

During late spring 1998, the U.S. government decided that the conference Eizenstat had announced the previous December would be held in Washington, D.C., in December 1998 and that it would be cosponsored by the Department of

State and the United States Holocaust Memorial Museum. Planning began in earnest in June 1998, and it was determined that NARA should be involved. Since this conference would be more diplomatic, political, and legal in nature, I was urged to have NARA hold a more records- and research-oriented conference the day after the Washington Conference. NARA assistant archivist Michael Kurtz quickly endorsed the idea, and the planning for a NARA symposium began.

The Washington Conference on Holocaust-Era Assets was held from November 30 to December 3, 1998. Attending were more than 400 representatives from forty-three countries and a dozen nongovernmental organizations. Among the U.S. delegation were Kurtz and myself. Kurtz presented a paper on the importance of NARA's holdings and during one night of the conference NARA hosted a reception for the conference delegates in the rotunda of the National Archives Building. An important aspect of the conference was opening closed archives to researchers. "A key to success in all the areas of this conference has addressed— and in all aspects of Holocaust-era assets—is the openness and accessibility of archives," Eizenstat stated in his concluding remarks. He added that the United States vigorously supported the archival openness declaration of the Task Force for International Cooperation on Holocaust Education, Remembrance and Research.[17] Speaking about archival openness, Eizenstat took the opportunity to thank NARA for its work in helping his interagency group and the foreign commissions. In his concluding statement, conference chairman Judge Abner J. Mikva noted that NARA's research room had become the center of international study of the assets issues.[18]

The NARA-sponsored Symposium on Records and Research Related to Holocaust-Era Assets was held at Archives II on December 4. More than 400 people, including representatives of numerous foreign governments, attended this event. More than sixty speakers took part in the symposium, and Eizenstat gave the keynote address, in which he stated that "it is truly remarkable to reflect on the sheer amount of research that is being conducted and the new archival sources that have been unearthed in just the past few years." Furthermore, he added, "I am particularly proud to say that our country was a leader in this effort to advance the process of archival research. . . . The National Archives . . . has become a focal point of research, scholarship, and remembrance into the issues surrounding Holocaust-era assets." He concluded his remarks by stating that "The National Archives can be proud of the positive role it has played both in bringing justice, however belated, to the survivors and memory to the deceased."[19] During the course of the day NARA launched its assets Web site.[20]

In mid-December 1998 a three-day conference, sponsored by the United States Holocaust Memorial Museum and three Israeli universities, was held in Jerusalem and Tel Aviv. The conference was entitled "New Records—New Perspectives: World War II, the Holocaust, and the Rise of the State of Israel." Archives were a key focus of the various panels. I spoke about NARA's holdings and challenged the historians to push their governments for increased openness of records and their archival institutions to prepare more and better finding aids.[21] By the end of 1998, the importance of archives as a result of Holocaust-era assets research had been clearly demonstrated. On November 18, 1998 the *Washington Post* quoted Miriam Kleiman as stating, "What's in College Park has rewritten the history of World War II. No question." Reporter John Marks in the December 14, 1998, issue of the *U.S. News & World Report* wrote, "since 1996, when the Holocaust restitution effort gained new momentum" archival institutions "have become drivers of world events. Their contents have forced apologies from governments, opened long-dormant bank accounts, unlocked the secrets of art museums, and compelled corporations to defend their reputations." Actually it has done much more. At the end of the year Lord Janner, who headed the London-based Holocaust Educational Trust, stated that the "hunt for Nazi loot has turned into the greatest treasure hunt in history. We don't know where it will end."[22] Although not knowing where it would end, everyone involved in the various issues knew that much research and negotiations lay ahead of them.

1999: RESEARCH AND NEGOTIATION

President Clinton in January 1999 issued an executive order establishing the Nazi War Criminal Records Interagency Working Group (IWG) to oversee the implementation of the Nazi War Crimes Records Disclosure Act of 1998. This group is composed of representatives of seven federal agencies and three public members appointed by the president. The executive order provided that NARA would chair the group, and Kurtz was so named. NARA was also charged with providing support for the group.[23] Once Sandy Berger, the national security adviser, issued a "tasker" to the federal agencies on February 22, the IWG set in motion the machinery to facilitate the identification of relevant records and their declassification.

In February 1999, the German government and German banks and businesses held negotiations with representatives of law firms, the World Jewish Congress, and the U.S. government to settle the slave-labor lawsuits. The U.S. government wanted to quickly resolve the lawsuits to ease German–U.S. tensions but also so that a last measure of justice could be done to the victims before they all had died. To show their good faith, in February 1999 a group of twelve leading German companies, including Volkswagen, set up the "Memory, Responsibility, and Future Fund." Its aim is to raise funds from German companies to offer to surviving forced laborers. During 1999 the German government agreed to compensate Holocaust survivors in the former Soviet bloc, thereby reversing their Cold War policy against such compensation.

At the first meeting of the Presidential Advisory Commission on Holocaust-Era Assets in the United States (PCHA), in spring 1999, I and two others made presentations about avenues of research and the records available. I brought to the meeting a copy of a 1,100-page finding aid to Holocaust-era assets records held by NARA that had just been published[24] to demonstrate the research task facing the commission researchers. The PCHA's researchers, often numbering over fifteen a day, began their research at Archives II in late spring 1999. They concentrated their research into art, gold, and financial asset issues. Given the quantity of records, the variety of issues the PCHA wanted to be addressed, and the complexities of the research, it appeared that it would be impossible for the commission to complete its work by the end of 1999. Congress, realizing this, extended the life of the commission to the end of 2000.

The media continued to be most interested in NARA and its holdings. In May I gave a presentation in Kansas City to the annual meeting of the Investigative Reporters and Editors (IRE), who were finding that archives were an untapped and important source for investigative stories. My talk and the continuing interest in the Holocaust-era assets story resulted in more journalists pressing NARA for information. To better inform the reporters, in January 2000 I gave a presentation at the National Press Club in Washington to a meeting of the IRE on utilizing NARA's holdings.

President Clinton during summer 1999 promoted Eizenstat to be the deputy secretary of the Treasury. At the White House ceremony announcing the nomination, Clinton made it abundantly clear that Eizenstat would still remain the administration's point man on Holocaust-era assets issues. He was subsequently given the additional title of the special representative of the president and the secretary of state for Holocaust issues. With Eizenstat leaving the Department of State, that agency during the summer created an Office of the Special Envoy for Holocaust Issues to address all issues relating to Holocaust-era assets issues and named J.D. Bindenagel to head the office with ambassadorial rank. NARA has subsequently closely worked with this office on many issues.

Eizenstat and Bindenagel during the summer and fall met with the German government and German corporations to work out a settlement. The Germans were offering about $1.5 billion, but in August lawyers representing victims demanded $20 billion. In October talks adjourned after failing to reach agreement. At that time about thirty-five German companies were participating in the fund. Germany was now offering about $3 billion, half from firms and half from the government. In November talks came closer to a deal but still failed to reach agreement. The Germans offered about $4 billion—$2.5 billion from the fifty companies participating in the fund and $1.5 billion from the government. In December the parties agreed in principle to a settlement worth about $4.8 billion.[25]

In December a class-action lawsuit was filed in the U.S. District Court in San Francisco against the Vatican Bank and the Franciscan Order. They were charged with receiving and laundering hundreds of millions of dollars of gold and other assets looted from victims of Croatia's Ustasha regime during World War II. In mid-September 2000, the judge ruled that the Swiss National Bank (SNB) could be added to the class-action lawsuit.[26]

JANUARY–JUNE 2000

As the year 2000 began, looted art continued to be a major issue. In late April at a joint New York University-International Foundation of Art Researchers conference and again in May at the annual meeting of the American Association of Museums, looted art was a major concern. At both conferences I gave talks about NARA's holdings and how art provenance researchers could best utilize them. Many provenance researchers understood the importance of NARA's holdings but found them daunting to use. To address this concern, Kurtz and I decided to hold a meeting with the art community to address their interests and concerns. In mid-August NARA sponsored an all-day meeting of representatives of the art world, including museums, provenance researchers, and auction houses, to discuss records relating to art provenance and claims research. Growing out of the meeting was an agreement that NARA would work with the art world to make its holdings more accessible. A project team was put in place to ensure that NARA met the needs of the provenance and claims researchers.

On May 1 Eizenstat, in an address before the U.S. Chamber of Commerce, called on American companies whose subsidiaries in Germany during World War II had used slave labor to contribute to a newly created compensation fund. This call prompted several companies to begin doing research at NARA to determine what their subsidiaries did during the war.

As the summer began, the IWG was overseeing the relatively massive declassification of records as required by the Nazi War Crimes Records Disclosure Act of 1998. In late June a major release was made of 400,000 pages of OSS records. By the end of the summer some 2.5 million pages were declassified and released at NARA. Among these records were those of the Army Counter Intelligence Corps, the Federal Bureau of Investigation, and the Department of State.

A SUMMER AND FALL OF SETTLEMENTS

During summer 2000 some Holocaust-era assets issues were coming to fruition, while others still are to be resolved. There were still some fifty-five lawsuits in American courts. In early July Spain agreed to contribute $1.5 million to a fund for Holocaust survivors who are Sephardic Jews. In mid-July France announced it would pay Holocaust orphans compensation. Earlier in the year the French government announced that the 1.4 billion francs of unclaimed funds it held and the 1 billion francs held by financial institutions would go to a "National Foundation for Memory" intended to teach future generations about the Holocaust. Also in mid-July the Dutch government and financial institutions agreed to provide $325.5 million to cover property and assets looted from Dutch Jews during the war. In late September Belgium announced that Belgium's government, banks, and insurance industry were setting up a fund to compensate Belgian Holocaust victims for assets stolen during World War II.

During the mid- and late summer agreements were reached with Europe's second-largest insurance group, Assicurazioni Generali, and efforts were initiated with France's AXA and Switzerland's Winterthur and Zurich Allied. These companies, along with Allianz AG and several Dutch companies, are members of the International Commission on Holocaust-Era Insurance Claims

(ICHEC).[27] The agreement with Assicurazioni Generali obliges it to pay all valid claims from Holocaust survivors and heirs; to give the commission access to its archives; and to post on its Web site more than 21,000 names of the firm's policyholders; Assicurazioni Generali also will give a foundation in Jerusalem the responsibility of deciding which claims are valid. At this point Assicurazioni Generali had pledged $100 million to pay claimants, and by the agreement if the total sum of compensation exceeds that figure, Assicurazioni Generali will pay the full sum of claims.

A settlement was signed in mid-July by representatives from Germany, the United States, Eastern Europe, and Israel, and U.S. attorneys to provide Nazi-era victims of forced and slave labor $4.8 billion, half from the German government and half from German companies.[28] The German legislature quickly approved the settlement. At this point more than 3,100 firms had pledged money. As a way of encouraging additional contributions, the U.S. government agreed to give $10 million to the new slave-labor fund.

Although a Swiss bank settlement had been reached in August 1998, the task of working out the details still remained in the courts. In December 1999 the Volcker Committee issued a report saying that some 54,000 Swiss accounts had probable or possible links to Holocaust victims. As of late July, 600,000 people had returned questionnaires in an effort to be included in the class-action settlement. Judge Edward R. Korman in the U.S. District Court in Brooklyn, in late July, gave final approval to a $1.25 billion accord to settle claims of Holocaust survivors who had sued a group of Swiss banks. At the time he gave his approval, the lawsuit had expanded to include Jehovah's Witnesses, the Roma, the disabled, and homosexuals. Korman's approval provided that money could begin to be distributed to the plaintiffs and their heirs by the end of the year. Korman also ruled that smaller Swiss banks had to give more information on Holocaust-related bank accounts, while the government and companies had to provide information on World War II refugees and forced laborers by an August 25 deadline.

Switzerland's two biggest banks, Crédit Suisse Group and UBS AG, during the first days of August, announced that they had officially accepted an amended version of the $1.25 billion settlement.[29] Four Swiss insurers—Baloise, Helvetia Patria, Rentenanstalt/Swiss Life, and reinsurance group Swiss Re—added $50 million to the settlement amid claims that some life insurance policies of Holocaust survivors had not been honored. Korman's order prompted a great many Swiss corporations to examine the slave-labor use of their wartime subsidiaries. Failure to identify themselves could lead to new lawsuits by slave laborers and their families. During August more than thirty-five Swiss companies so identified themselves. Among the first was the bank UBS, which had owned a factory in Germany that used slave laborers from a concentration camp. Also identifying themselves were the food giant Nestlé, the life-sciences group Novartis, and the pharmaceutical company Roche. Other companies said they could rule out any use of slave labor but were signing up anyway—thus gaining protection against separate U.S. lawsuits. Nestlé announced in August that it was giving about $14 million toward the settlement fund. They were followed in September by Novartis and Roche, both of whom announced that they would each pay about $14 million into the fund in the expectation that it would cover any possible claims against them.

During the first part of September, a special master appointed by the court announced that some $800 million would pay for Holocaust-era bank accounts and about $100 million would be reserved for "looted assets" claimants. The latter would cover former slave/forced laborers and other categories of asset-related claimants. The special master said former forced and slave laborers—whether or not they worked for Swiss subsidiaries—should receive $500 and $1,000 respectively from the Swiss fund in addition to whatever they obtain from the German fund, and that refugees who were denied entry to Switzerland should receive up to $2,500. A fairness hearing was held in late November after which Judge Korman approved an allocation of funds. The distribution plan will give $800 million to people who charged that Swiss banks had prevented them from withdrawing their money. Former forced laborers in German plants owned by Swiss companies can get a maximum of $1,000 per person. Refugees who were turned back at the Swiss border can claim as much as $2,500 each. Some $100 million was set aside to repay those whose assets, which were looted by the Nazis, ended up in Switzerland.

On September 11 in New York City a World Jewish Congress event was held to honor key people, such as Bronfman and Eizenstat, involved in the recovery of Holocaust-Era assets. President Clinton, speaking at the event, stated that "Of course, we can never compensate the victims and their families for what was lost. It is beyond our power to restore life or even to rewrite history. But we have made progress towards setting history straight, and providing compensation for lost or stolen assets, and forced or slave labor. We have an especially sacred obligation to elderly survivors, particularly the double victims who endured first the Holocaust and then a half-century of communism. For their sake, there can be no denying the past or delaying the compensation. We must also meet our obligations to the future, to seek the truth and follow where it leads." Following this event in mid-September, U.S. negotiators led by Eizenstat began pushing Austria to set up a $150 million interim fund to help speed payments to some 21,000 Jewish Holocaust survivors. Austria had already put forward a $415 million restitution plan for Nazi-era forced laborers, hoping that a settlement would bring "legal closure" to claims against Austrian companies.[30]

VILNIUS FORUM

During the first week of October in the Lithuanian capital of Vilnius representatives of thirty-seven nations and seventeen nongovernmental organizations met at the Vilnius Forum on Looted Cultural Property. The meeting had been a provision of a Council of Europe Assembly resolution in late 1999 that called for a European conference that would focus on the return of cultural property and legislative reform. Some of the representatives, including me, were archivists and were present because of the acknowledged importance of archival records in provenance and other looted cultural assets research. In his keynote address, Eizenstat talked about the importance of archives and urged the conference to adopt a resolution relating to openness of archives. My presentation not only focused on NARA's accomplishments but also cited tasks that archival institutions should undertake to facilitate research on Holocaust-era assets records.

The forum adopted a declaration that had six sections dealing with the restitution of looted cultural property. The second section stated, "the Vilnius Forum asks governments, museums, the art trade and other relevant agencies to provide all information necessary to such restitution. This will include the identification of looted assets; the identification and provision of access to archives, public and commercial; and the provision of all data on claims from the Holocaust era until today. Governments and other bodies . . . are asked to make such information available on publicly accessible websites and further to co-operate in establishing hyperlinks to a centralized website in association with the Council of Europe. The Forum further encourages governments, museums, the art trade and other relevant agencies to co-operate and share information to ensure that archives remain open and accessible and operate in as transparent a manner as possible."[31]

Just before the conference ended, Eizenstat flew to Vienna to continue his negotiations with the Austrians, quickly reaching an agreement with Austrian Chancellor Wolfgang Schüssel that would establish a $380 million fund to compensate people forced into hard labor by the Nazis during World War II. The fund will be financed by both the Austrian government and businesses that profited from slave laborers.

THE WINTER OF 2000–2001

During the final weeks of the Clinton Administration in January 2001, much was accomplished in the efforts to compensate victims of the Holocaust and their heirs. The Presidential Advisory Commission on Holocaust Assets in the United States submitted its report and recommendations to the president.[32] On January 17, after a winter of negotiations, the Austrians agreed to a $500 million settlement package, including monies for forced and slave laborers, unpaid insurance policies, and property claims. The next day French and U.S. negotiators reached a settlement that would compensate Holocaust victims for lost assets. French banks will pay more than $72 million to 64,000 known account holders and other undocumented claimants.

CONCLUSION

By the fall of 2000 much had been accomplished toward bringing justice and compensation to victims of Nazi persecution, but those working so hard to achieve the financial settlements knew that no amount of money could ever compensate for the atrocities of World War II. They also know that much still needs to be done, and done quickly as the number of Holocaust survivors decreases every year. Most survivors are in their 80s, and an estimated 1 to 1.5 percent die each month. Many issues, both old and new, are still unresolved. Undoubtedly, interest in Holocaust-era assets issues will continue for years, if not decades. As Gregg Rickman noted recently, the efforts of the past several years had opened Pandora's box and "once opened, it would be impossible to close. Fifty years ago the world did not care about the looted assets of Holocaust victims. Today, it does."[33] Just as certainly, archival research throughout the world will accompany the interest in the various asset-related issues. Archives have served during the past four and one-half years, and will in the future serve, as important resources in the search for truth and justice, and as Stuart Eizenstat frequently says, turning history into justice.

NOTES

1. A general overview of the assets taken can be found in Richard Z. Chesnoff, *Pack of Thieves: How Hitler and Europe Plundered the Jews and Committed the Greatest Theft in History* (New York: Doubleday, 1999).

2. Margaret Clarke, a Federal Economic Administration historian, in 1946 wrote a 193-page history of the Safehaven Program, "Safehaven Study." The study was never published. A copy of it is at NARA in the Records of the Federal Economic Administration (RG 169). Many policy records relating to the Safehaven Program are available in *Foreign Relations of the United States* (FRUS): *FRUS* 2 (1944): 213–251; *FRUS* 2 (1945): 852–932; and *FRUS* 5 (1946): 202–220.

3. Greg Bradsher, "Nazi Gold: The Merkers Mine Treasure," *Prologue* 31 (Spring 1999): 7–21.

4. Arthur L. Smith, Jr., *Hitler's Gold: The Story of the Nazi War Loot* (Washington, D.C.: Berg, 1996); Ian Sayer and Douglas Botting, *Nazi Gold* (New York: Congdon and Weed, 1984); Sidney Zabludoff, *Movements of Nazi Gold: Uncovering the Trail*, Institute of the World Jewish Congress Policy Study No. 10 (Jerusalem, Israel: Institute of theWorld Jewish Congress, 1997).

5. It has been reported numerous times that the reason that all the attention is now being focused on Nazi-looted gold and Jewish assets in Swiss banks is that most of the records remained classified for fifty years. We have had to explain that there is no such thing as a "fifty-year rule." In fact about 50 percent of the relevant records were never classified. Of those that were classified, approximately 75 percent were declassified by 1982, 15 percent were declassified in 1982–1989, 5 percent in 1990–1994, and 5 percent in 1995–1997. A relatively very small number of records remain classified.

6. Foreign and Commonwealth Office, General Services Command, History Notes, *Nazi Gold: Information from the British Archives*, No. 11 (London: Foreign and Commonwealth Office, Sept. 1996). See also Foreign and Commonwealth Office, General Services Command, History Notes, *Nazi Gold: Information from the British Archives*, 2d ed., No. 11 (London: Foreign and Commonwealth Office, Jan. 1997); Foreign and Commonwealth Office, General Services Command, History Notes, Nazi Gold: Information

from the British Archives, *Part II: Monetary Gold, Non-monetary Gold and the Tripartite Gold Commission*, No. 12 (London: Foreign and Commonwealth Office, May 1997).

7. Accessioned and made available during spring 1997 were Army Security Agency intercepts of communications between the Swiss legation in Washington and the Swiss Foreign Ministry in Bern, Switzerland, relating to Allied negotiations with Switzerland in 1946; Central Intelligence Agency profiles of Emil Puhl, vice president of the Reichsbank, and Thomas McKittrick, the wartime president of the Bank for International Settlements; and although their records are not federal records, the Federal Reserve Bank of New York sent NARA copies of pertinent materials.

8. It is interesting that the story does not end at this point, because in 1948 the U.S. Army did not microfilm all the records and both those filmed and those not filmed were turned over to the successor bank, and they have since disappeared. During the past several years there has been a search throughout Europe to locate the original records, and the Germans have issued a massive report explaining their disappearance. The German report has not satisfied everyone, but interest in the search has recently waned.

9. U.S. Department of State, *U.S. and Allied Efforts to Recover and Restore Gold and Other Assets Stolen or Hidden by Germany During World War II: Preliminary Study*, co-ordinated by Stuart E. Eizenstat and prepared by William Z. Slany, Department of State Publication 10468 (May 1997). The report and the appendix were immediately made available at the Department of State's Web site and sold by the U.S. Government Printing Office. Subsequently the U.S. House of Representatives reproduced the finding aid as part of the printed Banking Committee hearings of May 15, 1997, on Swiss banks and attempts to recover assets belonging to the victims of the Holocaust.

10. Foreign and Commonwealth Office, *Nazi Gold: The London Conference* 2–4 December 1997 (London: Stationary Office, 1998).

11. In September 1998 the TGC terminated its activities; it gave the small amount of gold it still controlled to the Bank of England to hold until such time an agreement was reached on the gold that was still owed to the former Yugoslavia. The TGC records were transferred to the French National Archives and copies of key documents were given to the British Public Record Office and to NARA.

12. A good background on looted art and the U.S. involvement is Peter Harcerode and Brendan Pittaway, *The Lost Masters: The Looting of Europe's Treasurehouses* (London: Victor Gollancz, 1999).

13. The $5 million for archival research, though authorized by Congress, was never appropriated.

14. U.S. Department of State, U.S. and Allied Wartime and Postwar Relations and Negotiations with Argentina, Portugal, Spain, Sweden, and Turkey on Looted Gold and German External Assets and U.S. Concerns About the Fate of the Wartime Ustasha Treasury: *Supplement to Preliminary Study of U.S. and Allied Efforts to Recover and Restore Gold and Other Assets Stolen or Hidden by Germany During World War II*, coordinated by Stuart E. Eizenstat and prepared by William Slany, Department of State Publication 10557 (June 1998).

15. Hearing on H.R. 3662–U.S. Holocaust Assets Commission Act of 1998, Thursday, June 4, 1998, Room 2128, Rayburn House Office Building, U.S. House of Representatives, Committee on Banking and financial Services, Washington, D.C.

16. Harclerode and Pittaway, *Lost Masters*, p. 210.

17. J.D. Bindenagel, ed., *Proceedings of the Washington Conference on Holocaust-Era Assets* November 30–December 3, 1998 (Washington, D.C.: Government Printing Office, 1999), p. 129.

18. Ibid., pp. 139, 429, 430.

19. The quotes are from an eight-page speech prepared for delivery by Ambassador Stuart E. Eizenstat, Undersecretary of State for Economic, Business, and Agricultural Affairs, Symposium on Records and Research Relating to Holocaust-Era Assets, National Archives and Records Administration, College Park, Maryland, Dec. 4, 1998, p. 2. Copy in possession of the author.

20. The Web site address is nara.gov/research/assets.

21. Greg Bradsher, "Holocaust-Era Assets Records and Research at the National Archives," *Journal of Israeli History* 8 (Summer–Autumn 1997): 283–286.

22. Harclerode and Pittaway, *Lost Masters*, p. 351.

23. Five NARA staff members, including myself, serve as the IWG staff. The IWG Web site address is nara.gov/iwg.

24. Greg Bradsher, *Holocaust-Era Assets: A Finding Aid to Records at the National Archives at College Park, Maryland* (Washington, D.C.: National Archives and Records Administration, 1999).

25. In March 2000 an agreement was reached on how the compensation would be allocated: about $4 billion to be paid in individual compensation and the remainder to cover property losses and other projects.

26. The judge ruled that the SNB, which is party to the $1.25 billion global agreement between Swiss banks and Jewish organizations, could be named in the current lawsuit because the Serb victims of the Ustasha regime were not mentioned in the global settlement. The court also allowed the lawsuit to add a number of other unidentified Swiss, Austrian, Argentine, and Brazilian banks.

27. The commission has received 30,000 claims since it began accepting them in February. It forwards them to insurance companies. If they refuse to pay, or if the claimant finds a counteroffer to be too small, appeals can be made to special panels established by the commission. Successful claimants receive ten times the value of the original policy in order to approximate roughly its purchasing power of a half-century ago. The only person authorized to act to dismiss future claims will be the ICHEC chair. Leverage against the companies, all of which have subsidiaries in the United States, are laws in at least six states authorizing insurance commissioners to forbid companies from doing business in the state if they refuse to cooperate with the commission.

28. About 240,000 Nazi-era slave laborers—who were meant to be worked to death but survived—will receive payments of up to $7,000; and about one million forced laborers, who toiled under somewhat less punishing conditions, will receive about $2,500.

29. The amendments included, among other things, references to looted artworks, insurance, and forced laborers, as well as creating a database of the bank accounts.

30. Under the plan, compensation would mainly be paid to Eastern Europe, the home of most of the 150,00 survivors who qualify. But Jewish groups and U.S. lawyers who are suing the country and its companies on behalf of Holocaust survivors have attacked the plan, charging that the Austrians have almost entirely excluded Jews from getting any benefits. Further, they have accused Austria of dragging its feet on returning property—including an estimated $1.225 billion of long-term apartment leases—that were stolen from Jews.

31. The conference's Web site is vilniusforum.lt/proceedings/index.htm. It contains substantial documentation on the conference, including speeches given and papers presented.

32. *Plunder and Restitution: The U.S. and Holocaust Victims' Assets; Findings and Recommendations of the Presidential Advisory Commission on Holocaust Assets in the United States and Staff Report* (Washington, D.C.: Presidential Advisory Commission on Holocaust Assets in the United States, 2000).

33. Gregg Rickman, *Swiss Banks and Jewish Souls* (New Brunswick, N.J.: Transaction, 1999) p. 278.

"They Should Have Destroyed More": The Destruction of Public Records by the South African State in the Final Years of Apartheid, 1990–1994

Verne Harris

Under apartheid, the terrain of social memory, as with all social space, was a site of struggle. In the crudest sense it was a struggle of remembering against forgetting, of oppositional memory fighting a life-and-death struggle against a systematic forgetting engineered by the state. The realities, of course, were a little more complex. Forgetting, for instance, was an important element in the struggles against apartheid—forgetting the half-truths, the distorted interpretations, and lies of the apartheid regime. And the notions of "oppositional memory" and "state memory" themselves are problematic. They are artificial constructs, obscuring the sometimes fierce internal contestation in both spaces. Then there is the question of memory and imagination. Memory is never a faithful reflection of process, of "reality." It is shaped, reshaped, figured, reconfigured, by the dance of imagination, so that beyond the dynamics of remembering and forgetting, a more profound characterization of the struggle in social memory is one of narrative against narrative, story against story.

Nevertheless, it is true to say that the tools of forgetfulness, of state-imposed amnesia, were crucial to the exercise of power in apartheid South Africa. The state generated huge information resources, which it secreted jealously from public view. It routinely destroyed public records in order to keep certain processes secret. More chilling tools for erasing memory were also widely utilized, with many thousands of oppositional voices eliminated through media censorship, various forms of banning, detention without trial, imprisonment, informal harassment, and assassination. As this essay recounts, the tools of forgetfulness were also important to the transfer of power—between 1990 and 1994 the state engaged in a large-scale sanitization of its memory resources, a sanitization designed to keep certain information out of the hands of a future democratic government.

Soon after the initiation in 1990 of the process toward a negotiated settlement in South Africa, a number of individuals and structures in opposition to the state began to express fears that such a sanitization would take place. By 1994 it was clear that these fears had been well founded.[1] It is not surprising, then, when the South African Truth and Reconciliation Commission (TRC) was established in 1995 to shine a light into the apartheid system's darkest caverns,[2] one of its specific mandates was "to determine what articles have been destroyed by any person in order to conceal violations of human rights or acts associated with a political objective."[3] This mandate provided the basis for a focused investigation into the destruction of public records by the state. Given the complexity and extent of the apartheid state, adequate coverage by the investigation of *all* state structures and records systems proved impossible, and the TRC decided to limit the investigation to state structures subject to national archival legislation,[4] thus excluding parastatals, statutory bodies that had not voluntarily submitted to the operation of the Archives Act, "privatized" bodies, and "homeland" structures.[5] The "homelands" were responsible for the management of their own records, in some cases in terms of their own archival legislation. The investigation further concentrated its energies on the activities of the security establishment—preliminary research made it clear that initiatives for systematic destruction of public records originated and were felt most acutely there.[6]

This essay relies heavily on the work and findings of the TRC investigation, thus reproducing in large measure both its emphases and its limitations.[7] From the TRC's inception late in 1995, I carried responsibility for liaison between it and the National Archives. When the investigation into records destruction got underway, I was released to become an integral part of the investigative team, an involvement that endured from late 1996 until mid-1998. During 1998 I was contracted by the TRC to collate information it had gathered and to draft sections of the final report dealing with the destruction of records.[8] This essay also draws on my own interrogation of National Archives' documentation of records destruction up to 1994 (all of which was made available to the TRC) and of subsequent follow-up investigations by the National Archives.

I begin with an account of state record keeping, official secrecy, and the destruction of records under apartheid, before detailing the preelection purge of 1990–1994. The question of accountability is then explored, and in the conclusion I offer an assessment of the purge's impact—broadly on social memory and more specifically on the TRC's work—and an outline of lessons to be learned from it by a democratic state.

STATE RECORD KEEPING AND OFFICIAL SECRECY

Apartheid's bureaucracy was huge and complex and intruded into almost every aspect of South African citizens' lives. Controls over racial classification, employment, movement, association, purchase of property, recreation, and so on, all were documented—usually in a multilayered process—by thousands of state offices across the country. This was supplemented by the record of surveillance activities by the Security Police, Military Intelligence, the National Intelligence Service, and numerous other state bodies, including those of the homelands. Large quantities of records were confiscated as well from individuals and organizations opposed to apartheid. An army of bureaucrats—servicing registries, strong rooms, and computer systems—managed this formidable information resource. It is tempting to focus on the unique aspects of information gathering and record keeping by the apartheid state, but they need to be seen in a broader, international context. One of the distinctive features of the late twentieth century state—and globalization is rapidly creating a universal pattern—is its massive accumulation of information, particularly about its own citizens. It does this both through programs with a service rationale and through the activities of bodies charged with surveillance mandates. The "new" information technologies—the pace of their development means that they are always new—provide the state with a capacity for this massive accumulation, which is growing exponentially.

What the state does with all the information at its disposal, and how accessible that information is to citizens, are key issues. Under apartheid, the state's memory resources were hoarded with a pathological attention to detail. While all governments are uncomfortable with the notion of transparency and prefer to operate beyond the glare of public scrutiny, in apartheid South Africa state secrecy was a *modus operandi*. Interlocking legislation restricted access to, and the dissemination of, information on vast areas of public life. These restrictions were manipulated to secure an extraordinary degree of opacity in government, and the country's formal information systems became grossly distorted in support of official propaganda. The fundamental guideline for public access to public records was provided by the 1962 Archives Act (which was amended in 1964, 1969, 1977, and 1979). The 1962 act—the forerunners of which were the 1922 Public Archives Act and the 1953 Archives Act—established that access was a privilege to be granted by bureaucrats unless legislation recognized the right of access to specific categories of records. The number of record categories covered by such legislation was insignificant—for instance, records older than thirty years in the custody of the State Archives Service,[9] and deceased estate files in the custody of masters of the Supreme Court. On the other hand, the discretionary power enjoyed by bureaucrats was severely circumscribed by a range of legislation containing secrecy clauses.

Even within state structures, the management of information was framed by an obsession with secrecy. Every bureaucrat was graded in terms of a rigorous security clearance procedure, the grading level determining an individual's right of access to information. This procedure meshed with a pervasive system of information grading—commonly referred to as "classification"—defined by perceived security risks. The Protection of Information Act, and various legislative forerunners, promised severe punitive action against individuals defying the system.

The Archives Act charged the director of archives (the chief executive official of the State Archives Service) with "the custody, care and control of archives." "Archives" were defined as "any documents or records received or created in a government office or an office of a local authority during the conduct of affairs in such office and which are from their nature or in terms of any other Act of Parliament not required then to be dealt with otherwise than in accordance with or in terms of the provisions of this Act." So the State Archives Service had wide-ranging powers over the management of public records at central, provincial, and local government levels from the moment of their creation or acquisition. However, the words "from their nature," as I elaborate below, left the boundaries around the term *archives* far from clear. Also unclear was who should determine the records that by their nature should not fall under archival legislation. Other provisions of the act elaborated on specific aspects of records management—the physical care of records, their management in terms of approved "filing systems," their conversion to microform, and their accessibility, inspection, and ultimate disposal. Comparison with the archival legislation of other countries reveals that the powers enjoyed by the State Archives Service over the active records of the state were amongst the most extensive of any national archives service in the world.

The legal disposal of public records involved either their transfer into the custody of a State Archives Service repository or their destruction under the terms of a disposal authority. Until 1979 it was the responsibility of the Archives Commission—a statutory body appointed by the responsible Cabinet minister—to authorize the destruction of public records. However, while this authority had been vested with the commission since 1926, by the 1960s the commission had become a rubber stamp for recommendations made by the director of archives. A 1979 amendment to the Archives Act recognized this *de facto* situation by empowering the director of archives to authorize destruction. The act made it a criminal offense to willfully damage a public record, or to remove or destroy such a record other than under the terms of the act or any other law. As with all national archive services, the State Archives Service was obliged by limited resources to select only a small proportion of public records for archival preservation. To date, no study has been made of the impact on the archival record of the service's selection program. What is clear is that state secrecy ensured that this program was neither transparent nor accountable to the public, and that it was sustained by bodies (the commission and the service) reflective of the apartheid system and shaped by its ideology.

Needless to say, efficacy in implementation is the most important test of powerful legal instruments. In practice, the service was hampered by inadequate resources and by its junior status in government. Empowered legislatively for the first time in 1922, the service had undergone a number of name changes and been moved successively from the departments of: Interior; Union Education;

Education, Arts and Science; and, finally, to National Education. As with all the service's staff members, the director of archives occupied a public service position and was appointed through the standard public service mechanisms and procedures. Only a small proportion of government offices were effectively reached by the service's records management program. The inspection function, crucial to the auditing mandate of the Archives Act, was no more than a token gesture. This, combined with the state's disregard for accountability and the director of archives' relatively junior ranking in the public service hierarchy, rendered the service almost powerless to resist state organs obstructing its legitimate activities and flagrantly ignoring or defying its legal instruments. Especially problematic were bodies located within the security establishment. With the exception of the South African Defense Force and the Department of Prison Services, the service did not subject these bodies' records systems to professional supervision. Indeed, there is no evidence of professional liaison between the service and other branches of the security establishment before 1990. It is not clear whether this abrogation of responsibility was the result of orders from higher authority or it was simply the result of the service's leadership being intimidated by the security establishment's powerful position. The consequence was that the establishment was a law unto itself in the management of its own records.

Also of crucial importance—and devastating in its consequence—was the vulnerability of the Archives Act's definition of *archives* to divergent interpretations of the words "from their nature." It is not clear what the act's drafters intended to exclude from the definition by these words, although in his speech of January 31, 1962, to the Senate, the minister of Education, Arts, and Science indicated that the words were designed to accommodate requirements for secret records.[10] The authority of the act over various categories of public records was challenged unsuccessfully on this basis in the period immediately after the act's passage into law. However, until 1991, the status of classified (in terms of security grading) records in relation to the Archives Act received no legal scrutiny. In that year it emerged that the National Intelligence Service had destroyed the sound recording of a meeting between imprisoned African National Congress leader Nelson Mandela and State President P.W. Botha. The State Archives Service challenged the legality of the destruction on the grounds that the director of archives had not authorized it. On December 10, 1991, the state president's office secured a state legal opinion (299/1991) indicating that "sensitive" documents—those requiring secrecy—were by their nature not "archives" and therefore not subject to the Archives Act. Subsequently the National Intelligence Service also acquired a state legal opinion (308/1991, December 17, 1991), which produced a similar finding. The legal scrutiny underpinning these opinions revealed that the security establishment had since the Archives Act's inception regarded classified records as falling outside the act's ambit and had implemented a governmentwide policy for the routine destruction of such records.

RECORDS DESTRUCTION UP TO 1990

In the period 1960–1994, first the Archives Commission and later the director of archives issued a total of more than 4,000 record disposal authorizations to state offices. As I indicated earlier, it remains to be assessed to what extent the interests of the apartheid state were accommodated in this selection process. Within budgetary and other constraints, the State Archives Service monitored implementation of these disposal authorizations to ensure that public records were destroyed under archival authorization and only after the lapsing of appropriate retention periods. Numerous cases of alleged or actual unauthorized destruction were investigated. Most involved disasters such as fires and flooding, and in some cases it was clear that negligence had played a role. However, in not a single instance was the State Archives Service able to identify sinister motivation such as the deliberate destruction of documentary evidence. Over many years a dispute was sustained with Central Statistical Services (CIS) over their routine destruction of census returns and related records without proper archival authorization. CIS's legislative mandate required the agency to ensure the confidentiality of such records, and they adopted the position that only destruction could achieve this. The loopholes in the Archives Act's definition of archives gave CIS the space to outmaneuver the State Archives Service successfully.

Incredibly, the service's monitoring activities did not detect a governmentwide policy for the destruction of classified records until 1991. It is not clear when this policy was first implemented, but it was certainly in place by 1978. In that year all government departments received guidelines for the protection of classified information, signed by the prime minister and empowering department heads to authorize destruction outside the ambit of the Archives Act. The guidelines did not explicitly challenge the Archives Act's ambit. Rather, they simply authorized destruction without mentioning the Archives Act at all.[11] This was in direct conflict with a standing directive of the State Archives Service that indicated that all classified records were to be regarded provisionally as archival until the State Archives Service had physically appraised them. The guidelines were updated in 1984 by the National Intelligence Service under the state president's signature.[12] How widespread or stringent was their implementation by state offices remains unclear. Certainly within the security establishment they were implemented rigorously. The South African Defense Force utilized a similar parallel set of guidelines from at least 1971. Like their civilian counterparts, military archivists in the South African Defense Force Archives appear not to have been aware of their existence.

The great majority of the records generated by the security establishment was classified and therefore subject to the guidelines' provisions for destruction. In essence the guidelines on the one hand obliged agency heads to destroy certain categories of record in the interests of security, and on the other gave discretionary power to destroy records that had lost their functional usefulness. The TRC investigation revealed evidence of widespread implementation, particularly rigorous in structures of the National Security Management System, the

National Intelligence Service, the Security Police, and the South African Defense Force. The National Security Management System (NSMS) was set up in the early 1980s to coordinate state action against antiapartheid activities. It was headed by the State Security Council, ostensibly subordinate to Cabinet but by the end of the 1980s supreme on issues relating to security. The council ran a huge network of substructures reaching into every part of the country, relying mainly on security establishment resources but drawing in almost all organs of the state. When the public debate on the destruction of classified records occurred in 1993 (recounted later in this essay), the head of the Security Secretariat maintained that a full set of NSMS records were being preserved and that only duplicate copies were being destroyed. On the contrary, the official responsible for the management of these records from 1980 to 1990 was later to inform the TRC that the guidelines for destruction were fully implemented throughout that period. It is not surprising that the documentary residue of the NSMS contains numerous and substantial gaps.

The National Intelligence Service (NIS) was established in 1980, inheriting the functions of the Bureau of State Security (1968–1978) and the Department of National Security (1978–1980). The systematic routine destruction of NIS records began at least as early as 1982. On December 1, 1982, the service's top management adopted a set of guidelines (Directive 0/01) that authorized divisional heads and regional representatives to destroy annually records that no longer possessed security relevance. It proved impossible for the TRC investigation to determine records disposal procedures in the pre-1980 era, but the evidence suggests that NIS procedures were applied to any records that had survived.

The Security Police was a branch of the South African Police (SAP). With the approval of the director of archives, they managed their records according to records systems approved by the director for use throughout the SAP but in physically separate record sets classified as secret or confidential. Standing SAP instructions indicated that no secret or confidential records could be destroyed without written authorization from the director of archives. In the period 1960–1994 no such authorizations were given. The TRC investigation determined that throughout this period Security Police records were routinely destroyed in accordance with internal retention and disposal arrangements. In the main this state of affairs seems to have obtained in the support-function records rather than in the operational records. Huge volumes of operational records were generated at head office, regional, and local levels. To cope more effectively with them, a microfilming project was initiated, probably in the 1970s. Originals of microfilmed records were apparently destroyed, but not systematically. From 1983 onward a computerized database of operational records was created. Again, it appears as if certain original records were destroyed after the core data had been captured on the database. Nevertheless, in 1990 the Security Police retained huge quantities of operational records in locations throughout the country, a large proportion still in paper form.

The South African Defense Force (SADF) enjoyed a special status within the framework of the Archives Act. It managed its own archives repository (the SADF Archives) and, from the late 1960s, provided its own records management service (through the SADF Archives) to SADF structures. Both functions were supervised by the State Archives Service. Standing orders required that records be destroyed only in accordance with authorizations signed by the director of archives, and that destruction certificates be submitted to the SADF Archives. However, as I have already indicated, from at least 1971 conflicting standing orders authorized the routine destruction of classified records without reference to the SADF Archives, the director of archives, or the Archives Act. The evidence suggests that substantial volumes of records were destroyed in this way without any archival intervention. There is also evidence of large-scale destruction of records generated by bodies related in one or other way to the SADF. The South West Africa Territory Force was a joint South African/Namibian force established to operate in conjunction with SADF operations in Namibia. Starting in December 1998 its records were subjected to systematic appraisal. Decisions on which records were to be destroyed were authorized by the commanding officer of the South West Africa Territory Force. There was no consultation with the civilian archives repository in Windhoek, the SADF Archives, or the State Archives Service. Records that survived this exercise were placed in the custody of the SADF Archives.

The Civil Cooperation Bureau was a special unit established to disrupt or eliminate persons considered to be enemies of the state. It reported to the SADF's Special Forces division. The Harms Commission of Enquiry into Certain Alleged Irregularities, which reported in 1989, revealed that all the bureau's records had either been destroyed or been illegally removed. The records of Koevoet, the notorious counterinsurgency unit that operated out of Namibia, were reported as having all disappeared in transit between Windhoek and Pretoria.

Between 1960 and 1990, through its appraisal function and the monitoring of state offices, the State Archives Service had sought to control the destruction of public records and to ensure the preservation of records with archival value. Nevertheless, by 1990 there was a well-established practice within state structures of routinely destroying classified records outside the ambit of the Archives Act. Within the security establishment there was an ethos in the management of its own records characterized by almost complete autonomy from the intervention of the State Archives Service. Nevertheless, throughout the state substantial and archivally rich classified information resources were being maintained. Particularly in the security establishment, a prevailing sense of being in control supported the preservation of records that in more uncertain circumstances would surely have been destroyed.

THE PREELECTION PURGE

Uncertainty for state structures was heralded by the February 1990 lifting of the ban on the African National Congress and numerous other antiapartheid organizations, and the subsequent initiation of formal negotiations toward the official dismantling of apartheid. Apprehension about certain public records passing out of the then government's control became prevalent. There was particular concern about such records being used against the government and its operatives by a future democratic government. The first state agency to act decisively was the National Intelligence Service (NIS). In 1990 it decided to replace its 1982 guidelines for records destruction with a far more rigorous process to be managed by an interdivisional Standing Re-evaluation Committee. New guidelines were given to the committee in October 1991. The guidelines required the destruction of paper-based records unless there were very good reasons for their retention. "Security relevant" records were to be kept on microfilm or in electronic form, where they were most secure and easier to destroy or erase quickly. Continued retention was to be reviewed annually. In addition, documentation of covert operations was to be categorized according to criteria relevant to sensitivity and security, and references to the most sensitive documentation were to be removed from the electronic information retrieval system. None of this documentation was to be kept longer than six years. Top management elaborative guidelines issued in February 1992 make it clear that one of the purposes of this exercise was to sanitize the image of both the government and the NIS in a new political environment.[13] Initially, the new guidelines did not accommodate Treasury requirements for the management of financial records. However, in 1992, after conferring with the auditor-general and the director of archives, the NIS director-general requested ministerial approval for the destruction of financial authorizations, vouchers, and related documentation. The minister of Justice and National Intelligence gave his approval on July 3, 1992.

Implementation of the new NIS policy gained momentum in 1992 but reached its greatest intensity in 1993. Mass destruction of records took place at this time, embracing all media and all structures. In a six- to eight-month period in 1993, NIS headquarters alone destroyed approximately forty-four tons of paper and microfilm records, utilizing the Pretoria Iscor furnace and another facility outside Johannesburg. The evidence suggests that many operatives took the opportunity to "clean up" their offices, irrespective of the guidelines. Systematic destruction exercises continued until late in 1994, with many of the surviving minutes of chief directorate, directorate, and divisional meetings and most administrative records covering the period 1989–1994 being destroyed at this late stage. NIS's own requirements for the preparation of destruction certificates were seldom observed. The result was a massive purging of NIS's corporate memory. This was supplemented by the unauthorized *ad hoc* removal of documents by individuals for their own purposes. Any attempt to quantify this phenomenon was beyond the resources of the TRC investigation. Very little pre-1990 material survives in the paper-based, microform, or electronic systems, and the documentary residue for the period 1990–1994 has been substantially sanitized. The one seemingly intact records series is minutes of senior management meetings, which covers the period 1980–1994.

In 1992 the Security Police followed the example set by NIS. In March of that year an instruction emanating from their head office ordered the destruction of all operational records, including nonpublic records confiscated from individuals and organizations. The TRC investigation was unable to determine either the precise source of this instruction or its precise content. The evidence suggests that it was received orally at both regional and local levels. The instruction embraced all media and required the destruction not only of records but also of all documentation about the records. In the months following the issuing of the instruction, massive and systematic destruction of records took place. In some cases records were removed to the head office for destruction. In others, destruction took place on site. In yet others, private companies like Nampak (a manufacturer of cardboard containers) and Sappi (a paper and board manufacturer) were utilized. With few exceptions, it would appear that Security Police offices implemented the instruction to the letter. In fact, some offices destroyed most, if not all, support function as well as operational records. There were exceptions. The investigation revealed that certain operational records from eleven regional and local offices were not destroyed. Several thousand files also survived in what had been the Security Police head office, most carrying dates after 1990. Eleven backup tapes of the head office computerized database were located, seven of which were still readable. And contrary to the March 1992 instruction, three offices kept lists of files forwarded to the head office for destruction.

As early as 1990, NIS's top management expressed the need for coordinated governmentwide action in the destruction of records. The first step taken in this direction related to the records of the NSMS, which was rapidly dismantled after February 1990. NIS was made the official custodian of NSMS records. On November 29, 1991, a circular instruction was sent to all government departments requiring them to transfer to NIS all NSMS-related records in their custody. While the stated purpose of the exercise was to enable the Security Secretariat to assemble a complete set of these records, it was clearly designed to facilitate systematic sanitization. The exercise was less than successful, and in July 1993 the head of the Security Secretariat, with explicit Cabinet approval, sent another circular to all government departments, recommending that they destroy all classified records that had been received by them from other sources, with the exception of those constituting authorization for financial expenditure or "other action." Special mention was made of documentation related to the NSMS. The impact of this circular was immediate and severe. Across the country government officials began purging the classified records under their care. At the time I was an archivist in the records management program of the State Archives Service. I had professional contacts in numerous government offices, and some of the more conscientious amongst them alerted me to the danger. When I briefed the director of archives, I discovered that he knew about the circular and "had the matter in hand." When nothing was done over the next week to stem what was clearly a massive governmentwide destruction exercise, I leaked the information to the African National Congress, the press, and Brian Currin, then National Director of Lawyers for Human Rights. In the public furor that followed, the state maintained that the step was merely designed to eliminate unnecessary duplicate copies of classified records, that all originals would be preserved, and that in any case classified records fell outside the ambit of the Archives Act. Currin then challenged the circular's validity in the Supreme Court, identifying the respondents as the state president, the minister of National Education, the director of archives, and the director-general of NIS. In his application, Currin argued that state legal opinions 299/1991 and 308/1991 were "wrong," and that the nature of "sensitive" records, including classified material, did not exclude them from the operation of the Archives Act. On September 27, 1993, all the parties reached agreement that from then on no public records would be dealt with otherwise than under the terms of the Archives Act.[14] Two days later the minister of Justice issued a news media statement in which he stated, "Cabinet is of the view that state documentation should be dealt with in terms of the Archives Act."[15]

Hopes that the loophole in the Archives Act had been removed proved vain. The settlement had not incorporated Currin's broader arguments, and the state exploited this to continue its "legal" destruction of records outside the operation of the Archives Act. The 1984 guidelines for the destruction of classified records were not withdrawn. In fact, as late as November 1994, *after* the installation of South Africa's first democratically elected government, NIS issued an updated version of the guidelines that still ignored the Archives Act. This action was a direct violation of the Currin settlement. The director of archives challenged NIS accordingly, and the guidelines were revised appropriately and rereleased in February 1995. In the wake of the Currin settlement, for the benefit of the media and oppositional groups, the state staged a charade of abiding by its provisions. A second circular was sent out to government departments qualifying the contents of the first. An interdepartmental working group was established to prepare guidelines for government offices on which categories of public record fell outside the ambit of the Archives Act. When the group produced draft guidelines, the director of archives (through the director general of National Education) sought a state legal opinion on their validity. The opinion (220/1993, November 2, 1993), without even referring to the Currin settlement, simply affirmed the findings of opinion 299/1991. However, the opinion did assert that decisions on destruction should not be left to individual department heads and recommended that an advisory mechanism should be created. This was never done.

The full extent of the Cabinet's duplicity emerged only during the TRC investigation. Unbeknownst to either Currin or the State Archives Service, on June 2, 1993, a month before the July Security Secretariat circular, the Cabinet had approved a new set of guidelines for the disposal of "state sensitive" documentation. These guidelines had their origin in meetings of NIS top management in 1990 and 1991, where it was decided to use NIS's own destruction guidelines as a point of departure for the preparation of governmentwide guidelines. The proposal was taken to the State Security Council, which adopted the guidelines in May 1993, subject to an NIS investigation of comparative practice internationally. There is no evidence that NIS conducted such an investigation. The following month the council proposed the guidelines to the Cabinet, which duly approved them. They empowered ministers to authorize the destruction of financial and related records outside parameters laid down by the Treasury, and heads of departments to authorize the destruction of all "state sensitive" records meeting certain loosely defined criteria.[16] The guidelines were distributed to all government departments. Carrying the weight of the highest authority in the land, their impact was severe. For instance, the State Archives Service's own parent body, the Department of National Education, promptly destroyed most of the files in its security-related filing system, despite the fact that the system was subject to a State Archives Service disposal authority that had earmarked the great majority of the files for archival preservation. Nevertheless, the evidence suggests that implementation was extremely uneven and shaped directly by an office's positioning in relation to the coercive aspects of apartheid administration.

It is unclear to what extent subsequent destruction exercises were in response to or shaped by the Cabinet-approved guidelines of June 1993. Clearly, however, senior managers in state structures regarded themselves as having been given the green light to sanitize records in their care. No records of the Kwazulu Intelligence Service (KWAZINT) survived. KWAZINT existed between 1986 and 1991 as a special NIS project managed in cooperation with the Kwazulu homeland. All project records were either sent to or managed by NIS. During 1995 the remaining former homeland intelligence services were integrated into the new civilian intelligence services, the National Intelligence Agency (NIA), and the South African Secret Service. It seems that before then very little records destruction had been effected by these services. On the other hand, between April and October 1995 an NIA Chief Directorate Research and Analysis Coordinating Committee subjected some of the records inherited from these services to a thorough reevaluation process. Working both on site and with records that had been transferred to NIA headquarters, the committee was mandated to identify for preservation records of value to NIA from both operational and historical perspectives. The TRC investigation revealed that less than 5 percent of the records were identified for preservation, almost none of them predating 1990, and that in practice the sole criterion for preservation seems to have been security relevance. The remaining records were subsequently destroyed, the last destruction exercise taking place as late as November 1996. This episode revealed the resilience of attitudes and values from the past. Not only did NIA, ostensibly a structure of the new democratic South African state, implement the sanitization policy of the apartheid state, in doing so it ignored the State Archives Service and defied moratoriums on the destruction of public records introduced in 1995.[17] After completion of the reevaluation process, large volumes of additional records were secured at NIA headquarters from the offices of the former Bophutatswana, Transkei, and Venda intelligence services.

The periods covered by these records are as follows: Bophutatswana Intelligence Service (1973–1995), Bophutatswana National Security Council (1987–1994), Transkei Intelligence Service (1969–1994), and Venda Intelligence Service (1979–1994).

The SADF responded decisively to the Cabinet-approved guidelines. In 1992 Lieutenant General Steyn, at the time the SADF chief of staff, had been appointed to investigate SADF intelligence activities. On November 23, 1992, all SADF structures had been informed that from then on records were to be destroyed only with the express approval of Steyn. However, on receipt of the Cabinet-approved guidelines, the chief of the SADF ordered their immediate implementation, thus effectively repealing Lieutenant General Steyn's instruction. Two joint teams consisting of inspector general and counterintelligence personnel were appointed to visit all units and to identify records for destruction. A countrywide destruction exercise followed. By and large this exercise failed to produce the required destruction certificates, making analysis of its impact extremely difficult. The TRC investigation was forced to seek a sense of the impact through probes into what it regarded as hot spots:

- Although subjected to close scrutiny during the 1993 destruction exercise, a surprisingly large volume of Military Intelligence files have survived. As one of the South African National Defense Force's (SANDF) legal team commented to me during the investigation, "They should have destroyed more." Another instance of being confronted by a ghost from the past. Three discrete file groups were identified at the SANDF Archives: group number 14, comprising 299 boxes of files covering the period 1977–1987; group number 21, comprising 254 boxes of files covering the period 1975–1987; and group number 30, comprising 529 boxes of files covering the period 1976–1996. Significant gaps were identified nevertheless. For instance, no record accumulations of the directorate Special Tasks or the Directorate Covert Collection could be found, and only a small accumulation of Contra-Mobilisation Projects (COMOPS).

- No record accumulation related to the Civilian Cooperation Bureau could be found.

- Spot checks revealed that not all personnel files could be made available, raising the question of whether such files had been destroyed.

- Spot checks suggested that substantial documentation of cross-border operations in neighboring countries had survived.

- Very little NSMS documentation managed by the SADF has survived. The only significant accumulation comprises fifty-four boxes of files (now in the SANDF Archives) generated in the Eastern Cape and preserved for use in the inquest conducted into the death of political activist Mathew Goniwe. However, some other NSMS documentation was identified in each of the three Military Intelligence file groups described above.

- A task group authorized by the chief of the SANDF in June 1994 managed the acquisition by the SANDF Archives of all extant records of the former defense forces of Transkei, Bophutatswana, Venda, and Ciskei. These forces had been amalgamated with the SADF and nonstatutory forces to form the SANDF in April 1994. Apart from

the 1,544 boxes of files secured from the Bophutatswana Defense Force, relatively insignificant documentary traces were secured: eighty boxes of files from the Transkei,
115 from the Ciskei, and 331 from Venda. Excluded from these figures are personnel
files, which were integrated with the SANDF's personnel file series. Clearly, then,
huge volumes of records generated by the defense forces of the former homelands
had been destroyed.

The limitations of the TRC investigation were exposed dramatically in 2001
when the South African History Archive (SAHA) put in a Promotion of Access to
Information Act request for a list of all extant apartheid-era military intelligence
records. Whereas the TRC, as detailed above, had been told about and given access to only three file groups, SAHA was provided with a list of forty-two file
groups, including the three examined by the TRC. This discovery carries considerable import. Not only does it provide evidence that broader TRC investigations were hindered by obstruction in the security establishment, it also places a
question mark behind the conclusions drawn in relation to the extent of the pre-
1994 purge. How many other caches of records are lurking in security establishment facilities?

This reservation notwithstanding, it seems that by May 1994, when the new
democratically elected government took office, a massive deletion of state documentary memory had taken place. This enforced amnesia was concentrated, for
obvious reasons, in the security establishment. Unlike their counterparts in the
former East Germany, Kampuchea, and other countries, South Africa's apartheid leaders had had plenty of time in which to do the job thoroughly. Despite
this, surprising pockets of public records survived the process, even within the security establishment. Some I have already detailed. There were others. From the
perspective of documenting resistance to apartheid, two are of particular interest.
First, the Department of Prison Services, despite routinely destroying classified
records in the pre-1990 period and acting on all the 1993 governmentwide
guidelines, preserved intact two significant file series: case files opened for every
security/political prisoner and case files opened for every prisoner under sentence of death. And second, the comprehensive accumulation of records generated by the Department of Justice's Security Legislation Directorate. The
directorate was established in 1982 and endured until 1991. Its predecessor was
the Internal Security Division, and before that, beginning in 1949, the function
was performed by various individuals in the department. Its function was to
make recommendations to the ministers of Justice and Law and Order on the
administration of security legislation—for instance, should an individual or organization be banned? should an individual be restricted? should a certain gathering be allowed? Legislation falling within its ambit included the Suppression of
Communism Act, Internal Security Act, Affected Organizations Act, Terrorism
Act, Unlawful Organizations Act, and Public Safety Act. It made recommendations on the basis of investigations initiated by the Security Police. Recommendations were supported by information gathered on its behalf by the Security
Police, NIS, and Military Intelligence. The evidence suggests that the director-

ate's records management was impeccable. Records were kept in accordance with State Archives Service and departmental directives, with disposal being performed in accordance with disposal authorizations issued by the Archives Commission and the director of archives. While the directorate did routinely destroy classified records received from other state offices in accordance with the NIS guidelines, they ignored all the 1993 disposal guidelines. The directorate's extant records, kept in excellent condition by the Ministry of Justice, comprise the following: a series of case files for individuals, spanning the period 1949–1991; a series of case files for organizations and for publications (the series for organizations includes files inherited by the directorate dating back to the 1920s); and policy, administrative, and other subject-based correspondence files.

Despite the large-scale destruction of records that had taken place during the negotiation process, as the April 1994 General Election loomed President De Klerk and his Cabinet became anxious about what remaining public records the new government would inherit. Late in 1993, the president's office asked the chief state law advisor whether representatives of De Klerk's government could retain custody of certain records after April 1994. A draft memorandum leading to the formal request cited an obscure British precedent and indicated that one of the motivations was to "keep this information out of the hands of future co-governors."[18] The records referred to were "gebruiksdokumentasie"—working documentation—including Cabinet minutes and the minutes of Cabinet committees, ministers' committees, and the State Security Council. At the time none of these records had been transferred into the custody of the State Archives Service, on the grounds that their "sensitive nature" excluded them from the operation of the Archives Act. In his opinion 207/1993 of December 22, 1993, the chief state law advisor indicated that such records could not be removed from the state's custody. Also in December 1993, President De Klerk referred the same question to Advocate S.A. Cilliers for an opinion. Advocate Cilliers responded on January 13, 1994, confirming the chief state law advisor's opinion, and went further by disagreeing with opinion 299/1991 and its affirmation of the legality of the destruction of "state sensitive" records on the authorization of departmental heads.[19] Subsequently Cabinet and Cabinet committee records were transferred to the State Archives Service, albeit with a Cabinet-imposed ten-year embargo on access. The service ignored the embargo, and access was managed from the outset under the terms of the Archives Act's access provisions. In 1995 and 1997 the surviving residue of State Security Council and related records was also transferred into archival custody. Why, one must ask, did De Klerk and his Cabinet not simply destroy these records? With approval already given for the destruction of numerous other records categories, why the fastidiousness over these? I suspect that the answer is twofold. On the one hand, they were high-profile records that both the news media and the new government would be eager to see after April 1994. On the other, the destruction of these records would directly involve the Cabinet. Consequently, it would be impossible to blame junior officials for misinterpreting disposal guidelines.

ACCOUNTABILITY

The routine destruction of classified public records outside the parameters of the Archives Act had begun well before 1990. Sanctioned by the head of state, the process was concentrated in South Africa's security establishment. Between 1990 and 1994 the process was broadened into a systematic endeavor authorized by the Cabinet and reached into all sectors of the state and embraced categories of record designated as "state sensitive." At the time and subsequently, those responsible maintained that the endeavor was designed simply to protect intelligence sources and the legitimate security interests of the state. The evidence demonstrates that the endeavor went far beyond such categories, constituting a systematic sanitization of official memory resources in anticipation of the nation's transition to democracy. Those responsible also maintained that the endeavor was entirely legal. They pointed to the state legal opinions secured by the state president's office, NIS, and the director general of National Education in 1991 and 1993, which ruled that "state sensitive" public records fell outside the definition of records that were subject to the Archives Act. This argument is deeply flawed.

First, the legal opinions were disputed by the State Archives Service, Advocate S.A. Cilliers, and Brian Currin, the National Director of Lawyers for Human Rights. The basis of Currin's successful legal intervention in 1993 was a rejection of the two 1991 opinions. Second, the public position adopted by the Cabinet itself was that all public records should be dealt with in terms of the Archives Act. Third, the state used the legal opinions selectively. For instance, the 1993 opinion's recommendation that an "advisory mechanism" on records destruction be created was never implemented. Fourth, the Cabinet's approval of the destruction of financial records outside requirements laid down by the Treasury was of dubious legal validity. And fifth, the legal opinions begged the question "In terms of what law are 'state sensitive' records to be destroyed?" Several officials involved in such destruction pointed to the Protection of Information Act, but that act makes no reference to the destruction of documents.

Ultimately the question of legality is a nonissue. On the one hand, apartheid was characterized by "official lawlessness,"[20] with rules and actions that were perfectly legal but lacked legitimacy and bore little or no relation to the rule of law. On the other, it is clear that the sanitization of official memory resources would have taken place irrespective of legal constraints. As Brian Currin said of the 1993 settlement that followed his legal intervention, the only way to enforce the Archives Act would have been to "tie up their [the government's] hands and confiscate all the relevant machinery they can use to destroy documents."[21]

Given its legislative mandate, the State Archives Service was the principal state agency responsible for acting against the destruction of public records without archival authorization. In the 1990–1994 period of mass destruction, intervention by the service achieved nothing. It followed up by correspondence every allegation of illegal records destruction, engaged the security establishment in debate around the issue, registered its disagreement with the 1991 and 1993 legal opinions, and forced revision of NIS's 1994 *Guidelines for the Protection of Classified Information*. However, it was hamstrung by the apartheid system's disregard for accountability, by inadequate resources, by its junior status in government, and by a leadership that was intimidated by the security establishment and lacked the will to act decisively. I was a staff member of the service throughout this period and remember well how I and some of my junior colleagues pushed for such action while the leadership chose to sit on the fence. Earlier in this essay I recounted the inadequacy of leadership's response to the 1993 Security Secretariat circular authorizing the destruction of certain categories of classified records. To cite another instance, in June 1992 the Department of Foreign Affairs requested authority to destroy certain special projects files. When the director of archives indicated that they should be transferred into State Archives Service custody, Foreign Affairs withdrew their application and claimed that the files were in fact merely empty file covers. The director refused my calls for an investigation. More damning was the director's collusion with NIS in 1992, cited earlier in this essay, to secure authorization for the quick destruction of that agency's financial and related records. Specific instances aside, not once in the period 1990–1994 did the director authorize an investigative inspection of an office suspected of illegally destroying records. Not once did the director undertake a face-to-face meeting with a suspected perpetrator. And not once was the Archives Act used to institute an investigation of possible criminal charges in terms of the act.

What about intervention by the liberation movements? I joined the African National Congress (ANC) in 1990, and in 1992 I was appointed to its Archives Committee (a subcommittee of its Commission on Museums, Monuments and Heraldry). Within the committee and other structures in which I was involved there was an acute awareness of the danger that the apartheid state was planning a mass destruction of public records. The experience of Zimbabwe in the months preceding that country's independence, when huge quantities of public records were destroyed by the outgoing regime, was frequently cited in discussions. It was felt imperative that the issue be put on the agenda during negotiations with the apartheid government and that the ANC's leadership should call for a moratorium on the destruction of public records with immediate effect. The first formal recommendation for such a moratorium was made at a meeting of the Commission on Museums, Monuments and Heraldry in March 1992, and at the ANC's 1993 Conference on Culture and Development it was resolved that "there should be an immediate cessation of the destruction of all State records regardless of existing policy."[22] However, it proved impossible to mobilize the leadership behind the issue. It was not put on the table during the multiparty negotiation. Support for Currin's 1993 legal intervention was limited to a news release backing his endeavor. When the Transitional Executive Council was established in 1993, the liberation movements that participated failed to ensure that the enabling legislation addressed the question of a moratorium. Moreover, the Transitional Executive Council failed to take any action in the wake of the Currin settlement—the council was, in the words of Currin, "just paralyzed and didn't respond."[23] Action was to take place only in 1995. In June of that year the National Intelligence Coordinating Committee introduced a moratorium on the destruction of all "intelligence documents." On November 29, 1995, the Cabinet decided on a moratorium that applied to all records of the state, irrespective of their age and irrespective of whether the director of archives had authorized their destruction. This blanket moratorium endured until completion of the TRC's work in 1998, whereafter it was narrowed to the records of the security establishment. It will only be lifted when the TRC's amnesty process is concluded. These moratoriums, of course, came too late. It is also not clear how effectively the moratoriums were communicated to and enforced within security establishment structures. Certainly NIS and later NIA, as I pointed out earlier in this essay, continued destroying records after the introduction of the moratoriums, until as late as November 1996. It could be argued that more decisive intervention by the African National Congress and the other liberation movements would not have prevented, nor even curbed, the mass destruction. Nevertheless, this was a lever that sadly was not utilized.

In its findings on the destruction of public records in the period 1990–1994, the TRC distinguished between culpability and accountability.[24] The former implies wrongdoing, the latter shortcoming or negligence. Identified as culpable were

- The Cabinet and the State Security Council, for sanctioning, from at least 1993, a governmentwide purging of official memory resources.

- NIS, for beginning its purging exercise before Cabinet sanction was secured, initiating the process that led to the adoption of governmentwide destruction guidelines in 1993, defying the terms of the Currin settlement by failing to revise its *Guidelines for the Protection of Classified Information*, and of supervising, or at least of failing to prevent, the purging of NSMS records.

- The Security Police, also for beginning its purging exercise before Cabinet sanction was secured.

- The numerous individual state officials and operatives who used the cloak provided by the destruction endeavor to destroy or remove documents without authorization.

Also found culpable were the NIA officials directly responsible for the destruction of records until as late as November 1996, in defiance of the two government moratoriums. NIA's top management were held accountable for not preventing this destruction. For the period 1990–1994, the TRC assigned accountability as follows:

- The head of the Security Secretariat, for the consequences of his July 1993 circular to all government departments recommending the destruction of certain categories of classified records.

- The State Archives Service, for "the indecisive and ineffective steps it took to halt the destruction endeavor."

- The liberation movements, for failing "to exercise all the leverage at their disposal in acting against the endeavor."

CONCLUSION

It is far too early to come to any conclusions about the impact of the 1990–1994 purge on social memory in South Africa. Our knowledge of the purge relies heavily on the TRC investigation into records destruction, an investigation severely constrained by a number of factors. It operated with limited resources within extremely tight time frames. Of necessity, it had to rely on highly selective probes into hot spots, and in doing so was dependent to a greater or lesser degree on resources and cooperation made available by state structures still in the initial stages of transformation. While for the most part levels of support appeared to be excellent, cases of overt obstruction did occur.[25] As detailed earlier in this essay, the most blatant case of obstruction that we are aware of was exposed by the South African History Archive in 2001, when it was able to demonstrate the extent to which the TRC was deceived by Military Intelligence. This case of a successful hiding of substantial accumulations of records from the TRC investigation places a question mark behind all its findings. Clearly, much work remains to be done. Nevertheless, in my view, the TRC investigation gave us a sound grasp of the broader processes of records destruction—the big picture—and considerable insight into the impact of those processes within the security establishment. It remains for the National Archives and private researchers to extend these boundaries. What we can say at this stage is that the evidence suggests a considerable impact on social memory. Swaths of official documentary memory, particularly around the inner workings of the apartheid state's security apparatus, have been obliterated. Moreover, the apparent complete destruction of records confiscated from individuals and organizations over many years by the Security Police has removed arguably the country's richest accumulation of records documenting the struggles against apartheid. The overall work of the TRC suffered substantially as a result. In seeking to reconstruct and understand the past, so many pieces of that past's puzzle were missing. As the TRC itself indicated, "the destruction of state documentation probably did more to undermine the investigative work of the Commission than any other single factor."[26] As significant, it now appears, was the degree to which surviving state documentation was successfully hidden from the TRC's purview. For the most part the big picture—the fundamental shape and pattern of process—was as clear as any interrogation of the past can be, but so often the details, the nuances, the texture, the activities and experiences of individuals, remains absent. On the other hand, TRC investigation teams were often surprised by records accumulations that survived the purge. One has to ask why they survived. Imperfect central control over what was a vast bureaucracy? The presence of individuals with consciences in the lower reaches of the state? Determination to preserve information that could compromise the leadership of the new government? During the course of the investigation I saw several files that could create severe difficulties for people now prominent in the public and other sectors. At one point I remember one of my TRC colleagues turning to me with the comment: "Perhaps it would have been better if all these files had been destroyed."

More edifying has been the discovery of extensive accumulations of records detailing the apartheid state's dispossession of individuals' and communities' rights to land. The National Archives and the Department of Land Affairs have worked closely with the National Commission for the Restitution of Land Rights to identify substantial records series in state offices around the country that the commission is using to investigate land claims. Clearly, then, much work remains to be done before we have a comprehensive picture of the scale and consequences of the 1990–1994 purge.

Imperfect as our understanding of the purge might be, we know enough to have learned crucial lessons from it. Perhaps the most important is the necessity for transparency and accountability in government. As the transition to democracy has gathered momentum, "openness" and "disclosure" have become watchwords both within the state and in broader societal processes. This emphasis is underpinned by the new Constitution's recognition of the public right of access to information, particularly that held by the state.[27] It remains to be seen how well this lesson has been learned. Already evident is a strong countercurrent, fed by state officials and structures that are finding themselves blinded by all the light. There is now awareness within the state—honed by the impact of the records destruction moratoriums—that no state has the resources to preserve indefinitely all the information in its systems. Selection procedures, choosing what to remember and what to forget, are essential—this to support both the efficacy of archival programs and the protection of legitimate interests through confidentiality. Beyond the determining of memory's outer boundaries, the state is also becoming adept at crafting the hidden places—the "official secret"—within that memory. Take the TRC, torchbearer of disclosure, as an example. Some of its hearings were held *in camera*. Its records of protected witnesses were secret. Information on certain decision-making processes and of internal tensions and disputes was jealously kept out of the public arena. Its archive is subject to various access restrictions. Some democrats accept that a measure of official secrecy is desirable; most accept it as unavoidable. There are disturbing signs in post-apartheid South Africa that official secrecy is beginning to be embraced as a point of departure. In March 1999 the SANDF demanded the return of certain "top secret" documents it had submitted to the TRC—this followed the detention by the police of a Swiss journalist for possessing a copy of one of these SANDF documents, a document that he had been given by the TRC. The state has effected no meaningful changes to the inherited systems of information classification and staff security clearance. With increasing frequency, the news media are running into government communications officials who constitute brick walls rather than gateways. At the same time heat directed against news media freedom by the state is gathering fuel. And "open democracy" legislation—which will provide for freedom of information, the protection of personal information, and the protection of whistleblowers from the state—has been through a protracted gestation cloaked in secrecy.[28] It seems that for South Africans, particularly lawyers, journalists, and activists, learning how to wrestle effectively with the "official secret" will be essential. The degree to which they are successful will be a crucial measure of South Africa's democratization.

The purge also highlighted the need for a democratic state to take appropriate measures to prevent the sanitizing of official memory resources. The cornerstone for such measures is the provision of suitably powerful legal instruments to a state agency responsible for the auditing of public record keeping and, ideally, for managing public archives services as well. In many respects the 1962 Archives Act constituted such an instrument, but it possessed four fatal flaws. First, many state offices were excluded, wholly or partially, from its operation. Second, its definition of archives (public records) contained loopholes that the apartheid state was able to exploit ruthlessly. Third, the penalty for conviction on a charge of destroying a public record without archival authorization was a laughable fine of 200 Rand.[29] This did not constitute a deterrent. And fourth, it provided no mechanisms for ensuring accountability and transparency in the selection of public records for preservation by the director of archives. All these flaws have been rectified by the National Archives of South Africa Act of 1996, and the national government has put in place mechanisms to ensure that archival legislation passed by the provinces follows the same model.

Needless to say, a powerful legal instrument without appropriate executive action is nothing more than a dead letter. This was recognized by the TRC in three of its recommendations:[30]

- The government should provide the National Archives with the resources it requires to give life to the legislation. The power to inspect governmental bodies, for instance, is rendered meaningless if the resources to exercise it are not made available. Current budgetary allocations to the National Archives are woefully inadequate.

- The government should take steps to ensure that the positioning of the National Archives within the state supports its function as the auditor of government record keeping. Currently, as with the State Archives Service in the past, the National Archives is positioned as a junior subcomponent of a noncentral national department and lacks both the status and the autonomy it requires to perform the auditing function. Unfortunately, this TRC recommendation loses its force through contradictory elaboration—at one and the same time it advocates independent agency status (the ideal) and positioning within either the office of the president or that of the deputy president.

- The security establishment should not be allowed to escape the operation of the National Archives of South Africa Act. While the act brings security bodies firmly within its ambit, it does allow for various exclusionary options.[31] It is conceded that a special status for such bodies appropriate to the sensitivity of the records they generate would be legitimate, but that they should remain fully subject to the professional supervision of the National Archives.

The TRC also made several recommendations related to redressing the imbalances imposed by the purge on official memory.[32] A number relate to ensuring that the National Archives secures control over the records of the security establishment that have survived the purge. To date only two of the many records accumulations concerned have been transferred into the National Archives' custody, and of the remainder not one has been either inspected or subjected to an archival audit by the National Archives. In addition, the TRC recommended as follows:

- The security establishment should make every attempt to locate and retrieve documents removed without authorization by operatives of apartheid security structures. To my knowledge, nothing has been done in this regard.

- The South African government should acknowledge that, in terms of internationally recognized archival principles, the extant records of the South West Africa Territory Force (currently in the custody of the SANDF Archives) properly belong in Namibia and must be returned to the Namibian government. It was noted that an agreement between South Africa and Namibia covering equivalent civilian records was already in place. To date this recommendation has not been acted on.

- The National Archives should be given the necessary resources to take transfer of, process professionally, and make available to the public the TRC's own records (which fill many of the gaps in official memory resources). After a long tussle with the Department of Justice, the National Archives has at last been given the go-ahead to take custody of the TRC's records when the TRC office finally closes down, probably early in 2002.

- The National Archives should be given the necessary resources to fill the gaps in official memory resources through the collection of nonpublic records and the promotion of oral history projects. To date the National Archives has not received a significant infusion of resources for these purposes.

I find the TRC recommendations compelling. It remains to be seen what the state makes of them. To date the signs are mixed. Three years down the line there has been no formal government response to the TRC recommendations. It is hoped that a response will be forthcoming once the TRC completes its work and submits the codicil to the final report. On the other hand, the National Archives has sought either to promote the recommendations, where its mandate and resources allow, or to implement them. However, in every case the National Archives is reliant on higher authority to give full effect to the recommendations.

NOTES

1. Between 1988 and 1994, I was an archivist in the Pretoria records management division of the South African State Archives Service. Rumors were rife within the public service, and by early 1993 I had enough evidence from sources in various governmental bodies to know that destruction was widespread. When it became clear that the State Archives Service was unable or unwilling to act decisively, I began leaking information on the destruction to the African National Congress, other oppositional structures, and the news media. The celebrated 1993 Currin case discussed later in this essay pushed the issue firmly onto center stage in the news media. And the Harms and Goldstone commissions of inquiry as well as the Goniwe inquest revealed substantial evidence of systematic destruction of records.

2. The seventeen-member Truth and Reconciliation Commission was given four principal functions: to establish as complete a picture as possible of the causes, nature, and extent of gross human-rights violations committed in South Africa between 1960 and 1994; to facilitate the granting of amnesty to perpetrators of gross human-rights violations associated with a political objective; to recommend appropriate reparation for the victims of gross human-rights violations; and to compile a report of its activities, findings, and recommendations. The commission's final report was submitted to President Nelson Mandela in October 1998, but the work of the commission's Amnesty Committee proceeded and is anticipated to continue for some time.

3. South Africa, Promotion of National Unity and Reconciliation Act (Act Number 34 of 1995) §4(d).

4. South Africa, The Archives Act (Act Number 6 of 1962). See in particular the definition of a "government office" in §1.

5. The apartheid government allocated a homeland to each of South Africa's major African ethnic "groups." In terms of separate development policy, these Africans were to exercise full political rights only in these homelands. The ultimate goal was to establish each homeland as an independent country—by 1994 four of them had taken "independence."

6. Each of the security establishment's structures was subjected to close scrutiny by a joint team comprising representatives of the structure concerned, the TRC, the Human Rights Commission, and the National Archives.

7. The work of this investigation is reflected in the following sections of the TRC's final report: South Africa, Truth and Reconciliation Commission, *Final Report*, vol. 1, ch. 8, and vol. 5, ch. 8, pp. 62, 66, 67, and 100–108 (Cape Town, 1998).

8. My work was subsequently edited by the TRC editorial team, but I was involved in the editing process. In preparing this essay I had a choice between quoting extensively from the published version or of assuming that my role in its authorship precluded the need for what would be a clumsy nicety. I chose the latter course, working always in the first instance from my first draft for the TRC and quoting from the published version only in instances where that seemed appropriate.

9. The State Archives Service became the National Archives on January 1, 1997. See South Africa, National Archives of South Africa Act (Act Number 43 of 1996).

10. South Africa, *Debates of the Senate* (1962).

11. The guidelines were referenced as EM 9–12. The relevant paragraphs are 31 and 32.

12. The updated guidelines were referenced as SP 2/8/1.

13. These elaborative guidelines are reproduced as Appendices 2 and 3 to vol. 1, ch. 8, of the TRC's final report. See TRC, *Final Report.*

14. South Africa, Supreme Court, Transvaal Provincial Division, Case No. 19304/93.

15. The statement was issued in Afrikaans. This is my own translation of the text.

16. The guidelines are reproduced as Appendix 1 to vol. 1, ch. 8, of the TRC's final report. See TRC, *Final Report.*

17. The moratoriums are discussed later in this essay.

18. The text was in Afrikaans. This is my own translation.

19. Advocate Cilliers's opinion is dated January 13, 1993, but this is clearly a dating error.

20. Christopher Merrett, *A Culture of Censorship: Secrecy and Intellectual Repression in South Africa* (Cape Town: David Philip and University of Natal Press, 1994), p. 203.

21. TRC, *Final Report*, vol. 1, ch. 8, p. 232.

22. I quote this from my own conference notes.

23. TRC, *Final Report*, vol. 1, ch. 8, p. 234.

24. TRC, *Final Report*, vol. 1, ch. 8, pp. 235–236.

25. The TRC acknowledged excellent support that it received from South Africa's National Archives and various security establishment structures, but it noted obstruction encountered in work with the SANDF. See TRC, *Final Report*, vol. 1, ch. 8, pp. 202–204, 216. Numerous minor instances of obstruction were not noted by the TRC.

26. TRC, *Final Report*, vol. 1, ch. 8, p. 204.

27. The new Constitution also recognizes the right of access to information held by persons other than the state "that is required for the exercise or protection of any rights." South Africa, *Constitution*, § 32(1).

28. The state held the Open Democracy Bill under consideration for about five years. At the last moment, the state decided to exclude provisions for the protection of personal information and of whistleblowers—both to be dealt with in separate legislation. In January 2000 the legislature passed the *Promotion of Access to Information Act*, which defines the right of access to information held both by the state and by persons other than the state. This act became effective in March 2001. The Protected Disclosures Act, which provides for the protection of whistleblowers, was also passed in 2000.

29. This was the equivalent of about U.S. $24 dollars at the current exchange rate (August 2001). The *National Archives of South Africa Act* (Act Number 43 of 1996), § 16(1), has changed the penalty to "a fine or imprisonment for a period not exceeding two years or both such fine and imprisonment."

30. TRC, *Final Report*, vol. 5, ch. 8, p. 345.

31. The act allows for certain categories of public records identified by the national archivist to remain in the custody of the creating agency rather than be transferred into the custody of the National Archives. It allows for public records to remain in the custody of the creating agency if another Act of Parliament requires it. And it allows for a governmental body to be exempted from any provision of the act with the concurrence of the national archivist, the National Archives Commission, and the responsible minister.

32. TRC, *Final Report*, vol. 5, ch. 8, p. 346.

Trying to Write "Comprehensive and Accurate" History of the Foreign Relations of the United States: An Archival Perspective[1]

Anne Van Camp

For something approximating the truth beyond the day's spin on events, we need genuine history. The U.S. government, however, has grown so addicted to the drug of secrecy injected regularly during the Cold War that it seems to believe it has the right to protect its secrets from its own citizens forever.

Eric Alterman[2]

One hallmark of a society's openness is the degree of public access to the archives and records of its government. While the United States is indisputably a world leader in providing open access to government information, current public policy for handling and releasing classified government information is still in need of much reform. The end of the Cold War sparked a renewed effort on the part of historians, journalists, and legislators to open much of the historical information that was kept closed for national security reasons for too many years.

Yet even today, over a decade since the breakup of the Soviet Union and the various events that now mark the end of the Cold War, few of the necessary reforms to open our historical files have been achieved. Appropriate legislation to enforce the systematic release of historical information is lacking. Adequate systems for managing and providing access to government information—especially records in electronic form—are not in place. And many federal agencies remain recalcitrant in complying with the requirements to release historically important records.

This article will examine aspects of current policy controlling the management of the federal government's classified records and will explain in particular the role of the Historical Advisory Committee (HAC) to the U.S. State Department in trying to effect change in opening the historical records of our nation's foreign relations so that an accurate and comprehensive history can be written.

BACKGROUND OF THE HISTORICAL ADVISORY COMMITTEE TO THE STATE DEPARTMENT

One of the responsibilities of the U.S. State Department since the presidency of Abraham Lincoln has been to compile and publish the important records of the government's foreign policy, a series entitled the *Foreign Relations of the United States* (*FRUS*). The formal mandate for the series required that it be complete and accurate and serve as the official record of the nation's foreign policy. It was also intended to be a timely publication getting the record out as soon as possible. Over the years, the ability of the State Department historians to meet this mandate effectively has been compromised by several factors. The growing volume of records being generated by the government, the growing volume of records having security restrictions, and the growing number of government agencies participating in the making of foreign policy have all contributed to the near demise of the credibility of this important government resource.

For many years, the State Department had invited a board of distinguished diplomatic historians to serve in an advisory capacity for the *FRUS* series. Over time the board became increasingly disturbed by the lack of timeliness of the publication and the lack of completeness that the volumes were able to achieve. The situation reached a climax in 1990 when a volume was published in the *FRUS* series covering the events in Iran in 1952–1954. The historical community was outraged at the omission of information about the intelligence community and its role in bringing about the fall of the government in Iran. In fact, the volume was criticized by one reviewer as being fraudulent history.[3] While many of the details of the Iran episode had already been published in several other sources, the government had not and would not officially release any information about the incident.

This publication, coupled with other problems the committee encountered in gaining access to important classified information and even in getting accurate information on the universe of records in existence, led to the resignation of the chair of the committee, Professor Warren Cohen.[4] This act of protest sparked a public outrage over the degradation of the *FRUS* series and an increasing government embarrassment for the overly protective classification policies impeding access to important historical information.

It was clear to the historical profession, journalists, scientific researchers, archivists, and the interested public that serious reform was needed. In 1991, a new law was passed to help rectify the problems: Public Law 102–138, Title IV—Foreign Relations of the United States Historical Series. This new law included provisions that deadlines for the publication of the series would not exceed thirty years from the dates of the events; volumes must be a thorough, accurate, and reliable documentary record of major U.S. foreign policy decisions and significant U.S. diplomatic activity; and editing principles should cover inclusion of facts of importance and guidelines about omissions. In addition, the law required access of State Department historians to records from all U.S. agencies, and that the State Department declassify and transfer its records to the National Archives at the thirty-year point. The law also established a nine-member *FRUS* advisory committee, including six members from designated professional associations and three at-large members. Members of the committee were required to have or obtain security clearances adequate to provide appropriate oversight for the work of the committee. The advisory committee was to meet quarterly or more if necessary. The advisory committee's charter required its members to review records and advise and make recommendations to the historian of the State Department on all aspects of preparation and publication of the *FRUS* series, as well as to review State Department procedures for declassification of department records, for their transfer to the National Archives, and for their availability for public inspection and copying. Finally, the committee was directed to report annually to the secretary of state and provide an accounting of its reviews.[5]

EARLY PROGRESS

In meeting its responsibilities, the committee began by focusing on the broad tasks assigned in the law: (1) ensuring that the *FRUS* series remain "thorough, accurate, and reliable," constituting a "comprehensive documentation of the major foreign policy decisions and actions of the U.S. government"; (2) ensuring that the FRUS would be published no later than thirty years after the events; and (3) monitoring the declassification and transfer to the National Archives all State Department historical records as scheduled.

The committee's accomplishments in the area of ensuring accurate and reliable volumes centered on the establishment of procedures for getting better access to documentation across the government and for streamlining the clearance processes for classified materials. Agreements regarding access for the State Department historians were secured with nearly every relevant government agency, notably including the Department of Defense and the Treasury Department. A timeline for publications with clear benchmarks was developed as a tool for use in planning research and the clearance process. The advisory committee members all gained security clearances allowing them to provide adequate oversight and advice to the historian's office. Several appeals procedures were built into the State Department's publication process, and the work of the historians gained a much higher profile at the very highest levels of the department.

Issues surrounding declassification of the State Department's records consumed a great deal of time and attention from the committee. In examining the process and trying to find ways of streamlining this work, the committee became increasingly aware of the poor record policies that govern historical materials not only in the State Department but also throughout the government. From the beginning, the committee members were struck by the overly restrictive declassification standards that were being applied to the release of information and the time-consuming, labor-intensive processes that were in place to review records for release—literally a page-by-page, and often line-by-line, review was conducted for each document requested for release.

The committee's early recommendations for bulk declassification of most records that were thirty years old or older met with extreme resistance from the State Department's declassification staff. A small working group was then assigned to look more closely at the process and make alternative recommendations. The working group included representatives from the historian's office, the advisory committee, the National Archives, and the State Department's declassification unit. It was clear that the working group would need to be creative in solving the problem, for the estimate given for using the existing process was that it would take nearly twenty years before the bulk of the 1963 files would be open—obviously not an acceptable way to meet the thirty-year mandate.

The working group recommendations included the creation of a State Department Center for Declassification that would review records for their clearance prior to being transferred to the National Archives. Foreign service officers retired from the State Department would be used for declassification review and they would be encouraged by the department management to pursue an aggressive policy of openness.

The advantages were that the reviewers would be familiar with the subject matter and its sensitivities and could thus review the materials quickly. It was hoped that they would learn how to assess the risk of releasing in bulk large series of records. The selection of retired foreign service officers was intended to speed the process and increase the volume of released records by eliminating the need for reviewers from the National Archives to declassify based on guidelines written by State Department officials but often too opaque for consistent application by NARA declassifiers. Previously, classified records sent to NARA would be handled along with all other classified materials from other agencies and would be placed in a priority queue awaiting systematic, mandatory, or special-access requests for release.

Despite early reservations from the State Department declassification unit about whether they would ever be able to meet the timelines, and despite the early reservations from some members of the advisory committee that retired foreign service officers would embrace the policy of openness and the timeliness recommended, the progress within the first few years was extraordinary. Department reviewers used a combination of risk assessment of records to determine their sensitivities, rapid review of records known to hold minimal sensitivities, and more considered review of records known to hold continuing sensitive information and "equities" from other agencies. The volume of documentation reviewed and released under this process continues to be staggering. In the first year of the program, the State Department released more than sixteen million pages of historical records totaling nearly 6,265 cubic feet. As a result of this approach, the withholding rate, or the number of documents that continued to remain classified, was about 3 percent of the total number of records reviewed, and the vast majority of those records were withheld because of "other agency equities." This means that agencies other than the State Department (e.g., the Central Intelligence Agency) hold continuing interest in the information and the State Department does not have the authority to release that information without consent from the other agency.

The advisory committee remained concerned about this 3 percent of withheld records, and several suggestions were made on how to get other agencies to review these items in a timelier fashion. Some agencies, including the Department of Defense, were willing to give declassification authority to the State Department reviewers to declassify on their behalf. The concept of interagency review teams was proposed but was not embraced. In some cases agencies were persuaded to go to the National Archives and review the records that contained their equities. However, this was not a consistent practice throughout the government, and each agency brought different criteria to the process. In addition, the committee recommended that any records thirty years old and older that have been reviewed and remain classified be rereviewed systematically every five years until they can be released. Without this provision, the records would not be reviewed again unless a researcher requested their review.

The State Department demonstrated that with experience and will (and perhaps with the insistence of a committee with legislated mandates), changes could be made to the declassification process. Low-risk materials can be easily identified and released with no harm to the agency. High-risk materials can be identified and dealt with in a rapid fashion by trained and efficient reviewers. Other agency equities and resistance to more liberal openings remain obstacles to fuller release of the State Department's records.

The role of the HAC in effecting some of the changes was significant. In a July 1, 1994, letter to Secretary of State Warren Christopher, the HAC chairman, Warren Kimball, stated that: "Reflecting on nearly three years of activity by the HAC since the 'Foreign Relations Act' became law, I am struck by three things: first, how effective an independent public interest advisory committee like this can be, and how essential it has been for us to have the force of law behind us in our dealing with both career officials and political appointees; second, how much more of our time and effort has been required than any of us expected; and third, how much can be accomplished, quickly and cost-effectively, when responsible officials become actively involved with the issues facing the HAC and press an agenda of openness rather than secrecy."[6]

From the archival perspective, two important changes occurred in this process. First, the department takes a much more active approach in the declassification of its own records. Instead of shifting the bulk of the responsibility for handling large amounts of classified documents to the National Archives when records are transferred, the bulk of the work is being done before the records are transferred, thereby releasing more information in a timely manner. Second, there is a greater sensitivity to the need to review the entire universe of the department's records—in other words, a systematic review of the records is now a matter of course, rather than a selective review of only those records requested for review.

As work continued on trying to improve declassification procedures, it was clear that while the State Department was making progress, there was no efficient way to ensure that similar progress would be made government-wide. And this caused an enduring problem in holding up publication of the *FRUS* series, because documents from other agencies were crucial to the publications. The only way to effect this kind of government-wide policy was through a new executive order. As the drafting of President Bill Clinton's new executive order dealing with classified national security information began in early 1995, the HAC made several suggestions, including a twenty-five year mandatory declassification review timeline; clear benchmarks for measuring declassification activity; and the creation of an advisory council of public citizens to provide oversight for reviewing progress in these areas.

EXECUTIVE ORDER 12958

Protection of national security information has been prescribed by a series of executive orders, beginning with President Franklin D. Roosevelt in 1940. These executive orders identified categories of information that should be protected, how materials should be classified, and often noted how such materials should be declassified. Nearly every president after Roosevelt issued a new executive order clarifying or changing some aspects of these procedures. Beginning with President Harry S Truman, each new executive order issued carried the intent of easing secrecy and opening records in a timelier fashion. President Ronald Reagan's executive order of 1982 on this issue reversed a nearly thirty-year trend toward liberalizing access and in fact instituted policies that would allow some information already released to be reclassified.[7]

President Clinton's Executive Order 12958, issued in April 1995, addresses some of the major problems regarding access to classified information. It takes into account the end of the Cold War and the need for change in the climate of secrecy in government. Executive Order 12958 and its implementing directives, issued in October 1995, make significant changes in policy on both the classification and declassification of government information. It contains a considerable emphasis on the need to change the government attitude toward national security information. President Clinton states in the preamble to the order: "Our democratic principles require that the American people be informed of the activities of their Government. Also, our Nation's progress depends on the free flow of information. Nevertheless, throughout our history, the national interest has required that certain information be maintained in confidence in order to protect our citizens, our democratic institutions and our participation within the community of nations. Protecting information critical to our Nation's security remains a priority. In recent years however, dramatic changes have altered, although not eliminated, the national security threats that we confront. These changes provide a greater opportunity to emphasize our commitment to open government."[8]

Changes in the new order significantly tighten the guidelines for original classification so that the volume of newly created classified information should diminish considerably. Time limits and reasons for classifying must accompany original records when they are created. An automatic declassification deadline is built into the order, requiring that all historical records twenty-five years old and older were to be opened by the year 2000. While some categories of materials may be exempted from automatic declassification, those materials must be reviewed and justified for exemption prior to the required opening date.

The executive order also gives some new and important responsibilities to the National Archives and to other agencies with respect to their management of their records and their relationship with the National Archives. All records scheduled for disposal or retention by NARA are covered by the automatic declassification mandate. Originating agencies are given clear directions on their responsibility for "cooperating with NARA in developing schedules for the declassification of records in the National Archives and the presidential libraries to ensure that declassification is accomplished in a timely manner." Agencies are also instructed to consult with NARA in establishing their own declassification programs and in reviewing records in their holdings to ensure that appropriate procedures are established for maintaining the integrity of the records. Agencies are also directed to provide NARA with accurate information about their declassification actions when they transfer records to NARA.[9]

Originating agencies are now directed to take all reasonable steps to declassify information contained in records determined to have permanent historical value before they are accessioned into the National Archives. And they are expected "to the extent possible . . . [to] adopt a system of records management that will facilitate the public release of documents at the time such documents are declassified."[10]

Oversight for implementation of all aspects of the executive order is the responsibility of the Information Security Oversight Office (ISOO), formerly attached to the Office of Management and Budget, and now reporting to the National Archives. This move offers the potential for NARA to become a major influence in setting direction for the handling and management of classified information through its life cycle, and for insuring good recordkeeping practices throughout the government.

It is conceivable that better records management and sound administration of classified records—in keeping with life-cycle management of classified information—could ultimately relieve the government of much of the costly burden of meeting the overwhelming quantity of mandatory document review (MDR) requests and Freedom of Information Act (FOIA) requests. If at the time records were created the classification given to them also included the date the document should be released or reviewed for release, and if that were tracked effectively throughout the life of the record, an enormous improvement would be achieved. To effectively make this positive change, the mindset for change must extend to records creating agencies government-wide and particularly to NARA.

To date, the Information Security Oversight Office has been passive in asserting its role in the oversight and implementation process. The office has been given unprecedented authority for monitoring and advising on the implementation of the executive order and yet it has done little to actively pursue those directives. The advisory council stipulated in the Clinton executive order of 1995 was never appointed, and NARA has not seized the opportunity to use the ISOO as a means of proactively working with other government agencies to develop strong declassification guidelines and strategies.

While some agencies have complied with the spirit of the executive order, many have found ways to postpone action, file for major exemptions, and in other ways avoid compliance with the demands for more aggressive declassification of historical government information. In particular, the Central Intelligence Agency and the Department of Defense have been the least forthcoming in the release of their historical records and most creative in finding obstructionist tactics. No other agency has the experience or advantage that the State Department has, and the model of its success should be replicated by other agencies. Without good guidance and strong oversight, there will certainly continue to be inconsistent and unarchival policies that will impede access to the vast amount of historical documentation that should be open to the public.

POSSIBLE ALTERNATIVE SOLUTIONS

On April 30, 1994, legislation was passed creating the Commission on Protecting and Reducing Government Secrecy (Title IX of the Foreign Relations Authorization Act, 1994–1995). Initially introduced by Senator Daniel Patrick Moynihan, the legislation called for "comprehensive proposals for reform" that are designed "to reduce the volume of information classified and thereby to strengthen the protection of legitimately classified information."[11] Senator Moynihan's concerns were reflected in the findings section of the law. He states, "During the Cold War an extensive secrecy system developed which limited public access to information and reduced the ability of the public to participate with full knowledge in the process of governmental decisionmaking." Also, "the burden of managing more than six million newly classified documents every year has led to tremendous administrative expense, reduced communication within the government and within the scientific community, reduced communication between the government and the people of the United States, and the selective and unauthorized public disclosure of classified information."[12]

The commission organized its research around four topics: classification, declassification, personnel security issues, and how technology affects the protection and reduction of secrecy both now and in the future. The report of the commission was released in 1997, and one of its major recommendations was for new legislation to create and empower an interagency, government-wide program to address the serious issues that impede access to government information.

The Historical Advisory Committee of the State Department took an active role in support of Senator Moynihan's initiative. Advice from HAC focused on the need for systematic declassification of historical records and a strong oversight mechanism to ensure that appropriate procedures would be in place to support compliance with a national security information policy. A related issue on which the HAC has taken a strong stand is the need to avoid selective, topical, targeted openings of records such as those conducted by the President John F. Kennedy Assassination Records Review Board in 1998.[13] In fact, while the Moynihan Commission was conducting its research, the HAC sent them a strong resolution that stated, "Intentionally or not, 'targeted' openings become a form of information control. Such practices allow government agencies and commissions to determine which part of the archival record will be opened to the public and thereby threaten to distort the public record."[14]

More recently, the Nazi War Crimes Disclosure Act–H.R. 4007, has placed an enormous burden on agencies holding relevant records. As important as this project continues to be, this is the kind of program that must take into account the need to provide adequate resources so that continuing programs of systematic declassification are not abandoned or diminished in the process. William Slany, the historian of the U.S. State Department, stated this position eloquently in his testimony before the Subcommittee on Government Management, Information and Technology of the House Government Reform and Oversight Committee on July 14, 1998: "Even as I recognize the urgency of moving to complete the overdue disclosure of the record of Nazi war crimes, I must remind you of the concerns of my colleagues in the State Department and other agencies of the costs and consequences of assigning special legislative priority to the declassification of these records. The Cold War has left federal agencies the legacy of a huge backlog of classified records. President Clinton's Executive Order of April 1995 directed us to liquidate this Cold War backlog by the year 2000. Programs to achieve what the President mandated strain the resources of agency declassifiers and records managers all around Washington. The Department of State has taken the lead in opening for public view the agency's main foreign affairs record and should achieve the mandated twenty-five year disclosure goal by the end of this decade. State's success is the result of the commitment of its leadership and the assignment of the right resources and direction to get the job done. . . . Special declassification programs like that mandated by H.R. 4007 may have the effect of overwhelming agency records managers and declassifiers and threaten to disrupt the ongoing efforts to meet the President's important goals in an orderly, systematic fashion."[15]

Senator Moynihan's efforts have continued, and the originally proposed "Public Interest Declassification Act of 1999" was ultimately passed in January

2001 as part of the "Intelligence Authorization Act for Fiscal Year 2001."[16] Within this act, H.R. 5630, Title VII—Declassification of Information, section 703, deals with the creation of a Public Interest Declassification Board, and section 704 deals with the identification, collection, and review for declassification of information of archival value or extraordinary public interest. As passed, it lacks many of the original intentions to reinforce the tenets of the Executive Order 12958, including the mandate for classified historical records to be automatically declassified within twenty-five years of their creation.

The Public Interest Declassification Board as defined in the law has as its purposes "to advise the President . . . and other executive branch officials on the systematic, thorough, coordinated, and comprehensive identification, collection, review for declassification and release . . . of declassified records and materials that are of archival value including records and materials of extraordinary public interest; to promote the fullest possible public access to a thorough, accurate, and reliable documentary record of significant United States national security decisions and . . . activities; To provide recommendations to the President for . . . declassification of information of extraordinary public interest that does not undermine the national security of the United States to be undertaken in accordance with a declassification program that has been established or may be established by the President by Executive Order; and to advise . . . on policies deriving from the issuance by the President of Executive orders regarding the classification and declassification of national security information."[17]

Membership on the board is to include nine citizens appointed by the president and designated congressional leaders. The members will all be required to have adequate security clearances and the director of the Information Security Oversight Office will serve as the executive secretary of the board. Section 704 of the legislation addresses other specific responsibilities of the board, including briefings on agency declassification programs, recommendations on agency declassification programs, and recommendations on special searches for records of extraordinary public interest.

If the board so interprets its mandate, it may achieve the goal of providing sound guidance and recommendations across agencies on declassification processes. The language of the act allows for broad interpretation of the selective declassification approach of materials of "extraordinary public interest" to be determined by these politically appointed individuals. It also suggests in several places that a new executive order could be introduced that may or may not be in the same spirit as the Clinton executive order.[18]

The bill could go a long way in reversing some of the current backlash against release of records starting with the congressionally mandated revision of the classified information review process that was instated in 1999 as a result of the Energy Department's fear of the inadvertent disclosure of restricted data.[19] When the Senate was considering the Kyl amendment to the Defense Authorization Act in 1999, an amendment that called for page-by-page review and rereview of Defense records, Page Miller noted in her newsletter, "there is a frenzy of activity to try to deny access to any documents that may have information on how to develop nuclear weapons. Unfortunately many older historical records that have no sensitive weapons information in them have been caught up in this frantic activity.... Despite the imprecise language of the amendment, it sends a strong message that efforts to increase openness to older historical records are no longer in favor."[20] Other recent stories about alleged leaks of information from the Los Alamos Laboratory have fueled this backlash.

It is important to remember that since 1995 and the release of Executive Order 12958, there have been nearly 600 million pages of historical documents that have been declassified and released with no instances of breach of national security, loss of life, or breakdown in foreign relations.[21] The number of records released each year since 1995 has increased significantly, especially during the first three years.

THE CURRENT SITUATION

Despite setbacks, progress within the State Department continues and, as new challenges arise, the HAC continues to help find appropriate solutions. With regard to the department's record for declassifying and transferring records to the National Archives, it is one of the few agencies that are very close to meeting the mandate of the executive order. While exemplary progress has been made with historical paper files, the complications of dealing with electronic records are now a major concern.

Since 1973, the State Department's Central Cable files have been created and stored in electronic form in a classified system within the State Department. The records from the earliest years of this system now fall within the mandated period when they should be reviewed, declassified, and transferred to the National Archives for public availability. While both agencies have been aware of this problem for several years and the HAC has continued to monitor activity in this area, NARA has been very slow in addressing the urgency of this problem and possibly will not be ready to accept the Cable files and make them accessible in electronic form within the mandated time. While NARA is currently developing an electronic access system that will be available within the National Archives, it is anticipated that public access via the Internet to this system may not be ready until 2005.

The State Department has been responsible about managing this information over time and has successfully migrated the data to a more modern electronic information-management system, but the complications of transferring data to a NARA system are enormous. Issues include maintaining a classified set of data and one that has been reviewed and declassified for public access—inserting "electronic outcards" for example. Removing a few years of cables at a time takes them out of the fuller system and presents serious concerns for making sure that records can continue to be accessed and integrated into the larger system of information that will provide their accurate context over time. As a contingency measure, the State Department has agreed to maintain their own records until the National Archives is in a position to provide adequate protection and access to the information. Until these issues can be resolved, the State Department will provide access to the declassified portions of this record for the public through its Web-accessible Electronic Reading Room.

The historian's office continues to struggle with the publication deadlines, and one of the major stumbling blocks is the inability to get critical documents declassified by other agencies in a timely and adequate manner. In 1997 a high level panel was formed with representatives of the secretary of state, the national security adviser, and the director of Central Intelligence. The purpose of the panel was to help resolve interagency disagreements on release of information and for reviewing highly classified documentation on major covert actions, intelligence activities, and other relevant issues selected for inclusion in the *FRUS* volumes. While the panel has met and reviewed several cases, the record of release of information has been disappointing and continues to impede the ability of State Department historians to produce a full and accurate historical record, particularly with respect to the role of intelligence in foreign policy.[22]

One example of this continuing struggle to obtain important documentation concerns the President's Foreign Intelligence Advisory Board (PFIAB). Access to records of this board has been consistently denied to the State Department historians and to the members of the JFK Assassination Records Review Board as well. The records are unique and critically important to understanding foreign policy and the president's role in this regard. According to Steve Aftergood in a recent issue of *Secrecy News*, "In a last-minute good deed that has gone entirely unnoted, President Clinton on January 19, rejected an appeal by the PFIAB and directed that hundreds of pages of historical records . . . be released to the National Archives." As Aftergood noted, "the PFIAB, possibly confusing the United States with some other country, has contended that it 'owns' its records and they are beyond the reach of the law."[23] President Clinton's directive sets a very important precedent for opening these exceptionally important records.

Declassification issues are not the only impediments to making the *FRUS* series into the timely and accurate record of foreign policy it is intended to be. The issues that brought the series into crisis eleven years ago continue to be of concern. The growing volume of information; the new forms of media to be examined, including audiotapes and electronic records; and new kinds of information that should be considered part of the foreign relations record such as social, cultural, and economic institutional information all contribute to the challenge of this publication series.

All these issues combined prompted the HAC to consider an initiative to modernize the *FRUS* series. Beginning in January 1999, this project was intended to rethink and redesign the process of ensuring that users of the *FRUS* series could gain access to the fullest possible record in the timeliest fashion. In July 1999 the HAC approved a new "mission and purpose" statement for the series that reads as follows: "To enhance United States Government and public knowledge of the development of the government's role in history of American foreign relations and to provide a public record that assists the public and its representatives in understanding and assessing the actions of their government."[24]

To achieve the goals of this statement, steps have been taken to increase the volume of documents that can be released, to accelerate the opening of the historical record, to provide detailed guides to the archival record of U.S. foreign policy, and to promote identification and preservation of those records. The new *FRUS* series is envisioned as a multilevel access project that includes core and critical publications of the major themes and issues of U.S. foreign policy. These will likely be printed and made available in electronic form. Related to these volumes will be access guides pointing to the bulk of related archival records, and in time larger quantities of complete documents will be made electronically available with or without annotation. Progress on the implementation of these reforms will appear in the record of the activities of the HAC.

Future progress will depend on several things. The State Department's continued support of the historian's office is crucial. Providing adequate resources and high-level support are essential. Better interagency coordination and government-wide improvement in providing access to the full and complete record of the nation's history must be achieved. This certainly includes a more rational approach to the protection of those secrets that must be protected while opening as much as possible the records of the actions of the entire government. Only with these reforms will the public overcome its cynicism toward public officials and their actions and be reassured that they are getting a complete and accurate history of our national foreign policy.

As Abraham Lincoln once said, "Let the people know the facts and the country will be saved."

NOTES

The Archives of the Historical Advisory Committee—including annual reports, minutes of meetings, and correspondence—are located in the State Department public reading room. Many of the items cited here may be found in the Archives of the Historical Advisory Committee.

1. Since 1990, I have served as a representative of the Historical Advisory Committee of the State Department. My appointment was the first appointment of an archivist to the committee. In the preceding decades, the committee had been composed almost singularly of diplomatic historians and political scientists. All the committee members have learned a great deal about the scope of the problems surrounding access to historical government records. Learning about the inner workings of bureaucracy across the government, coupled with the appallingly inadequate guidelines and standards for managing government information, drove the committee to pursue every avenue for change and reform of recordkeeping policies and systems. Our efforts did result in real change and progress in opening vast amounts of records, in streamlining processes, and in engaging in real reform. The lessons learned by this committee should help inform similar efforts in the future.

This article was written in part as a product of the author's participation in the 1996 Research Fellowship Program for the Study of Modern Archives administered by the Bentley Historical Library, University of Michigan, and funded by the Andrew W. Mellon Foundation, the National Endowment for the Humanities, and the University of Michigan. The author remains extremely grateful for that support.

2. Eric Alterman, "America's Secret History" (May 6, 1999), available at IntellectualCapital.com.

3. Bruce R. Kuniholm, "Foreign Relations, Public Relations, Accountability and Understanding," *Perspectives* 28 (May/June 1990): pp. 1–12.

4. Ibid.

5. The legislation governing the Historical Advisory Committee is *Public Law 102–138, Title IV*, "Foreign Relations of the United States Historical Series," Oct. 28, 1991. The Charter of the Advisory Committee on Historical Diplomatic Documentation is updated annually and can be obtained in printed form from the Office of the Historian, Bureau of Public Affairs, U.S. Department of State.

6. Letter from the HAC Chairman Warren Kimball to Secretary of State Warren Christopher, July 1994.

7. Charles R. McClure, Peter Hernon, and Harold C. Relyea, eds., *United States Government Information Policies: Views and Perspectives* (Norwood, N.J.: Ablex, 1989). In particular, see Harold Relyea, "Historical Development of Federal Information Policy," pp. 25–50, in that volume.

8. U.S. Executive Office of the President, Executive Order 12958, Classified National Security Information, Apr. 17, 1995. Available at fas.org/sgp/clinton/eo12958.html.

9. U.S. Office of Management and Budget, Information Security Oversight Office, *Classified National Security Information, Final Rule, Federal Register* 60 (Washington, D.C.: Office of the Federal Register, National Archives and Records Administration, Oct. 13, 1995), pp. 53491–53502.

10. Ibid.

11. U.S. Commission on Protecting and Reducing Government Secrecy, *Report* (Washington, D.C.: Government Printing Office, 1997). Available at fas.org/sgp/library/moynihan/index.html. See also Public Access Roundtable, *Summary of Proceedings*, May 16, 1996 (Department of State Records Service Center, PA/HO Files).

12. Ibid.

13. U.S. Assassination Records Review Board, *Final Report* (Washington, D.C.: Government Printing Office, 1998). Available at fas.org/sgp/advisory/arrb98/index.html.

14. U.S. Department of State, Advisory Committee on Historical Diplomatic Documentation to the United States Department of State, *Resolution of the State Department Advisory Committee on Historical Diplomatic Documentation*, June 7, 1996.

15. U.S. Congress. House. Committee on Government Reform and Oversight, Subcommittee on Government Management, Information, and Technology, *H.R. 4007 and S. 1379, The Nazi War Crimes Disclosure Act: Hearing*, Testimony of William Z. Slany, July 14, 1998 (Washington, D.C.: Government Printing Office, 1999). Available at fas.org/sgp/congress/hr071498/slany.html.

16. Public Law Number 106–567.

17. Ibid.

18. Ibid.

19. U.S. National Archives and Records Administration, Information Security Oversight Office, *1998 Report to the President*, Aug. 31, 1999. See page 8 for information on the National Defense Authorization Act for FY 1999, section 3161, "Protection Against Inadvertent Release of Restricted Data and Formerly Restricted Data." Available at fas.org/sgp/isoo/isoo98.html.

20. *NCC Washington Update* 5, no. 18 (June 1, 1999). Available at h-net.msu.edu/~ncc/ncc99/ncc9918june1.html.

21. U.S. National Archives and Records Administration, Information Security Oversight Office, *1998 Report to the President*, Aug. 31, 1999, p. 4. Available at fas.org/sgp/isoo/isoo98.html.

22. U.S. Department of State, Advisory Committee on Historical Diplomatic Documentation to the United States Department of State, *Report for FY 1999*, Mar. 27, 2000. Available at fas.org/sgp/advisory/state/hac99.html.

23. Steve Aftergood, "PFIAB Documents Released by Clinton," *Secrecy News*, Mar. 19, 2001. Available at fas.org/sgp/news/secrecy/2001/03/031901.html.

24. U.S. Department of State, Advisory Committee on Historical Diplomatic Documentation to the United States Department of State, *Report for FY 1999*, Mar. 27, 2000. Available at fas.org/sgp/advisory/state/hac99.html.

TRUST

What You Get Is Not What You See: Forgery and the Corruption of Recordkeeping Systems

David B. Gracy II

Documentary forgery, especially through polluting recordkeeping systems, is a crime against society. Few see it that way, however. Some forgers consider that having their work accepted as genuine is a harmless and fun way to embarrass "the experts." Others approach it as a legitimate means of changing history to suit the forger's view of how history should be, or should have been. Still others pursue forgery as lucrative employment that offers them the added excitement and challenge of living on the edge. What all these individuals gain in personal fulfillment pales in comparison to what society loses in the compromise of our understanding of the progress and development that has brought us to the present. In truth, their illicit work robs us of our humanity. Since building upon the experience of others is the most fundamental distinguishing characteristic that makes us human, contaminating this body of knowledge cheats us all. Consequently, exposing forgery of records, particularly by protecting the integrity of recordkeeping systems, is as fundamental a work as society—in particular archivists and other records keepers as its agents—must undertake. This is no easy job. Forgers are clever.

THE HOFMANN CASE: THE ART OF FORGERY

Dated October 23, 1830, the simple one and one-half-page handwritten letter from Martin Harris to W.W. Phelps of Canandaigua, New York, described a bizarre event that Harris had witnessed three years earlier.

In the fall of the year 1827 I hear Joseph Smith found a gold bible I take Joseph aside & he says it is true I found it 4 years ago with my stone but only just got it because of the enchantment of the old spirit come to me 3 times in the same dream & says dig up the gold but when I take it up the next morning the spirit transfigured himself from a white salamander in the bottom of the hole & struck me three times & held the treasure & would not let me have it because I lay it down to cover over the hole when the spirit says do not lay it down.[1]

Harris's account of Prophet Joseph Smith's finding of the golden plates—the very plates the translation of which constitutes the text of the Book of Mormon, the foundation of the Church of Jesus Christ of Latter-Day Saints—seriously contradicted Smith's own account of the event. More than just contradicting details, the Harris account in fact called into question the divine character of the discovery. The salamander was no divine being, no equivalent of an angel sent from God. It was a symbol commonly found in folk medicine and magic. The letter suggested that what Prophet Smith called divine communication was nothing more than a hallucination sprung from dabbling in folk medicine. In short, if valid, the letter undermined the divinity of the 150-year-old worldwide church.

Where had this letter been for the 153 years between the time it purportedly had been written and 1983 when it surfaced? No one knew. Where and how did it surface? That could be traced through a Mormon dealer in stampless covers, a specialty of philately that concentrated on postal markings used prior to the introduction of stamps in the late 1840s. The Mormon dealer had bought the letter from a New Hampshire dealer in philately. Since dealers in postal marking frequently pay little or no attention to the content of the pieces of mail they are handling, that nothing more was known of the provenance was hardly unusual.

The letter had the look and feel of the genuine article. Both the Federal Bureau of Investigation and a manuscript dealer prominent for his role in unmasking the Hitler diary forgeries corroborated that. In comparing the ink of the Salamander Letter, as it came to be called, with that of unquestioned documents of the period, forensic investigators concluded that it exhibited the chemical composition of iron gall ink in common use during the period. Though no test could determine when the ink had been applied, "there is no evidence to suggest that these documents were prepared at a time other than their reported dates," the report concluded. Those who looked closely at the handwriting saw a script that flowed naturally. Clearly the writing was not labored as so often is the case when one writer is trying consciously to mimic characteristics of the handwriting of another.[2]

In 1983 the Salamander Letter appeared to be genuine, and leaders of the Mormon Church worried. As subsequent events showed, the letter in fact was the work of a forger, a disillusioned Mormon, Mark Hofmann. Having lost his faith, Hofmann determined to use his talents to discredit the church. The method he chose was changing the history of the church, that is, creating documents the contents of which would call into question its very foundations. "I believed that the documents that I created could have been a part of Mormon history," Hofmann testified during his trial for murder. "In effect, I guess, the questions I asked myself in deciding on a forgery[,] one of the questions was, what could have been? I had a concept of church history and I followed that concept."[3]

Succeeding at the work that Hofmann undertook of forging nineteenth-century documents required mastery of a wide range of capabilities and knowledge, including especially manual dexterity and an artistic ability to be able to produce flawless, flowing handwriting in the style of a specific other person; chemistry to be able to create ink that would test positive for ink of the period; sources of blank sheets of contemporary paper and contemporary postal markings; historical research to command the known facts so fully that even incidental facts, such as the mail route and days of delivery appropriate for the fabricated letter, would be accurate; and, finally, imagination sufficient to create fictional content so real among the known facts that, virtually without question, it would be taken for genuine.

Mastering these, every would-be forger possesses the capability of changing our history. Success rests on more, however, than simply the historical credibility and technical dexterity incorporated into the forgery. To succeed, the forger must introduce the fabrication in such a way that it is accepted as genuine. That means the forger has to provide a history of the item—its provenance—so convincing as to minimize the likelihood of serious questions being asked, or at least that squares so closely with known facts that it can withstand investigation.

Hofmann did this the harder way, using two conventions. First, he set up discovery of the document so that someone other than, or at least in addition to, himself found it and began to recognize its value. Second, he suggested—or, better yet, let the document suggest—connections among historical individuals that victims could readily see and uncritically accept.

The means by which Hofmann brought to light his fabrication of the Anthon Transcript on April 16, 1980, his earliest major forgery, demonstrated his command of the technique. That Wednesday he sat leafing through a 1668 Bible he recently had acquired, when he noticed that some of the pages did not turn freely. Two were adhered to each other, and something seemed to be secured between them. Naturally sharing his curiosity at such an unexpected and unusual circumstance, he called his wife to where he was sitting to show her. As she watched, Hofmann separated the Bible pages. Stuck to one of the pages was a piece of yellow paper folded many times and sealed by the same black adhesive that held it to the page. Hofmann and his wife worked gently to open the puzzling document, but as they worked, the sheet tore. To avoid damaging the document further, they halted their efforts. They could see what appeared to be the signature of Joseph Smith. Doralee Hofmann could vouch for the freak discovery.

The following day, Hofmann took the Bible with its remarkable document to archivist A.J. "Jeff" Simonds at Utah State University. Could the Smith signature be authentic? Hofmann asked. Quite possibly so, Simonds thought after comparison with Joseph Smith signatures in the archives. The most striking part of the document to Simonds was not the signature. It was the hieroglyphics on the other side of the document. Putting two and two together, Simonds arrived at a startling thought. If these were the hieroglyphics that Joseph Smith said he had copied from the golden plates, which Smith associate Martin Harris subsequently had taken to New York to show to Professor Charles Anthon, and which subsequently had disappeared—then this was a find of unimaginable proportions. "Mark and I just sort of collapsed when it dawned on us that this, indeed, might have been the original paper which Martin Harris took to New York. I told Mark that he should take the paper to [the] LDS Church Archives for final verification," Simonds recalled.[4]

The genius in the provenances that Hofmann fabricated was wonderfully elegant in its simplicity. By placing others at the center of the discovery, he created an atmosphere in which the discoverers, not he, the forger Hofmann, would recognize the real value of the find. Assessing and recognizing the value for themselves, the persons joining him in the discovery shifted attention from Hofmann who actually had brought the item forward. The point, pure and simple, was to give the victims just enough information to secure their interest, after which the forger could rely on them to build and support the case on behalf of the authenticity of the fraudulent item.

The more difficult, more challenging, and at the same time more insidious means of introducing forgeries such that they will be accepted as genuine is by inserting them into a genuine document or into a recordkeeping system whose integrity is taken for granted. Two avenues for this are open to the forger. One is offering yet other forgeries as valid documents against which to compare the questioned document. In this, Hofmann again proved his mettle. One of the first means of analysis anyone should apply to a questioned document is comparison of the handwriting of the questioned document against that of a known genuine item. So it was with the 1830 Martin Harris letter. Unfortunately, no genuine writing of Martin Harris was known to exist beyond his signature. Then a book dealer friend of Mark Hofmann innocently called to Hofmann's attention an 1830 imprint of the *Book of Common Prayer* only notable, if at all, because it contained the signature of one Nathan Harris, a brother, Hofmann said, of Martin Harris. Hofmann bought the book and left. Five days later, he returned to the bookstore with the little volume in hand and news of a remarkable find. In it in several places appeared the handwriting of Martin Harris. Pleased, Hofmann offered to compensate the bookstore for the true value of the book. He arranged to pay not just the original $50 purchase price, but $1,000, an amount calculated as half the true value of the item adorned with the Martin Harris writing. Those interested in the Salamander Letter recognized that the value of the book lay far beyond its worth in dollars. "Hofmann has purchased a volume of Nathanial Harris from Kirtland[, Ohio,] which evidently has Martin Harris' handwriting in it in several places which corresponds perfectly to the 1830 Harris to Phelps letter," Ron Barney of the Historical Department of the LDS Church declared.[5] Mark Hofmann had succeeded in having his own free-flowing version of Martin Harris's scrawl accepted as genuine.

In time, Hofmann promised more forgeries than he could deliver. Aggravating his situation, he had spent beyond his means and failed to sell his fabrication of the first item printed in the United States, the Oath of a Freeman of 1638, the income from which sale he counted on to settle accounts. To free himself from this situation, he resorted to murder. After killing one creditor and the innocent wife of the creditor's business partner, a third bomb exploded prematurely, nearly killing Hofmann himself. His explanation of the incident led to his discovery, after which he was arrested, tried, convicted for murder, and, in a plea bargain struck to learn about his forgery techniques, sentenced to life in prison.

THE REAVIS CASE: SALTING THE ARCHIVES WITH FORGERIES

The other means of corrupting the genuine record on which investigators want to rely for comparisons of handwriting, as well as for technical features of the media used during the period for creating documents, is surreptitiously slipping the forgery into a file of records in an archives, or a similar records repository, so that, when discovered, the item will be taken as genuine simply by its association with the long-unquestioned documents with which it is found. A variation is to alter, commonly by addition, the information contained in an unquestioned document. This corruption, through which the forger simultaneously takes advantage of and compromises an established recordkeeping system, is especially evil. In the first place, the victim innocently encounters the forged document in a context that gives little reason for questioning its validity. In the second place, this action jeopardizes the integrity of documentation on which society depends. It casts a shroud of suspicion over a far larger body of documentation than occurs when an item is brought forward by itself.

At this industry, James Addison Reavis excelled in his time, the latter half of the nineteenth century. In one of the grandest claims in the United States ever made and sustained by forgery, Reavis asserted ownership to some 11 million acres of southern Arizona and a bit of southern New Mexico. At the base of the claim lay a supposed grant from the Crown of Spain to a cousin of a governor of New Mexico, Don Pedro de Peralta. Few paid much mind to the claim until Collis P. Huntington in 1874 seized upon it as a weapon with which to block his rival, Jay Gould, from building a competing railroad line to the Pacific Ocean along the southern route through Arizona. To validate the claim, Reavis in 1880 traveled to Guadalajara and Mexico City. He studied the script of Spanish colonial documents until he, an accomplished forger of handwriting, had mastered the ability to reproduce it. At the same time, he made friends with the archivists, who shared his feigned pride in noble Spanish ancestry. Then, enjoying lax supervision, he doctored a wide array of documents, in some instances adding the Peralta name, in other instances inserting entire pages.

As proficient as Reavis was in mimicking the handwriting, he understood the importance of the provenance that gave the forgeries life—and he took the creation of a provenance to a level above simple documents. He brought forward a supposed actual descendant of Don Miguel Silva Jesus de Peralta, the second Baron de Peralta. Traveling on a train in California in 1877, Reavis spotted a young woman whom he approached and gave to understand that her resemblance to the wife of the second baron must be more than coincidence. Reavis sent the waif to finishing school and turned her into the noble Doña Carmelita Sofia Loreta Micaela de Maso y de Peralta. At the same time, he visited the church of the parish in San Bernardino, California, in which, he said, she had been born and carefully added her name to the baptismal record, and then obtained a baptismal certificate based on the record in the church register.

Late in 1885, Reavis and Doña Carmelita Sofia, whom by that time he had married, traveled to Spain for a two-year stay. To further solidify his claim, the Baron de Peralta y Córdoba, as Reavis began calling himself, visited the Archives of the Indies in Seville, where he continued his practice of inserting bogus information, usually entire pages, into documents in the archives, after which he requested certified copies. The archivists became suspicious, because uniformly he asked for certification not of the entire document, but only of individual pages. Since they were the pages that he had inserted, his action called attention to those pages, which the archivists readily observed did not correspond in all regards with the other pages of the documents in which they were found. In particular, they lacked the stamp of the archives that appeared on every other page of each document.

Back in the United States, enough questions had been raised around the Peralta claim that the scheme began to collapse. Investigators who visited the American, Mexican, and Spanish archives from which Reavis had obtained certified copies found serious discrepancies when they inspected the documents. In documents in which Reavis had inserted the Peralta name, he had carelessly inserted it only once, not at every appropriate place throughout the document, giving away the fact that the name had not been in the original version. Those who read Spanish noted, too, certain misspellings that Reavis had inserted, no doubt for effect, but which never would have been written by a native speaker. Specifically, Reavis from time to time added a second letter "l" to a word. The double "l" in Spanish is pronounced as "y," which yields a different, not a misspelled, word. Then they noticed that the writing had been done with a pen that left the telltale lines of a steel point characteristic of the end of the nineteenth century, not the characteristic line of a quill pen with which the vast majority of the document had been written. One of the most damaging pieces of evidence investigators found in the baptismal record book in San Bernardino. No real question had been raised about the baptismal record until, in searching for it, someone noticed that no entry for it existed in the index—the only instance of such an omission. In 1896 Reavis was convicted of forgery, sent to prison for two years, and deserted by his wife.[6]

FORGERY AND ITS MEANINGS

The two cases of Hofmann and Reavis, among the scores of cases of forgers that have occurred in the United States during the past two centuries, must make everyone responsible for records, and archivists especially, sensitive to the ever-present likelihood of encountering a forgery, or at the least being asked whether a given document is what it is purported to be. The cases should alert every researcher who relies on records of any sort, and especially on historical records, to be sensitive to the possibility that documentation, especially that concerning a prominent individual, is not what it is purported to be. Finally, every citizen who relies on the sanctity of recordkeeping systems and the integrity of individual records within those systems, especially systems of government, the contents of which are fundamental to entitling citizens to benefits, rights, and privileges, ought never cavalierly to take the incorruptibility of the system for granted.

The clear conclusion to be drawn from the Hofmann and Reavis cases is that what you see in a document may not be what you get. As records show, such has been the case for at least the past 2,500 years. Students of classical Greece point to writings and records of the results of athletic contests in which the actual outcomes and accounts of those outcomes as recorded by the losers vary in such a way that it is clear that the loser consciously sought to create a record that mitigated or reversed the actual outcome. Such forgeries were detected contemporaneously on the basis either of blatant inconsistency with known facts or of anachronism in the style of lettering in which the forged document was written compared to the style contemporary with the period in which the document purportedly was produced. For their term for forgery, the ancient Greeks drew on the root word *plasma*, meaning to form or mold, one sense of which was to form or mold deceitfully (plasma is the root from which our word *plastic* comes). As the practice apparently became more common, the Romans coined at least two words for it. *Falsum*, the legal term for fraud, referred to anything deceptive and was related to *fallere*, meaning to deceive. *Subicere* meant simply to introduce falsely or to put forward as genuine.[7]

By contrast with the concepts of "molding" and "false" on which the ancient Greeks and Romans grounded their words for the act of forgery, the English at the dawn of the Renaissance drew from the Latin *fabricare*, "to forge," meaning simply to make. This root carried no negative connotation at all. Over time the word was endowed with specific meanings, one being working with metal, as we still use it. Another related to production of records, specifically to the act of producing—"forging"—an agreement, most commonly a treaty between powers, which was physically attested to and documented with a written instrument. Not until 1574 did the term *forgery* first appear in English carrying the negative connotation of the creation or alteration of a written document with the intent to defraud (replacing *falsum*, which had continued in use through the medieval period). In the literary world, the change represented a moralizing of the concept of forgery, distinguishing between acceptable fiction and reprehensible fraudulent concoction. Those whose property, or position in society, or livelihood was grounded in information contained in records, that is who relied on the integrity of records, in the sixteenth century, took serious exception to the number of spurious documents in existence and being generated to defraud the rightful owners of their property and rights. Taking the act of forgery out of common law, where it had applied only to the king's seal, to counterfeiting money, and to documents submitted in a court of law, they secured an act of Parliament in 1562–1563 imposing severe civil and criminal penalties for creating such falsifications.

The principal point of debate in the definition of forgery is the intent of the forger. The *Encyclopaedia Britannica* (14th edition) defines forgery as alteration of an original document or wholesale production of a document that never existed as of the date on the document, both done with the intent to deceive or defraud. Without such intent, the fabricator produces merely a fake or a copy. As the intention of the creator commonly is difficult to substantiate, this aspect of the definition has proven to be the most challenging to show. Yet the commonly accepted connotation of the term *forgery* incorporates at its heart the concept of deception.

By this definition, Samuel Johnson was not a forger. Yet he knowingly created spurious accounts of actual events. For four years, for the *Gentleman's Magazine*, Johnson received notes of speeches from reporters who attended sessions of Parliament, which he was to correct and polish so as to produce an "enriched" text. Sometimes he received only the names of the speakers and the part they had taken in the debate. In these worst cases, to Johnson then fell the task of creating the texts of the speeches, that is, of literally putting words in the mouths of the speakers. He did not do it with the intent of deceiving anyone. Nevertheless, it was not work that he enjoyed, and shortly before his death "he expressed a regret for his having been the author of fictions, which had passed for realities."[8]

The line between purposeful deception and working with supposedly good intention to fabricate a scene more representative of reality than any actual scene—that line between permissible fiction and reprehensible fraudulent concoction—cannot help but be a moving target. Not everyone who has straddled the line has done so with the same circumspection as Johnson. One of the most obvious cases in point is that of arguably the most famous photograph to come out of the American Civil War, the image of the dead Confederate sharpshooter, rifle leaned against the protective rock wall beside him, in the Devil's Den on the battlefield at Gettysburg. Taken by Alexander Gardner three days after the conclusion of the battle, the image hardly could have been more contemporary to the event. Yet Gardner composed the scene, moving the body, as Gardner's own photographs show, some 40 feet to the location in which he situated it to project the heart-wrenching mood he wished to convey. The caption with which he accompanied the image characterized the soldier dying "while memories of home grew dearer as the field of carnage faded before him." Gardner's work became so famous that his name for the location of the body—"Devil's Den"—became the accepted name of the place. Many veterans who returned to the battlefield years later even noted that they recalled having seen the body exactly as Alexander had pictured it. To this day, the site is a common stop on tourists' treks across the battlefield.[9]

THE SOCIETAL IMPLICATIONS OF FORGERY: THE HITLER DIARIES AND OTHER CASES

Because our society relies so heavily on documentation as the basis of valid information, the acceptance of a document as being what it is purported to be, and thus as being as true and accurate in its content as the author was able to make it—this fact positions forgeries as having a terribly detrimental and damaging affect on those immediately concerned with the content of a document, on those associated with those immediately affected, and so on ad infinitum. The effect of forgeries hardly can be measured. We have no way of assessing the ill effect of successful forgeries—those that go undetected and whose misinformation becomes accepted fact. Only from studying the impact of known—that is, unsuccessful—forgeries while they were believed to be genuine can we gain insight into the magnitude of the impact on society—real and potential—of spurious documents. And from what we have learned from the testimony of forgers who have commented on the results of their forgeries and from victims whose lives or relationships have been changed by forgeries, even for a short time, the consequences of documentary forgeries are substantial.

During the short period in 1982 between the time the Hitler diaries became common knowledge and began to be published on the one hand and the moment they were shown to be a forgery on the other hand, their existence even affected relations among nations. The diaries painted a man different from the one known to history up to that time. The diaries portrayed Hitler as a man more interested in peace for having authorized the peace mission of Rudolph Hess, more compassionate for having consciously permitted the British army to escape annihilation at Dunkirk, and less anti-Semitic since he complained of the acts of fanatics over whom he lacked full control and blamed atrocities on subordinates. This Hitler was guilty at most of not controlling his fanatical followers.

As parts of the diaries became known, those who saw the Hitler documented in archival records as a demonic figure objected strenuously to the depiction of the leader of the Third Reich as being normal and human. One prominent British government official warned, "even if the diaries were found to be genuine, they must not be believed. We are dealing here with one of the masters of propaganda, an arch-liar." Were the diaries genuine, he argued, they would be "genuine fiction" rather than "fictional fiction." In the politics of countries, the Soviet Union branded the diaries the work of the Central Intelligence Agency of the United States, while the Americans suspected the Communists of being behind the diaries; each side believed that the other had produced them for the purpose of sowing discord. The press carried the diaries as headline news.

The fallout from the hoax was significant. It left the reputation of the press, more interested in a scoop than in truth, severely tarnished. In concrete terms, four editors in three countries lost their jobs as a result of their parts in the events. The magazine *Stern*, which owned the principal rights to the diaries, lost millions of dollars. Further, the reputations of distinguished British historian Hugh Trevor-Roper and of document examiner Ordway Hilton, both of whom had declared the diaries genuine, never fully recovered.[10]

The Vrain Denis Lucas forgeries of the second half of the nineteenth century strained relations between the scientific communities of France and Great Britain. Lucas's principal patron, Michel Chasles, a prominent member of the French Academy of Sciences, longed for France to have a more robust history in the realm of scientific discovery than it had enjoyed. Lucas obliged him. The prolific forger created documents that credited Pascal with discovering gravity more than three decades before Isaac Newton of Great Britain and gave to Galileo, rather than to the Dutch Huygens, the distinction of having discovered the first moon of Saturn. Of whatever lack in French achievement Chasles complained, Lucas claimed to find—that is, created—one or more documents to rectify it. For a few years, disputes over the validity of the documents diverted attention from scholarly pursuits to arguing over credit for intellectual contributions to the world.[11]

The several Hofmann forgeries that appeared over a span of several years caused many people to question the validity of the Church of Jesus Christ of Latter-Day Saints. The leaders specifically had to debate the best course to take in the midst of the continuing appearance of important, but troubling, documents. Paying out a great deal of the church's treasure to acquire several of the documents seemed to validate the documents that called into question the church's very foundation. Salting away the documents in the vault of the First Presidency only made matters worse, as that act left the impression that documented truth was not a commodity highly valued by the church. Along the way, document dealer Charles Hamilton of New York, called upon to give his opinion on the genuineness of one of the documents, declared it valid, a tarnish on his reputation that he later regretted. Finally, after Hofmann fell into deep financial distress, only one truly effective avenue of escape occurred to him—murder. And two people lost their lives as a result.

The effect of the James Addison Reavis forgeries clouded property deeds in Arizona for decades. Reavis commonly demanded and obtained quit-claim deeds from those he found living on the land he claimed. The work of undoing all those deeds as a result of the exposure of his forgery was no little undertaking. In the meantime, persons wanting to sell affected property encountered difficulty concluding the transactions.

For western Pennsylvania, the case of the Horn Papers, the first large-scale forgery of historical documents in the United States for the purpose, at least in part, of changing history, created problems of historical understanding and of genealogy for years. From the mid-1930s until 1946, the massive accumulation of supposed papers of the Horn family of western Pennsylvania of the second half of the eighteenth century were treated by most as genuine historical documentation. The owner, a Horn descendent, gave speeches enthusiastically received, generously donated to museums objects from his family's accumulation, and enjoyed the status of a celebrity. The information he produced from the papers extended genealogical knowledge of local families and prominent individuals alike to an unprecedented degree for that period and added in remarkable detail to knowledge of the place and period. In time, as a means of trying to answer the questions raised about the validity of the papers, local historians published the documents in two substantial volumes, supplemented by a third containing genuine contemporary documents anticipated to be useful for dealing with conflicting data in the papers. Once scrutinized, the documents and associated artifacts were shown conclusively to be spurious.

Writing shortly after a special committee of the American Historical Association concluded its study of the documents by declaring all the Horn Papers to be forgeries, two historians observed on the impact of the bogus documents that

Many genealogists have already incorporated Horn data in their reports of various family lines, and as a result the national headquarters of the Daughters of the American Revolution has had to take precautions to cope with them. The praiseworthy campaign to raise funds to restore the Jonathan Hager House in Hagerstown, Maryland, is meeting opposition from individuals, who were *always* against expending money on such project, and who now cite *The Horn Papers* affair as reason for non-cooperation. Thus the poison works on. And, undoubtedly, for years to come some unwary individuals will continue to be misled by the documents' fascinating historical fictions, and other persons will continue to use the story of the false diaries as a weapon against legitimate and valuable historical enterprise.[12]

The nefarious work of Major George Gordon Byron in the nineteenth century, who claimed to be the illegitimate son of the British romantic poet Lord Byron, has clouded and confused knowledge of Lord Byron and his contemporaries, especially Percy Bysshe Shelley and John Keats. Major Byron operated by claiming to be writing a biography of his father, and for his projected work borrowed documents. These he copied and then returned the originals. From the copies, he lifted phrases, clauses, even sentences, which he wove together, adding detail of his own invention, to create new and very genuine-sounding, but totally bogus, letters. An eager public hungry to possess something of the popular poets provided a ready market for the major's pen. Some of the documents were published contemporaneously as genuine. Even from early on, distinguishing genuine from spurious Byron, Shelley, and Keats documents has proven to be distressingly difficult. Some maintain that as a result of Major Byron's work, the true lives of the three poets never can be known.[13]

Author Clifford Irving set out on a lark early in the 1970s to create an autobiography of Howard Hughes. It was an incredibly bold scheme, as Irving had no more knowledge of Hughes than anyone else who read newspapers and news magazines. Most astounding of all, the subject of the faked autobiography was very much alive. Irving bet that the recluse would not surface to dispute the work, and that, if he did, no one would believe him. Further, Irving thought that his forgery would have no real impact. Were he caught, he believed, he could simply return the money he had received for the writing and then walk away. "If things get too hot or even if they don't you can always go to them and tell them it's a hoax. The money will be there and then we've got an unauthorized biography or a novel."[14] "We weren't stealing anything," he moralized. "For whatever we received, we would be giving fair value. Not that it would be what I represented it to be—the authorized biography of Howard Hughes—but it would be a book. 'An important book,' I added. 'And a *good* book.' "[15] What Irving saw himself producing was not history, but rather entertainment. "Think what a great book could be done, what a great character could be created—using the known facts about the man and inventing the rest," he thought.[16] "Make sure the book's got plenty of soul-vomit," his wife counseled. "That's what the kitchen maids like to read."[17] Sometimes "feeling playful or adventurous, we launched out into the murky waters of Howard's philosophy: his theory of corruption in American family life, of germs, of a universe in which an atom in a man's toe might contain an entire solar system. Nothing was too outrageous. 'The wilder the story,' I explained to Dick, 'the deeper their need to believe it. And, of course, it's less checkable.' "[18] Ultimately, "if they could manufacture a pseudo-Hughes and set him in opposition to the real Hughes, there was a strong likelihood that people might accept the pseudo-version. After all, the real Hughes, eternally locked in his air-conditioned nightmare, was already totally incredible. Reconstituting the old man would be almost a service to reality."[19] In the forger's hands, an important figure in aviation, the oil industry, and the first half of the twentieth century in America would have moved from mystery to almost pure fiction, hardly a service to society. In any case, the scheme was exposed before the book was published, and, not permitted simply to return the money, Irving was convicted for his deeds and sent to jail.[20]

In 2001, some 166 years after his death, the manner in which American icon David Crockett met his fate at the Alamo on March 6, 1836, is fuel for charges that one sentence in the manuscript account of the Texas Revolution written by Mexican army officer Enrique De la Peña, if not the entire document, is a blatant forgery written to discredit Crockett. De la Peña reported that Crockett, along with a handful of others, surrendered and that all were summarily executed on orders of the commander of the Mexican Army, General Antonio López de Santa Anna. At least three books and numerous articles carry the arguments that have ranged over historical fact, language translation, and forensic examination of the document. At stake in the controversy is the image of an icon of the American westward movement.[21]

FORGERY SCHOLARSHIP

Clearly, historical documents touch nerves and excite passions ranging from personal reputation to local pride to national prestige. The depth of feeling ignited by forgery, magnified by the repercussions of the fraud, establish forgery of historical documents as a fertile field for investigation. Intense study of events depicted in, issues raised by, and documents bearing on or affected by a forgery has contributed significantly to the understanding of periods, places, events, and issues of various characters brought into focus by questioned documents. As one scholar has put it: "A good forgery is like a shot of adrenaline in the blood-stream of culture."[22] This adrenaline is injected from two sources. The most obvious is with the study required of those engaged in exposing forgeries. Equally, it must occur with the forger, whose success hinges in significant part on thorough knowledge of the time, place, and people in which and among whom the forgery is set. Mark Hofmann's documents altering the history of the Mormon Church are a prime example. The results of the study of the forger and of the investigator, when combined, have led to a richer understanding of the past and especially of the production of documents, both genuine ones of a former period and modern ones created to resemble ones of that former period.

The silver lining of richer knowledge resulting from investigating forgery is harder to concede when forgery compromises systems for keeping official records—as those of birth, landholding, and museum acquisition—and for keeping records of all kinds as documentary heritage. Such records are fundamental to the smooth and efficient operation of society. The problem is particularly acute for records keepers and recordkeeping systems in which a principal basis for presuming the validity of a document resides in the presence of the document within a file whose integrity is known because the file is maintained by a public agency.

In recordkeeping systems growing out of the ancient Greek and subsequent Roman system of substantiating validity, authenticity was grounded in filing a document with a public authority, either a designated government office or a private notary public licensed for the purpose. Once filed, the genuineness of the document could be shown by obtaining a certificate from the record keeper. Here, one must be careful. Certifications issued by archivists vouch only for the accuracy of the copy as a copy, not for the integrity of the information in the document. In other words, were a forgery successfully inserted into a file in an archive and a certified copy requested of it, the archivist could and would issue a certification vouching both for its presence in the file and for the faithfulness of the reproduction. In the hands of a James Addison Reavis, the certification is passed as something it is not—that is, as a guarantee of content rather than of faithfulness of reproduction. The certification is offered with the implication that, because the item being certified is present in the file, it has been part of the file from the time that the records were created and was used for the purpose for which purportedly it was created, in short, that it is a genuine document or part of one.

When spurious documents are found to have been inserted into archival records, archivists make note for all potential users of the questions surrounding the documents and the known facts regarding the history of the file prior to the apparent insertion. On the other side of the coin, were a fraudulent document used in conducting the work done by the creator of the records in carrying out or documenting the business of that creator, and were this fact discovered only much later, the archivist would have the charge of maintaining the document as it lay as part of the surviving record, because the file had not been corrupted after leaving the creator's hands.

Essential, then, to detecting forgery is a knowledge of recordkeeping systems and of the structure of documents. For recordkeeping systems, the investigator wants a deep understanding of the technology and conventions of creation, use, and management of records in the office at specific moments, as well as of the ways in which these functions have changed with the passage of time. For documents, the investigator seeks knowledge of the structure of each different form of document of the time and place from which a supposed document came. So fundamental is this understanding that it formed the basis of the science of diplomatics, which originated in France near the end of the seventeenth century in response to the need for a systematic means of distinguishing genuine documents from spurious ones.

Without systematic knowledge of the structure and media of documents of different times and places, the techniques of forgery had outstripped the science of detection. Neither courts, nor anyone else, had a sound basis outside of anachronism for exposing fraudulent documents. Then in 1681, Jean Mabillon published *De Re Diplomatica*, introducing the science of diplomatics—that is, of criticism and authentication of a document based on structural and writing characteristics of the document. The term *diplomatics* takes it name from the Greek word *diploo*, meaning "fold." It referred to the fold of a parchment or paper on which two identical copies of a treaty, or similar document, had been executed, one copy of which went to each of the two parties to the agreement. Before the identical copies were separated, crosshatching was laid down between them. After separation, the genuineness of either copy could be demonstrated conclusively simply by matching the crosshatching. Until Mabillon published his work, such physical comparison constituted the only foolproof means of proving or disproving authenticity. Without the other copy, and in the case of any other form of document than an agreement, no incontestable means of authentication existed.

The basis on which diplomatics rests is that writing, which is the record of an act, by virtue of having been part of the conduct of the act, has a probative value. The goal of the science of diplomatics, then, is validation of the record of an act as proof of the validity of the act itself. It works by analysis of the two principal aspects of a document—its construction and structure (codicology) and its calligraphy (paleography). Diplomatics requires establishment of a bank of information on the codicology and paleography of every kind of document produced by a given office at a given date, sometimes even including by a given scribe. Diplomatics is based squarely on comparison of one document against a known exemplar, or genuine example, of the time and place of the questioned document. Content is not the focus of diplomatics. A diplomatist studies each of the parts of a document—such as complementary opening, complementary close, date, and authentications—to determine whether those on the questioned document are appropriate to a document of the time and place from which the questioned document is said to have originated, whether they appear in the proper location and in the proper form, and whether any expected elements are missing.

In diplomatics, one distinguishes three kinds of authenticity—diplomatic, historical, and legal. Documents that are diplomatically authentic are written according to the practice of the time and place indicated in the text and are signed with the names of persons competent to create such documents. Historically authentic documents are accurate to the knowledge of their creator in their information content. Finally, documents said to be legally authentic carry their own authentication by a designated authority, for example, a notary attesting to their genuineness. Of course, it is possible for a document to be authentic in one or two but not all three aspects. For example, a birth certificate that bears the proper authenticating signatures and follows the form prescribed for such documents, but which contains a mistake in the date of birth, is said to be legally and diplomatically authentic, but historically false. A document valid in all three regards is said to be genuine.[23]

Forensic analysis is closely related to diplomatics in the approach that it offers for distinguishing genuine from false documents. In regard to study of documents, forensic science consists of two fields—chemistry and handwriting analysis. Questioned document examiners, who are experts in analysis of handwriting, typically work only with contemporary cases. The handwriting comparisons they conduct occur as a result of legal cases in which the suspected forger is able to, indeed is compelled to, produce samples specifically for analysis. Dealers in historical manuscripts, rather than questioned document examiners, provide expertise in authentication of the handwriting of historical figures. Until the beginning of the twentieth century, forensic analysis of documents was rudimentary at best. The first two major texts in the field were published only around the beginning of the century, being William E. Hagan's *Treatise on Disputed Handwriting and the Determination of Genuine from Forged Signatures* (1894) and Albert S. Osborn's *Questioned Documents: A Study of Questioned Documents with an Outline of Methods by Which the Facts May Be Discovered and Shown* (1910). The Osborn book itself preceded by almost twenty years construction of the first forensics laboratory in the United States.

Any perusal of works on detection of and on specific cases of documentary forgery will yield the reader a long list of characteristics and features to review when studying incongruous historical documents. How much evidence must be amassed to put the investigator on safe ground to declare a document either spurious or genuine will be determined in each case. Consequently, investigation of as many of the characteristics and features as possible must be the best advice to anyone questioning the validity of any piece of writing.

CONCLUSION

Forgers are cunning and are ever sharpening their personal skills and their management of new technologies in their drive to create false documents so true to sight and analysis that the creations are mistaken for what they are purported to be. Worse, forgers recognize that they are at their cleverest when their work is accepted as a legitimate part of a recordkeeping system whose integrity is unquestioned. While the triumph of the forger is personal, the loss occasioned by the legitimizing of a forgery is societal. Acceptance of deliberately false information robs everyone of a healthy understanding of history, thereby jeopardizes a clear sense of the present, and, consequently, compromises the search for the best course into the future.

The extent to which the forger succeeds is determined directly by the vigilance of the records keeper and the citizen. Vigilance relies upon serendipitous discovery, which in turn can happen only when the potential victim possesses, refreshes, and routinely brings to bear enough pertinent knowledge to question the seemingly genuine but somehow incongruous document. Keeping records safe from forgers is everybody's business, because in modern society records define who we are. Holding the key to our identity as individuals, as a nation, and as a people, records rank among the most important pillars of, and likely are the most vulnerable foundation of, modern society. In guarding against forgeries, records keeper and citizen alike occupy front-line positions.

NOTES

1. Richard E. Turley, Jr., *Victims: The LDS Church and the Mark Hofmann Case* (Urbana: University of Illinois Press, 1992), pp. 79–80. Accounts of the Hofmann forgery presented in this essay are based on Turley's book. For the Salamander Letter, see Turley's chapter 5, "The Salamander Letter." See also Joseph Rosenblum, *Practice to Deceive: The Amazing Stories of Literary Forgery's Most Notorious Practitioners* (New Castle, Del.: Oak Knoll, 2000), pp. 295–342; Kenneth Rendell, *Forging History: The Detection of Fake Letters and Documents* (Norman: University of Oklahoma Press, 1994), pp. 124–140; Charles Hamilton, *Great Forgers and Famous Fakes: The Manuscript Forgers of America and How They Duped the Experts*, 2d ed. (Lakewood, Colo.: Glenbridge, 1996), pp. 269–288.

2. Turley, *Victims*, p. 244.

3. Ibid., p. 316.

4. Ibid., pp. 24–39.

5. Ibid., pp. 129, 128.

6. E.H. Cookridge, *The Baron of Arizona* (New York: John Day, 1967), and Donald M. Powell, *The Peralta Grant: James Addison Reavis and the Barony of Arizona* (Norman: University of Oklahoma Press, 1960). Those who love Class B movies will enjoy hooting at *The Baron of Arizona*, a 1950 release written and directed by Samuel Fuller and produced by Carl K. Hittleman for Lippert Productions. Vincent Price stared as Reavis, Ellen Drew as Sofia (Carmelita).

7. I am grateful to Benjamin B. Gracy of the University of New Mexico for his research on the ancient Greek and the classical and medieval Latin terms covering forg-

ery. See Ian Haywood, *Faking It: Art and the Politics of Forgery* (New York: St. Martin's Press, 1987), pp. 1–18.

8. Haywood, *Faking It*, p. 64.

9. William A. Frassanito, *Early Photography at Gettysburg* (Gettysburg, Pa.: Thomas, 1995).

10. Haywood, *Faking It*, pp. 4–5; Robert Harris, *Selling Hitler: The Story of the Hitler Diaries* (Boston: Faber and Faber, 1986), p. 20.

11. Henri Leonard Bordier, *Prince of Forgers*, edited by Joseph Rosenblum (New Castle, Del.: Oak Knoll, 1998).

12. Arthur Pierce Middleton and Douglas Adair, "The Mystery of the Horn Papers," *William and Mary Quarterly*, 3d ser., 4 (Oct. 1947): 409–445. The quotation appears on page 442.

13. Rosenblum, *Practice to Deceive*, pp. 199–231.

14. Clifford Irving, *What Really Happened: His Untold Story of the Hughes Affair* (New York: Grove Press, 1972), p. 75.

15. Clifford Irving, *Project Octavo* (London: Allison & Busby, 1977), p. 73.

16. Ibid., p. 7.

17. Ibid., p. 22.

18. Ibid., p. 145.

19. Stephen Fay, et al., *Hoax: The Inside Story of the Howard Hughes—Clifford Irving Affair* (n.p.: Andre Deutsch, 1972), p. 63.

20. Irving, *Project Octavo*, p. 370. In 1999 terrificbooks.com of Santa Fe, New Mexico, issued the book under the title *The Autobiography of Howard Hughes*.

21. Bill Groneman, *Death of a Legend: The Myth and Mystery Surrounding the Death of Davy Crockett* (Plano, Tex.: Republic of Texas Press, 1999); James E. Crisp, "The Little Book That Wasn't There: The Myth and Mystery of the de la Peña Diary," *Southwestern Historical Quarterly* 98 (Oct. 1994): 262–296.

22. Haywood, *Faking It*, p. 67.

23. Luciana Duranti, "Diplomatics: New Uses for an Old Science," *Archivaria* 28 (Summer 1989): 7–27, 29.

The Jamaican Financial Crisis: Accounting for the Collapse of Jamaica's Indigenous Commercial Banks

Victoria L. Lemieux

From the beginning of the 1990s, symptoms of fundamental problems in the Jamaican financial sector began to appear. By mid-1996, it was apparent that the financial sector was in a crisis, a crisis that would lead to the insolvency and technical failure of all of Jamaica's indigenous commercial banks in the span of two years. In response to the growing crisis, in January 1997 the government of Jamaica established the Financial Sector Adjustment Company (FINSAC), Limited, to address the liquidity and solvency problems within the sector through a process of intervention, rehabilitation, and divestment. The FINSAC bailout has cost the Jamaican government and taxpayers some Jamaican $130 billion (roughly U.S. $3.2 billion) during the longest period of negative economic growth in the country's history. The financial crisis has driven the country into an enormous debt trap from which, at present, it is difficult to see how it will recover. At the time of writing, the country's ratio of total debt servicing to total revenue ran at an astounding 82.5 percent. In 1999 the government's efforts to raise funds through higher taxes to cover the debt led to riots and protests across the country that had serious economic and social ramifications. Moreover, the government has had to drastically reduce spending on critical social programs such as education and health as well as on maintenance of the country's infrastructure of roads and water and waste-disposal systems. Given the economic and social impact of these bank failures, it is clearly important to fully understand all the factors contributing to their collapse.

This essay presents a case study of the failure of Jamaica's indigenous commercial banks and identifies records creation and recordkeeping practices as important factors in the bank collapses. The case study draws upon a number of interviews conducted by the author with FINSAC officials and former directors and managers of failed Jamaican commercial banks as well as on-site examinations of recordkeeping systems in both failed and viable commercial banks. The case study begins with the factors typically cited as explanations for the collapse of the banks. Explanations of the bank failures typically have focused on the state of the country's economy, a weak regulatory framework, cronyism and corruption, and management incompetence in evaluating new areas of business risk. Though these factors are partly to blame, the argument will be made that none of them provides a fully satisfactory explanation for the collapse of the country's indigenous commercial banks. Information about particular record-making and recordkeeping practices in the failed banks will be used to explain how and why these practices have contributed to the bank failures. The case will be made that as a result of the failed banks' practices of records creation and recordkeeping, managers and directors in these financial institutions lacked the trustworthy and timely accounting and management information they needed to maintain effective control of the banks' operations, to assess and manage their financial positions and risk exposures, and to prevent fraud. The record-making and recordkeeping practices in the failed banks, combined with other internal and external factors, led to the banks' collapse. This discussion is followed by an exploration of underlying causes of the banks' records creation and recordkeeping practices. Then discussion will address how these practices have affected social accountability for the bank failures, arguing that in the aftermath of the failures, the banks' records creation and recordkeeping practices also have hampered efforts by the Jamaican government to rehabilitate the country's financial sector. Finally, the case study concludes with some general observations about the lessons to be learned from the Jamaican experience.

FACTORS CONTRIBUTING TO THE COLLAPSE OF JAMAICA'S INDIGENOUS COMMERCIAL BANKS

A number of cumulative and dynamically interrelated factors can be cited as having contributed to the problems experienced in the Jamaican commercial banks. These problems ultimately saw the country's entire financial system become a "weak and vulnerable 'house of cards' ready to fall to the ground."[1] The contributory factors can be grouped into two broad categories. First, environmental factors originating outside the banks. Second, internal factors originating inside the banks and relating to the way that they conducted their business.

Environmental Factors

Analysts and commentators point to a number of environmental factors as having contributed to the collapse of Jamaica's indigenous commercial banks. Principal among these is the government of Jamaica's macroeconomic policy and failure to properly regulate the financial sector.

In the years leading up to the collapse of Jamaica's indigenous commercial banks, the country experienced rising interest rates, increases in the foreign-exchange rate, and rising inflation. A number of reasons for the country's macroeconomic instability have been advanced; but there is a growing consensus that liberalization policies that formed part of World Bank Structural Adjustment Programs (SAPs) contributed to Jamaica's macroeconomic instability.

From the mid-1980s to the early 1990s, in accordance with the conditions of International Monetary Fund (IMF) loans to the country, the Jamaican government introduced a number of structural reforms leading to liberalization of the country's trade regime, foreign-exchange markets, and financial markets. With liberalization and structural adjustment came a devaluation of the Jamaican dollar. Not only did the exchange rate increase, but also between 1990 and 1993 inflation was averaging 49 percent. In 1991 it reached its highest point, 80 percent. The necessity of supporting the Jamaican dollar and the inflationary environment led the Jamaican government to raise interest rates. In December 1993 short-term lending rates rose to more than 61 percent.

Although the government had hoped that interest rate increases would buttress the faltering Jamaican dollar and cool off the inflationary economy by tightening the money supply, its policy had the opposite effect. Banks, rather than taking the signal to tighten up lending, speculated that the government's high interest rate policy was a short-term measure and continued to lend freely, attracted by the profit potential of high-interest-bearing loans. These loans, made at exceptionally high and ultimately unsustainable interest rates, later became nonperforming.

The banks' problems were compounded by the fact that high inflation resulted in an overvaluation of their assets, especially property, which often served as collateral for loans and in which they had invested heavily. The high interest rate environment also encouraged individual investors to place their money in short-term, high-yielding instruments, such as time deposits. In 1994, time deposits grew by 71 percent over the previous year. Ultimately, the mix of short-term high-yielding time deposits and long-term loans created a mismatch between assets and liabilities in several banks that sowed the seeds of the banks' liquidity problems.

Another of the elements of the government's liberalization policy involved bank regulatory reform. The existing legislative framework, dating from 1961, made it all too easy for financial institutions to take advantage of regulatory arbitrage. For example, the Bank of Jamaica had no regulatory control over building societies, and many commercial banks took advantage of this legislative loophole by selling problem loans to the building societies in order to remove bad loans from their books.

To address regulatory weaknesses, in 1992 the earlier banking act was repealed and replaced with a new act, and new legislation was passed to better monitor building societies. The new legislation proved to have a number of weaknesses that contributed to later problems the banks experienced. To address these weaknesses, the Bank of Jamaica established a special task force in 1995 to "fast-track" appropriate amendments to the 1992 Banking Act. These legislative changes came into force in 1997. But they came too late.

Besides the legislative weaknesses, the bank supervisory structure was designed to deal only with a small number of commercial banks. Liberalization and the de facto easing of restrictions on licenses for the establishment of financial institutions, however, encouraged growth in the banking sector. As the sector grew in size, inspections were performed less regularly and the time lag between inspections and issuance of reports became too long. Moreover, supervisors could not deal with specialist areas, particularly those related to loopholes and gaps in the legislation. The fact that there was no overarching authority to regulate the rising number of financial conglomerates and no legal regulations to facilitate the exchange of information between authorities or the disclosure of information to the public and analysts also prevented proper supervision of Jamaican commercial banks.

Internal Factors

While macroeconomic instability and a weak regulatory framework certainly contributed to the collapse of Jamaica's indigenous commercial banks, the fact that the foreign-owned Bank of Nova Scotia among others profited in the same period as the indigenous banks were failing suggests that these environmental factors alone cannot explain the failure of Jamaica's indigenous commercial banks.

It is possible to argue that the success of the foreign banks can be attributed to the fact that they simply had deeper pockets and bigger reputations to trade on. While capitalization must not be dismissed as a factor—since it is known that at least one of the foreign-owned banks received what amounted to a bailout from its parent company after having experienced some of the same operating problems as the failed indigenous banks—it is also apparent that another foreign bank needed no additional support from its parent and did not suffer from the operating problems that characterized the indigenous banks. Directors and managers in this viable bank made very different, obviously more prudent, decisions when faced with the same macroeconomic conditions and regulatory environment.

Explanations for the imprudent decisions and actions taken by directors and managers of the failed banks generally can be grouped into two categories. "Sharp" practice—practices that are illegal, bordering on the illegal, or self-serving—and management incompetence.

Many observers of the Jamaican financial crisis argue that directors and managers in the failed banks were engaging in "loophole mining," self-dealing, and speculation. For example, several commentators suggest that the banks' problems arose because senior directors and managers deliberately used "creative accounting" with respect to asset valuation and income recognition in order to avoid having to set aside funds to provide for a growing number of nonperforming assets.

While there is evidence to support the argument that some directors and managers in the failed Jamaican banks were engaged in sharp practice motivated by self-interest and opportunism, this argument alone cannot explain the sheer pervasiveness of the imprudent decisions and actions taken by directors and managers of the failed banks. In addition, the argument rests on the assumption that the failed banks' directors and senior managers knew exactly what they were doing and had adequate control over their operations and risks at all times. However, public statements by a number of commentators and data collected by the author equally indicate that the banks' directors and senior managers in many cases did not recognize the full extent of the risks they faced. Far from being "masterminds," the failed banks' directors and managers seemed not to know what was going on or, if they did, not to know how to deal with it.

Many analysts have argued that Jamaican bankers' inability to recognize and control risks and operational problems was due to the fact that they lacked sufficient management expertise and training, particularly in dealing with new financial products and services in a more volatile market environment and in dealing with the management of noncore businesses, such as hotels. Consequently, they did not know enough to put in place proper internal controls and risk management mechanisms appropriate to the new business areas and environments in which they were working.

Nevertheless, it is also clear that Jamaican commercial bankers were not totally remiss in establishing internal operating accountabilities and controls to aid in identifying and managing areas of risk. Indeed, bank regulation required them to establish many accountabilities and controls and to report regularly on their level of compliance. Despite gaps in their internal control and risk-management procedures, they had put a number of accountabilities and controls in place. Nevertheless, time and again, bankers in the failed banks were unable to control and monitor their operations effectively despite the internal accountabilities and controls they had established, even when such controls were *not* subject to override by managers and employees. This raises the question of why.

RECORDS CREATION AND RECORD KEEPING
AS CONTRIBUTING FACTORS

Data collected by the author indicate that an inadequate basis of information contributed to the weakness of the banks' systems of accountability and control. A good basis of information for accountability is particularly critical to achieving and maintaining internal control in large hierarchical organizations such as were the Jamaican commercial banks. The reason is that decentralization and specialization naturally bring about operational inefficiency because no one person has all the information relevant to the enterprise's activities. As a result, individual members of an enterprise will have some freedom to choose their own actions. If there is any divergence between the members' goals or objectives and those of their managers or the enterprise, inefficiencies can arise. For example, employees may make decisions to take actions in their own best interests that are detrimental to the broader aims of the enterprise, such as in cases of fraud. For this reason, directors and managers of large hierarchical organizations rely on formal internal accountabilities to monitor and control the decisions and actions of their subordinates. Moreover, this information is crucial as a basis for directors' and managers' own decisions and actions in developing business strategy.

For these reasons, communication of information is essential to the operation of formal internal accountability systems in large hierarchical organizations. In addition, it is preferable that the communication of information be in recorded form because records, in their generally accepted greater capacity to capture and fix meaning, have a greater relative capacity to communicate meaning over organizational space and time. Therefore, records provide the means by which standards of performance are communicated to the members of enterprises as well as how individuals give and are held to account for their performance in formal systems of internal accountability.

Turning to look first at the communication of performance standards, there were weaknesses in the banks that collapsed. In formal accountability systems, standards of performance usually are communicated through policies, procedures, directives, and documentation of a similar nature. The absence of such records clearly contributed to the internal operating problems experienced by the banks that failed and was linked to weaknesses in their internal control and risk-management practices. However, even when such documents did exist, performance standards were not being followed.

Commentators typically have pointed to weak management oversight and control coupled with a weak internal audit function in the failed banks as reasons that even documented performance standards were not properly implemented. While there is certainly evidence to suggest that this was the case, it assumes that employees were sufficiently aware of existing policies and overlooks the failure to communicate policies effectively as a factor that prevented their proper implementation. In contrast to the received wisdom, evidence gathered by the author suggests that weak compliance with internal operating rules and standards of performance in the failed banks also was linked to problems with how rules and standards of performance were communicated. For example, policies, procedures, and directives did not flow as they should have to those responsible for their implementation. Nor were they regularly reviewed to ensure their continuing relevance.

In commenting on the communication and management of policies, procedures, and directives, one interview subject spoke of the problems encountered:

In some cases they were there but you had to look for [them]. In that, although there is a procedures manual, a document that states how they should operate, you find that there are several amendments and these amendments are given in the form of a memo. [They] do not necessarily . . . hit the manual but [are] in a separate file. So the information is kind of sketchy in some cases. Where [there] is an issue you have to run the light [investigate] to some extent on the people involved in the process.[2]

Another respondent commented that a new person joining the bank would see that the policy manual "is five years behind but the [amendments are] somewhere around in the organization which you cannot find."[3]

As a result, informal and predominantly oral communication of practices "the way we do it around here" prevailed, with resultant ambiguity about organizational practices and standards of performance.

Problems with the communication and management of policies, procedures, and directives were linked to the fact that the failed banks were not systematically managing the creation, review, distribution, and filing of these documents. In other words, the problems arose from weak management of the records creation and recordkeeping processes. Each operational area was separately responsible for codifying policies, procedures, and directives relating to the functions it performed. In the absence of a central coordinating unit with responsibility for the management of the organization's codified business rules, there was no way of ensuring that operating units codified consistently and regularly or of ensuring that they systematically reviewed existing policies, procedures, and directives to incorporate changes necessary to correct operating problems or address new product innovations.

Furthermore, no single unit was responsible for compiling all policies to maintain an official current version of the various policy manuals or a historical record of superseded policies in the event that questions arose about past decisions based on earlier rules. Nor was there a single distribution list to ensure that all relevant persons received new versions or that new employees received important information about business rules. Moreover, no clear procedures existed for updating policy manuals as amendments were issued, with the result that manuals became outdated and new policies, procedures, and directives were difficult to find. In many cases, individuals continued to work in accordance with outdated business practice.

As the banks grew in size and came to have more complex organizational structures, lack of control over the management of their policies, procedures, and directives became more pronounced and detrimental to operations. There were more units creating policies and procedures and an increasing number of staff members to whom policy and procedure documents had to be distributed. In the absence of any coordination over the development and communication of documented business rules and performance standards, the banks' documentation of policies, procedures, and directives became more erratic and uncontrolled. Moreover, growth and product innovation created a need for rapid revision of existing policies so that version control in this increasingly complex environment became of increasing importance. Since no version control was in place, personnel were often unaware of operational standards and requirements, and management was increasingly unable to hold staff to account and maintain internal control.

Effective operation of formal internal systems of accountability relies not only on records to communicate performance standards. Records are also essential in the communication of accounts of decisions and actions taken by accountable persons, for records form the basis on which those to whom others are accountable (i.e., managers and directors) judge their decisions and actions. In turn, managers and directors use the information communicated in the accounts as the basis for their own decisions and actions in maintaining operational control, managing risks, and deciding business strategy. Evidence gathered from the failed Jamaican commercial banks reveals that accounting information required for effective accountability was not available. As a result, directors and managers experienced difficulties in maintaining control over their banks' operations and in obtaining the information needed to make prudent decisions about risk exposures and management of their balance sheets.

It is worth noting at this point that commentators frequently have attributed these problems with accounting information to ineffective "management information systems." The way various commentators use this terminology, however, indicates that they all have very different ideas about what management information systems actually comprise. For example, some respondents use the term to refer to the banks' computerized transaction processing and core accounting systems. Others use it to refer to the reporting functionality of information systems (whether computerized or manual) that supported management review and decision making. Still others use the term quite liberally to refer to all computerized information systems in the banks.

Despite their different conceptualizations of management information systems, persons with whom the author spoke all described pervasive problems in accessing trustworthy and timely accounting and management information. In the words of one interview subject,

I would have to say that one of the big problems that faced Jamaica is [that] the management information systems . . . were absolutely atrocious; nobody could get anything out of them and if I was a manager I would not have a clue as to what was going on in my bank.[4]

Lack of trustworthy accounting information led to problems that had serious repercussions. Without timely and accurate information about their bank's financial position, managers were unable to accurately assess the quality of their asset portfolios, make adequate provisions against loss, prevent a mismatch between assets and liabilities, manage their cash flows, and keep down the costs of their funds. The banks' failure to perform these critical functions effectively, or even perform them at all in some cases, in combination with market conditions at the time, resulted in a number of life-threatening problems. For example, a rising number of nonperforming assets funded by short-term liabilities led to liquidity problems. The banks' profitability further declined as overhead expenses increased from losses due to fraud and the banks' inability to manage their cash flow effectively, which led to penalties for failing to adhere to statutory deposit ratios, which again increased costs of operation. All these factors taken together spelled disaster for these commercial banks.

One of the reasons typically given for the failed banks' information-related problems is the level and quality of computerization of their transaction processing and accounting processes. Proponents of this argument suggest that replacement of manual systems or improved computer systems for transaction processing and accounting would have resulted in better quality and more accessible accounting and management information. While it is certainly true that the banks still handled processing and accounting for certain types of transactions manually and also that their existing computerized transaction processing and accounting systems were seriously flawed, explanations attributing the banks' information-related problems solely to the level or quality of their computerization tend to overlook the significance of original records of business transactions, or source documents, in the production of trustworthy and timely accounts.

While the level and quality of computerization of the banks' transaction processing and accounting systems clearly was a factor in the poor quality of their accounting and management information, a number of problems with source documentation also created errors and omissions in the production of the failed banks' accounts and accounting reports. Interview subjects gave numerous examples of missing source documentation. They cited instances when these records were unavailable because they were not created in the first place, were lost or destroyed (either accidentally or purposely), or so disorganized as to be impossible to retrieve. The following are just a few examples uncovered of the banks' source documentation problems.

- Many loan files lacked key documentation or contained documentation that was incomplete. Problems included obsolete financial statements, poor and incomplete appraisals, unsatisfactory and incomplete loan information, no documentation relating to site visits, and insurance documentation that was not current.

- There were unrecorded deposits dating from 1993 in the failed banks approaching Jamaican $200 million (approximately U.S. $4.5 million).

- Bank guarantees were issued at the officer level and often not reported, secured, or documented in the bank's official records.

- There was a lack of proper documentation of banks' investments of its own funds handled by brokers.

- An internal audit conducted at one of the failed banks uncovered many instances of incomplete and missing documentation in the treasury and foreign-exchange trading operations.

- Documentation relating to the transfer of funds between companies was incomplete. Often the origination of fund transfers was not clear.

- The banks failed to create documentation on their various subsidiary companies and the nature of the relationships between the various companies in their financial groups.

- Customer information files were incomplete and inaccurate.

- There was poor documentation of fixed assets.

Interviewees described how the absence, incompleteness, and inaccuracy of records prevented the banks from monitoring their balance sheets, reconciling accounts, managing their risk exposures, and preventing fraud. In addition, because of missing records, FINSAC was unable to verify many transactions, forcing it to write them off. This is how missing and untrustworthy records contributed to poor control in the failed banks, were a factor in the banks' decline, and later ended up costing FINSAC, and ultimately the government and taxpayers, additional sums of money.

There are three main ways in which source documentation contributed to the information-related problems of the failed banks. First, records of original transactions provided the foundation for the construction of accounts and, by extension, the basis for internal and external accountabilities. Thus, weaknesses in source documentation "rippled out" to affect the trustworthiness of the accounting information upon which managers and directors of the banks relied to control operations, assess their financial positions and risks, and control fraud. The failure to record loans and guarantees resulted in omissions in the banks' accounts that presented a misleading picture of their asset portfolios. Moreover, incomplete and inaccurate internal vouchers resulted in a high incidence of misposted transactions and difficulties in the subsequent sorting out of errors. Missing, incomplete, and error-ridden source documentation, coupled with system-related problems and limitations in the production of trial balances, balance sheets, and other management and financial accounting reports, had a cumulatively disastrous effect for the failed banks. There were distortions and inaccuracies in the banks' accounts that prevented them from assessing and managing the risks associated with their loan portfolios and other assets, managing liquidity, and assessing profitability and their financial positions. Consequently, in many cases directors and managers had no basis for determining their banks' true financial positions and risk exposures. This finding goes against the received wisdom that all distortions and inaccuracies in the banks' accounts were deliberate attempts at "creative accounting" on the part of the banks' directors and managers.

Second, source documentation also provides an essential means of verifying the accuracy and validity of those accounts through processes of proofing the entry of transactions, account balancing, and reconciliation. Here again, the banks had problems with their records. Retrieval of source documents for the purposes of clearing up transaction entry errors, account imbalances, or reconciliation of accounts was difficult or impossible because of the manner in which the banks kept transaction records. So chaotic was the way in which these records were kept that, in response to concern about the public release of individuals' financial details as a result of the banking crisis, Jamaica's minister of finance was prompted to remark of two of the banks that "Having seen the way that records were kept . . . I have no doubt that they'd lose, if not all, at least most of the pieces of information."[5]

Interview subjects described the state in which one of the banks kept daily transaction vouchers as follows:

> We went on this occasion. . . . because we needed to get some documents for our law-
> yers, who had requested some specific files and we went with the lawyers to see how
> easy it would be to locate these documents. On arrival we saw the door was open and a
> number of boxes were scattered outside on the steps. We went up the steps and there
> was one guy at the back leafing through stuff in a box. . . . So we actually went there and
> what we encountered was a room filled with boxes, torn and untorn, all dumped in the
> middle of the room in no particular order. . . . So we had to climb on top of the pile and try
> and re-arrange the boxes in some sort of order to try and figure out what was what. We
> also had to compete with the rats.[6]

Under these conditions of storage, retrieval of the records for account verification purposes, and therefore the construction of trustworthy accounts, was impeded. In terms of the effect that records storage had on the banks' ability to
reconcile their accounts, a 1999 Ministry of Finance and Planning paper stated
that FINSAC discovered over 5,000 unreconciled accounts in four of the failed
Jamaican commercial banks! A former director of one of the failed banks attributed the lack of reconciliation of accounts directly to a problem with locating
source records. While, arguably, part of the problem the failed banks experienced with account reconciliation related to the fact that bank directors and
managers did not take steps to ensure that this function was being performed on
a timely basis, records-related problems were certainly a contributing factor.
The director commented that

> We have accounts here that haven't balanced, been reconciled for years. Mainly be-
> cause they just can't get the source documents. They are nowhere to be found. Either
> they were lost at the branches, they were not maintained at the branches, or [they were
> lost] in transit, . . . or they were filed somewhere or destroyed. And we have had to write
> off millions, literally millions, of dollars, because we just do not have the information to
> reconcile accounts.[7]

In 1998 alone the bank had to write off Jamaican $120 million (approximately
U.S. $2.7 million) because it was unable to reconcile accounts. Had the banks'
directors and managers ensured that source documents were properly maintained, such losses might have been avoided.

Third, source documents provide the primary means for the banks to prove
their legal right to certain assets. Poor documentation of asset and collateral on
assets prevented the banks from exercising their rights. For example, many loan
files lacked key documentation or contained documentation that was incomplete. According to one subject,

> When someone wants a loan you take security such as a guarantee, a mortgage, a lien on
> the house, a chattel mortgage something like that [and] they sign a promissory note. You
> then arrange to debit their account for the payment, or the interest payments. You have

agreed on the interest rates. In some of the records we received on the loans we took over ... the documentation of loans was [poor].[8]

This subject went on to note that, even when the documentation was created and gathered initially, that

Sometimes [we are] not even being able to find the files on those loans. ... Some [loan files] did not have signed notes. ... [For] some the title had been lost ... [T]hey had taken it to the Titles Office to have the assignment noted and it [was] not computerized at the Titles Office or it got lost. Or it was never there. So as a banker you would have no proof that you took that security. Or it had gone down to the bureau to have the stamp duty put on it and it never came back. Or it got stuck in the black box because the branches may be computerized but they are totally reliant on the supporting agencies.[9]

As of the end of 1999, one of the failed banks with a comparatively well managed system for its securities could claim documentation was complete on only some 70 percent of files. When the economic situation turned sour and many individuals and businesses defaulted on loans, the banks—and consequently FINSAC, because it took over the loans of the failed institutions—were unable to recover on their assets because of inadequate documentation in their credit and securities files. In the end, the high number of nonperforming loans on which the banks could not recover had to be written off, thereby weakening the banks' liquidity positions and capital adequacy and contributing to their collapse.

Investment was another area in which the banks were unable to protect their legal rights because of inadequate documentation. As one FINSAC official explained, the reason was that certain banks bought, held, transferred, and disposed of stocks that they owned through brokers. In order to avoid paying taxes on these investments, the banks sometimes had brokers purchase these shares in the brokers' names rather than in the name of the bank. These share transfers were not properly documented and, as a result, it later proved impossible for the banks to verify share ownership. The inability to validate investment transactions resulted in one loss that amounted to Jamaican $100 million (approximately U.S. $2.32 million).

The banks' microfilming practices contributed to losses from fraud as well. Bank officers were often unable to retrieve microfilmed checks and other documents because of the poor quality of the microfilm, which was often completely black or blank. Owing to their inability to retrieve microfilmed copies of checks, the banks were often unable to pursue legal action in cases of suspected fraud.

Despite the critical importance of original records of financial transactions, the manner in which the failed Jamaican commercial banks created and kept source documentation contributed to errors and omissions in accounting records, prevented proper verification of accounts, and kept them from pursuing legal claims in cases of loan defaults, investment ownership, and fraud. All the problems combined and contributed to the banks' downward spiral into eventual insolvency and failure.

FACTORS CONTRIBUTING TO RECORDS-RELATED PROBLEMS IN JAMAICA'S INDIGENOUS COMMERCIAL BANKS

The previous section has illustrated how records creation and recordkeeping practices contributed to the poor decision making and internal operating problems in the failed banks. These practices were the result of decisions and actions that the banks' directors, managers, and employees took every day in performing their duties. In making decisions and taking actions with respect to records creation and record keeping, these individuals were guided by their own motivations and incentives influenced by the organizational and broader social context in which they worked as well as by limitations of the technology they used to create and keep records.

Data collected by the author points to the fact that a number of directors, managers, and employees were motivated by self-interest and greed. However, in looking for root causes of source documentation problems in the failed Jamaican commercial banks it would be all too easy to point to sharp practice on the part of some managers, directors, and employees and leave explanations at that. Certainly, investigations uncovered examples linking the absence or incompleteness of records with sharp practice (such as the failure to write up loans and properly document investments). Nevertheless, the banks' recordkeeping problems were so widespread that the sharp practices of a relative few cannot explain all failures to document or document properly. Moreover, it does not account for the disorganized way in which the banks stored their source documents. Other explanations must be sought.

What is clear is that all processes concerned with the making and keeping of records were relatively uncontrolled in the failed Jamaican commercial banks. The reason was either an absence of bankwide policies and procedures relating to records-related activities or weak monitoring and enforcement of existing policies and procedures. In the absence of effective internal accountabilities and controls over records creation and record keeping, the banks' officers made decisions about how records should be created and kept according to their own preferences, personal standards, and motivations. In many cases, the factors that drove how individuals created and kept records produced results that were not in the best interests of the banks and, indeed, were detrimental over the long term.

For example, broad cultural influences affected the making of records in the failed banks. Interview subjects pointed to the fact that because Jamaica is a small society, many deals were made on the basis of personal contacts. In commenting on this phenomenon, Jamaica's minister of finance has stated that in a small community, decisions cannot be made dispassionately, noting that you can have rules but "sooner or later you get a call."[10] He also has observed that the tendency to do business with friends or known associates in the context of a small society militates against the creation of documentation (because the other party is known to the banker and there is greater trust), adding that this was the reason that some of the loan documentation in the failed banks was nonexistent or incomplete.

Some subjects point to a generally held belief that Jamaican people favor oral forms of communication and therefore are less likely to make records. As one interview subject remarked, "It is very difficult to get [employees] to put this information down on paper. Maybe it is because we are not very literate in that we don't like writing letters and writing memos and that sort of thing. We just don't do it."[11] This cultural aversion to record making was clearly evident among the Jamaican employees in the banks that failed. In contrast, Jamaican employees working in foreign-owned banks created documents where their counterparts in the failed banks did not. This difference in behavior among people from the same cultural background can be attributed to the fact that in the foreign-owned banks the cultural values of the foreign parent company, reflecting the broader cultural values of a society more oriented to making records, placed greater emphasis and importance on documenting transactions. The organizational culture reflected this value system, and the bank promulgated and enforced clear rules and structures to ensure that proper documentation was made and kept. In the failed banks, where documentation was poor, it was the cultural predilection not to document *coupled with* an organizational absence of effective accountability for the making of records, which led to failures to account. Without polices, procedures, standards, and guidelines in this area, or because of weak enforcement of those that existed, individual motivations and cultural disincentives to record making had full play.

Similarly, organizational cultural factors influenced how the banks kept their records. In the absence of general standards for the organization and management of records stores and weak enforcement of existing general standards, each manager and the individuals to whom they assigned responsibility for the day-to-day keeping of records organized and managed records in their custody according to their own preferences, level of knowledge, and priorities.

Managers had little time for the recordkeeping function, being busy with other pressing operational priorities and generally perceiving the records management function as relatively unimportant. A comment by one subject reflects the generally held attitude to record keeping:

Simply because I don't think that records management—although it's probably one of our most, one of our highest risks area—it's not something that is looked at as very important. . . . [However, when] you can't find a document everybody starts to jump all over each other. But the time, the money, et cetera, is not something that I think people focus [on] enough to say that this is such an important project let us carry it through to the bitter end. You see? . . . Something is always more important. There is always another major blaze that somebody has to go and [put] out and [consequently, records management goes] to the back end.[12]

Thus, managers assigned responsibility to lower-level—untrained clerical—staff for the organization and management of current records stores in their custody and the transfer of noncurrent records to secondary records stores. In many cases, these untrained staff lacked the knowledge of the banks' policies and procedures and records management principles and practices to carry out their duties effectively. In addition, because branch and unit managers saw the recordkeeping function as a low priority, they provided little to no oversight over how clerical staff performed their recordkeeping duties. As a result, staff charged with the oversight of records stores had little incentive to ensure that records were properly managed, even if they did identify ways in which the organization or management of the stores under their control might be improved.

In addition, as the banks grew, increasing decentralization of decision making and action led to a concomitant decentralization of records stores. This also contributed to inconsistency in the organization and management of records by multiplying the number of stores and the number of employees responsible for them, each with his or her own motivation influencing decisions and actions with respect to record keeping.

The banks' approach to the organization and management of stores of source documents led to noncompliance with records management policies and procedures and inconsistencies in the way in which records stores were organized and managed. In the long run, these recordkeeping practices produced disorganized and poorly managed records stores from which important records were missing.

Technical factors also contributed to some of the problems that the failed banks experienced with their source documents, since each technology used in the creation and keeping of records had its own inherent advantages and limitations. Decisions of the banks' directors and managers with respect to how different technologies were deployed played a critical role in determining the extent to which technology helped or hindered accounting and accountability for financial transactions. The banks' use of microfilm to produce backups of documents transported between branches and central processing units and to retain copies of processed checks returned to customers or other banks provides an example. Despite the advantages of microfilm technology for these purposes, the technology had limitations that the banks failed to address. Microfilm usage requires that microfilm cameras be serviced regularly, that camera operators receive proper training, that microfilm be sent for processing on a timely basis, and that the quality of film images be checked after processing. As the banks had not established clear procedures for microfilming activities nor assigned responsibility for the microfilming activities to a supervising officer, the limitations of microfilm as a technology of record inscription and storage were not addressed and, consequently, the banks were unable to retrieve copies of documents of critical importance to verify the reliability of their accounts and pursue cases of fraud.

Not only did the failed banks' records creation and recordkeeping practices contribute to the internal operating problems that led to their demise, but they have also been factors preventing social accountability for the collapse of Jamaica's indigenous commercial banks. Starting in 1997, FINSAC took over the operation of a number of the failed Jamaican commercial banks. At that time, there were many allegations of fraud and corruption with respect to the operation of the banks. To address the allegations, FINSAC established a team of foreign and local forensic auditors to investigate. Because of the inaccessibility of source documentation and other accounting records, however, the auditors have found their work extremely difficult. As one forensic auditor commented, "What you are finding is that our work is being severely hampered by the record keeping or the lack thereof."[13] Explaining the consequences of poor record keeping, this subject went on to state that "The court demands that you have certain types of evidence, and if you don't have that it jeopardizes the whole case. . . . They need to see the books and all that sort of information, and if you don't have things like returned checks, then you know it goes a long way in subverting the whole process."[14] FINSAC has been able to pursue legal action against very few of the directors and managers of the failed commercial banks accused of illegal activities because documentary evidence with which to build cases is lacking.

CONCLUSION

The failure of Jamaica's indigenous commercial banks has had a profound negative effect on the Jamaican economy and society. As a result of the forced rescue of the failed banks, the country has incurred an enormous foreign and domestic debt burden. Consequently, the Jamaican government has been forced to raise taxes to generate revenue and to reduce expenditure on social programs and maintenance of the country's infrastructure. Under these conditions, the overall standard of living for the average Jamaican has become increasingly difficult to sustain, and a sense of frustration and hopelessness has invaded the national psyche. For this reason, it is imperative to fully understand all the reasons for the collapse.

While explanations of the bank failures typically have focused on the state of the country's economy, a weak regulatory framework, sharp practice, and management incompetence, this case study has shown that an absence of essential information about standards of operation as well as accounting and management information—the result of the banks' records creation and recordkeeping practices—was an important contributing factor in the bank failures. As a result of these practices, the banks' directors and managers were simply unable to obtain the quality of information they needed to maintain effective control of the banks' operations, monitor and manage their financial positions and risk exposures, and prevent fraud. Moreover, in the aftermath of the collapse, the absence of critical records has also hampered efforts by the Jamaican government and FINSAC to rehabilitate the Jamaican financial sector and bring legal action against certain former directors and managers.

Contrary to the belief that the banks' information-related problems were largely intentional coverups or resulted from the level or quality of computerization in the transaction processing and accounting areas, many of the information-related problems resulted from the absence of effective enterprisewide systems of accountability for records creation and storage of source documents. In the absence of effective records-related accountabilities and controls, individuals with diverse motivations who were influenced by a wide range of social factors made choices about how to create and keep these records, and those choices did not support the production of trustworthy and timely accounts and therefore the effective operation of the banks' internal systems of accountability. Since the Jamaican banking community has tended to conceive of information-related problems only in terms of deliberate avoidance of records creation or tampering with records, information technology failures, and other non-systemic risks, they have not recognized the cumulative negative effect of systemically negligent records creation and record keeping. The value of this case study lies in uncovering the effects that the failed indigenous banks' habitual records practices had on internal and social accountabilities for the banks' operations and in highlighting the importance of clear standards of accountability for and control of records. We hope that lessons learned from this experience can be used to avoid repeating the same mistakes.

NOTES

1. Financial Sector Adjustment Company, Limited, *Annual Report* (Kingston, Jamaica, 1998), p. 8.

2. Subject A-2. Personal interview, Kingston, Jamaica, May 19, 1999. Interview subjects are identified by alphanumerical code rather than by name in order to protect their identities.

3. Subject A-10. Personal interview, Kingston, Jamaica, June 17, 1999.

4. Subject A-1. Personal interview, Kingston, Jamaica, May 19, 1999.

5. Omar Davies, "Introductory Statements," *Symposium on the Crisis of the Jamaican Financial Services Sector* (Kingston, Jamaica: University of the West Indies, Nov. 27, 1999). Author's transcription from tape-recorded proceedings.

6. Subject A-4. Personal interview, Kingston, Jamaica, May 20, 1999.

7. Subject A-18. Personal interview, Kingston, Jamaica, Aug. 3, 1999.

8. Subject A-3. Personal interview, Kingston, Jamaica, May 20, 1999.

9. Ibid.

10. Davies, "Introductory Statements."

11. Subject A-18. Personal interview, Kingston, Jamaica, Aug. 3, 1999.

12. Subject A-17. Personal interview, Kingston, Jamaica, Aug. 2, 1999.

13. Subject F-1. Personal interview, Kingston, Jamaica, May 9, 2000.

14. Ibid.

The Anchors of Community Trust and Academic Liberty: The Fabrikant Affair

Barbara L. Craig

AUDITS AND ACCOUNTABILITY

Members of a community usually trust their colleagues and those in positions of responsibility who act on their behalf or have power over them. For this gift of trust we expect honest behavior in return. These expectations are largely met by the audit, a more or less formal process in organizations that proves that people have exercised the diligence expected of those with personal and corporate responsibilities. Derived from the Latin verb *audire*, to hear, the audit has taken on the sense of a review of actions, after the fact, through examining documents that authorized actions and recorded their details. The audit gives us the power and the opportunity to "listen" or to revisit what has taken place. Audits to prove due diligence express continuing accountability and are a regular part of good business practice.[1]

Accountability anchors trust and is a cornerstone of moral behavior. This larger role may not be seen clearly. The formal controls of accounting, emphasizing procedures and rules rather than the community bond these nurture, may overshadow the social purpose of the audit, which is to reestablish the balance of trust among members of a community through the exercise of judgment on those things for which we are accountable. A robust freedom to act within our community is fully realized when trust is anchored in a habit of clear records. Responsible recordkeeping practices that are sensitive to their part in cementing the bonds of trust give us the best way of returning to the past to relive its contingencies without ambiguity—the planned and the contingent intersect in our documents.

While organizations generally assign formal responsibilities for making records, the proper discharge of these obligations relies on the willingness of individuals to comply. Without the full participation of members, trust in a community ultimately will be undermined. The reasons for neglect may not be fraudulent nor even a product of a purpose. Formal requirements to keep records may seem to be onerous, and their need may not be fully grasped in academic environments where freedom is guarded fiercely and bureaucratic strictures are perceived as encroachments. However, the need for constraint on the exercise of free action only becomes apparent when we consider that acts that are legitimate, accepted, and acceptable need a foundation of trust built by transparent records and proved in the audit. Freedom that is robust and defensible emerges logically, not paradoxically, from the attention paid to keeping complete and comprehensive records. Far from being only a lesser responsibility with only a brief claim on our attention, record making and keeping must be living commitments if they are to thrive. When these habits lose their robustness or fall into abeyance, when audits are perfunctory or superficial, or when the absence of records is seen as an expression of the liberty of a person or an office, freedoms are ultimately compromised, and actions—however legitimate and honest they may be—are open to questioning.

ACADEMIC INSTITUTIONS AND THE FABRIKANT AFFAIR

Academic institutions are bound by the laws that govern other types of public or private organizations, and they have rules and procedures for their business that are similar to those of any large, complex enterprise. However, the academic mission is unique. It emphasizes scholarship, the free interplay of ideas, and the pursuit of research untrammeled by restrictions of politics, profit, or popularity. The university values honesty and supports broad freedom to pursue the scholarly goals of its members and peers. While the academy and the institution in which it lives at times can seem to be two distinct cultures with differing values—freedom versus procedural rules—the Fabrikant affair amply illustrates the symbiosis between real academic freedom and clear institutional accountability.[2]

On August 24, 1992, Valery Fabrikant, a professor in the Faculty of Engineering and Computer Science at Concordia University in Montreal, shot five of his colleagues at the university's main downtown campus, killing four. Fabrikant briefly held hostages before surrendering to the police. He was tried and convicted of murder in 1993 and is currently serving a life sentence. Although the shooting generated investigations into matters related to the crime, the Fabrikant affair spawned a number of special inquiries, or audits, commissioned by Concordia to provide it with advice for making changes in the university's practices to redress deficiencies and revitalize sound ideals. The results of these investigations touched the heart of the university and had implications for academic life as a whole.

The history of Fabrikant at Concordia University, even before the events of August 1992, was as intricate as it was uneasy. Aspects of his contractual relationship with the university, first as a part-time contract researcher, and then as a sessional teacher and ultimately in a tenure-track position, were under review by committees of his peers at the university.[3] Fabrikant initiated a grievance alleging that he was unfairly denied tenure by his department and the university, and that his entitlement to sabbatical leave was not correctly calculated according to the university's agreed formula. He was a well-known correspondent with officers of the university on a number of matters over the years since his arrival in 1979. Recently, in formal letters and often in informal conversations, Fabrikant alleged that colleagues in his department were in conflict of interest as employees of the university. This conflict arose from their position as grantees of federal research agencies, notably the National Engineering and Science Research Council (or NESERC), and as contractors for private paid work as consultants and contract holders from outside agencies and private companies.

The allegations were serious enough, but of equal concern was Fabrikant's behavior disrupting the normal course of university life and creating an atmosphere of disquiet and concern. In early 1992 a number of investigations had taken place into Fabrikant's grievances about his employment relationship with the university and his allegations against colleagues.[4] In June 1992 the university decided to set in motion an independent investigation of Fabrikant's charges that colleagues in the Faculty of Engineering and Computer Science were improperly using grant funds and that some had assumed credit for research they had not done in coauthored published papers. In July NESERC asked the university formally to investigate these charges and by August plans were well underway.[5] The investigations were suspended after the shootings on August 24.

THE FABRIKANT AFFAIR AND RECORDS

Immediately after the criminal investigation were concluded and Valery Fabrikant was tried and convicted, the university commissioned three investigations. In September 1993 the board of governors resolved to appoint an external investigator to review "all the documents related to the employment history of Valery Fabrikant at Concordia University." John Scott Cowan was appointed to undertake this investigation on November 10, 1993.[6] The board also appointed Harry Arthurs, Roger A. Blais, and Jon H. Thompson to conduct an independent inquiry into issues related to scientific and academic integrity at Concordia University. Their mandate is provided as Appendix A to the report. Finally, the dean of the Faculty of Engineering and Computer Science commissioned an audit of the research, contract, and discretionary accounts held by Concordia from 1980 to 1992.[7]

These inquiries into the several issues surrounding Fabrikant's allegations and the university's response to them were based on interviews with key informants and principals to the matters under review, and to a greater or lesser degree, on the records of the university. The importance of clear records for a thorough review of past actions was underscored by the principals who conducted each of the independent reviews. While the investigators were able to interview individuals who could speak from firsthand experience about what they knew to be true, a full view of events from a number of perspectives and in a number of contexts could be had only by revisiting the records of many departments and committees of the university. These proved to be inadequate to the expectations people had of them.

Concordia's archives holds the historical records of the university and its predecessors and actively documents certain aspects of Montreal life through an active appraisal and acquisition program in special areas. The archives staff also provides the university with advice on current recordkeeping practices.[8] When requested, the staff helps recordkeeping units on technical matters, including classification of records, file maintenance, and security. The archives also operate a secure place for the custody for dormant records under the control of approved records schedules. The staff provides reference to dormant records in their custody and expedites duly authorized destruction of records at the end of their scheduled period of retention. The first efforts in record management were in the research and financial services areas. These units keep central files to satisfy internal rules for demonstrating fiduciary responsibility for funds that are largely provided by outside agencies. While the archive service has been establishing additional agreed-upon controls over all records—including standards for classification, compliance with laws and regulations, and schedules for destruction—responsibility for making and keeping clear, unambiguous, and open records resides with all members of the community. No central service department is a surrogate for personal commitment to responsible record keeping and ethical dealings. The achievements of the archives since its official formation in 1985 are significant, but as a small unit it relies on the cooperation of university officers and faculty to ensure that the comprehensive spirit of responsible records management is expressed in everyday actions. Compliance with approved classification schemes and records schedules is largely voluntary.

Each of the investigators into the Fabrikant affair discussed the importance of records, to their work and to the university, and pointed to the inadequacies that they found—in essence it was not possible to view the past clearly, largely because the records were incomplete.[9] Their reports spoke explicitly about the vital importance of personal and community ethics for the healthy life of an academic community and especially for research: its costs must be paid, its results give us new knowledge, and its authors reap academic rewards of recognition, promotion, and credit for their work in peer-reviewed publications. Each investigation, in its own way, relied on records to revisit events in the past, and each one of the reports spoke about the importance of clear and consistent record keeping as the grounding for accountability and the best insurance against risk.[10]

The Cowan Report addressed administrative issues surrounding Fabrikant's employment relationship with Concordia. Cowan concluded that the officers of the university were hampered in reacting to Fabrikant's complaints because the system of record keeping did not provide adequate management information. The university could not rely on a stable source for institutional memory that would support business when officers of long standing were no longer in place to fill in the memory gaps.[11] Specific gaps in Fabrikant's employment records were noted.[12] Recommendation 3 in the Cowan Report urged the university to improve its record keeping and to take "other steps to create and maintain an institutional memory."[13]

Administrators responsible for handling Fabrikant's appeals and charges were unable to refer to either accessible or complete documents of the many official attempts to settle the grievances, appeals, and claims pressed on the university and its officers by Fabrikant over a number of years. An unclear history in documents bred uncertainty and may have compromised effective actions of managers as well as peer reviews of academic performance and achievements. Cowan concluded that if proper records had been kept and were available to those who needed them, many of the actions taken by successive administrators and university committees might have been different because fuller knowledge of the events and circumstances surrounding them would have been accessible. Records would have helped officials separate issues of employment from those related to either academic competencies or improper behavior and clarified the remedies available for complaints.

The Levi Report provided a forensic assessment of certain accounts based on a review of the source documents maintained to support actions on those accounts.[14] Philip Levi's detailed review uncovered irregularities in claims and unexpectedly high activities in journaling between accounts.[15] The forensic auditor and the other investigators in their reviews were guided by law, the internal rules of Concordia University, and the requirements of the agencies who give money to the university. The auditor's evidence was entirely documentary.[16] His conclusions about the appropriateness of the financial behavior, measured against best practices and the relevant internal rules, found "irregularities, inconsistencies and abuses."[17] In some cases funds awarded to principal investigators for research were not used according to the rules of the grantor or of the university. The complexity of the university's accounting procedures, the institution's highly differentiated structure, and the fast expansion of research and contracting activities in the 1980s and later created an environment in which assiduous personal and corporate vigilance was needed to ensure that all rules were met in letter and, more important, in spirit.[18]

Auditors focus on the minutiae of financial disbursements recorded in the bills, claims for reimbursement, invoices, receipts, stubs, and other documents accumulated in pursuit of legitimate university business. These items proved to be wanting in some of the accounts the auditor examined, while in others the charges were for items that were not eligible for reimbursement according to terms of the grant. The Levi Report "confirmed that certain research funds were used for purposes other than those intended."[19] The auditor underscored, however, that ethical leadership comes from examples and deeds and not from memoranda.[20] While no wrongdoing of a criminal nature was charged, the forensic auditor's findings generated sufficient concerns that he recommended many changes in the university's procedures and processes for controlling the disbursement of funds from accounts and for receiving and using money on contract. These recommendations aimed at strengthening the university's financial accounting by improving the clarity and completeness of procedures that authorized payments and transfers. The Levi Report offered many concrete suggestions for reestablishing responsibility for due process and for encouraging personal responsibility for proper actions.

The Arthurs et al. Report reviewed the larger contexts in which the university operates, as a corporation with legal responsibilities and as an academic enterprise with missions to teach and to undertake pure and applied research. The report focused on the concept of accountability, which the authors saw as ensuring the governors and supporters of the university that its employees, especially members of the faculties, "devote themselves primarily to the tasks for which they are paid and to which, by their very acceptance of a university position, they are committed—the teaching of students and the disinterested pursuit and dissemination of knowledge."[21] While recognizing these aims, the report acknowledged that achieving them was not simple and that there were a number of ways in which the aims could be recognized in practice. The report established four tests for accountability procedures: They must accommodate all groups in the university and be supported and promoted by all. They must be sufficiently broad to accommodate the university's various academic communities while at the same time ensuring general compliance for all. All relevant information must be duly reported; and that compliance must be universal, allowing no exceptions or exemptions. The report concluded that these conditions did not exist and, among other points, directed attention to the inability of static procedures to keep pace with the growth in the university.[22] The Arthurs et al. Report found that existing rules were not universally understood or applied. Moreover, the report pointed to the absence of an agreed code of ethics that, the report suggested, was important in establishing an unambiguous framework for the discharge of research responsibilities in an academic setting.[23]

CONCLUSION: LESSONS LEARNED

A lesson renewed from the Fabrikant affair is that a robust freedom to pursue academic inquiry is neither easily nor automatically secured. A cornerstone is a trust anchored freely in personal accountability, a trust sustained largely through personal and corporate commitment to transparent records. These are as important to the academic enterprise as they are to government and business, perhaps more so because freedoms nurtured in the university are vulnerable to erosion by the demands of an increasingly profit-driven and product-oriented society whose values are shaped by money.

No claim can be advanced for the power of records that would ensure that the contingent conditions that led to the dreadful events at Concordia in August 1992 would be prevented in the future. Pointing out the flaws in actions based on records of their performance does not assure that when these are corrected there would be any different outcome. Good records kept well cannot correct malevolent personal behavior nor can they make better inherent human flaws. However, they do have the power to establish a basis of trust within a community and beyond it. That trust cannot be broken if actions can be defended and revisited in documents honestly prepared and kept. They are at their best in dispelling doubt and accounting for official work.

The external reviews undertaken in the wake of the August 1992 shootings underscored the value of the audit as a concept; each review, in its own way, expressed a form of audit, one being personal and historical, one being financial, and the third being moral. The changes made by Concordia pursuant to the reviews were important and significant, especially the university's renewed commitment to unambiguous codes ensuring the ethical treatment of people, money, and responsibilities.[24] In the future, accountability will rest largely, as before, on the foundations of trust built by honesty in a community. The best guarantor of that trust remains the record of actions that provides evidence for the audit. Our documents are ourselves.

NOTES

1. The literature on accountability is considerable, especially in areas of public policy. The following selected items illustrate recent discussions of four aspects: policy implementation, multiple accountabilities, borders of authority, and the role of documents and traditions. Jorgen Gronnegaard Christensen, "Corporatism, Administrative Regimes and the Mis-management of Public Funds [in Denmark]," *Scandinavian Political Studies* 16, no. 3 (1993): 201–225; Thomas Christiansen, "Tensions of European Governance: Politicized Bureaucracy and Multiple Accountability in the European Commission," *Journal of European Public Policy* 4 no. 1 (Mar. 1997): 73–90; Arthur Edwards, "Scientific Expertise and Policy-making: The Intermediary Role of the Public Sphere," *Science and Public Policy* 26 no. 3 (June 1999): 163–170; Carsten Gronbech, "The Scandinavian Tradition of Open Government and the European Union: Problems of Compatibility?" *Journal of European Public Policy* 5, no. 1 (Mar. 1998): 185–199; Mary Henkel, "Teaching Quality Assessments: Public Accountability and Academic Autonomy in Higher Education," *Evaluation* 3, no. 1 (Jan. 1997): 9–24; "Symposium on Accountability in Public Administration: Reconciling Democracy, Efficiency and Ethics." a theme issue of the *International Review of Administrative Sciences* 66, no. 1 (Mar. 2000): 15–159; and Ray C. Rist, "Management Accountability: The Signals Sent by Auditing and Evaluation," *Journal of Public Policy* 9, no. 3 (July–Sept. 1989): 355–369.

2. In 1991 the rector of Concordia contributed to a volume on accountability in the university sector. The article situates the fast growth of universities in Quebec since the 1970s and reviews the impact of draconian changes in public policy and financing.

Patrick Kenniff, "The University Perspective on Funding, Autonomy and Accountability: A View from Concordia," in James Cutt and Rodney Dobell, eds., *Public Purse, Public Purpose: Autonomy and Accountability in the Groves of Academe* (Halifax: Institute for Research on Public Policy, 1992), pp. 223–234.

3. The complex history of Fabrikant's employment at Concordia—from December 1979 when he was hired as a part-time research assistant in the Department of Engineering and Computer Science through his appointment as a probationary associate professor in 1990 to the tenure and promotion formalities related to the terms of his initial appointment in the winter and spring of 1992—is reviewed in detail in John Scott Cowan, "Lessons from the Fabrikant File: A Report to the Board of Governors of Concordia University, An Independent Review of the Employment History of Valery Fabrikant at Concordia University, with Particular Emphasis on Concrete Measures to Enhance the Future Ability of the University to Deal with a Wide Range of Issues Raised by the Case in Question" (May 1994) (hereafter the Cowan Report) Part 2, pp. 12–31. Report downloaded from uwaterloo.ca/web-docs/documents/cowan on Oct. 10, 2000. A copy of the report can also be found at the Concordia University Archives.

4. The intensification of action by Fabrikant, including a history of his written communications and e-mail activities leading up to and continuing as part of his grievance concerning sabbatical entitlement and tenure are summarized in the Cowan Report, pp. 25–28.

5. See Cowan Report, pp. 25 and 29.

6. The full text of the board resolution and further mandate to John Scott Cowan is provided as Appendixes A and B to the Cowan Report, pp. 38–41.

7. The archives service at Concordia University has a full set of the public documents produced by the formal inquiries undertaken in the wake of the events of August 1992. These files include the university's press releases, clippings from the public press and the university's newspapers, articles from Canadian journals, and copies of the reports from the three special investigations commissioned by the university. These reports are the Cowan Report; Harry W. Arthurs, Roger A. Blais, and Jon Thompson, "Integrity in Scholarship. A Report to Concordia University by the Independent Committee of Inquiry into Academic and Scientific Integrity" (Apr. 1994; hereafter the Arthurs et al. Report); Philip C. Levi, "Concordia University Special Audit Report on Specific Accounts of the Faculty of Engineering and Computer Science" (July 1994; hereafter the Levi Report); and Levi, "Concordia University Supplement to the Special Audit on Specific Accounts of the Faculty of Engineering and Computer Science" (July 1994; hereafter the Levi Report Supplement). The minutes of the board of governors from 1974 are available on the Web site of the Concordia archives (no attachments are included) at archives3.concordia.ca.

8. A record management program was begun in 1985. The first task was a complete inventory of records. Schedules were developed for several key areas and new file plans developed. (Oral communication with the archivist, Nancy Marrelli, Aug. 24, 2000.)

9. The external reviews commissioned by Concordia commented generally on the confused state of record keeping and the lack of clarity in the documentary trail. It seems obvious that these were expected and that their absence had an impact on the reviewers' assessment of the situation. See, for example, the Arthurs et al. Report, p. 23, the Cowan Report, p. 3, the Levi Report, p. 6, and the Levi Report Supplement, p. 14.

10. Levi Report Supplement, p. 10.

11. Cowan Report, pp. 8–9.

12. Ibid., pp. 12–13.

13. Ibid., p. 34.

14. The destruction of scheduled records was halted by the archives after the shootings.

15. Journal entries can be used to move funds among accounts when, for example, a debit may have been charged to an account in error. In this case the journal entry would restore the balances of the original accounts by moving money from one fund to the other. There are many reasons why money is moved among accounts, and auditors expect to find a certain number of journal entries.

16. Levi Report includes the detailed investigations of the auditor into special accounts of the Faculty of Engineering and Computer Science. The Levi Report Supplement contains more general recommendations for procedural changes that seemed useful as part of a broader measure to correct internal accounting and compliance with existing rules and more informed review of the information offered in source documents that are attached to disbursements from accounts held as a trust from an outside grantor.

17. Levi Report Supplement, p. 1.

18. Ibid., pp. 2–8.

19. NESERC froze certain research accounts at Concordia on July 1994, but the vast majority of accounts were not frozen. "Concordia Releases Engineering Audit" *Information Release*, July 15, 1994.

20. Levi Report Supplement, p. 9, citing J.G. Dies of Harvard Business School.

21. Arthurs et al. Report, p. 10.

22. Ibid. The relevant rules and procedures in force at Concordia University as guides to academic conduct have four main provenances: the collective agreement between the university and the Concordia University Faculty Association; the policies contained in the Contract Research Handbook prepared by the university's Office of Research Services; the accounting procedures of the university's Treasury; and a host of practices, either customary or formal, at the level of department or unit. See the "Arthurs et al. Report," p. 15.

23. Ibid., pp. 22, 26, 70–71.

24. The university agreed to put new mechanisms in place to correct the problems identified by the forensic auditor. An associate vice-rector of finance, with experience as a financial manager, was appointed as an "independent financial expert" to oversee changes to accounting and to enhance the treasury's ability to support the university's finances with policies, procedures, and controls. The university publicized its commitment to implement a code of ethics and to include procedures emerging from this code as part of the collective agreement. A summary of actions taken in response to the auditors is provided in a university press release, "Concordia Releases Engineering Audit," July 15, 1994.

Records and the Public Interest: The "Heiner Affair" in Queensland, Australia

Chris Hurley

In Australia, government archives authorities have discretion to allow or forbid the destruction of public records. Should they exercise this discretion to safeguard the rights and entitlements of private citizens or merely on "historical" grounds? Should government archivists prevent hasty destruction of official documents that may provide evidence of government liability or wrongdoing? Who determines the public interest in retention and balances individual concerns against public benefit? These and related questions were raised in the Report of the Senate Select Committee on Unresolved Whistleblower Cases entitled *The Public Interest Revisited* (Oct. 1995). The report dealt, inter alia, with the shredding of the Heiner documents in Queensland. In the course of the Senate's inquiry, Queensland authorities argued that it was no business of the state archivist to be concerned with disposal other than to determine what documents should be kept for reasons "of historical public interest."

In 1999 the Forde Inquiry was set up by Peter Beattie's Labor government to investigate and recommend reforms to stamp out widespread abuse (both physical and sexual) in Queensland's institutions for teenagers and children. Ten years earlier, a more modest investigation was begun by retired magistrate, Noel Heiner, into allegations made by the staff of one such institution, the John Oxley Youth Center (JOYC), against its manager, Peter Coyne. The Heiner Inquiry had been terminated by an earlier Labor government under Premier Wayne Goss. The Goss Cabinet not only silenced Heiner, they ordered all his records destroyed. The consent of the state's archivist to this destruction was formally sought and obtained.

A HISTORY OF THE AFFAIR

On March 23, 1990, Kate McGuchin, a senior archivist at the Queensland State Archives (QSA), returned to her office and wrote up a note for file:

Ken Littleboy from Cabinet Office collected me from Queensland State Archive[s] on March 23, 1990 at 2.30 p.m. We went to the Executive Building and collected the records of the inquiry by Mr. N.J. Heiner, that Lee McGregor and myself had inspected on February 23, 1990. We took the box of records to the Family Services Building where I took possession of the records and myself and Trevor Walsh from the Department destroyed them in a shredding machine. All the records were destroyed—paper, cassettes and computer disc.[1]

Trevor Walsh also recorded the event in a note for file written up on April 2, 1990:

It is confirmed that on Friday, March 23, 1990, Ms. Kate McGuchin, officer of the State Archivist, destroyed the relevant material from the Heiner Inquiry in my presence. I confirmed with Ms. McGuchin that she would notify the Secretary to Cabinet that she had carried out the decision of Cabinet.[2]

This simple administrative act was solemnized by the trappings of state power. It was ordered by ministers of the Crown, who formally set their decision down in the minutes of Cabinet. It was carried out after obtaining advice from the Crown's most senior law officer. Sanction for it was given by the state archivist. An officer of the Cabinet Office escorted an archivist to the seat of political power, the Executive Building, where the records were handed over to the archivist and an officer of the government department where the records had originated. Together they proceeded to a place of lawful destruction and carried out the directive.

Like a Tudor political execution, the act had all the appurtenances of law and process. We can, however, glimpse beneath the surface a naked power in operation that would brook no denial. It took many years, a succession of investigations and hearings, the singular determination of one of the victims of that power (Kevin Lindeberg), and a tireless newspaper campaign (by Bruce Grundy of the *Weekend Independent*) for most of the truth behind this destruction to become known.

The records shredded that Friday afternoon contained details of allegations made against Peter Coyne. After his interview with Heiner, Coyne asked to know what allegations were being made against him. He asked to see the documents that Heiner had gathered (as he was entitled to do under the regulations governing staffing matters) and this was followed by a second demand—this time from Coyne's lawyers—accusing Coyne's employer, the Department of Family Services (DFS), of denying their client justice.

The Crown solicitor advised that the manner in which the inquiry had been established did not confer complete immunity from legal action for damages upon Heiner or those who had spoken with him. In the face of this advice and Heiner's unwillingness to continue in these circumstances, the inquiry was terminated by the Goss Government. The next day, Coyne's lawyers put their request to see the documents in writing. Over the next few weeks, the matter escalated until it was being considered in the Cabinet room itself.

It is clear that by this stage the Queensland government, in its various arms and manifestations, was formulating a policy of preventing Coyne and his lawyers from getting access to the Heiner records and of frustrating his attempts to take the matter to court. The lengths to which, ultimately, some would go to carry out this policy became an important element in what came to be called the Heiner Affair.

The roots of the Heiner Affair go back to 1989. After decades of corrupt government under the National party (uncovered by the Fitzgerald Royal Commission), the Aherne Administration was trying to repair the National party's reputation before an impending election in which Wayne Goss's Labor party, long condemned to the political wilderness, was destined to sweep to power.

In September 1989 DFS received complaints from youth workers at JOYC alleging mismanagement and mistreatment of inmates. On October 1, Labor candidate Ann Warner gave an interview to the *Sunday Sun* claiming she had been informed by staff at JOYC that children were being handcuffed to fences overnight and sedated with drugs. She called for a review of management procedures. On October 23, the minister for Family Services (Beryce Nelson) announced an inquiry and on November 2 approved the appointment of Noel Heiner to conduct it.

Heiner was still at work when Labor swept into office in December. Ann Warner, by then minister for Family Services and Aboriginal and Islander Affairs herself, was to claim (years later) that she and her Cabinet colleagues had no idea that Heiner's records had anything to do with inmate abuse. Within months, the Heiner Inquiry was brought to a halt and Coyne was soon relocated to other duties and, one year later, paid off on condition that he keep silent about the circumstances leading up to and surrounding his relocation (a payment later found to have been illegal). Meanwhile, Cabinet ordered the destruction of Heiner's records, and Kevin Lindeberg (Coyne's union representative), the one man who refused to be keep quiet about it, was sacked.

For ten years, Lindeberg pursued a lonely and courageous campaign to obtain justice. Despite ridicule and attempts to besmirch his character, he gradually obtained a hearing—in the Australian Senate and amongst senior police officers, the media, political scientists, lawyers, ethicists, and (belatedly) archivists and record keepers. In 1999 he sought to have the affair considered by the Forde Inquiry because by that time some hint of the allegations against Coyne had emerged. Forde refused to hear him on the grounds that the Heiner Affair fell outside her terms of reference.

Those terms of reference were set by the government of Peter Beattie, many of whose members had sat around the Cabinet table with Wayne Goss ten years earlier and ordered the destruction of Noel Heiner's records.

By this stage, there were good grounds for Forde to have investigated a link between the shredded records and the very kind of inmate abuse she was investigating. This could have raised serious doubts over the reasons given by the Goss and Beattie Governments for ordering the shredding and raised the specter that it was just one more instance of a system of covering-up those abuses by politicians, bureaucrats, staff, and union officials—the perpetuation of which was (it could be alleged) the true motive for the shredding. If, instead of being shredded, the Heiner records had seen the light of day in Coyne's lawsuit, the whole sorry mess might have been exposed a decade earlier.

It could have been further argued before the Forde Inquiry that this system of officially sanctioned cover-up (if proven) was the real cause of the abuses that Forde was investigating and that her inquiry was, therefore, attacking the symptoms, not the root, of the evil. None of this has ever been properly investigated, and it may now never be because the records in question no longer exist. One person, however, knows what they contained, a person who has never been interrogated in any of the inquiries that have been held into the matter, a person who, by law, had to examine the records and give permission for their destruction—the state archivist.

On February 23, 1990, the Queensland Cabinet Office asked the state archivist, Lee McGregor, to give urgent approval for the destruction of the Heiner records, as required by the Libraries and Archives Act of 1988. The letter advised the archivist that "During the course of the investigation, questions were raised concerning the possibility of legal action against Mr. Heiner and informants.... I am ... advised that the material could not be fairly described as 'Cabinet documents' ... and any claim by the Crown for 'Crown Privilege' would, therefore have little chance of success in order to maintain ... confidentiality."[3] The archivist was told that the government's motivation in seeking destruction was to prevent access ("to maintain confidentiality") and so thwart any defamation action that might be taken. This was also spelled out in a note made by Lee McGregor of a telephone conversation that she had that same day with Ken Littleboy (acting principal cabinet officer):

Cabinet feels that they [the Heiner records] contain much defamatory material and would prefer them destroyed.... I pointed out that in general, if material is worth keeping, it should be kept regardless and a long closure period put on it. Freedom of Information legislation [which had not yet been enacted in Queensland] would have to consider areas such as this where defamation laws may make it extremely difficult for the government to grant access to this type of material.... One carton of records was delivered to my office and Kate McGuchin and myself went through them. The records consisted mainly of tapes and transcripts of interviews ... plus a small quantity of related notes and correspondence. On the transcript of Peter Coyne it was clearly stated that the proceedings were being recorded solely for Mr. Heiner's use. In general the interviewees complained about various aspects of the management style, staff transferred from another Youth Center were the main complainants. Most of the correspondence consisted of copies of letters and reports which would be in the Family Services Department's own records.[4]

The question whether a government's wish to prevent legitimate access to documents constitutes a valid reason for the archivist to consent to their destruction was, therefore, a matter to be considered by Lee McGregor from the outset. As far as we know, however, she was not informed that Coyne and his lawyers were actually seeking access at this time. After examining the material, she gave her approval on the same day. A decision to carry out the destruction was taken in Cabinet on March 5, 1990, in the full knowledge that Coyne's lawyers were seeking access to the material.

For months afterward, Coyne and his lawyers were stonewalled. The administration did not reveal that destruction had been decided on or, after the event, that it had taken place. Negotiations continued as if the records they wanted to make their case were still in existence. During this time, Coyne approached the state archivist for information, seeking her reassurance that she would not approve the destruction until his case had been heard. Lee McGregor sent a fax to Trevor Walsh, the departmental officer who was handling Coyne's demands: "Trevor—This is a letter received from Peter Coyne. I spoke to him briefly by phone yesterday before receiving his letter and indicated that I would not comment on the matter. Lee McGregor, May 18, 1990."[5]

The copy of this fax, subsequently obtained from departmental files by Kevin Lindeberg under freedom-of-information law is annotated "I rang Lee McGregor and advised that there is no need to respond to Mr. Coyne's letter but that she should refer him back to me if he re-contacts her. I advised Ms. McGregor that the matter is being handled by Crown Sol[icitor]."[6]

Even after Coyne and his lawyers were finally informed that the records they wanted had been destroyed, the work of cover-up continued. Not all the records had been destroyed on March 23, 1990. Heiner had worked with copies of the allegations. The originals were still in departmental files and, to avoid disclosure, they were subsequently handed over to the union whose members had first made allegations against Coyne—contrary to the Crown solicitor's advice. That advice was based on yet more copies supplied to the Crown solicitor by the department. These copies were quietly shredded later on without further reference to the state archivist, but these things were not discovered until years later—after three Senate committees of inquiry had investigated the matter—by two barristers appointed by a new Queensland government in 1996 to clear matters up.

Was the Goss Government, which decided to terminate the Heiner Inquiry and destroy the records, acting under labor union pressure to protect the interests of union members? Coyne belonged to one union (the Queensland Professional Officers' Association) and his complaining staff to another (the Queensland State Services Union). When the government's actions were subsequently called into question, the attorney general stated that the Goss Government's sole motivation was to protect Noel Heiner and his informants from defamation action. This explanation was repeated years later by the Beattie Government. The motives behind the government's determination to destroy the documents may never be known and subsequently became the subject of argument. Government ministers and their apologists have always claimed that they were merely acting for the best to tidy up someone else's mess.

Another explanation is that in the lead-up to an election, a row between union members and their boss was used to get publicity for politically damaging allegations against the doomed national government. After the election, it became apparent that the allegations revealed details of inmate abuse that, if disclosed, would reflect unfavorably not only upon the beleaguered Coyne (and the government that had employed him), but also on the staff who participated in the abuse, the union to which they belonged, and the responsible department. Now that there was no further political advantage to be gained, it could be alleged, the Labor government was anxious to oblige its union supporters by burying the allegations and returning to the status quo; a system in which neither staff nor management was anxious to discuss inmate abuse publicly. The suspicion lingers, therefore, that these things were known for years and that the real reason for the shredding was a continuing system of coverup and suppression by government, the unions, and the bureaucracy.

The critical period, in view of what followed, was between January 15, when Coyne sought copies of the complaints from the department, and February 7, when department head Ruth Matchett terminated the Heiner Inquiry. In that interval, the state's Crown solicitor gave a series of advisings to the effect that Heiner and the complainants were not covered by the usual protections from prosecution because of flaws in the way the inquiry had been set up.

By this stage at the latest, consideration of the issue had passed beyond the bureaucrats and involved the Cabinet Office (in effect, the government). On February 13, 1990, Matchett allocated Coyne to other duties and on the same day Stuart P. Tait, acting Cabinet secretary, sought Crown Solicitor Kenneth O'Shea's advice on how to go about destroying the evidence. The Crown solicitor's advice subsequently became the subject of legal dispute. He said that destroying the evidence would not be obstruction of justice because legal proceedings had not formally commenced in the courts and would not commence until papers were served in court. In that case the only obstacle he saw to destruction was the need to obtain the approval of the state's archivist.

In 1993 the Senate Select Committee on Public Interest Whistleblowing was established, whose report, *In the Public Interest*, was issued in August 1994. They recommended that Queensland take action on a number of unresolved whistleblower cases. Queensland's Premier Wayne Goss refused. This led the Senate to establish the Select Committee on Unresolved Whistleblower Cases in December 1994. This committee completed its work by publishing *The Public Interest Revisited* in October 1995. One of the unresolved cases investigated by the committee involved the shredding of official documents. The case is generally referred to as "The Shredding of the Heiner Documents."

The Queensland government refused to cooperate with the Senate inquiry, though it did supply (directly or indirectly) much of the documentary material that is now published in appendices to the committee's report. The Queensland Criminal Justice Commission (CJC), however, did appear and give evidence. The CJC's involvement comes about because it dealt with some of the cases (including the Heiner Documents Case) investigated by the first Senate inquiry. In part, the Queensland government's refusal to participate was based on a view that CJC was the appropriate body to deal with these cases and had already done so. Dissatisfied whistleblowers called into question the adequacy of CJC's methods and conclusions. Because CJC did appear, give evidence, and submit itself to examination by the committee, the second Senate inquiry became to some extent a review of CJC's handling of the cases referred to the committee.

Australia is a common-law country in which the power of the courts to impose procedural restrictions on quasi-judicial and administrative processes can be regarded as a blessing or a curse (or both). In recent years, a series of corruption scandals involving the highest levels of government in several Australian states has led to the establishment of anticorruption bodies who both investigate and reach findings on alleged official wrongdoing by politicians and public employees. Such bodies are intended to be able to combat corruption by stepping outside the normal restrictions of court procedure and discovering truth untrammeled by the limitations of the burden of proof and the adversarial process to be found in courts. Their work has been frustrated, however, by political resistance and judicial interference.

The courts have resented and distrusted the operation of these quasi-judicial bodies and have consistently cut back their freedom to operate outside the ordinary rules of evidence and procedure. Politicians have used this judicial reluctance to uphold the powers of anti-corruption bodies to challenge any adverse findings against them on fine legal arguments that the courts have been eager to allow—significantly limiting the anticorruption bodies by forcing them to act, ineffectively, within the limitations of court rules.

One issue that has severely limited the fight against corruption has been the difficulty in defining high misdemeanors. When High Court Justice Lionel Murphy was accused of exerting improper influence over a lower court then hearing charges against his "little mate," Morgan Ryan, eminent lawyers sprang to his defense on the argument that such action, even if established as true, was insufficient to remove him—that the standard of conduct expected of a High Court judge was no higher than that applying to an unconvicted felon. In effect, it was argued that he could be removed only for a criminal conviction.

Politicians and the courts have leapt onto this argument with alacrity. The test of corruption for a government employee is more demanding. A public servant can be found to be corrupt for conduct that is criminal or in breach of a code of discipline or conduct to which he is subject or subscribes. Using the Murphy defense, high officials and politicians, because they are not subject to a disciplinary regime or written standard of conduct, can be found to be corrupt only if they commit a criminal act. In New South Wales, the Independent Commission Against Corruption (ICAC) found that the premier, Nick Greiner, had acted improperly when he offered a government position as an inducement for a member of Parliament to resign so that a by-election, expected to be favorable to his government, would be held. The finding was thrown out in court, in part, on this reasoning. Because there was no applicable law or code of conduct that prohibited a head of government from acting in that way, it was not possible for anyone, even ICAC, to say whether such action was improper. The powers and effectiveness of the anticorruption bodies have been weakened every time politicians have used the courts to overturn their findings. The difficulty would be removed if Australian politicians adopted codes of discipline or conduct applicable to themselves, but they have shown no enthusiasm for doing so.

It is with this background in mind that the CJC's difficulty must be understood. Since it is reasonably clear that the driving force for the document destruction came from Cabinet itself, a finding of simple impropriety might not have been possible under the Greiner doctrine. A more terrible possibility, that the entire Queensland Cabinet (unless it could claim Crown privilege) had engaged in a criminal conspiracy in breach of the Queensland Criminal Code would, if pursued, have undoubtedly been challenged up to the highest court in the land using every last dollar of taxpayers' money to overturn so odious a finding. This would have tied up CJC and its resources interminably and arguably provided a political will to curb its powers and its budget. In view of the very definite role played by Cabinet in the decision, a lesser finding of misconduct against one or more of the officials involved might have been, politically speaking, just as dangerous. In fact, the CJC has found itself in a dispute of one kind or another and under attack from successive governments whenever its pursuit of corruption has ruffled political feathers.

SHOULD RECORDS BE DESTROYED IF THEY ARE REQUIRED IN EVIDENCE?

Any person who, knowing that any book, document, or other thing of any kind, is or may be required in evidence in a judicial proceeding, willfully destroys it or renders it illegible or undecipherable or incapable of identification, with the intent thereby to prevent it from being used in evidence, is guilty of a misdemeanor, and is liable to imprisonment with hard labor for three years. (Queensland Criminal Code, section 129)

It is clear that, once legal proceedings have commenced, it is a serious matter for one litigant to destroy documents that have been subpoenaed by the other party. When Crown Solicitor O'Shea advised in January 1990 on status of the Heiner Inquiry, he recommended (January 23) that the documents gathered by Heiner should be destroyed if it was decided to terminate the process, possibly believing them at that stage to be Heiner's private property. He noted, however, that "This advice is predicated on the fact that no legal action has been commenced which requires the production of those files."[7]

There is no dispute that, when the archivist's approval for destruction was subsequently sought, proceedings had not yet been launched in the formal sense before a court and had not begun before the records were eventually destroyed in March. It is apparent, however, that the Queensland government and those involved in the shredding were aware of the possibility that legal action could be taken and, to varying degrees, the likelihood that this would occur. It is also apparent that Coyne's wish to see the records and his intention to take legal action was known and that there was determination to thwart him:

Hon. Senator Eric Abetz: Did that not alert you or the CJC that there was something of some importance to Mr. Coyne there? Documents had been shredded, but the official advice to him that they had been shredded and the final advice received was two months after the event?

Mr. [Michael] Barnes: I do not see that the delay is either here or there. There is no doubt that the documents were destroyed at a time when cabinet well knew that Coyne wanted access to them. There is no doubt about that at all. . . .

Senator Abetz: Is there no doubt in your mind that cabinet knew that Coyne wanted the documents?

Mr. Barnes: I am confident that is the case.[8]

It has been argued in defense of the Queensland government that there was no legal obstacle to destruction and that the government was within its rights in proceeding with the destruction. In a ministerial statement to Parliament,[9] the Queensland attorney general objected to criticism that the records were subject to "pending" legal proceedings—arguing that, since proceedings had not yet commenced, a distinction had to be drawn between legal proceedings that had been commenced or instituted and could thus be described as pending and those that were "intended," "foreshadowed," or "threatened." In the words of Crown Solicitor O'Shea, "There is an abundance of authority to show that a civil action or proceeding is not pending until the originating proceeding (Writ, Summons or Motion) has been filed in the Court. . . . All the threats in the world to commence a Civil proceeding (or a Criminal one) do not make it pending, for the purposes of Section 129 of the Criminal Code."[10] In response to this, it has been argued that the O'Shea view is splitting hairs in anything other than a strict legal sense, that the government should have behaved as a "model litigant," and, knowing that proceedings were contemplated (or "threatened"), should have held its hand. In the words of one submission, "The simple fact is that, by seeking to destroy these documents, the Crown has removed a prospective litigant of his rights. This cannot in any true sense of the word be in accordance with our democratic principles."[11]

The distinction between destroying documents after legal proceedings are under way and destroying them to prevent legal proceedings being commenced was lost on some:

Senator [Christabel] Charmarette: I am then saying that to me, from a lay point of view, to actually destroy the documents to prevent litigation being on foot seems very similar. Are you now saying that to actually use as your rationale for the destruction to prevent litigation being on foot is somehow different from litigation being on foot?

Mr. Barnes: Yes. With respect, I say it is a lot different. What you do with your own property before litigation is commenced, I suggest, is quite different from what you do with it after it is commenced.[12]

A middle path between the Charmarette view and the Barnes view would have been found in a 1989 textbook on the subject if anyone had thought of looking:

One important question is when the duty to preserve evidence commences. It is clear that the duty to preserve evidences attaches no later that the date on which the spoliator receives notice that litigation has formally began. The difficult question is how much earlier the duty extends. A strong argument can be made that the duty to preserve evidence attaches at the point when the spoliator knew or should have known that litigation is likely to be instituted. For example, if defendants were allowed to destroy evidence without fear of tort liability after being contacted by opposing counsel concerning settlement, but before a complaint had been filed, there would be a strong incentive to destroy unfavorable evidence. If the spoliation tort is to function effectively to deter destruction of evidence and compensate the victims of such destruction, the duty to preserve must commence as soon as it is reasonably foreseeable that legal proceedings will be instituted.

The cases support the proposition that the duty attaches before litigation is formally begun. In *Smith v. Superior Court* (151 Cal. App. 3d 491, 198 Cal. Rptr. 829 (1984)) ... the complaint alleged that destruction had occurred before suit was brought but after the defendant had been contacted by plaintiff's counsel. (Id. at 495, 198 Cal. Rptr. at 832).

Likewise, in *Velasco v. Commercial Building Maintenance Co.* (169 Cal. App. 3d 874, 215 Cal. Rptr. 504 (1985)) ... it appears that the destruction of evidence occurred before any legal proceedings had been instituted. (Id. at 876, 215 Cal. Rptr. at 505). In *Hazen v. Municipality of Anchorage*, the opinion strongly suggests that the destruction of evidence had occurred before the underlying lawsuit was filed. (718 P.2d 456, 458–59 (Alaska 1986).[13]

The crucial point here is that the CJC (an investigative body established by Parliament) appears to have found as a matter of fact that the Cabinet acted to destroy documents for the express purpose of preventing Coyne's litigation from succeeding:

Senator Abetz: Does the CJC agree from its investigation that the documentation was shredded because there was fear that litigation might flow from that documentation if it were not destroyed?

Mr. Barnes: The papers seem to suggest that both of the matters I have raised with you—the possibility of litigation and the concern that the people who had been induced to come forward to give evidence could be victimized—were foremost in the minds of the people who made the decision. But, with respect, I cannot look into their minds and see which of those issues was predominant. . . . [14]

Senator Abetz: I am trying to get a handle on this. What seems to have occurred is that, with the potential threat of a defamation suit, Cabinet decided to shred the documents because they were of no historical value, knowing full well that it may be the material evidence on which a potential litigant would rely to pursue or prosecute his case.

Mr. Barnes: I think that probably is a fair summary. As a result of the actions, the correspondence and the communications, I think they believed that Coyne was considering suing the people who gave evidence before Heiner for defamation. As you say, the Crown Solicitor's advice seems quite clear that that was a potential and, consistent with that advice, cabinet decided that they would prevent that from happening.[15]

The archivist's position was somewhat different. Although she knew that Cabinet's wish to have the records destroyed was motivated by a desire to ensure that evidence would not be available to support an action for defamation, she was not (apparently) given the information she would have needed to be able to make a judgment on whether there was a reasonable prospect of such litigation pending. A defense of the archivist's conduct could be mounted (on this point) on the basis that, from her point of view, it was not "reasonably foreseeable" that legal proceedings would be instituted.

A distinction can be made between cases where "what you do with your own property before litigation is commenced" is for some unspecified (probably unknowable) purpose, and the Heiner case where a competent investigative body has concluded that records were destroyed to prevent litigation from commencing. Yet no one seems to have been prepared to contemplate the possibility that this conclusion by the CJC about Cabinet's intent (if it could be sustained) could have established a prima facie basis for establishing criminal intent in a prosecution under the Queensland Crimes Act. For a criminal offense to be established, however, the courts require proof of criminal intent (mens rea) and the absence of such proof was the CJC's main line of defense.

The CJC's contention was that Cabinet was acting in good faith on advice received from the Crown solicitor, though it (the CJC) would not make an evaluation of whether O'Shea's advice was good. The CJC went on to argue "In our submission, there is not a scintilla of evidence to indicate that when the Queensland Government decided to shred the documents it had any reason to believe that it was acting unlawfully. It had cognizance of, and was acting in accordance with, legal advice provided to it by the Crown Solicitor. . . . In those circumstances, there was no possibility of establishing that the members of the Cabinet had committed a criminal offence. . . . At this point the Commission had discharged its function."[16]

Counsel for Lindeberg (I.D.F. Callinan QC and R.D. Peterson) argued that the CJC's interpretation was too narrow. They drew attention to a recent High Court decision in *R v. Rogerson and Ors*:

[I]t is enough that an act has a tendency to deflect or frustrate a prosecution or disciplinary proceedings before a judicial tribunal which the accused contemplates may possibly be implemented. (Justice Mason)

A conspiracy to pervert the course of justice may be entered into though no proceedings before a court or before any other competent judicial authority are pending. (Justices Brennan and Toohey)[17]

The U.S. courts take an equally strong line in condemning the destruction of records as an "obstruction of justice," and the whole issue appears to have received greater consideration there than in Australian courts. The question was reviewed at some length by Fedders and Guttenplan in the *Notre Dame Lawyer* in 1980: "Whether a company has an *ad hoc* search and destroy operation or a regular records retention program, management and counsel must consider a federal criminal statutory scheme which renders the destruction of documents illegal if it interferes with judicial, administrative or legislative investigations or proceedings. . . . If a party to a civil proceeding has destroyed records, a negative inference may be drawn from that fact and exploited for its prejudicial value at trial."[18]

Federal statutes in the United States restrain destruction of documents (or any evidence) in judicial proceedings and U.S. courts also have had to consider at what stage in proceedings a criminal liability arises:

[T]he courts . . . have concluded that only ongoing or pending judicial proceedings . . . fall within the section's . . . language. . . . The courts reason that a person unaware of the pendency of a proceeding could not have the requisite intent to obstruct justice. . . . The courts justify their literal interpretation. . . . with the maxim that criminal statutes should be strictly construed. . . . Although the substantive offense of obstruction of justice requires a pending proceeding, otherwise punishable conduct which precedes pendency is not immune from prosecution. In *United States v. Perlstein* the Third Circuit affirmed convictions for conspiracy to obstruct justice even though the conspirators were not found guilty of the substantive crime. . . . The court stated: " . . . there is nothing to prevent a conspiracy to obstruct the due administration of justice in a proceeding which becomes pending in the future from being cognizable under section 37" [antecedent of present conspiracy statute, 18 U.S.C. § 371].[19]

The same principle is applied even more widely to obstruction of proceedings undertaken by departments, agencies, and committees:

Courts have expressed various views as to the time at which an agency's activity first qualifies as a "proceeding" . . . : when the agency is notified of potential violations; when pre-investigation begins; when an informal inquiry begins; or when a formal order is issued directing investigation to begin. . . . As one court explained: "[T]he growth and expansion of agency activities have resulted in a meaning being given to 'proceeding' which is much more inclusive and which no longer limits itself to formal activities in a court of law. Rather, the investigation or search for the true facts . . . is not ruled as a non-proceeding simply because it is preliminary to indictment and trial." [20]

The question whether an Australian court would follow U.S. precedent and entertain charges of conspiracy with regard to "punishable conduct which precedes pendency" does not appear to have been discussed. It is apparent from all this that the legal issue is far from clear and, in any case, conviction by a court of members of a government for a decision taken in the Cabinet would be unprecedented. It is at least arguable, however, that the view taken by the Queensland Crown solicitor and the CJC (in effect, that no issue of obstruction arises until proceedings have actually commenced regardless of circumstances or intent) is too narrow. The CJC's contention that there is no evidence of criminal intent is dubious, to say the least. The record shows that it was Cabinet's intention to prevent Coyne from getting the documents and using them in a legal action he was contemplating. Having formed this intention, which may or may not have been criminal, the government sought legal advice on how to carry it through. CJC seems to have reached a conclusion that whatever criminality may have been involved in forming an intention to destroy records in these circumstances, it is removed once a lawyer says you can do it!

Insofar as this is a question of criminal liability, archivists and record managers can only try to stay in touch with unfolding developments in the courts and endeavor to ensure that their conduct does not implicate them (wittingly) in a conspiracy to obstruct justice or (unwittingly) in smoothing the path of others so bent. The exercise of the archivist's discretion, however, involves issues that go beyond questions of criminal liability. The CJC argued that its jurisdiction was limited to a consideration of "official misconduct" and that "conduct will not amount to official misconduct unless it constitutes a criminal offence or a disciplinary breach that provides reasonable grounds for termination of [a] person's services."[21]

In the case of ministers (who are not subject to a disciplinary regime), conduct must amount to a criminal offense. Archivists, like anybody else, must avoid crime. The question we must now consider is what their role and responsibility is beyond that. Politicians' defense against findings of official misconduct amounts to this: if they can't put me in jail for it or sack me for it, it isn't corrupt. The professional concern goes to the further issue: whether the state archivist was (or should have been) apprised of the wish of potential litigants to have the records and what weight (if any) that knowledge should have been given when deciding whether to approve the request for destruction.

Barristers Anthony J.H. Morris and Edward J.C. Howard, who investigated the affair in 1996, recommended, inter alia, that a person seeking to destroy official records should be required to sign a certificate assuring the archivist that: "all information supplied in support of the request is true and accurate; the certifying officer is not aware of any facts or circumstances that have not been disclosed; and the certifying officer has no reason to suppose the records are wanted in pending or future court proceedings or under any statutory schemes of access." These are lawyers' solutions—relevant to particular instances—and there is no reason that we should not tighten up archival appraisal procedures by introducing such measures. This can be done at any time by government archivists without waiting for legislative amendment, and the next time one of them finds himself or herself in a similar situation we can now ask why they did not seek such assurances.

There is no suggestion that a failure by an archivist to evaluate and determine the rights and entitlements of potential litigants is, in itself, misconduct. Indeed, one reason for giving the above lengthy account of one of the legal issues to which the Heiner case gives rise is to suggest the impossibility of reducing the archivist's responsibility to a case-by-case adjudication of such matters. The above account distills lengthy, convoluted, and confusing argument before the Senate committee gathered over many months. It eliminates many claims and counterclaims advanced during the hearing of evidence. Learned lawyers expended much breath and ink first establishing and then arguing differing interpretations of the facts.

If eminent lawyers and investigators with all the benefits of hindsight and the leisure to consider matters from every angle cannot reach agreement, it is simply preposterous to say that the archivist, confronted with the necessity of reaching a decision in circumstances similar to those in which Lee McGregor found herself on February 23, 1990, could have done so. That is not the nature of the archivist's discretion. It will be seen, therefore, that whether or not the archivist is required to consider or to be apprised of the wishes of potential litigants in a particular case is not central. We may even agree with Barnes that establishing whether potential litigants have legally enforceable rights to records proposed for destruction has "nothing to do with the archivist."

It is not the job of the archivist to adjudicate disputed rights or to second-guess the courts on a particular case. The archivist cannot be expected to evaluate the potential probative value or status as evidence of this or that folder of documents that she is asked to examine. No more can she be expected to evaluate the potential historical value of folders of records placed in front of her. The whole process of calling upon the archivist for an opinion unrelated to context of any kind about the value of a heap of records (whether for history, litigation, or any other purpose) is deeply flawed. Such ad hoc evaluations may need to be carried out occasionally and for exceptional reasons, but they do not and should not be allowed to be represented as the "norm" for archival appraisal.

The archivist's job is to identify rules and policies governing disposal of categories of records (not to examine heaps of them), to analyze administrative processes (not to investigate particular instances), to consider the reasons (pro and con) that records should be kept and for how long, and to establish a regime to ensure that records are kept for as long as necessary and for no longer. Ministers and officials need to be told that they cannot expect to come to the archivist as

Tait did and to get approval on a case-by-case basis to destroy a particular set of records except in the most extraordinary circumstances, which they will be called upon to explain and justify. If, despite all this, an archive chooses to establish ad hoc evaluation as the norm, then it does indeed impose upon itself the obligation to investigate the circumstances of each particular case.

Common sense indicates how the archivist's discretion must be exercised: "there needs to be some regulation on the period of time that certain records must be kept" (see below). It is the archivist's job to determine and enforce those periods and to establish a disposal regime in which they are routinely applied without reference back to the archivist in every instance. It is when determining the period that the archivist is concerned with analyzing the purposes for which records belonging to each category are or may be needed—including the interests of potential litigants.

WHAT CAN (AND SHOULD) THE ARCHIVIST DO?

These [records of legal value] are records which involve long and short term rights of the council or of private citizens and which are enforceable by the courts; e.g. contracts, tender documents, building approval permits, leases, title deeds, etc. . . . In general, the record should be retained long enough to ensure that the rights of the council and of any individual concerned are fully protected. (Queensland State Archives, *General Disposal Schedule for Local Government Records in Queensland*)

There appears to be agreement that the archivist was not informed that the records had been sought or that legal action was contemplated. So far, so good. From this point on, things are less clear. A variety of reasons have been suggested for Cabinet's wish to have the records destroyed. Barnes, for the CJC, suggested, "It is clear that Cabinet made the decision to destroy the documents knowing full well that Coyne wished access to them. It may be that Cabinet made that decision to destroy the documents on the basis that, in its view, the public interest in protecting the people who gave evidence before Heiner outweighed Coyne's private interest in having access to them."[22]

The Senate committee found that a "more pragmatic" explanation could be inferred from Crown Solicitor O'Shea's advice of January 23, 1990: "Naturally Mr. Heiner is concerned about any risk of legal action which may be instituted against him for his part in the inquiry and it would appear appropriate for cabinet to be approached for an indication that should any proceedings be commenced against Mr. Heiner because of his involvement in this inquiry, the government will stand behind him in relation to his legal costs and also in the unlikely event of any order for damages against him."[23] The committee then concluded that: "The most plausible explanation for the shredding of the documents was to protect the public purse from the expenses of litigation. If in so doing, the rights of an individual (Mr. Coyne) were negated, as he and others assert, some would argue that they were sacrificed for a reason."[24]

All these speculations involve, in some degree or another, a balancing of reasons for destruction against reasons for retention. They are things that might have been in the minds of Cabinet members when they came to consider whether the records *should* be destroyed. The CJC and the Crown solicitor contend that responsibility for making this decision (for balancing the reasons for and against destruction) lay with the Queensland government, not with the archivist (who, according to the CJC, was limited to a consideration of historical value). Their critics counter that the Queensland state archivist is not limited to questions of historical value and that she too had a responsibility to weigh all relevant considerations in reaching her decision.

On the most altruistic representation of the case, that given by the attorney general in explanation of his own and his colleagues' actions, the Queensland Cabinet was acting as an honest broker between the contending parties, reaching a difficult decision in the best interests of all concerned. Cabinet was impartial, disinterested, reasonable, and acting in good faith. A difficult balance had to be struck between competing interests, but Cabinet could be trusted as an appropriate arbiter.

On any other view, Cabinet was an interested party—not standing above the fray but directly involved. No fair evaluation of the competing claims could be found there. It may be that, on the balance of considerations, destruction of the records was "reasonable," but the Queensland Cabinet was not a fit body to decide that because it had reasons of its own for preferring one outcome over another.

The Queensland government certainly wanted to protect its own interests in threatened legal proceedings. This is a perfectly legitimate aspiration, but it cannot then be suggested that the government itself had no interest in the outcome of the disposal decision. It was a potential party to litigation (or, at least, potentially liable for costs or damages awarded against potentially litigating parties): "there will be no report [JOYC staff were assured]. Thus the risk of staff being exposed to legal action is reduced. I want to remind you all however of the current Government policy regarding the legal liability of Crown employees—which you all are. In short, the Crown will accept full responsibility for all claims arising out of a Crown employee's due performance of his/her duties provided these duties have been carried out conscientiously and diligently."[25]

Cabinet could not plausibly assume legal liability in the matter and then be said to be impartially weighing the rights and interest in preservation of its adversaries in the threatened litigation. In destroying the records, Cabinet usurped the role of the court (the only body that could have impartially determined the issues between the contending parties) by preempting the possibility of legal action by the government's adversaries to resolve the matter there. There is nothing wrong with governments seeking to protect their own interests. But governments are also charged with protecting the interests of individual citizens, and the two sets of interests may at times be in conflict. When the Queensland government preempted court action by destroying documents, it was acting in its own interests. It cannot then turn around and claim to be acting in everyone's best interest. Only an independent arbiter can claim that, and in determining whether official records should be destroyed, that is the role of an independent state archivist.

The only way a truly fair and equitable outcome could have been reached (which might well have been that, on the balance of interests involved, the records should have been destroyed) would have been for the matter to have been judged by a truly independent authority, with no interest in the outcome, that could be trusted to fairly evaluate and (where necessary) protect the citizen's rights and entitlements against the concern of government to defend itself against potential legal action. This kind of reasoning has long been advanced as the rationale for an independent archive authority capable of evaluating disposal action by balancing, amongst other things, the competing interests of government and its citizens in the destruction or preservation of records. Such reasoning was used by a U.S. district court in 1980 when issuing an injunction to prevent the National Archives and Records Service of the United States (NARS) and the Federal Bureau of Investigation (FBI) from proceeding with a scheduled destruction of records sought under the Freedom of Information Act (FOIA) (or potentially subject to FOIA requests). The court allowed the injunction in part on the argument that NARS had not taken sufficient account of the rights of members of the public, including persons claiming to have suffered legal wrongs. The court ruled that

It is thus clear that the Archivist never discharged his statutory responsibility to make independent judgments concerning the record retention and destruction practices of the [FBI]. This neglect, without more, fatally flaws the legality of any further destruction of records by the FBI. . . . Congress has determined that federal recordkeeping shall accommodate not only the operational and administrative needs of the particular agencies but also the right of the people of this nation to know what their government has been doing. The thrust of the laws Congress has enacted is that governmental records belong to the American people and should be accessible to them. . . . The thrust of the actions of the FBI, perhaps naturally so, has been to preserve what is necessary or useful for its operations. The Archives, which should have safeguarded the interests of both the FBI and the public, in practice considered only the former.[26]

Of more significance is the role of an independent archives authority in preventing the untoward destruction of evidence of government corruption and wrongdoing by establishing a regime of records management that supports the public interest in government accountability. A government whose right to destroy records is limited by an independent evaluation only of their historical value can remove at will all evidence of corruption and wrongdoing and thereby effectively frustrate the fight against corruption.

The Crown solicitor's justification for the government's action gradually narrows down to an analogy between government and any other private litigant:

In a free society, a person (and this includes the Crown) does not need to find an enabling law to enable that person to destroy his or her own property. In a free society a person (which, as I said, includes the Crown) may do what he likes with his property, including destroying it, unless there is some positive law preventing its destruction. . . . Had the Heiner documents been the property of Mr. Heiner, and not the Crown's, he could have destroyed them without the Chief Archivist's permission but, because we ultimately came to the conclusion that the property in them was in the Crown, the Chief Archivist's permission was necessary and, in my opinion, she was quite entitled in the circumstances to grant that permission.[27]

There is no suggestion here that Queensland's public records belong to the people. According to Crown Solicitor O'Shea, Queensland's public records belong to the government and the government has no obligation or responsibility to its citizens, which is not analogous to that of any other "person" in a free society (except to submit proposed destructions to the archivist for approval). The government is not just any other private litigant. The state has a responsibility to safeguard citizen's rights and entitlements. Parliament has established a system of checks and balances, amongst which the requirement for the Queensland government to submit its intention to destroy public records for independent assessment by the state archivist may be included. Where a conflict (or potential conflict) may be found between the executive's actions and the citizen's interests, the latter must be protected by the intervention of an *independent* authority, free from potential control by the executive, whose job it is (in part) to look out for the citizen and, in the final analysis, to weigh competing interests in retention or destruction. That is why, in matters relating to disposal of public records, it is the archivist and not the executive or any of its arms who must decide.

It appears, however, that the state archivist of Queensland was never placed in possession of the facts that would have enabled her to make such an evaluation. On the view put forward by the CJC, there was no reason to do so. In this view, government agencies are required to keep "full and accurate records" for no other reason than ensuring that a good historical record can subsequently be extracted:

Mr. Barnes: [W]e have to look at the Archivist, because Mr. Lindeberg is concerned that her actions in authorizing the destruction were inappropriate. . . . The archivist's duty is to preserve public records which may be of historical public interest; her duty is not to preserve documents which other people may want to access for some personal or private reason. She has a duty to protect documents that will reflect the history of the state. . . . In my submission, the fact that people may have been wanting to see these documents—and there is no doubt the government knew that Coyne wanted to see the documents—does not bear on the archivist's decision about whether these are documents that the public should have a right to access forevermore. . . . That is the nature of the discretion she exercises. The question about whether people have a right to access these documents is properly to be determined between the department, the owner of the document, and the people who say they have got that right. That is nothing to do with the Archivist, so I suggest to you that the fact that was not conveyed to the Archivist is neither here nor there. That has no bearing on the exercise of her discretion.[28]

Accountability through records management ultimately involves a concern with what records are created. This was recognized in Queensland, whose archives law imposed on agencies a statutory obligation to create and maintain "full" or "complete" and "accurate" records. On the CJC's argument before the Senate committee, these provisions have no other purpose than to compel government agencies to create materials for historical study.

It is legitimate to ask whether it was the intention of the Queensland legislature, when passing the archives law, that the archives should be limited to historical matters. To put the matter bluntly, on what words in the Queensland act does CJC base its argument that Queensland State Archives should ignore any other reason it may perceive for keeping records even though they have no value for historical research, any public interest (other than the need for a historical record) bearing adversely on the agency's wishes to destroy the records, or "the fact that people may have been wanting to see" the records, when considering whether to agree or withhold consent to an agency's request for approval to destroy records? The Queensland Crown solicitor, on the other hand, asked only what actions of the state archivist were expressly permitted or prohibited. Neither view sought to evaluate the propriety of the manner in which the discretion was exercised—namely whether it was done fairly and justly.

Propriety is more than legality. It is not necessary to argue that illegality has occurred in order to say that fairness and justice required the archivist to consider whether the records were needed to satisfy the rights and entitlements (or merely the wishes and curiosity) of an individual citizen, that the Queensland government was derelict in failing to supply her with relevant information on that issue, and that the archivist should have taken steps to satisfy herself on this point before approving the destruction. The argument for narrowing the discretion rests on two mutually inconsistent planks. First, the narrow legal arguments of Crown Solicitor O'Shea that there was no objection to destruction absent legal proceedings that had actually been instituted or "some positive law preventing" it, that the government clearly had the right to destroy "its own property" in accordance "with a Statutory regime which permitted its destruction," and that the archivist had a "wide discretion . . . to authorize destruction" and was "clearly within her rights" in so authorizing it[29] on this occasion. Second, the policy argument launched by CJC representative Barnes that the archivist's discretion is a narrow one—limited to questions "of historical public interest"[30] and that other reasons that might exist for retaining records have "nothing to do with the Archivist."

Taken separately, either argument might be sustainable (though the O'Shea view is clearly unhelpful in determining what factors the archivist must consider). Taken together, they make nonsense. On the one hand, destruction is a matter for the archivist alone using a wide discretion in the exercise of which she is not obliged to consider any matter pertaining to citizens' rights or interests because *there is no express legal or statutory* obligation for her to do so. On the other hand, the archivist exercises a narrow discretion and is precluded from giving consideration to citizens' rights or interests because such consideration is ultra vires despite the fact that *there is no express legal or statutory* restriction preventing it. In the absence of statutory appraisal criteria, with no case law to speak of, and within the scope of archive laws that mandate a role for the archivist in records management, her responsibilities cannot be limited except by statutory provisions that expressly *prevent* her from considering relevant matters or from asking for relevant information—even if there is no obligation to provide it.

The bewilderment of nonprofessionals when archives laws fail them instinctively seeks redress in a wider view of recordkeeping responsibilities. This was apparent in testimony given before the Senate committee in another (unrelated) matter involving "missing documents" sought under freedom-of-information laws:

Senator Abetz: As a matter of principle you talk about the disappearing of documents, and previously we have heard what the criminal code here requires when legal proceedings are underfoot and whether you are allowed to destroy documents. From your experience, do you believe that the current law is sufficient or do you think it ought to be extended to make it an offense to destroy documents which a person must reasonably believe capable of being used in proceedings sometime in the future?

Mr. Peter Stewart Jesser: I am not even sure whether it is as specific as that. An organization must keep archival records for some period—so that it can conduct an investigation or just as normal correspondence, it must surely keep back-up discs for 12 months or two years or something like that. It seems to me to be slightly unreasonable to say, "We don't keep any back-ups" or "We don't know what happened last week in our correspondence. It has all disappeared." I think that there needs to be some regulation on the period of time that certain records must be kept.[31]

Of course an organization must keep archival records for some period "so that it can conduct . . . normal correspondence." Of course "certain records must be kept." The basic human need for records could be put more expertly but hardly more eloquently. It is the very basis of the recordkeeper's mission, their reason for being, the most fundamental thing about them. It is not, however, in legal opinions or through statutory provisions alone that this need will be satisfied. We know that it must be satisfied by establishing a reliable and trustworthy recordkeeping regime and through the integrity and diligence of record keepers.

If the archivist asks for relevant information and it is not provided, she can refuse to agree to destruction. If false information is provided, then the responsibility for thwarting her attempt to inform herself of relevant considerations is placed clearly where it belongs—on the agency that trades in untruth—and the propriety of the agency's action can be judged by an appropriate authority. If the archivist doesn't even try to find out what needs the records may serve before she agrees to their destruction, the propriety of exercising the discretion in this manner may be questioned.

There are other ways the prudent archivist might ensure that citizens' interests in record retention are protected. Archival regulation of disposal does not derogate from, or in any way substitute for, other mechanisms of control and accountability. What then is the "value added" by the archives? Clearly, it is that agencies must submit their records practices to external scrutiny. This provides additional safeguard for the public interest in records retention (to ensure that governments cannot "cover up" and a safeguard too for individual citizens in conflict with government. It also establishes routine procedures for documenting the decisions taken (through archives' disposal schedules and destruction authorities) so that if any question of what was authorized later arises, it can be settled by reference to those records. Finally, it should be pointed out that it provides the public servants who are records creators with some measure of protection from undue political interference in the process of keeping and destroying "full and accurate" records.

No minister or official determined to destroy or falsify the record will be prevented by archives law from doing so. What archive procedures do is to establish a norm, a routine procedure, from which such actions can and usually will be seen to depart, thus making detection more likely. If such routine procedures are established under archives laws, departures from them (which can't always be prevented) will at least be obvious and will be seen to be outside acceptable limits. The value of the archives regime is that it establishes a benchmark (a test) by which good and bad behavior can be measured and it creates an environment in which departures from the benchmark are more likely to be detected. Just as financial auditing has been effectively applied to both public and private enterprise, so to can archival regulation be applied—if there is the will to do it. Statutory provision simply provides the basis and authority for doing so.

Is the regulatory role detrimental to efficient administration? Certainly, archives procedures overlay administration with "additional" requirements, but do they add to the "burden" on chief administrators? Good archives and records management practices are, after all, meant to assist and foster efficient administration, not to weigh it down with unnecessary burdens. How, it might reasonably be asked, is the regulation of disposal for the purposes of accountability any more of an interference in "efficient management" than regulation of disposal for research purposes? Nor can it be argued that these safeguards represent an increased workload on top of current practice. Quite the contrary. Nothing could be more wasteful of resources than the cumbersome case-by-case appraisal that routinely passes for archival evaluation. If attention were paid instead to developing and implementing disposal policies and establishing recordkeeping regimes that focused on documentation of government activity (of which disposal is merely an expression) rather than evaluation of files and folders when requested to do so, it would be a much better use of available resources. Needless to say, under such a regime cases like the Heiner Affair would not arise because the opportunity to destroy the Heiner documents as a unique case without regard to routine procedure, would simply not have been available. All that money could have been saved if Cabinet need not have met about it, the Crown solicitor need not have deliberated about it, and the CJC need not have investigated it or subsequently defended its actions.

Why, in any case, should it be accepted that accountability requirements should be subordinate to efficiency? What tenable view of public sector efficiency could be based on a refusal to acknowledge and serve the public interest in accountable administration? For such arguments to be sustained, the alleged "inefficiencies" and costs of accountability itself would have to be demonstrated, not merely assumed.

Should record creators be the sole judges of the public interest in preserving their records? Clearly not, since all mechanisms of accountability provide some kind of external and independent judgment about what constitutes public interest and weighs in the balance, where necessary, individual rights and entitlements with public interest represented by governmental policy. These judgments necessarily cut across the responsibility that a government agency has for efficient management.

The better view is that departments and agencies must be responsible for efficient administration subject to compliance with the rules and regulations established by or in accordance with the law to serve the needs of government, the public interest, and the individual citizen. If this "infringes" on administrative independence, archives law must similarly infringe because archives laws are concerned with the survival of full and accurate records upon which such accountability mechanisms depend for their effectiveness. No government or private organization concerned with its own operational efficiency and ultimate survival (let alone any concern for the public interest) could acknowledge such "independence" from accountability. History (and in Australia, very recent history too) tells us that inefficiency, corruption, and mismanagement thrive in the dark, not under the spotlight.

The Queensland Electoral and Administrative Review Commission found that its investigation of alleged irregularities in electoral redistribution was thwarted by the lack of an adequate public record. It concluded that the state's archives system had to be upgraded and strengthened. Can anyone suppose, as CJC would apparently have us believe, that EARC's concern was for the lack of an adequate *historical* record? The Western Australian Royal Commission into the W.A., Inc., scandals concluded that its investigations were hampered by gaps in the official record. It recommended that the Western Australian archives system should be upgraded and strengthened. It is nonsense to suggest, as CJC must contend, that the Royal Commission was worried solely about the impact on scholars.

If there is to be external regulation of records management in the service of accountability—an obligation to create full and accurate records, manage them properly, and keep them for purposes other than those of the agency that produced them—where is it provided for apart from the archives laws? Whether the archives has a broad or narrow role comes down to this: *Can an archives au-*

thority, having a general power to approve or disallow applications by government
agencies to destroy public records, limit its consideration of the matters upon which it
must satisfy itself before granting its consent to a consideration of historical research
purposes only in the absence of the clearest indication from the legislature that this is
what was intended?

Archives laws provide the *only* general statutory regulation of which records
are kept and which destroyed. Other mechanisms such as freedom-of-information legislation, the ombudsman, the courts, inquiries, and reviews, are all limited and circumscribed in their effect by what records do in fact exist when they
are brought in to deal with a particular instance. They very often have to be in-
voked by an interested party. They are not in a position usually to intervene before the fact. No prior decision to destroy relevant records can be overturned or
ameliorated by the operation of those mechanisms.

The point was several times made that the government did not advise QSA
of the possibility of litigation and that it would be unreasonable to expect QSA
to be able to find out in such cases whether proceedings were in prospect. It is
clear that no archive can expect to be aware of all potential uses for records relating to a particular matter. There are, however, steps that may be taken by the
prudent archivist to limit the ill effects of the absence of "legal or legislative provision" requiring or enabling the archives to inquire more closely into the circumstances of each case. Archivists might refuse to grant approval for destruction relating to a particular matter in any circumstances (or only in exceptional
circumstances, where the agency makes a special case). The archivist could establish routine procedures governing the timing and processes for disposing of
records belonging to different categories of records and then treat with suspicion any request to destroy records that relate to a particular instance outside
these normal procedures.

On this basis, QSA's response to Cabinet's request would have been "no, we
have determined that records of inquiries such as this are to be destroyed X
years after the termination of the inquiry, and we see no reason to depart from
normal practice in this case." Cabinet would then have been obliged to postpone
the proposed action and deal with the records in a routine rather than an extraordinary way or else explain to the archivist the reasons it was in haste to get
rid of them. In reaching its decision on the disposal of inquiry records (in advance of any request for approval on a specific instance), QSA would have already considered the balance of possible uses to which records of this type
might be put and have come to an evaluation of the competing interests (including the entitlements of citizens wanting to subpoena records in legal action
against the government)—on general terms and not in relation to any particular
case before government at the time a request for approval was received. Such
generalized rules of administrative action—though they could not be guaranteed to work to the citizen's advantage in all cases—would at least establish a
minimum standard of routine conduct under which victimization would be
more difficult.

Another way is for archivists to place a caveat on all destruction approvals voiding the permission in specified circumstances—a general instruction to departments that makes void any destruction approval where a freedom-of-information request has been lodged, for example. It would be possible (and, in the light of the Heiner case, arguably desirable) for government archives to issue generalized instructions making explicit the position of records due for destruction when the agency has been made aware of a citizen's intention to take action to obtain access. It is unlikely that an indefinite postponement of destruction could be made in such cases, and it might indeed be determined that no postponement of any kind should be mandated. But at least a policy would exist, a standard would have been established, a benchmark would be provided to test the propriety of agencies' actions in particular instances, there would be evidence that the matter had been considered, and citizens aggrieved by the outcome in a particular case could be assured they had not been singled out and know why they were unable to get any further.

NOTES

Unless otherwise stated, all references are to the volumes of material compiled in 1995 by the Parliament of the Commonwealth of Australia, Senate Select Committee on Unresolved Whistleblower Cases. The committee's report (October 1995) was entitled *The Public Interest Revisited* and is referred to by title only, followed by a page reference. Materials gathered or received by the committee were published in seven volumes under the title *Submissions, Supplementary Submissions and Other Written Material Authorised to be Published*, of which three are cited here as follows: Volume 1: *Queensland Government* (cited as *Submissions*, vol. 1), Volume 2: *Criminal Justice Commission* (cited as *Submissions*, vol. 2), and Volume 3: *Shredding of the Heiner Documents* (cited as *Submissions*, vol. 3). The official Hansard report of transcripts of evidence taken by the committee is cited as *Transcript*, followed by the date of the hearing and the page in the report of that day's proceedings. The report of an independent investigation undertaken in 1996 by lawyers Anthony J.H. Morris QC and Edward J.C. Howard entitled *Report to the Premier of Queensland and the Queensland Cabinet of an Investigation into Allegations by Mr. Kevin Lindeberg* is cited as *Morris/Howard*.

1. *Morris/Howard*, p. 65.
2. Ibid., p. 65.
3. Ibid., Attachment F.
4. Ibid., pp. 59–60.
5. From departmental files obtained by Kevin Lindeberg under freedom-of-information laws on May 27, 1996.
6. Ibid.
7. *Public Interest Revisited*, p. 52.
8. *Transcript* (Canberra, May 29, 1995), p. 682.
9. *Submissions*, vol. 1, Ministerial Statement of Senate Select Committee on Unresolved Whistleblower Cases made to the Queensland Parliament by the State's Attorney-General (p. 17), enclosed in a Submission of the Queensland Premier dated February 21, 1995.

10. *Submissions,* vol. 1, Memorandum dated March 21, 1995 from Crown Solicitor, Queensland, to Minister for Justice (p. 2), tabled in the Queensland Parliament under a Ministerial statement made on March 30, 1995 by the Honourable Dean Wells, Minister for Justice, Attorney-General and Minister for the Arts and enclosed in a Submission of the Queensland Premier dated March 31, 1995.

11. *Submissions,* vol. 3, Submission by R.D. Peterson, LLB, dated May 5, 1995 (p. 2), enclosed in a letter to the committee on May 8, 1995.

12. *Transcript* (Brisbane, Feb. 23, 1995), p. 103.

13. Jamie S. Gorelick, Stephen Marzen, and Lawrence Solum, *Destruction of Evidence* (New York: Wiley, 1989), pp. 154–155.

14. Ibid., p. 105.

15. *Transcript* (Canberra, May 29, 1995), p. 696.

16. *Public Interest Revisited,* p. 59.

17. "R v. Rogerson and Ors," *Australian Law Journal and Reports* 66 (1992): 500, 502, 503.

18. John M. Fedders and Lauryn H. Guttenplan, "Document Retention and Destruction: Practical, Legal and Ethical Considerations," *Notre Dame Lawyer* 56 (Oct. 1980): 5–64. Quote taken from pp. 7–8.

19. Ibid., pp. 23–24.

20. Ibid., p. 24.

21. *Submissions,* vol. 2. Submission by Queensland Criminal Justice Commission, February 1995 (pp. 2–3).

22. *Public Interest Revisited,* p. 58.

23. Ibid., pp. 58–59.

24. Ibid., p. 59.

25. *Submissions,* vol. 1, Speech made by the Acting Director-General to the staff at the John Oxley Youth Centre on February 13, 1990, attached as Document 17 to a Submission to the committee made by the Queensland Cabinet Office, July 31, 1995.

26. *American Friends Service Committee, et al., v. William H. Webster, et al.* (720 F.2d 29), pp. 230, 235.

27. *Submissions,* vol. 1, Memorandum dated March 21, 1995 from Crown Solicitor, Queensland, to Minister for Justice (pp. 10–11), tabled in the Queensland Parliament under a Ministerial statement made on March 30, 1995 by the Honourable Dean Wells, Minister for Justice, Attorney-General and Minister for the Arts and enclosed in a Submission of the Queensland Premier dated March 31, 1995.

28. *Transcript* (Brisbane, Feb. 23, 1995), p. 108.

29. *Submissions* vol. 1, Memorandum dated March 21, 1995 from Crown Solicitor, Queensland, to Minister for Justice (pp. 5–10), tabled in the Queensland Parliament under a Ministerial statement made on March 30, 1995 by the Honourable Dean Wells, Minister for Justice, Attorney-General and Minister for the Arts and enclosed in a Submission of the Queensland Premier dated March 31, 1995.

30. *Transcript* (Brisbane, Feb. 23, 1995), p. 108.

31. *Transcript* (Brisbane, Mar. 16, 1995), pp. 407–408.

Index

About the Editors and Contributors

RICHARD J. COX is a professor in Library and Information Science at the University of Pittsburgh, School of Information Sciences, where he is responsible for the archives concentration in the Master in Library Science degree. Prior to his current position he worked at the New York State Archives and Records Administration, Alabama Department of Archives and History, the City of Baltimore, and the Maryland Historical Society. He chaired the Society of American Archivists (SAA) committee that drafted new graduate archival education guidelines adopted by its council in 1988, served for four years as a member of that association's Committee on Education and Professional Development, and was a member of the society's governing council from 1986 through 1989. Dr. Cox served as editor of the *American Archivist* from 1991 through 1995. He has written extensively on archival and records management topics and has published six books in this area: *American Archival Analysis: The Recent Development of the Archival Profession in the United States* (1990)—winner of the Waldo Gifford Leland Award given by the Society of American Archivists; *Managing Institutional Archives: Foundational Principles and Practices* (1992); *The First Generation of Electronic Records Archivists in the United States: A Study in Professionalization* (1994); *Documenting Localities* (1996); *Closing an Era: Historical Perspectives on Modern Archives and Records Management* (2000); and *Managing Records As Evidence and Information* (2001).

DAVID A. WALLACE is an assistant professor at the School of Information, University of Michigan, where he teaches in the areas of archives and records management. Between 1988 and 1992, he served as records/systems/database manager at the National Security Archive in Washington, D.C., a nonprofit research library of declassified U.S. government records. While at the NSA he also served as technical editor to their *Making of U.S. Foreign Policy* series. From 1993–1994 he served as a research assistant to the University of Pittsburgh's project, Functional Requirements for Evidence in Recordkeeping, and as a contributing editor to *Archives and Museum Informatics: Cultural Heritage Informatics Quarterly*. From 1994 to 1996, he served as a staff member to the U.S. Advisory Council on the National Information Infrastructure. In 1997 he completed a dissertation analyzing the White House e-mail "PROFS" case and is reworking the manuscript for publication. In 2001, he won the Britt Literary Award from the Association of Record Managers and Administrators (ARMA) International for an article he wrote on electronic mail. The Britt Literary Award is given to the best article appearing in ARMA's *Information Management Journal*.

KIMBERLY BARATA is the research manager, Rights and Records Institute, International Records Management Trust, London, United Kingdom. She has written widely about archives and records management issues.

GREG BRADSHER is director, Holocaust-Era Assets Records Project, National Archives and Records Administration (NARA). Dr. Bradsher is also a member of the Interagency Group on Nazi Assets, works closely with the Interagency Working Group—Nazi War Crimes Records Disclosure Act and the U.S. Holocaust Assets Presidential Advisory Commission, served as a member of the U.S. Delegation to the Washington Conference on Holocaust-Era Assets, participated in international conferences in Switzerland and Israel, and served as the director of NARA's Symposium, Holocaust-Era Assets Records and Research. He has written several articles and given numerous presentations about the search for records relating to Holocaust-era assets. His 300-page finding aid to Holocaust-era assets was published in 1997 by the Department of State and a revised 1,200-page version was published by NARA in February 1999.

PIERS CAIN has extensive operational experience in a wide range of organizations, including business, international financial institutions, and local government. Formerly the founding director of the International Records Management Trust's Rights and Records Institute, in 2001, Mr. Cain co-founded the Missenden Group. As a director he provides consultancy advice, international development advice, training, and research. He has extensive consultancy experience, particularly focusing on personnel and payroll information systems as part of governmentwide civil service reform programs. He has worked in a variety of countries overseas, including Cameroon, Ghana, Malaysia, Namibia, Uganda, Ukraine, Tanzania, Gambia, and Zimbabwe. He is on the editorial board of *Archives and Museum Informatics* and has served as international liaison member of the International Standards Organization (ISO) Technical Committee 46, Sub-Committee 11 Archives/Records Management.

ROBIN L. CHANDLER is the manager of the Online Archive of California (OAC), a digital information resource of the California Digital Library (CDL). Prior to working at the CDL, she was head of Archives and Special Collections at the University of California, San Francisco, where she directed the Tobacco Control Archives (TCA). Ms. Chandler has served as archivist for the Stanford Linear Accelerator Center, has worked in the archival programs at Stanford University Special Collections and the Naitonal Maritime Museum, San Francisco, and is currently president of the Society of California Archivists.

TERRY COOK is visiting professor in the archival studies program at the University of Manitoba, where he teaches in the areas of appraisal and electronic records. He had been a senior archival officer at the National Archives of Canada for many years until his retirement in 1998. He is internationally renown for his major contributions to the appraisal and electronic record programs of the National Archives for Canadian government records, as well as his many significant publications on a wide range of archival subjects. His most recent publication activity has been editing the forthcoming *Electronic Records Practice: Lessons from the National Archives of Canada.*

BARBARA L. CRAIG is an associate professor of archives in the Faculty of Information Studies of the University of Toronto. Prior to her appointment in 1973, Barbara was an archivist at the Archives of Ontario and most recently at York University, where she was university archivist and head of Archives and Special Collections. Barbara has been chair of the Ontario Council of Archives, officer of the Association of Canadian Archivists in many capacities, and a director of the Ontario Women's History Network. She is the immediate past chair of the Canadian Council of Archives Preservation Committee, current reviews editor for the *American Archivist*, and an active participant in the growing Health Archives Information Group (HAIG) in Ontario. Barbara has undertaken research into hospital archives in Canada, the United States, and the United Kingdom. She has consulted widely on the establishment of institutional archives. Her interests lie in the integration of archives with their institutions and with broader themes of cultural memory, genres of records, office ecologies, and the history of records and archives. She has published widely on the history of record keeping, on the history of medicine and medical archives, and archival theory. A second and revised edition of her *Medical Archives: What They Are and How to Keep Them* was published in 1999. She is currently writing a book on archival appraisal.

SHELLEY DAVIS worked for sixteen years as a historian for the federal government, spending nine years with the Department of Defense and eight years as the only historian to ever work for the Internal Revenue Service. At the end of 1995 Ms. Davis resigned from her position with the IRS in protest the agency's failure to halt the illegal destruction of government documents, including its historical record. Ms. Davis subsequently wrote a book about her experiences with the IRS, *Unbridled Power: Inside the Secret Culture of the IRS* (1997). She has testified before Congress on numerous occasions about government record keeping and accountability and is a recognized expert on IRS history and record keeping.

DAVID B. GRACY II, archivist, historian, and educator, is the Governor Bill Daniel Professor in Archival Enterprise in the Graduate School of Library and Information Science at the University of Texas at Austin, where he teaches a course in the nature, detection, and impact on society of forged historical and literary documents. A former president of the Society of American Archivists, he has served as university archivist at Georgia State University and director of the Texas State Archives.

VERNE HARRIS is the director of the South African History Archive. Previously he was with South Africa's State Archives Service for thirteen years before becoming a deputy director in the National Archives established in 1997. He has published widely in the fields of archives, records management, history, music, and fiction. He participated in a number of key processes leading to the transformation of South Africa's apartheid public records system: from 1992 to 1993 he served on the African National Congress' Archives Subcommittee; in 1995 he chaired the working committee of the Consultative Forum that drafted the National Archives of South Africa Act; and from 1997 to 1998 he was a member of the Truth and Reconciliation Commission's investigative team responsible for investigating the destruction of records by the apartheid state. He was editor of the *South African Archives Journal* between 1988 and 1998.

CHRIS HURLEY has been general manager (Archives Business) at Archives New Zealand since 1997 and was acting chief archivist of New Zealand from 1998 to 2000. He has also worked in government archives programs in Australia, both federal (Australian Archives, 1971–1980) and state (Public Record Office of Victoria, 1981–1997). He helped prepare the 1983 federal Archives Act in Australia and was a consultant on archives legislation for Queensland and New South Wales and for the Australian Law Reform Commission's Review of the federal Archives Act. His other special interest is archival documentation and standards, and he is well known in Australia and elsewhere for his writing on these subjects. He has taught in these areas in both Sydney and Melbourne and has served on boards and committees of professional associations in archives and records management in Australia and elsewhere.

VICTORIA L. LEMIEUX has long service as a government archivist, presently holding a position as campus records manager for the University of the West Indies' Mona Campus in Kingston, Jamaica. Ms. Lemieux is a frequent contributor to journals in archival science and administration.

JAMES M. O'TOOLE is associate professor of history at Boston College. After a career as an archivist for the New England Genealogical Society, the Massachusetts State Archives, and the Archives of the Roman Catholic Archdiocese of Boston, he turned to teaching. For fifteen years, he was a member of the history department of the University of Massachusetts, Boston, where he directed the M.A. program in history and archival methods. In addition to numerous publications on the history of American religion, he is the author and editor of many articles and books on archives, including *Understanding Archives and Manuscripts* (1990) and *The Records of American Business* (1997). He served as a consultant and expert witness during the Martin Luther King, Jr., Papers trial.

DAWN ROUTLEDGE is the archives development officer for the Regions of the National Council on Archives. She was formerly the researcher for the International Records Management Trust, carrying out projects in Ghana, Namibia, and Tanzania. During 1999 Ms. Routledge worked with the Trust as project manager on the Management of Public Sector Records Study Program until its successful launch. She is a graduate of the University College London School of Library, Archive and Information Studies with an M.A. in Archives and Records Management. Prior to this, she developed a wide range of skills in organizations including Kings College London and the Corporation of London.

SUSAN STORCH received a B.A. from McGill University in Montreal in 1990 and an M.A. in History and Archival Methods from the University of Massachusetts, Boston, in 1994. She worked on the Human Radiation Experiments project at Lawrence Berkeley National Laboratory from 1994 to 1995, was project archivist for Tobacco Control at the University of California, San Francisco, from 1995 to 1996, and was university archivist at the University of Oregon from 1996 to 2001. Currently she is a project archivist at the Judah L. Magnes Museum in Berkeley, California, and works as an archival consultant in the Bay Area.

ANNE VAN CAMP is currently manager of Member Initiatives for the Research Libraries Group, Inc. Prior to going to RLG, she was director of the Archives of the Hoover Institution at Stanford University for eight years. Before that she was vice president for Information Services at the Chase Manhattan Bank. She is currently serving on the Historical Advisory Committee for the U.S. State Department. A fellow of the Society of American Archivists, she remains active in archival professional activities both nationally and internationally.

JUSTUS WAMUKOYA is a senor lecturer and head of Archives and Records Management in the Faculty of Information Sciences at Moi University, Eldoret, Kenya. He has worked extensively in Gambia, Ghana, Kenya, Sierra Leone, Uganda, and Tanzania as a resource person on records and archives workshops sponsored by the Association of Commonwealth Archivists and Records Managers (ACARM), in collaboration with the International Records Management Trust (IRMT). In addition to teaching and consulting, Dr. Wamukoya is a trainer for the United Nations Population Fund (UNFPA) on advocacy and communication of population information and was recently appointed a member of the Kenya Public Archives Advisory Council (PAAC) for a period of two years. Justus has published a number of articles in refereed journals and is an active